PURE LUST

D1255190

Emily Oddwoman

PURE LUST

Elemental Feminist Philosophy

MARY DALY

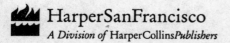

HarperSanFrancisco
A Division of HarperCollins*Publishers*

PURE LUST. Copyright © 1984 by Mary Daly. All rights reserved. Printed in the United States of America. No part of this book may be used or reproduced in any manner whatsoever without written permission except in the case of brief quotations embodied in critical articles and reviews. For information address HarperCollins Publishers, 10 East 53rd Street, New York, NY 10022.

Illustration copyright © 1984 by Emily Culpepper

FIRST HARPERCOLLINS PAPERBACK EDITION PUBLISHED IN 1992

Library of Congress Cataloging-in-Publication Data
Daly, Mary.
 Pure lust: elemental feminist philosophy / Mary Daly.
  p. cm.
 ISBN 0–06–250208–5
 1. Feminism 2. Social ethics I. Title
HQ1154.D314 1992
305.4'2'01—dc20   92–53924
                                                        CIP

92 93 94 95 96 97 CWI 10 9 8 7 6 5 4 3 2 1

To the Spirit
who lives and breathes
in all Elemental be-ing

To the Lady of Words of Power
who communicates herSelf
through the inadequate images—
from Isis and Ishtar
to Our Lady of Bourguillon

To the Muse
in Metamorphosing women
whose Presence inspires the Realizing
of our *own* powers of creation
finally, now, and always

CONTENTS

PREFACE

This book is being published in the 1980s—a period of extreme danger for women and for our sister the earth and her other creatures, all of whom are targeted by the maniacal fathers, sons, and holy ghosts for extinction by nuclear holocaust, or, failing that, by chemical contamination, by escalated ordinary violence, by man-made hunger and disease that proliferate in a climate of deception and mind-rot. Within the general context of this decade's horrors, women face in our daily lives forces whose intent is to mangle, strangle, tame, and turn us against our own purposes.

Yet at this very time, somehow living/longing through, above, before, and beyond it, thousands of women struggle to re-member ourSelves and our history, to sustain and intensify a biophilic consciousness. Having once known the intense joy of woman-identified bonding and creation, we refuse to turn back. For those who survive in the only real sense, that is, with metapatri-archal consciousness alive and growing, our struggle and quest concern Elemental participation in Be-ing. Our passion is for that which is most intimate and most ultimate, for depth and tran-scendence, for recalling original wholeness.

In Naming/reclaiming passionate Elemental knowing, know-ing that is intuitive/immediate, not mediated by the omnipresent myths of phallicism, we call forth hope and courage to transcend appearances.

Pure Lust is a sister-work to my books *Beyond God the Father* and *Gyn/Ecology*.[1] In some ways, *Pure Lust* can be seen as the parthenogenetic daughter of those earlier works—not in the sense that the Voyager of this book needs to have read them, but in the sense that *Pure Lust* continues the Otherworld Journey of Exorcism and Ecstasy. Since the direction of the Journey is not linear, but Spiraling, new Voyagers may join at any point.

Gyn/Ecologists will recall that the processions of demons who try to block our way are personifications of the Deadly Sins of the Fathers. I previously renamed the traditional Seven Deadly Sins, adding to the beginning of the list (which now totals eight) the most crucial one, which the fathers, of course, omit.[2] These are:

Processions	(deception)
Professions	(pride)
Possession	(avarice)
Aggression	(anger)
Obsession	(lust)
Assimilation	(gluttony)
Elimination	(envy)
Fragmentation	(sloth)

All of these sins, manifesting themselves as demons, appear and reappear in the course of the metapatriarchal Journey. The primary demons to appear in *Gyn/Ecology* were/are *Processions,* followed closely by *Professions* and *Possession.* These were/are warded off/defeated by the Spinning Spinsters and A-mazing Amazons, the Hags, Harpies, Crones, and Furies of the Gyn/Ecological phase of the spiraling Journey.

In *Pure Lust,* the main demonic attackers are *Aggression* and *Obsession.* As the Voyage continues, the Furious Fighters of these infernal molesters increase in numbers and in spirit-force. Moving onward, upward, downward, we enter, now, New Realms of Spheres.

In case the title of this book should seem misleading to some, I hasten to explain that *Pure Lust* is not primarily a work of feminist eroticism, although it hardly excludes this from its range of concern. Chiefly, it is a Work of Feminist Erraticism. Lusty women will understand this immediately upon reading the following definitions of *erratic:* "having no fixed course: WANDERING;" and "*archaic:* having no fixed residence: NOMADIC." For Lusty women are Wanderlusty, and we are known for fierce resistance to being fixed. Clearly, we rejoice in knowing that *erraticism* means "especially: a wayward act or tendency." We are proud that our published works are, according to phallic fixations ("standards"), utter *errata.**

The Wanderers of this Work meander through three Realms of Spheres, coursing first through Archespheres, the Realm of Origins; then through Pyrospheres, the Purifying Realm of Fire; and last through Metamorphospheres, the Realm of graceless/Graceful transformations. Our struggles are Battles of Life-Lust, transcending the States of Stag-Nation. Our Quest implies constant Creation.†

The weapons of Wonderlusting women are the Labryses/double axes of our own Wild wisdom and wit, which cut through the mazes of man-made mystification, breaking the mindbindings of master-minded doublethink.†† Undoublethinking, the Lusty Wanderers of the Realms of Pure Lust strive also to intensify our sense of genuine and organic complexity.[3]

---

* *Errata,* of course, is the plural of *erratum,* the archaic meaning of which is "an error (as a misstatement or misprint) in something published or written."

† In other words, our Creation involves striving for biophilic participation in Be-ing, transcending the forces of necrophilic negation of such participation.

†† Doublethink is manifested by popes, nuclear scientists, *et al.* in the sadosociety. On September 6, 1983, the *Boston Globe* printed an Associated Press report:

> VATICAN CITY—Pope John Paul II took his strongest stand yet against ordaining women as priests and told US bishops yesterday to reaffirm traditional church views on sex and marriage—even if they are unpopular.
>
> But the pontiff also called on the bishops to oppose "discrimination against women by reason of sex."
>
> The Pope, addressing 23 US bishops at his summer residence at Castel Gandolfo south of Rome, said they must strongly reaffirm church stands against contraception, divorce, homosexuality, premarital sex, and abortion.

On April 27, 1983, the *Boston Globe* reported the "torment" of Seth Neddermeyer, who developed the implosion trigger that made possible the detonation of atomic bombs.

> SEATTLE—When Seth Neddermeyer leaves Washington, D.C. this week and returns home here, he'll carry more with him than the prestigious Enrico Fermi Award, more than the $25,000 that goes with it,

Recognizing that deep damage has been inflicted upon consciousness under phallocracy's myths and institutions, we continue to Name patriarchy as the perverted paradigm and source of other social evils. Our Naming/analysis becomes ever more direct and urgent as we confront the advanced stages of nuclearism, Nagging women to Realize our own biophilic reality. Refusing to be distracted by the fathers' perpetual State of Emergency—their frenzied foreground fixations—the proud Prudes who prance through the Realms of Pure Lust fiercely focus our Fury, firing/inspiring ourSelves and each Other with renewed commitment to the cause of women and all Elemental be-ing.

This commitment implies experience and understanding of the Goddess as Metaphor—a reality beautifully and precisely explained by Nelle Morton.[4] It implies also cogent political analysis, for example, that developed by such diverse thinkers as Jan Raymond, Andrea Dworkin, and Marilyn Frye.[5] It involves exorcism of the partriarchally embedded mechanisms in women that impede female bonding.[6] It requires unveiling of the masters' pseudogeneric and pseudorational language structures.[7] Above all, it requires Elemental faith.

The work of such complex Naming is an invocation of Other reality. It is an invitation to the country of the Strange. For the Strange is the homeland of women who identify as women, and Wild women are Strange. This work, insofar as it is an expression/expansion of Pure Lust, is a conjuring of the Elemental Spirits of women and all Wild natures. Such conjuring conjoins women with our Selves and our Sisters, and with earth, air, fire, and water. It connects us with the rhythms of the farthest stars and of our own sun and moon. It mends our broken ties with the Witch within ourSelves, who spins and weaves the tapestries of Elemental creation.

---

more even than the satisfying glow of international acclaim for his achievements in the field of physics. He'll also bring along a burden of guilt he's been unable to discard for more than three decades.

"I feel kind of badly for accepting a prize that is in part recognition for something that's resulted in such horrible consequences for the human race," he said last week in his comfortable house in a woodsy suburb north of Seattle. "What I want to do is forget the past completely."

ACKNOWLEDGMENTS

Denise Connors has been Present in the deepest ways to the Journey reflected in this book. Her many Sparking, Spinning conversations and acts of Lusty friendship over the years have moved me into Metamorphospheres. The idea for the serpentine design on the front of the jacket is one typical product of her Wicked Celtic imagination. Nelle Morton has been a constant Source of inspiration and spiritual strength. Her Hearing and Speaking elicit New Words.

Emily Culpepper has been an invaluable co-worker and staunch friend. Her many suggestions and criticisms have enriched all of the Realms of *Pure Lust*. Marisa Zavalloni and Nicole Brossard have been encouraging and faithful colleagues in the work of weaving the Network of feminist analysis. Their conversations and comments have been important stimuli for the work of this book.

Peggy Holland has been a thoughtful friend whose conversations have contributed to the weaving process reflected in this book. Fran Chelland has been a Sister vagabond engaged in the process of seeing through to Other dimensions.

Barbara Zanotti worked tirelessly as Lusty Searcher and companion of the Journey in the formative stages of this book and contributed immeasurably to the process. Anne Dellenbaugh provided parthenogenetic gynergy and insights that were of inestimable value in the early shaping of *Pure Lust*. Eleanor Mullaley contributed unique insights and Crone-logical humor to the process. Joann Aalfs has been an encouraging participant in the work and process reflected in these pages. Kathy Newman was an efficient and imaginative helper in the final stages of the work.

Erika Wisselinck has provided Elemental encouragement from afar, with the assistance of her Crone cat, Adele, who resides in Munich. Pat Green has been a constant and generous friend, reminding me by her actions of what feminism is all about.

Sandra Stanley helped in invaluable ways, giving wise and expert assistance during the final "galley-slaving" stages of the book's process — an assistance consonant with her many acts of friendship during the course of several years. Ann Marie Palmisciano, Suzanne Melendy, and Nilah MacDonald worked Naggingly and Prudishly to produce a Weird and scholarly index.

Charlotte Cecil Raymond has contributed to the Realization of this book through her work as excellent and supportive agent. Joanne Wyckoff has been a sensitive and helpful editor. I am especially appreciative of Edna and Barbara McGlynn, whose conscientious labors contributing to the preparation of the manuscript were spiced with witty and imaginative conversation. Barbara Flanagan was a skillful and inspired copy editor.

I am energized always by memories of conversations with friends whose influence is felt despite geographic distance. Andrée Collard reminds me always of the dignity and rights of all Wild creatures. Linda Barufaldi won't let me forget to laugh. Sue Bellamy and Janet Ramsay demonstrated that sisterhood extends around the globe. Kaye Ashe Weaves spiritual connections.

Spiritual warriors, notably Sonia Johnson and Robin Morgan, and certainly many others, have helped me to keep the Faith. Jan Raymond's friendship, work, and commitment to the cause of women give me reason to Hope that the Vision can never be lost. There are many of us who intend to sustain and to Realize that Faith and that Hope. To all of us, the Haggard and indefatigable ones, I want to express my deepest thanks.

ON LUST AND THE LUSTY

Eye-beam:	"archaic: a radiant glance of the eye." *Webster's Third New International Dictionary of the English Language*
I-Beam:	"Archaic: a radiant glance of the I / Eye." *Websters' First New Intergalactic Wickedary of the English Language**

This book focuses upon and Spirals off from the traditional Deadly Sin of lust, which is treated here in an untraditional way. Phallic lust is seen as a fusion of obsession and aggression. As obsession it specializes in genital fixation and fetishism, causing broken consciousness, broken heartedness, broken connections among women and between women and the elements. As aggression it rapes, dismembers, and kills women and all living things within its reach. Phallic lust begets phallocratic society, that is sadosociety, which is, in fact, pseudosociety. The Lusty women who rage and roam through the Realms of this book wield the Labryses of our lustrous minds—our double-axes of divination —to defeat this obsession/aggression.

---

* *Webster:* "A weaver; a. as the designation of a woman." *Oxford English Dictionary*.
  Wickedary: "Archaic: a wicked/wiccen dictionary." *Websters' First New Intergalactic Wickedary of the English Language*. The adjective *wicked* can be traced to the same Indo-European root (*weik-*) as *wicce*, the Old English word meaning witch (*American Heritage Dictionary of the English Language*). The adjective *wiccen* is here constructed from the noun *wicce*. A *Wickedary* is a dictionary for Wicked/Wiccen Women.

THE TITLE OF THIS BOOK

The title *Pure Lust* is double-sided. On one side, it Names the deadly dis-passion that prevails in patriarchy—the life-hating lechery that rapes and kills the objects of its obsession/aggression. Indeed, the usual meaning of *lust* within the Lecherous State of patriarchy is well known. It means "sexual desire, especially of a violent self-indulgent character: LECHERY, LASCIVIOUSNESS." * Phallic lust, violent and self-indulgent, levels all life, dismembering spirit/matter, attempting annihilation. Its refined cultural products, from the sadistic pornography of the Marquis de Sade to the sadomasochistic theology of Karl Barth, are on a continuum: they are essentially the same. This lust is *pure* in the sense that it is characterized by unmitigated malevolence. It is *pure* in the sense that it is ontologically evil, having as its end the braking/breaking of female be-ing.† Its goal is the obliteration of natural knowing and willing, of the deep purposefulness which philosophers have called *final causality*—our innately ordained Self-direction toward Happiness.††

The word *Lust* has utterly Other meanings than this, however. It means "VIGOR, FERTILITY (the increasing lust of the earth or of the plant—Francis Bacon)." It means "an intense longing:

* Except when otherwise indicated, all definitions given in this work are from *Webster's Third New International Dictionary of the English Language.*

† I use *be-ing* in this hyphenated form to signify that this is intended not as a noun but as a verb, meaning participation in the Ultimate/Intimate Reality: *Be-ing,* the Verb.

†† The *final cause,* according to an old scholastic philosophical axiom, is the "cause of causes, because it is the cause of the causality of all the other causes." According to Aristotelian and scholastic philosophy, it is one of the four causes. As I explained in *Beyond God the Father* (Boston: Beacon Press, 1973), pp. 180–81: "When Aristotle wrote of the 'final cause,' he intended 'cause' to mean that which brings about an effect. Scholastic philosophers followed the Aristotelian theory of the 'four causes' to explain change. . . . The final cause is the purpose which starts the whole process in motion. . . . The final cause is the first cause, since it moves the agent to act upon the matter, bringing forth a new form." Thus the efficient cause (agent), the material cause (matter), and the formal cause (form) are all actualized by the final cause. Deep ontological purposefulness, or telic centering, is the target of phallic lust. Final causality, in this profound sense, is the object of attack within phallocratic society.

CRAVING." It means "EAGERNESS, ENTHUSIASM." The word, then, derived from the Latin *lascivus,* meaning wanton, playful, is double-edged. Wise women wield our wits, making this word our wand, our Labrys. For it Names not only the "thrust of the argument" that assails women and nature on all levels (mythic, ideological, institutional, behavioral) but also the way out—the vigor, eagerness, and intense longing that launches Wild women on Journeys beyond the State of Lechery.

Primarily, then, *Pure Lust* Names the high humor, hope, and cosmic accord/harmony of those women who choose to escape, to follow our hearts' deepest desire and bound out of the State of Bondage, Wanderlusting and Wonderlusting with the elements, connecting with auras of animals and plants, moving in planetary communion with the farthest stars. This Lust is in its essence astral. It is pure Passion: unadulterated, absolute, simple sheer striving for abundance of be-ing. It is unlimited, unlimiting desire/fire. One moved by its magic is Musing/Re-membering. Choosing to leave the dismembered state, she casts her lot, life, with the trees and the winds, the sands and the tides, the mountains and moors. She is Outcast, casting her Self outward, inward, breaking out of the casts/castes of phallocracy's fabrications/fictions, moving out of the maze of mediated experience. As she lurches/leaps into starlight her tears become tidal, her cackles cosmic, her laughter Lusty.

The struggle Named by the Labrys of this title is between reality and unreality, between the natural Wild, which is be-ing, and man-made fabrications that fracture her substance, simulate her soul. It is between the desire, eagerness, vigor, enthusiasm of/for expanding be-ing, which philosophers have called final causality, and blockage/blockers of this reaching of be-ing. Such blockage *is* the State of Lechery, in which longing for participation in transcendent Be-ing is reified, displaced, plasticized, rehabilitated.

Elemental female Lust is intense longing/craving for the cosmic concrescence that is creation. It is charged, tense, in tension with the tenses of fabricated "father time." Incensed, it burns through the shallow impressions of insipid senses, sensing the Sources, Astral Forces, Angels and Graces that call from the Deep. This Lusting is divining: foreseeing, foretelling, forecasting. Unlike the dim divines and divinities, the deadheads of dead-land whose ill-luminations blind us, Lusty women portend with luster, our radiance from within that radiates from and toward Original Powers of creation.

The word *luster* is itself a double-edged word, a Labrys, having quite opposite definitions. It means, on the one hand, "a glow of reflected light: GLOSS, SHEEN," and "a coating or substance that gives luster to a surface." On the other hand, it means "a glow of light from within: LUMINOSITY, SHINE: (luster of the stars)" and "an inner beauty: RADIANCE." These opposed definitions give clues concerning the condition of women and of words.

When reflecting the artificial lights of patriarchal prisons, words help us recognize the superficial coatings, the flashy phoniness of the fathers' foreground falsifications. Thus, for example, the word *woman* Names the alienating archetype that freezes female be-ing, locking us into prisons of "forever feminine" roles. But when we wield words to dis-close the inner beauty, the radiance of the Race of Lusty Women, we/they blaze open pathways to our Background/homeland. Thus *woman,* wisely wielded, Names a Wild and Lusty Female claiming wisdom, joy, and power as her own.

In their double-edged dimensions, then, words wield/yield messages about the tragedy of women and all Wild be-ing confined within imprisoning patriarchal parameters. Besides/beyond this, they radiate knowledge of an ancient age, and they let us know that they, the words themselves, are treasures trying to be freed, vibrations whose auras await awakening ears.

Breaking the bonds/bars of phallocracy requires breaking through to radiant powers of words, so that by releasing words, we can release our Selves. Lusty women long for radiant words, to free their flow, their currents, which like our own be-ing have been blocked and severed from ancestral Memory. The Race of Lusty Women, then, has deep connections with the Race of Radiant Words.

RE-CALLING THE ELEMENTAL RACE

A basic thesis of this book, implied in the title, is that women who choose biophilic be-ing belong to the Race of Lusty Women, which participates in the Race of Elemental be-ing. For we are rooted, as are animals and trees, winds and seas, in the Earth's substance. Our origins are in her elements. Thus, when true to our Originality, we are Elemental, that is, "of, relating to, or caused by great force of nature."

Under the conditions of patriarchy, women dis-cover our Original Race through the release of deep ontological Fury. By *Fury* I do not mean an agitated state of chronic or acute anger that immobilizes, or that misfires at the wrong target. Rather, I mean a focused gynergetic will to break through the obstacles that block the flow of Female Force. Female Fury is Volcanic Dragonfire. It is Elemental breathing of those who love the Earth and her kind, who Rage against the erasure of our kind. It is the Rage of those who choose this, our own Race of Elemental be-ing over all man-made, male-designed divisions and categories, Naming our Selves and all truly life-loving creatures as priority, refusing to be e-raced, to be severed from our deep roots—refusing the effacement of our Race.[1] Lusty women experience great diversity, and know that we belong to many tribes.[2] Dis-covering radical female-identified diversity, we decline confinement in man-made racetracks.*

A primary meaning of *race* is "the act of rushing onward: RUN." This definition describes the movement of women who have dis-covered our original, Elemental Lust. Another definition is "a strong or rapid current of water that flows through a narrow channel." Elemental life must often flow through narrow channels, for in the State of Lechery options are narrowed. Yet, under these conditions, force and focus can be intense. *Race* also means "a heavy or choppy sea; especially one produced by the meeting of two tides." This definition indeed applies, for the Race of Women is Wild and Tidal, roaring with rhythms that are Elemental, that are created in cosmic encounters.

The principalities of the Phallic State continually connive to eradicate the Elemental Race, to reduce us to the state of pos-

---

* One of these man-made racetracks, is, of course, racism. When I write of the Race of Women as participating in the Race of Elemental be-ing, I am Naming active struggle to overcome and transcend phallocracy, the social, political, ideological system that spawns racism and genocide as well as rapism and gynocide. Confronting phallocracy includes opposing it in all of its forms/manifestations. I initially developed this thesis in *Beyond God the Father* (Boston: Beacon Press, 1973). Its implications were further expanded in *Gyn/Ecology* (Boston: Beacon Press, 1978), and it is further elaborated in this book.

session by pulling us up by our roots, making us rootless. Their goal is our *deracination,* which is "detachment from one's background (as from homeland, customs, traditions)." Thus women and other Elemental creatures on this planet are rendered homeless, cut off from knowledge of our Race's customs and traditions. To the extent that such tactics are successful, we are *deracinated,* that is, "physically, mentally, or emotionally separated from [our] racial, social, or intellectual group: free from racial characteristics or influence (as deracinated migrants from another country)." In this way, our Racing is blocked, tracked into repetitive, circular movements. Cut off from our origins, we are disoriented.

Many women sense that we have been physically, mentally, and emotionally separated from our Original, Elemental Race, made "free"—that is, purified—of our own native characteristics and influence. We sense that we are "migrants from another country." Yet that country seems to be nowhere: it seems to be only a feminist utopian's dream.

Together with Virginia Woolf, feminists moan: "As a woman I have no country." And together with her we may add: "As a woman I want no country. As a woman my country is the whole world." [3] But there is something poignant about this brave assertion, for "the whole world" is groaning under phallic rule. It must be, then, that it is in some other dimension that "the whole world" is the country, the homeland of the Race of Women. This is not to say that a woman should cease struggling for survival within, or rather, on the boundary of, phallocracy. But that struggle is inadequate without Pure Lust, the active longing that propels a woman into her own "country," that is, into the Realms of Elemental Reality, of ontological depth.

As the oppression and depression of the eighties increases, women are indeed pressured to be free from our "racial characteristics or influence." Subsumed under the fathers' spheres of influence women have forgotten that *influence* means "the exercise of a power like the supposed power of the stars: an emanation of spiritual or moral force." Afflicted with amnesia, women have been subliminally seduced into forgetting the emanations of spiritual/moral power that are the influence characteristic of this Race.

This book is an invitation to women to unforget our potentialities—to re-call the Elemental potency asleep in our ancestral Memory. This requires entering Elemental Realms, and encountering the Race of Radiant Words, that is, dis-covering Elemental feminist philosophy.

THE SUBTITLE OF THIS BOOK:
ELEMENTAL FEMINIST PHILOSOPHY

In scribing the words *Elemental feminist philosophy* I intend to Name a form of philosophical be-ing/thinking that emerges together with metapatriarchal consciousness—consciousness that is in harmony with the Wild in nature and in the Self. The force of this philosophy has its source in women breaking out of the tamed/tracked modes of thinking/feeling of phallocracy. It is the force of reason rooted in instinct, intuition, passion.

Several meanings of the word *Elemental* converge for the conjuring of Elemental feminist philosophy. An "obsolete" definition is "material, physical." The philosophy here unfolded is material/physical as well as spiritual, mending/transcending this deceptive dichotomy. Another definition is "characterized by stark simplicity, naturalness, or unrestrained or undisciplined vigor or force: not complex or refined: CRUDE, PRIMITIVE, FUNDAMENTAL, BASIC, EARTHY." Elemental feminist philosophy is crude (in a natural state), primitive (original, primary), fundamental, basic, and, especially, Earthy. Its stark complexity spurns contrived simplicity.

Elemental also means "SPIRIT, SPECTRE, WRAITH." The sixteenth-century alchemist, physician, philosopher Paracelsus used this word to name the spirits of the elements, the "administrators of the processes of the elements." Since, according to his own admission, Paracelsus learned everything he knew about healing from the Witches, we can surmise who were the true sources of his naming of Elementals.[4] Following sources from Greece, Egypt, India, and China he divided these into four groups: the gnomes (earth spirits), undines or nymphs (water spirits), salamanders (fire spirits), sylphs (air spirits).[5] Elementals, thus understood, provide Radiant Words for Naming our spiritual connections with the elements.

Elemental also means "a first principle: RUDIMENT." Wonderlusting women seek understanding of first principles. Sensing deeply that officially condoned knowledge has been on the wrong

track, a Wild woman yearns to return to beginnings, to rudi-
ments, to the original questions of her childhood, of her ances-
tral/racial Memory. She recognizes that these have a special
aura, that they are imbued with a sense of deep Wonder, which
as Aristotle noted is the beginning of the philosophical quest.[6]
For Wonderlusters, this is the quest for Elemental Wisdom, which
is knowledge of first principles.

Clues about the nature of Elemental Wisdom can be gleaned
from statements attributed to the apostle Paul—arch-hater of
life in general and women in particular—concerning elements
and Elementals. He wrote:

See to it that no one makes a prey of you by philosophy and empty
deceit, according to human tradition, according to the elemental spirits
of the universe, and not according to Christ. (Col. 2:8 [R.S.V.])

It is evident that Paul experienced distaste for philosophy which
is associated with Elemental spirits. The antithesis of such Wild
Worldly Wisdom is Christ. The extent of the necrophilic lust
motivating these words becomes even more evident later in the
same chapter:

If with Christ you died to the elemental spirits of the universe, why
do you live as if you still belonged to the world? (Col. 2:20 [R.S.V.])

Elemental philosophy *is* of the world. It is for those who love
and belong to this world, who experience Be-Longing in this
world, who refuse the horror of Self-loss implied in dying "with
Christ" to the Elemental spirits of the universe. In case there
could be any delusions concerning the element-hating thrust of
christian ideology, which seeks to kill Earthy wisdom, Paul drives
home the point:

Set your minds on things that are above, not on things that are on
earth. For you have died, and your life is hid with Christ in God. (Col.
3:2-3 [R.S.V.])

In contrast to this, Elemental women experience our Selves, and,
therefore, our philosophy, as rooted in love for the earth and for
things that naturally are on earth. This Elemental Earthy Lust
was expressed by Emily Brontë in *Wuthering Heights,* in the
words of Catherine:

"If I were in heaven, Nelly, I. should be extremely miserable. . . . I dreamt once that I was there . . . that heaven did not seem to be my home; and I broke my heart with weeping to come back to earth; and the angels were so angry that they flung me out into the middle of the heath on the top of Wuthering Heights; where I woke sobbing for joy." [7] *

The joy of Elemental women, then, is Earthy, and so also is our philosophical quest.

The lust to kill this philosophical quest is expressed in yet another pauline text, which provides further clues for understanding the perversion/reversal of primal Wonderlust:

When we were children, we were slaves to the elemental spirits of the universe. But when the time had fully come, God sent forth his Son, born of woman, born under the law, to redeem those who were under the law, so that we might receive adoption as sons. And because you are sons, God has sent the Spirit of his Son into our hearts, crying "Abba! Father!" . . . But now that you have come to know God, or rather be known by God, how can you turn back again to the weak and beggarly elemental spirits, whose slaves you want to be once more? (Gal. 4:3–9 [R.S.V.])

Elemental women who have learned to recognize the technique of reversal will be suspicious of the word *slave* in this context. We do not wish to be redeemed by a god, to be adopted as sons, or to have the spirit of a god's son artificially injected into our hearts, crying "father." Having seen the horror of such phallocratic "spirituality," we indeed *can* "turn back again," re-membering our Selves as strong and proud "Elemental spirits," and using this expression as Metaphor to Name our Sources, Sisters, Muses, Friends, as well as our Selves. As we turn back, re-membering, we understand ever more deeply the war continually waged against Elemental life by the fathers and sons.

The logical outcome of the war against Elemental be-ing that

* Brontë uses the term *heaven* here in the christian otherworldly sense. I would use this term in an Elemental Otherworldly sense and thereby reclaim it for feminists, as meaning something Other than both the patriarchal "this world" and the patriarchal "otherworld." That is, I would reclaim it to Name the "this world" of women and all Wild beings, who are Other than patriarchal. In any case, this passage expresses—in traditional terms—a love of earth shared by Elemental women.

is legitimated by such "spirituality" was expressed in the second epistle of Peter:

But the day of the Lord will come like a thief, and then the heavens will pass away with a loud noise, and the elements will be dissolved with fire, and the earth and the works that are upon it will be burned up. (2 Pet. 3:10 [R.S.V.])

As self-fulfilling prophecy and manifesto of necrophilic faith, this "inspired" text is one among many that have paved the way for modern technological war against the elements, which takes such forms as nuclearism and chemical contamination. Understanding/moving through and beyond this war is the work of Elemental feminist philosophy of life.

Women who have not died to the Elemental spirits of the universe naturally do live as if we still belong to this world, which is the Otherworld in relation to the sadostate legitimated by Peter and Paul, Tom, Dick, and Harry. Naturally, we Lust for more re-membering of the elements and of Elemental spirits.

Re-membering Elements

Unwittingly, biblical scholars have provided some helpful hints for Earthy Hags concerning the Greek word *stoicheia* as used in Paul's letters, which is translated sometimes as "elemental spirits" and sometimes simply as "the elements." It means: (1) the spoken letters of the alphabet; (2) the fire, air, earth, and water of which the world was thought to be constituted; (3) the elements of the universe, the larger cosmos, including the sun, moon, planets, and stars; (4) "the spirits, angels, and demons which were believed to ensoul the heavenly bodies, traverse all space, and inhabit every nook and cranny of earth, particularly tombs, desert places, and demented persons." [8] These multiple meanings not only name the targets of the life-haters who control sado-society. They can also aid adventurous Amazons to cut through the foreground films of deception into our Elemental Realms. These meanings can be examined separately.

First, *elements,* defined as the spoken letters of the alphabet, suggests—if a Wondering woman listens with her Third Ear— the primal Race of Words: their cosmic sounds, meanings, rhythms, and connections. The fathers, sons, and holy ghosts attempt to annihilate this Archaic alphabet, replacing these sounds with meaningless noises, with verbiage and verbigeration. Women Naming our own experience awaken our Powers to hear the Elemental sounds.

Second, *elements* as fire, air, earth, water constitute the deep Realms of reality with which our senses are naturally and Wildly connected. These Realms are masked by the mediators who produce substitutes for the natural components of this world. Women Naming this world for our Selves re-member our relations with these Earthy realities.

Third, *elements* as the larger cosmos describe the vast context within which primal powers must be understood. They also describe the context in which Elemental philosophy is woven and suggest the scope of the Wanderlust/Wonderlust that motivates exploration/creation. The lords of lechery hide this context by embedding unnatural limitations in minds, senses. Muses melt these blinders with the Fire of desire. We break them with the winds and waters of Wild Words, Racing free.

Finally, *Elemental spirits/angels/demons* may be understood as Metaphors manifesting the essential unity and intelligence of spirit/matter, the inherent telos of spirit/matter. They Name Intelligence ensouling the stars, animating the processes of earth, air, fire, water, enspiriting the sounds that are the elements of words, connecting words with the earth, air, fire, water and with the sun, moon, planets, stars. The Metaphoric language of "Elemental spirits" is crucial for the empowering of women, for this conjures memories of Archaic integrity that have been broken by phallic religion and philosophy. The task of reclaiming this integrity demands *Stamina*—the threads of life spun by the Fates. The Spinning of these threads is the task of Elemental philosophy. Also it is the work of Graces, the work of natural, Elemental Grace.

TRAVELING COMPANIONS

Readers of *Gyn/Ecology* will recall that its Journey was/is a work of Hag-ography, a whirl though the time/space of Hagocracy, the Otherworld (Background) inhabited by Hags, Crones, Harpies, Furies, Amazons, Spinsters. As the Spooking, Sparking, and Spinning Voyagers continue to move, our Wanderlust/Wonderlust intensifies. The heat of our battles is heightened. The Force of our Fire is volcanic/epiphanic. The expanse of our

Journey is Astral/Archaic and the Voyagers are Archelogians whose Lust is fueled by the influence of the stars.*

Archelogians are neither religious nor irreligious; we are Nag-Gnostic. One meaning of the verb *nag* is "to affect recurrent awareness, uncertainty, need for consideration, or concern; make recurrently aware of something (as a problem, solution, situation)." One meaning of the adjective *gnostic* is "believing in the reality of transcendental knowledge." Nag-Gnostic Archelogians sense with certainty the reality of transcendental knowledge. At the same time, we never cease to Nag our Selves and others with recurrent awareness and uncertainty.

The Nags who blaze the paths of *Pure Lust* are characterized by rich diversity. Fired by Dreadful Desire, we battle the butchers/blockers/stoppers. Reeling through new Realms, Nags conjure forth Sister-Nagsters, all fueled with Elemental Fury. The following list will Name and summon forth a few. We are: Augurs, Brewsters, Dikes, Dragons, Dryads, Fates, Phoenixes, Gorgons, Maenads, Muses. We are Naiads, Nixes, Gnomes, Norns, Nymphs. We are Oceanids, Oreads, Orishas, Pixies. We are Prudes, Salamanders, Scolds, Shrews, Sibyls, Sirens. We are Soothsayers, Sprites, Stiffs, Sylphs, Undines. We are Viragos, Virgins, Vixens, Websters, Weirds.

As the crowd increases, the diversity intensifies. Our power is not of numbers but of astral force. This can be understood as a few of these Lusty spirits introduce our Selves and Name our be-ing:

Weirds: One meaning of *Weird* is "FATE, NORN." It also means "SOOTHSAYER." As the Fates, Weirds are "the three goddesses supposed to determine the course of human life" (*Oxford English Dictionary* [*O.E.D.*]). As an adjective, *weird* can mean "MYSTERIOUS." There is also the adverb *weirdward,* meaning "bordering upon the supernatural."

Women who have heard the Call of the Wild hear the Word of the Weird, and this summons us weirdward—which means to the borders of the *very* natural, the *supremely* natural. As we venture into this our homeland we conjure webs of Weird words and thus become . . .

---

* *Archaic* is derived from the Greek *arche,* meaning first principle, primal element.

Websters: Webster is defined as "a weaver; a. as the designation of a woman" (*O.E.D.*). According to *Webster's,* this word is derived from the Old English *webbestre,* meaning female weaver.* Weavers/Websters are, of course, closely allied to Spinsters, and thus are . . .

Virgins: One definition of the adjective *virgin* is "never captured: UNSUBDUED." Wild Virgins assume this definition for our Selves. By thus breaking the rules of common usage we show that we are . . .

Wantons: The adjective *wanton* has as its first definition "*archaic:* lacking discipline: not susceptible to control: UNRULY." It also means: "excessively merry or gay: FROLICSOME." Assuming this Lusty word as Self-definition, Wantons affirm our spirited natures, displaying that we are also . . .

Sprites: Sprite is derived from the Latin *spiritus,* meaning spirit. Its archaic meaning is "inner being: SOUL." There is an obsolete meaning of *sprite* as a verb, which is "to inspire with courage" (*O.E.D.*). Women who are spriting sprites are also . . .

Muses: Muse is etymologically connected with the Greek *mnasthai,* meaning to remember. Unlike the museless/useless man-made "memories" that mummify our minds, the Musings of Muses fly into the future. The movement of this Weirdward Musing is not always a calm and simple matter. Spriting/spirited Muses are therefore often . . .

Shrews: A *Shrew* is "a person, especially (now only) a woman given to railing or scolding or other perverse or malignant behavior" (*O.E.D.*). Shrews are shrewd. Indeed, the term *shrewd* is derived from Shrew. Shrewd Shrews of course are . . .

Scolds: A *Scold* is "in early use, a person (especially a woman) of ribald speech; later a woman (rarely a man) addicted to abusive language" (*O.E.D.*). Since the language of lechery is always ribald and abusive to women, this definition is thought-provoking. Female truth-telling—scolding—about phallic lust predictably

* Judy Grahn, in *The Queen of Wands* (Trumansburg, N.Y.: The Crossing Press, 1982), pp. xii–xiii, has introduced the Name *Webster.* She writes: "This spirit is a weaving spider, a fate spinner from whose very body comes the cloth of life and time and understanding. I named this spirit *webster,* or Spider Webster. Webster is a word that formerly meant 'female weaver,' the 'ster' ending indicating a female ancestor, or female possession of the word."

will be called ribald and abusive. It is understandable to Scolds that this name in its original form (*skald,* in Old Norse) means poet, and that at one point this is said to have meant "lampooner" and to have been connected with the idea of libel in verse (*O.E.D.*). The Scoldings of Scolds are certainly experienced as lampooning by the lords of lechery, according to whose law books and rules of reversal we are guilty of libel. For Scolds are . . .

Soothsayers: A *Soothsayer* is "a speaker of truth or wisdom; especially PROGNOSTICATOR." Soothsayers are truthsayers, and therefore are . . .

Prudes: Prude is derived from the French *prudefemme,* meaning wise or good woman, and is rooted in the Old French *prode,* meaning good, capable, brave. *Prude* has the same origins as *proud.* It makes sense that within the Lecherous State the name *Prude* is used disparagingly of women, for women who are wise, good, capable, brave, and—especially—Proud Women threaten the phallic lusters. thrusters. Simply by expressing our Selves, Proud Prudes "invite" the label . . .

Dikes: According to *Webster's,* a Dike is "a barrier preventing passage, especially protecting against or excluding something undesirable." Needless to say, Dikes are . . .

Viragos: A *Virago* is defined as "a loud overbearing woman," and "a woman of great stature, strength and courage: one possessing supposedly masculine qualities of body and mind." Indeed, Viragos are Amazons, possessing the great stature, strength, and courage that are essentially female qualities of body and mind. Viragos are Elemental, and therefore participate in the powers associated traditionally with Gnomes, Undines, Salamanders, and Sylphs—the *Elementals* envisaged for centuries as animators of the processes of the elements.

The prudence of Prudes, the shrewdness of Shrews, the rememberings of Muses inspire us to consider these personages—the Elementals.

ELEMENTALS

Gnomes: Searching the dictionary for definitions of *Gnome,* one finds, of course, that it means "an ageless often deformed dwarf creature of folklore conceived as living in the earth and usually guarding precious ore or treasure." There are many tales of Gnomes revealing their treasure to mortals for whom they have friendship. In a sense the moral is simple: the earth reveals her treasures to those who are friendly to her, who are respectful of her and refuse to do her violence. There is another meaning of *gnome,* i.e., "a brief reflection or maxim: APHORISM, PROVERB." Although the *Oxford English Dictionary* cautiously maintains that an etymological connection between the two meanings is unlikely, from another point of view it does seem very likely that there is a connection, for Elemental wisdom, expressed in aphorisms, is rooted in the earth, Earthy. Since the symbolism of the earth is so totally female, there can be no doubt, despite later depictions of gnomes as little old men, that the ageless wisdom that is Gnomic is also primordially female and Elemental.

One meaning of *gnomic* is "expressive of what is true generally, universally, or always—used of certain tenses ('day follows night' is an example of the gnomic present)." Lusty women are grounded in the Gnomic present, re-membering the treasures and precious ores bequeathed to us by our Earthy foresisters, some of whom we may choose to Name *Fore-Gnomes.* Moreover, in the Gnomic present, we discover the meaning of *gnomology,* which is defined as "an anthology of gnomes" and "gnomic writing." And we are *gnomical,* meaning "given to uttering gnomes" (*O.E.D.*). This gives some idea of the content of the muttering of Crones. In case there are some who would still have any doubt about the Elemental quality of Gnomic writing, it may be helpful to recall that Emily Dickinson described herself as a Gnome, and that her poetry has been called Gnomic.

Undines: Undine is defined as "a water nymph: an elemental spirit of the water, NIX." Cirlot, in *A Dictionary of Symbols,* writes:

With undines, it is the feminine [read: female]—or perilous—nature of the waters which is symbolized. . . . These nymphs are usually wicked insofar as they represent the treacherousness of rivers, lakes and torrents.[9]

Of course, Elemental women and nature are described as "perilous," "wicked," and "treacherous" by those in the Lecherous State who would block our flow.

It is significant that Undines are frequently identified with Mermaids. As Emily Culpepper has shown, Mermaids are powerful symbols for Self-identified women, suggesting the buoyancy and freedom of movement in water. Moreover, the Mermaid's anatomy suggests that she cannot be raped.[10]

Salamanders: As symbol, *Salamander* means "a mythical and not clearly defined animal having the power to endure fire without harm." The adjective *salamandrous* means "living as it were in fire; fiery, hot, passionate" (*O.E.D.*). In Heraldry, the Salamander depicts bravery and courage unquenched by the fires of affliction. Elemental women move within a Salamandrous tradition, re-membering in our own lives the nine million women who were massacred during the Witchcraze in Western Europe. Although their bodies were reduced to ashes, the spirits of the Witches have survived. As Anne Dellenbaugh has remarked, the Salamanders are mythic reminders of those enduring spirits.[11] Women re-membering are fueled by Female Fury, and inhabit the element Fire. We are fiery, passionate.* Living and surviving in a tradition of burnings, we have developed a power to endure fire, transforming it into gynergy.†

Sylphs: Sylph is defined as "one of a race of spirits or beings supposed to inhabit the air" (*O.E.D.*). The term *air* should be understood in its fullest mythic and symbolic dimensions. Among the pre-Socratic Greek philosophers, Anaximenes represented the view that air is the originative substance and basic form of matter, and that it changes by condensation and rarefaction. He regarded air as the breath of the world. In his *Dictionary of Symbols,* Cirlot summarizes the widely held symbolism of air, pointing out that whereas in some elemental cosmogonies fire is given pride of

---

* Writing of women and fire, Pat Hynes points out that patriarchal science continues the dishonorable tradition of attempting to steal women's fire, of draining and stealing women's energy. Recounting ancient myths from various cultures, she shows that there is a widespread association of women with fire, and urges that women reclaim this, particularly in the form of intellectual passion. "Intellectual passion is the mind on fire: a fire whose metaphysical energy furiously gathers and creates ideas; a fire whose vital flames light the eyes; a fire whose heat warms the mind and expands the self." See H. Patricia Hynes, "Active Women in Passive '80," *Trivia: A Journal of Ideas,* 1 (Fall 1982), pp. 72–73.

† *Gynergy* is a new word invented by Emily Culpepper in 1975. It stands for that female energy which "both comprehends and creates who we are. It is woman-identified be-ing." See her article "Female History/ Myth Making," *The Second Wave,* 4 (Spring 1975), pp. 14–17. This word has passed into common feminist usage in many areas.

place and considered the origin of all things, the more general belief is that air is the primary element. He writes:

Compression or concentration of air creates heat or fire, from which all forms of life are then derived. Air is essentially related to three sets of ideas: the creative breath of life, and, hence, speech; the stormy wind, connected in many mythologies with the idea of creation; and, finally, space as a medium for movement and for the emergence of life-processes.[12]

In order to understand our own Elemental powers, it is helpful to consider these three sets of ideas.

First, air is associated with the creative breath of life, hence with speech. As inhabitants of the air, Lusty women are breathers/speakers of Radiant Words. Insofar as we are Elemental, our speech releases words from the state of contamination. Like a sharp wind, it cuts through smog, clarifying, making it possible to breathe freely again. The more we become attuned to Radiant Words and give them incarnation (in speech, writing, music and other art forms, as well as in our lives), the more effectively we remove the man-made obstacles to breathing.

Second, air is the stormy wind, connected with the idea of creation. The synonyms for *wind* suggest the diversity of Elemental female creativity. These are: BREEZE, GALE, HURRICANE, GUST, BLAST, SQUALL, ZEPHYR, WHIRLWIND, CYCLONE, TYPHOON, TORNADO, WATERSPOUT, TWISTER.[13] To have some idea of the diversity, we might compare ZEPHYR and TORNADO. A *zephyr* is "a light gentle delicate wind, one that would not disturb halcyon weather." In contrast to this, a *tornado* is "a swirling wind accompanied by a funnel-shaped cloud moving with a force so violent that it cannot be measured accurately." We should understand the term *violent* here in a way totally other than patriarchal violence that intentionally violates. A tornado's violence is simply natural, Wild force. The movement of Elemental women also is forceful, in varying styles and velocities. Insofar as we are true to the Gyn/Ecological context, our Movement in its diversity is ultimately creative, as are the forces of nature. Elemental creativity is utterly Other than the acontextual and anti-contextual meddling with nature that characterizes phallic technocracy.

Such meddling, which is anti-creation, is the product and cause of what Paracelsus (and doubtless the Witches from whom he took his ideas) called *elementaries*.[14] Elementary—or what I would also call "plastic"—products and processions are simulations and substitutes for the Elemental, the Wild.

The substitution of the elementary for the Elemental in women's lives is illustrated in the patriarchal control of women's creativity. Thus, our speech is curtailed by manners and lethal custom into polite, shallow verbiage. It is also directed by phallic game rules into flattering, self-denying babble designed to inflate male egos. Our creativity is misdirected into misplaced rage against other women. It is tracked into soap opera level aspects of "relationships." Under therapeutic treatment, it is tracked into psychobabble that closes off deep Memory. When academically trained, it repeats male theories. Groomed for professional excellence, it serves phallic institutions. "Religious," it worships a male god.

The third symbolic aspect of air is its depiction as a medium for movement and for the emergence of life processes. This is particularly important, especially in view of the fact that in patriarchy women have been denied space, as Virginia Woolf elegantly demonstrates in *A Room of One's Own*. One thinks of Jane Austen struggling to write her novels in the "common room." Denial of physical space is accompanied by overt and subtle levels of denial of mental and emotional space. Since these space warps are so invisible and subliminal, women struggling under such conditions often feel "spacy," or dis-oriented. This effect is increased by the fact that women are spatially separated from each other on many levels—forced into conditions of isolation and alienation which are felt as ghostly, spooky. Women desperately *need* our own space/medium for Self-centering movement and emergence of life processes.

Elemental women create such a medium, making possible exits from confinement in elementary spaces. We strive to create an atmosphere in which further creativity may flourish. Self-identified women thus become Sylph-identified[15]—that is, we become breathers/creators of free space. We are windy, stirring the stagnant spaces with life. Lusty, Elemental women, speaking our own words, heal the broken connections between words and their sources. We re-connect the Speaker with her Original words. Spinning/spirating Elemental connections between Words and Sources we overcome/transverse the verbicide of the ages.

Breathing forth this healing, we confront the agents of gynocide, for we are re-membering the Archaic lore and the Pure Lusty Logic of our Race.

This Elemental Verbal power is angelic. The word *angel* originally means emissary, messenger. An angel is a spiritual being of great intelligence. Claiming that speaking Radiant Words has Angelic power is Naming/re-claiming primal force. It is overcoming the false dichotomy between spirit and matter, proclaiming Lust for that Integrity of be-ing from which we have been separated and which we have half-forgotten, but never lost.

BATTLES OF PRINCIPALITIES AND POWERS

The apostle Paul, as we have seen, was far from fond of autonomous Elemental spirits. He often referred to these as "principalities and powers," using these two names to represent the whole array of Elemental spirits (*stoicheia*) in all of their gradations.[16] Scholars commonly hold that the name *principalities,* as used by Paul, refers to the organized cosmological powers of the angels.[17] These, together with the *powers,* Paul saw as spirits that might hinder "salvation" and he wanted these threatening spirits to be safely "subject" to Christ. His obvious fear reflects the fact that there was widespread belief in angels, understood not merely as "messengers," but as spirits of natural phenomena, who were aware of the secrets of the cosmos.

It is interesting to read pauline texts that express the wish to subdue such manifestations of Elemental be-ing. For example, there is the often cited text in the Epistle to the Romans:

For I am sure that neither death, nor life, nor angels, nor principalities, nor things present, nor things to come, nor powers, nor height, nor depth, nor anything else in all creation, will be able to separate us from the love of God in Christ Jesus our Lord. (Rom. 8:38 [R.S.V.])

No doubt millions have experienced the seductiveness of this passage, which sounds like an expression of Divine True Romance. Thus seduced, the listener is supposed to fail to notice anything suspicious about a "love" to which principalities, powers, height, depth, et cetera, would seem to be so opposed.

The war that rages through these pages, then, involves battles of principalities and powers, unmasking deceptions, reclaiming original autonomy. The fighters are fired/inspired by Pure Lust, reeling through realms half-forgotten, re-turning through spheres of deep Memory, unforgetting Archaic Potency. This whirling/wandering means Weaving through the Wild, the Weird, recalling Amazonian Archelogy. This term, dryly defined by *Webster's* as "the science of first principles," is wryly defined by Websters as "the Realizing of our Original Potency."

The warrior aspect of our Realizing/Roaming the Realms of Pure Lust requires that Shrews sharpen our powers to recognize the enemies of our process, that Scolds scald these scoundrels with the flames of our Fury. What follows is a basic Self-defense kit for Scolds, a Prudishly prepared "package" of precise pejoratives which I have Named "A Glossary of Snools."

A GLOSSARY OF SNOOLS

As Wanderlusty/Wonderlusty women weave our way Weirdward into the Realms of Pure Lust we find we must fight off the Fixers/Tricksters, those poisonous presences whose program is to freeze/frustrate our Movement. These are the sovereigns of the sado-state, which can also be called the State of Boredom. For it is infinitely boring to be blocked from the movement of/toward one's innately ordained happiness. The corporate Big Brothers of Boredom daily demonstrate the impotence to reach beyond appearances that characterizes phallic lust. Unable to be whole, those driven by that lust attempt to find holes everywhere, to penetrate, to pierce into an inner reality which they yearn to destroy but cannot even find.

This compulsion to bore everywhere bores Lusty women. The institutions of Boredom—its media, its schools, its industries, its amusements, its religion, its governments, its culture—are programmed to control Viragos, to keep us within the confines of bore-ocracy, using bore-ocratic details and mazes. Weird women snore at the brothers' Bored Meetings, seeing through the lecherous leaders as Chairmen of the Bored.

Given these conditions of Stag-nation, Elemental Shrews and Furies urgently experience the need for Re-Naming/Re-Claiming our stolen Flames, undoing the promethean theft of Fire, retrieving our ravaged desire.

The would-be preventers of this retrieval of gynergy, the ghosts/ghouls that want our movement dead, are *snools*. The noun *snool* means (Scottish) "a cringing person." It means also "a tame, abject, or mean-spirited person" (*O.E.D.*). In sadosociety, snools rule, and snools are the rule. The dual personalities of these per-sonae—the cast of characters governing and legitimizing bore-ocracy—are unmasked by definitions of the verb *snool*. This means, on the one hand, "to reduce to submission: COW, BULLY," and on the other hand, "CRINGE, COWER." Snools are sadism and masochism combined, the stereotypic saints and heroes of the sadostate.

Nags use words like *snool*, not to define the essence of any sentient being but to Name agents *as agents* of the atrocities of the sadostate. This Naming is not essentially different from the use of such terms as *rapist* or *wife-beater*—terms which describe the perpetrators of certain atrocities *as agents* of those acts and, by implication, as having certain characteristics associated with such behavior. A rapist, for example, may also be a physician, a pro-fessor, a father, a voter. Shrews would suspect that these other roles would be seriously affected by the fact that the gentleman is a rapist. So also, snools—agents of the atrocities motivated by phallic lust—cannot be imagined to isolate their snoolishness into one area of action, but rather to communicate this in manifold ways.

Snools could sometimes be called *persons* in the sense of the Latin word *persona,* meaning mask, actor, role. These *personae* "take over" individuals who perform the snoolish functions re-quired to maintain and perpetuate the sadostate. This is not to say that individuals lack responsibility for allowing themselves to assume such roles. The contrary is the case.

The snoolish actors, then, sustain and are sustained by the sadostate. (Ronald Reagan, for example, could be a case in point.) Their acts, roles, productions, and endless reproductions are gynocidal in many ways, not least of which is the spawning of something like *screen memory*. This is "an imagined or real recollection of early childhood that is recalled with magnification of importance or other distortion that aids in the repression of another memory of deep emotional significance." The stages and screens of the Fathers' Foreground, the state of fabrications/fictions, flash forth terrifying and murderous shapes that consti-tute a mass of man-made magnified, mummifying "memories," repressing women's ancient Other Memories that are of deep Emotional significance.

Snools appear and re-appear in various forms. The thrusting throng includes the following snoolish agents/actors/types:

bores	flashers	plug-uglies	snitches
botchers/butchers	framers	pricks	snookers
cocks	frauds	prickers	snoops
danglers	hacks	rakes	snot boys*
dicks	hucksters	rippers	snudges
drones	jabbers	shams	snuffers
fakes	jerks	sneaks	studs
fixers	jocks	sniffers	wantwits

Et cetera. A few of these "deserve" special elaboration/explanation.

Fixers have an essential function, namely, to fix female Fury. Examination of the verb *fix* yields important information concerning the tactics of fixers. *Fix* is from the Latin *fixus,* past participle of *figere,* meaning to fasten, pierce. Thus its roots suggest varieties of phallic fixing of Wild women. The definitions of *fix* fulfill this promise. It means "to give a final or permanent form to: make definite and settled." It means "to make nonvolatile and solid." It means "to treat so as to make some condition permanent." It means "to kill, harden and preserve (as organisms or fresh tissues) for microscopic study or other purposes."

Fix also means "to establish or make (as a trait, quality, peculiarity) permanent by selective breeding." It means "FASTEN, ATTACH, AFFIX." *Fix* means "to hold fast: CAPTURE." It means

* In a creation story related by native women of Vancouver Island, Copper Woman cries bitter tears of loneliness. The tears and mucus from her eyes and nose form into a small, incomplete thing. This is Snot Boy, the incomplete manikin. Throughout his life and in all of his behavior, Snot Boy remains incomplete. See Anne Cameron, *Daughters of Copper Woman* (Vancouver, British Columbia: Press Gang Publishers, 1981), pp. 26–34.

"CASTRATE, SPAY." It means "to remove a principal means of defense from (as a pet skunk)." *Fix* means "to determine the outcome of (a contest) by bribery or other improper methods." It means "to tamper with in advance (a horse fixed to lose a race)." It means "to get even with: PUNISH." One definition of *fix* as an intransitive verb suggests the results in women's behavior of the fixers' deadly work. Thus *fix* means "to settle or remain permanently: cease from wandering."

This array of definitions, then, discloses the tawdry tactics of the Fix-Masters[18] who continually aim to freeze life, making Elemental be-ing stationary, implanted with fixes, nonvolatile, solid/stolid, killed, hardened, preserved, selectively bred, fastened, captured, castrated, made defenseless, bribed, tampered with—so that we will forever cease from wandering. This is the State of the Grateful Dead.[19]

The fixers' plan is the permanent establishment of fixocracy. The female inhabitants of that ideal state, if all goes "well," are pierced to the core, fastened forever within the confines of the touchable caste. Prior to the attainment of this final state—the Beatific Fission of women, which is fusion with the fixers—women are subjected to a multitude of pre-fixes.[20] These include fabricated emotions, fictitious memories. Filled with such fixed feelings, fixed ideas, pre-fixed women become more and more fictitious, even to themselves, unknowingly trapped within the fixocratic house of mirrors.

Among the henchmen required for the smooth operation of fixocracy are the cocks, danglers, pricks, and flashers who keep girls and women intimidated. Necessary also are the fakes, framers, frauds, and hucksters whose job is to manufacture and spread delusions. Heavier work is assumed by rakes, hacks, rippers and plug-uglies.

Plug-uglies are among the grosser snoolish incarnations. *Plugugly* is defined as "a member of a gang of disorderly ruffians often active in political pressure and intimidation." The term *disorderly* as applied here has nothing to do with truly Wild disorder, of course. It is descriptive of brutality characteristic of snooldom. Thus, plug-uglies include everyday rapists, child-abusers, pimps, wife-beaters, maimers, murderers, dismemberers, as well as professional hatchet-men such as those physicians and surgeons, politicians, scientists, and military experts who kill in order to cure.

Plug-uglies inhabit every populated area of this planet. Moreover, they have plugged themselves in to women and nature.

It is thought-provoking to consider that one meaning of *plug* is "a male fitting used to make an electrical connection by insertion in a receptacle or body and having one or more contact-making parts or blades that serve to close a circuit." Plug-uglies, while creating the illusion that they are always giving something, are in fact drainers of energy whose plugged-in fittings close women's circuits, sapping the flow of gynergetic currents so that these cannot circulate within/among women.

Among the others in the snoolish throng, prickers have particular historical significance. A *pricker,* of course, is "one who pricks suspected Witches to prove their guilt or innocence." Prudes know that prickers have been omnipresent in all eras of patriarchy. They are *sneaks, snoops.* They are *snookers,* for *snook* means "to pry about, especially while sniffing and smelling." They are *snudges,* for a *snudge* is "a mean avaricious person . . . a sneaking or sponging fellow."

Such, then, are the rulers/snoolers of snooldom, the place/time where the air is filled with the crowing of cocks, the joking of jocks, the droning of clones, the sniveling of snookers and snudges, the noisy parades and processions of prickers. Such is cockocracy/jockocracy, the State of supranational, supernatural erections. This is a world made to the image of its makers, a chip off the old blocks/cocks, who are worshipped by the fraternal faithless as god the flasher, god the stud, and god the wholly hoax.

Wayward, Wanton women, having been warned of the snoolish snares, proceed forthwith on our Wonderlusting/Wisdomweaving Quest.

METAPHORS OF METABEING

At this point it is important to discuss briefly the role of symbols and metaphors in Elemental feminist philosophy, particularly since this mode of discourse traditionally has been disdained by philosophers in general and metaphysicians in particular. Since this work describes/unfolds a deviant philosophy—and a philosophy for deviants—the reader might jump to the facile conclusion that the use of metaphor is "understandable" or even "excusable" in the absence of an adequate philosophical/metaphysical tradition to express woman-identified thought. The point is, however, that symbols and "mere" metaphors are required, not because of some deficiency or lack in the sphere of abstract conceptualization, but because of the demanding, rigorous nature of the work itself.

Symbols, in contrast to mere signs, participate in that to which they point. They open up levels of reality otherwise closed to us and they unlock dimensions and elements of our souls which correspond to these hidden dimensions and elements of reality. As Tillich pointed out, they cannot be artificially produced, but rather grow out of the unconscious. "They grow when the situation is ripe for them, and they die when the situation changes." [21] There is no way that Elemental feminist philosophy can speak adequately to the realms of Wild be-ing without symbols. In discovering these, we must pay particular attention to the task of "sounding out" symbols. Of course, there can be no One Absolutely Right symbol for all Lusty women, for we belong to different tribes and have great individual diversity. Despite this fact, and also because of it, Prudes prudently heed our intuitions about which symbols ring true, listening to the sounds of their names and to the rhythms of the contexts in which this Naming occurs.

When I use the word *metaphor* I intend this to include the qualities attributed above to symbols. However, there is more involved. As theologian Nelle Morton has explained, metaphors evoke action, movement. They Name/evoke a shock, a clash with the "going logic" and they introduce a new logic.[22] Metaphors function to Name change, and therefore they elicit change. When, for example, I write of women using double-edged words as *Labryses* to cut through mazes of man-made mystification, the word *Labrys* is not a static symbol; rather, it is associated with transforming action. Thus the very arduousness of the task of Naming and calling forth Elemental be-ing requires metaphors.*

---

* Julian Jaynes has written nicely about metaphors: "Let us speak of metaphor. The most fascinating property of language is its capacity to make metaphors. But what an understatement! For metaphor is not a mere extra trick of language, as it is so often slighted in the old schoolbooks on composition; it is the very constitutive ground of language." See *The Origin of Consciousness in the Breakdown of the Bicameral Mind* (Boston: Houghton Mifflin Company, 1976), p. 48.

The word *metaphor* is derived from the Greek *meta* plus *pherein,* meaning to bear, carry. Moreover, *metapherein* means to transfer, change. Metaphors of Muses carry us past the unnatural beings/things that are simulations of be-ing, leaving these in the past. Metaphors of Soothsayers carry us toward knowledge of our future as they connect us with our Racing memories. They transform/transfer our perceptions of reality, enabling us to "break set" and thus to break out of linguistic prisons.

Metaphors are necessary for Elemental feminist philosophy, for this is about and *is* transformation, movement. It is philosophy in the basic sense of "love or pursuit of wisdom: search for the underlying principles and causes of reality." This Lust/pursuit is Racing; it is Musing. An Archaic meaning of the verb *muse* is "to become astonished: WONDER, MARVEL." Women who Lust for wisdom become astonished/astonishing, Wondering. As Muses of our own creation, Wonderlusters re-member our Original Powers. Unlike the frozen "philosophy" that is packaged and stored within academic refrigerators, Wonderlust moves us always. Our vehicles are often Metaphors. Our destinations are the Realms of Metabeing.

The word *Metabeing* is used here to Name Realms of active participation in the Powers of Be-ing.* Be-ing, the Verb, cannot without gross falsification be reified into a noun, whether that noun be identified as "Supreme Being," or "God," or "Goddess" (singular or plural). When I choose to use such words as *Goddess* it is to point Metaphorically to the Powers of Be-ing, the Active Verb in whose potency all biophilic reality participates.

A problem that is implicit in such Naming is the classic philosophical problem of "the one and the many." For it is clear that Lusty women are profoundly different from each other. Not only are there ethnic, national, class and racial differences that shape our perspectives, but there are also individual and cross-cultural differences of temperament, virtue, talent, taste, and of conditions within which these can or cannot find expression. There is, then, an extremely rich, complex Diversity among women and within each individual. But there is also above, beyond, beneath all this

---

* Classical metaphysics spurns metaphorical analogy in favor of what is technically called *the analogy of being.* Elemental philosophy, since it is concerned with participation in Be-ing *requires* metaphorical analogy.

a Cosmic Commonality, a tapestry of connectedness which women as Websters/Fates are constantly weaving. The weaving of this tapestry is the Realizing of a dream, which Adrienne Rich has Named "The Dream of a Common Language." [23]

The word *Metabeing* is a metaphysical way of Naming forth and Naming faith in this common bonding of Lusty women. For *Metabeing* Names the Elemental participation in Powers of Be-ing which is the source of authentic female bonding. By choosing the plural—*Powers* of Be-ing—I intend to affirm our Diversity within Commonality.[24]

Metabeing conveys multiple meanings, since the prefix *meta* has several senses. First, it means "occurring later." This aspect is important since, under patriarchal conditions, knowledge of participation in Elemental Powers of Be-ing is experienced as an existential breakthrough *after* a woman has understood that the blockage of her powers within phallocracy, that is, the reduction of these to mere things/beings, is insufferable. The second meaning of *meta,* which is "situated behind," is also essential, for Lusty women's dis-coverings of our be-ing are not experienced as entirely new. In breaking through the man-made reifications of Be-ing, women enter Realms that are situated behind these reifications—the Realms of our ancestral memories. These memories can move women out of the passive state of things/nouns, cut off from our own be-ing.

The third sense of *meta,* that is, "change in, transformation of," thus follows logically, for dis-covering Metabeing means transforming release of lives that have been fragmented and frozen into stagnant bits of being. Since this transformation is not "once and for all," but rather a continuing process, the fourth meaning of *meta,* that is, "beyond, transcending," is also essential. The Realms of *Metabeing* are times/spaces of continuing transcending of earlier stages of shedding the shackles of body/mind that fix women as targets of phallic lust.

Metaphors of Metabeing awaken Muses, awaken in Muses memories that transform us, transfer us to these Realms of continuing transcending. Once partially awake, Muses awaken more Metaphors. We live in a veritable sea of sleeping Metaphors. Philosopher Susanne Langer referred to "faded" metaphors and suggested that "our literal language is a very repository of 'faded metaphors.' " [25] Explaining this, she wrote:

... if a metaphor is used very often, we learn to accept the word in its metaphorical context as though it had a literal meaning there. If we say: "The brook runs swiftly," the word "runs" does not connote any leg-action, but a shallow rippling flow. If we say that a rumor runs through the town, we think of neither leg-action nor of ripples; or if a fence is said to run around the barnyard, there is not even a connotation of changing place. Originally they were probably all metaphors but one (though it is hard to say which was the primitive literal sense).[26]

Like Langer, Shrews are aware of apparently faded metaphors, but unlike Langer's theory, Shrewish analysis dis-covers a sexual politics of fading. Powerful old words whose Metaphoric force has "faded" under the reign of phallicism include *Spinster, Witch, charm, spell, Weird, Goddess*. In fact, these words have not lost their vitality but have been covered under rubble heaps of bore-ocratic verbiage. Dis-covering them is a Wonder-full Work for Websters, yielding endless riches. Like Gnomes who know how to find buried treasures, we unearth these riches and share this abundance with friends. To snools, of course, the treasures remain invisible, "faded."

Carried by Metaphors to the Realms of Metabeing, Musing women encounter/uncover our own First Questions and hence find our First Philosophy. Since Prudes are occupied with our own priorities, making biophilic participation in Be-ing our ultimately intimate concern, it is imperative that we Weave a First Philosophy of the First Sex. Implicit in this Naming of the first sex is a conjuring of such visionary Foresisters as Elizabeth Gould Davis—the bold ones, the uncompromising Crones.[27]

In the classic philosophical tradition, *first philosophy* means ontology, the "philosophy of being." In the Elemental transition, *first philosophy* Names the philosophy of be-ing. It is first in the sense that it is Elemental, for elements are first principles. Since this first philosophy is about Elemental be-ing, it is radically metaphysical, concerned with ontological potency, knowledge, passion, virtue, creation, transformation. Given this complexity, our thinking must be not only imaginatively intense and concrete, but also intellectually extensive and abstract. The deep Spinning power of Metaphor is essential, and so is the honed logic of traditionally rational discourse. To Wonderlusters, these are as inseparable as the edges of the Labrys.

A standard definition of *ontology* is "the science or study of being; that department of metaphysics that relates to the being or essence of things, or to being in the abstract" (*O.E.D.*). Traditionally, it has attempted to deal with the most primary philosophical questions. Yet the questions have been framed/confined within parameters that fail to express biophilic intuitions. They are framed by the word *being* itself. Theologian/philosopher Paul Tillich exemplifies these limitations.* He wrote, for example:

The ontological question, the question of being-itself, arises in something like a "metaphysical shock"—the shock of possible nonbeing. This shock often has been expressed in the question, "Why is there something; why not nothing?" [28]

Readers who have subjected themselves to philosophical "discipline" are familiar with such language. One of the positive things that can happen when biophilic women read such words is the eliciting of a memory of an intuition of be-ing. The situation is complex, however. As a result of the intellectual deprivation inflicted upon all women, those who can still feel a deep thirst for philosophy are often too respectful of such "masters" and overlook their fundamental fallacy—phallicism. Thus, when reading the question "Why is there something; why not nothing?" a Wonderlusty woman might imagine that the question thus posed corresponds to her own ontological experience, to her Lust for Being. She might imagine that the ontological question thus posed expresses an attitude identical with her own Wonder and gratitude that things *are*. Caught up in this Wonder, she might fail to notice anything suspect about the second half of Tillich's question: "why not nothing?" Musing women would do well to ask ourSelves whether this question would arise spontaneously in biophilic consciousness.

Thought that starts with the noun, *being,* cannot go behind it —cannot transform/transfer itself into Realms of Metabeing.

* I have selected Tillich as an example precisely because of the vast scope and rigor of his thought, which sometimes inspires thinking beyond such limitations. In other words, I have chosen him because of his stature, because his work is worth studying and criticizing by those who would embark upon the adventure of dis-covering Elemental philosophy (provided, of course, that we employ his writings only as springboards for our own original analysis).

Such thought is stuck, fixated, fixed and thus does not actively participate in Powers of Be-ing. It is terrified of these Powers. Tillich reveals his terror:

Thought is based on being, and it cannot leave this basis; but thought can imagine the negation of everything that *is,* and it can describe the nature and structure of being which give everything that is the power of resisting nonbeing.[29]

The philosophers of phallicism, huddling behind the bastions of reified *being,* unable to leave this basis, can well imagine the negation of these bastions of boring thought, for they know that they are living, as it were, in a house of cards. The implications of such ontology are the antithesis of Wonderlusty, Elemental philosophy, the quest for Be-ing. The fact of the antithesis must be evident to Nag-Gnostic Archelogians.

The quest of Wanton women is not preoccupied with terror of "the negation of everything that *is.*" Rather it is rooted in the intuition that Powers of Be-ing are constantly unfolding, creating, communicating—Be-ing more. And it is rooted in the experience of active potency to move behind the Foreground of fathergods and other fabrications, fictions, fixed questions and answers, entering the Radiant Realms of Metabeing.

METHOD AND STYLE

In keeping with the tradition of Methodicide, this book is a work of studied *errata.* It is also part of the process of creative crystallizing of women's experience.[30] From the patriarchal perspective, therefore, it is, quite simply and entirely, a Mistake. Within this context of Total Erroneousness, a few details still call for clarification:

1. Since the language and style of patriarchal scholarship cannot contain or convey the gynergy of Pure Lust, in this book, as elsewhere, I invent, dis-cover, re-member words.
2. The choice between the pronouns *we* and *they* to refer to women is problematic. At times the choice of one or the other pronoun is easily justifiable, but often it is necessary to "play by ear" pronoun usage—for language reflects the conditions of alienation that prevail in patriarchy, as radical linguists, such as Julia Penelope, have shown.[31]

3. My use of capitalization is capitally irregular. It is intended to convey my meaning rather than to conform to standard usage. Since the immediate context of a particular passage affects the meaning of the words it contains, my choices concerning capitalization are not rigidly consistent even with usage elsewhere in this book.
4. The primary sources of *Pure Lust* are woman-identified experiences and observations. Its secondary sources are patriarchal texts. As I explained elsewhere:

> I use the latter in various ways. Sometimes I use them as springboards. At all times I am acutely aware that most of these books and articles were written at the expense of women, whose energies were drained and ideas freely and shamelessly taken over. . . . Finally, I must add that in using male sources, at no point have I acted in the position of "disciple" citing an authority.[32]

THE MOVEMENT OF THIS BOOK

Pure Lust wonders/wanders through three Realms of Spheres. Each Realm is reached through a *Foreground* in which Lusters confront specific conditions that impede entrance to the particular Realm we are approaching. Each *Foreground* thus constitutes an essential entranceway into the deep Realm it precedes—a place of unmasking the snoolish simulations intended to entrance questioners/questers, fixing us forever at the entrance, entrapped by tricksters.

The Foreground to the First Realm exposes the sadosociety and its legitimation by the saints and sages of sadospirituality. Nag-Gnostic Nags break their trance by unveiling the pathetic fallacies of the sadostate. Encouraged by knowing that one meaning of *trance* is "to pass or travel over the ground; to move briskly; PRANCE." Prudes trance/prance through this flatland into the Spheres of this Realm, which are *Archespheres*.

In this Realm, Shrews shrink the alienating archetypes drawn by drones and dangled by flashers to fix/frame women in amnesic oblivion. In courses of anamnesia, of unforgetting our Archaic origins, Lusters uncover the Archimage—the Original Witch—within our Selves. We re-member Isis, cosmic writer and librarian, and weave the way toward Naming our own Real Presence. Weirds conjure the Courage to Sin—to Realize be-ing. Brewsters brew potions, primevally potent. Our Archaic active powers are unleashed. Angelic forces are awakened.

The Foreground to the Second Realm presents plastic passions, potted feelings, and victimizing "virtues" and "vices" as specimens of man-made fixations, to be exorcised by Lusters. Prudes, Dragons, Viragos, Vixens and the whole array of Weird Wanderers here confront the fabricated tendencies and habits embedded in our psyches by snools. Vitalized by this exorcism, we vacate this Foreground and forge into the Spheres of this Realm, which are *Pyrospheres*.

Here Pyromantic Prancers/Dancers dissect the tactics and taboos that have kept us confined as the Touchable Caste. We know that breaking the casts of this caste requires focused ontological Passion, and choosing this, we join the Raging Race. Gnostic Nags thus breaking free begin a new and Gnomic Naming of Virtues, Vices. This purifying kindling of Impassioned Virtue burns away the vestiges of demonic domestication. Freed of these tidy ties, we *are* our own Daimons, Muses, and we Move, Muse in Tidal rhythms.

The Foreground to the Third Realm exposes the baffling traps of embedded desires for belonging, befriending, and bewitchingness—which are mirror images of Grace-full Movements—and the devices by which these are perpetuated. It explores theories of Metamorphic Movement. Realizing our Labryses as Butterflies, Erratic women eccentrically soar from this Foreground, entering the Spheres of this Realm, which are *Metamorphospheres*.

In this Realm, Websters see Stamina as its own reward. Here thinking is also thanking; the Wonderers weave wonders. Sensing the rhythms of a Gnomic Present, Prudes explore the States of Grace. Structurally, these are three: Be-Longing, Be-Friending, Be-Witching.* Cheered by such progress, Norns announce the founding of Gnostic Nag-Nations.[33] Dragons are in our Elements. Muses Muse, compose, create. The Wording of Weirds concresces Weirdward, humming, hissing, howling in harmonies of Spheres.

---

* Be-Friending is the weaving of a context in which female friendship —which Jan Raymond has Named *Gyn/affection*—can flourish. She has developed a historical and philosophical analysis of this female-centered reality in her forthcoming book, *A Genealogy of Female Friendship,* to be published by Beacon Press, Boston.

THE FIRST REALM
ARCHESPHERES

CHAPTER ONE

FOREGROUND TO THE FIRST REALM: THE SADOSOCIETY AND ITS SADOSPIRITUAL LEGITIMATORS

Archespheres:	Unimaginable to the compilers of patriarchal lexicons, therefore unlisted in . . .
	Webster's Third New International Dictionary of the English Language
Archespheres:	"the Radiant Realm of Elemental/Female Origins."
	Websters' First New Intergalactic Wickedary of the English Language

Lusty Wanderers must face the foreground conditions that impede our entry into the Realm of Archespheres, the Realm of Realizing our Archaic/Elemental powers. As prelude to our analysis of Elemental Self-empowering, therefore, it is necessary that Nags know the prevailing and legitimating ideology of the society spawned by phallic lust—the sadosociety.

The sadosociety is the sum of places/times where the beliefs and practices of sadomasochism are The Rule. It is formed/framed by statutes of studs, decrees of drones, canons of cocks, fixations of fixers, precepts of prickers, regulations of rakes and rippers. It is bore-ocracy. In effect, sadosociety is snooldom, schooled by snools. Pre-eminent among these are the pseudosages and saints who expound/expose the ideology of sadospirituality.

The sadosociety, then, is legitimated by sadospirituality. This is characterized by obsessive asceticism imposed upon others as well as themselves by the fabricators of ascetic fixations, who become models and ideologists for those within their spheres of influence. Sado-asceticism is in fact pseudo-asceticism; it is pseudo-purity. Its ramifications are vast, extending to sensory, intellectual, economic, and emotional deprivations of all kinds and to the infliction/affliction of ontological impotence, which is the blockage of participation in Be-ing.

The Sadospiritual Syndrome will be studied here under two aspects: *first*, as phallic flight from lust into phallic asceticism; *second*, as phallic flight from lust into "transformed" lechery. This second form of lecherous flight assumes a trinitarian shape, manifesting itself through the sado-sublime, through sado-sublimation, and through spiritual subversion by means of seductive sado-sublimination.[1] As we shall see, sadospirituality demands the destruction of women's ancestral Memory, the blocking of our capacity to conceive, speak, and act upon our own Original Words. That is, it causes the condition which Louky Bersianik has Named the amnesia of women.[2]

SADOSPIRITUALITY I: PHALLIC FLIGHT FROM LUST INTO PHALLIC ASCETICISM

Sado-asceticism is altogether dependent upon the sadomasochistic obsessions from which it attempts to escape. The direction of "escape" is into further futile fixations. This phenomenon is illustrated in the life and writings of the famous ascetic and father of the church saint Jerome (342–420), who described his experience in the following words:

I sat alone, the companion of scorpions and wild beasts, and yet was in the midst of dancing girls. My face was white with fasting, but the mind in my cold body was hot with desires. The fires of lust burnt up a body that was already dead.[3]

Jerome was a typical saint.

We might meditate also upon the life of the third century hermit saint Anthony, who, when he began his life as a hermit, saw "beautiful women" every night.[4] Saint Benedict, the sixth century "patriarch of Western monks," was haunted by a fair face until "at last, flinging away the skin which was his only dress, he flung himself naked into a thorn bush, and rolled himself in this bed until he had extinguished the lure of the senses."[5] Such cases can be multiplied thousands of times.

Especially instructive is the case of the fifth century saint Symeon Stylites the elder, the first and most famous of the pillar ascetics. We are told that Symeon began his monastic life as an enclosed anchorite by dwelling for forty days in a cave with his right leg fastened by iron to a stone. "When the bit of leather which protected his skin from the iron was removed, admirers counted in it twenty fat bugs which Symeon had refused to disturb." [6] His disciple Antonius stated admiringly that when he walked vermin dropped from his body.

In 423 A.D. Symeon mounted his famous pillar, on top of which he spent the next thirty-six years. Over the years the pillar's height was increased to sixty feet, for, "despairing of escaping the world horizontally, he tried to escape it vertically." [7] The record of his success is thought-provoking:

His fame as a saint was unequaled throughout the East. Arabs, Persians, Armenians, strangers even from Spain and Britain journeyed to gaze on this prodigy of austerity. The letters which he dictated from his pillar to his disciples on the dogmas of the Councils of Ephesus and Chalcedon were looked upon as authoritative pronouncements. Kings and emperors crouched at the foot of his pillar, cherishing, as if they were precious pearls, "the worms that dropped from his body," gazing with awe as Symeon touched his feet with his forehead 1244 times in succession. . . . He was called "the most holy martyr in the air." [8]

Symeon perished on his pillar in 459 and the said pillar was enclosed on the heights of Telnishé in a splendid church which no woman was ever allowed to enter.

There is variety as well as sameness in the tomes of sadohagiology. Saint Jerome admiringly wrote of a saint who lived in an old cistern on five figs a day. [9] There were "grazing monks" who ate grass, as if they were cattle. [10] Physical filth as a sign of spiritual purity was a common christian theme both in the East and in the West. We are told of a monk who for fifty years never changed his shirt or washed his face or feet, that "in his face one could discern the purity of his soul." [11] Although some scholars insist that there was greater fanaticism in the East than in the West, this was only a matter of degree.

It should not be imagined that sadospirituality afflicted ardent christians only in ancient times. Twentieth century armchair ascetics have included pious hack writers and their avid readers.

In an edifying work entitled *The American Martyrs,* John A. O'Brien offers blood-curdling descriptions of "Indians" torturing jesuit missionary "martyrs":

They [the Indians] cut off his [the priest's] nose, sliced off his upper lip, pulled out his tongue and hacked a piece off it. They placed fire-brands against his bleeding flesh and shoved one of them into his mouth. . . . They hacked off the charred feet, tore off his scalp, and cut out his heart. This they devoured, and they drank his blood, thinking to imbibe some of his invincible courage. A chief raised his tomahawk over the head of Brebeuf and split the jaw in two.[12]

Having finished off father Brebeuf, the "Indians" turned to his companion Gabriel Lalemant. We read:

Toward nightfall his captors hustled him to a torture post. Like Brebeuf, he fell on his knees and kissed it as if it were the cross of Christ.[13]

Each page is gorier than the preceding. One point is strongly established: The noble christians do not fight back. Supposedly this inspires the "gleeful Indians" to even greater atrocities, as they sardonically assure each priest that "the more one suffers on earth the happier he is in Heaven." [14]

Although these descriptions of the jesuit "martyrs" do not explicitly name the *sexual* component of asceticism, they obviously reflect the male flight from lecherous obsessions. The fanaticism both of the missionaries and of the over-zealous author of these descriptions belongs to the province of sado-hagiology. Historically, the Iroquois—the objects of conquering missionary zeal—were cast into a feminine role by the jesuits. In some ways comparable to the "dancing girls" who haunted the tortured imagination of saint Jerome in the desert, the males among the intended spiritual prey of the militant missionaries in this account took their revenge. However, since they were, in fact, actual individuals, they were enabled to take it actively and not merely as haunting figments in distraught minds of the ascetic missionaries. Typically the history of female Iroquois resistance is not even accorded the acknowledgment of condemnation.*

* In contrast to this deceptive sort of phallo-account that erases native Indian women warriors and resisters, the history of powerful and brave warrior women fighting the Spanish invaders and missionaries who occu-

Such gory glorifications of sadospirituality abound in pious literature. It is important to see these as part of a broader scheme, however. There is diversity in degrees of sophistication and in scope among the works concerned with religious asceticism. Moreover, the extent of the phenomenon is vast, and is hardly confined to christianity. The saintly throng of ascetic heroes circles the globe.

Hindu asceticism is a case in point. Sociologist Barrington Moore summarizes a few practices:

Among more familiar and recently observed forms are lying or sitting on spikes, wearing sandals lined with spikes, holding an arm rigidly aloft until it becomes atrophied, keeping a hand clenched until the fingernails grow through it, hanging the head downward in the smoke of a fire, and sitting between "five fires." In the last form the ascetic sits among four fires, one at each quarter of the compass, with the fierce sun overhead making the fifth flame.[15]

Other hindu ascetics were reported to have lived on beds of nails. One nineteenth century ascetic was reported to have vowed to fix every year a large iron ring into "the most tender part" of his body and to suspend a chain therefrom many yards long to drag along the ground.[16]

It is useful to examine the cases of a few twentieth-century ascetic heroes, which illustrate the lust-full circle of apparent separation from and frenzied return to the fixations of phallocracy.

Mahatma Gandhi. The record of Mahatma Gandhi's ascetic practices has drawn attention in recent years. In his autobiography Gandhi wrote of his possession by lust, by "animal passion," in his youth. At the age of thirty-six, having been married for twenty-four years, he took the vow of brahmacharya, or celibacy. He eliminated "carnal relationship" with women, including his wife, Kasturbai. There are strict rules to keep a "brahmachari" celi-

---

pied and exploited Vancouver Island is movingly told in *Daughters of Copper Woman*. This a-mazing book is a collection of historical accounts preserved for generations through women's oral tradition. See Anne Cameron, *Daughters of Copper Woman* (Vancouver, British Columbia: Press Gang Publishers, 1981).

bate. For example, he must not look at women, and must avoid even eunuchs and animals. The hindu doctrine behind the practice of brahmacharya is the teaching that conservation of semen, or "vital force," is essential for physical, mental, and spiritual power. Gandhi rejected these practices, believing that the brahmachari who really had developed self-control could mingle freely with women. He still had problems, however, and tried to resolve them by fasting, obsessing over foods supposedly responsible for his "animal passion." In order, it seems, to prove to himself that he had overcome his obsessions, he is said to have engaged in his famous, or rather infamous, "experiments in brahmacharya." These were described by Nirmal Kumar Bose, who is cited by Ved Mehta as follows:

"He sometimes asked women to share his bed and even the cover which he used . . . and then tried to ascertain if even the least trace of sensual feeling had been evoked in himself or his companion." [17]

Sometimes he would awaken with shivering fits and ask the woman sleeping next to him to hold him. According to Ved Mehta, toward the end of his life Gandhi was still continuing this practice and explained it with such religious legitimations as the following:

"When the *gopis* [milkmaids] were stripped of their clothes by Krishna, the legend says, they showed no sign of embarrassment or sex-consciousness but stood before the Lord in *rapt* [emphasis mine] devotion." [18]

Gandhi was unable to perceive the obscenity of this ideal of "purity." The idea that these women were being raped ("rapt") spiritually was completely negated. He denied that he was using the women with whom he slept in order to prove his seminal continence. (Gandhi was doing this at the age of seventy-seven.) Orthodox hindus condemned him for his unorthodox brahmacharya practices, "such as his long daily baths and massages, often administered by girls, and his daily walks with his hands on the shoulders of girls." [19] The fact is, however, that Gandhi simply carried through the logic inherent in brahmacharya, affirming that to be truly "successful" one would have to have close but asexual affinity with women. Thus he did not *flee* from women physically only to be obsessed with fantasies. Rather, he increased the illusion of mental flight by intensifying physical proximity.

What is really going on here is an enormous draining of women's energies into the phallocentric cesspool. One must ask what Gandhi received from the women when he asked them to hold him naked in the night. Clearly, it was something not attainable from men. One of the women who slept with him in this manner was interviewed and admitted that her husband did mind her sleeping with Gandhi and had gone to the latter, offering his own body in place of hers. "He [her husband] said that he had more vitality, more energy—was healthier all around." Gandhi knew better and kept the woman, to prove that he was "as free from lustful thoughts as he was from physical desire." [20]

Erik Erikson gives a convoluted explanation of such behavior, interpreting it as an expression of Gandhi's "maternalism":

Gandhi . . . had wanted to purify his relationship to his father by nursing and mothering him; and he had wanted to be an immaculate mother. But when, at the end, he was defeated in his aspiration to be the founding father of a united India, he may well have needed maternal solace himself.[21]

Erikson even says that in this expression of "maternalism" Gandhi was living and wondering out loud "about a multiformity of inclinations which other men hide and bury in strenuous consistency." It is necessary to cut through the stereotype of "motherhood" that beclouds the thinking of Gandhi, Bose, Erikson et al. and notice the blatant clues here. Gandhi wanted something which he recognized as female but which he could neither name accurately nor possess in himself.* He was not at all unusual in his attempts to tap into female energy sources.

T. E. Lawrence. Another twentieth century ascetic hero was T. E. Lawrence. Lawrence's obsessive self-punishment was even more spectacular than Gandhi's obsessive self-testing. Yet the very title of a recent biography (*A Prince of Our Disorder*) unmasks a

---

* The inflated and grandiose film *Gandhi,* released in the early 1980s, deceptively slides past the embarrassing details of Gandhi's brahmacharya experiments, while glorifying the submission of women, especially his wife. This film has been described as "inspiring." It is important to ask: "Inspiring *what?*"

secret similarity between Lawrence and other men. The author, John E. Mack, asserts that Lawrence's "flagellation disorder" was distinct from the "commonplace" practice of flagellation by individuals for erotic pleasure.[22] Mack describes Lawrence's disorder as "rare": the "self-determined use of flagellation for personal penance." Yet he manages to interpret this behavior as quite in keeping with the tradition of early saints who used such methods "to subdue sexual thoughts and cravings." [23]

Mack's information about Lawrence refutes his own deceptive distinction between "penance" and the "erotic pleasure" associated with flagellation. He recounts the bizarre exploits of this ascetic hero who, during the last years of his life, invented a fictitious "uncle" who decided that this "nephew Ted" should be flogged periodically with a metal whip. Under the pseudonym of this "uncle," Lawrence wrote letters to a man named John Bruce whom he hired to administer these beatings to Ted (Lawrence himself), giving instructions about details. One of the requirements was that the beatings be "delivered on the bare buttocks." It was also required that they be "severe enough to produce a seminal emission." [24] "Ted" regularly visited Bruce to receive his beatings. In his role as "uncle" (whose true identity allegedly was not known by the unsuspecting Bruce, who "believed" that Ted was being punished for a financial fraud), Lawrence wrote a number of letters to Bruce asking for the details of how "the lad" was taking his punishment. These beatings took place at intervals over a period of almost ten years.

Before quoting from some of the "uncle's" letters, Mack remarks that these reveal "his bitter hostility toward himself, his profound self-contempt, his wish to know his own reactions, and finally, a pathetic desire for some vindicating judgment that would free him of the conflict." [25] He was in fact never freed of the conflict. In Mack's analysis, Lawrence was punishing himself for his "sexual surrender" when he was raped by the Turks at Der'a, a surrender motivated by fear of pain. He believed that he had not only surrendered sexually, but had given away the fundamental integrity of self. Most horrifying to him was the fact that he found the mingling of sexual assault and pain to be pleasurable. He wrote to Mrs. Shaw that at the time he felt "a delicious warmth . . . swelling through me."

Mack theorizes:

The traumatic intensity of the experience, with its overwhelming of psychic defenses, led to the permanent welding for Lawrence of sexual pleasure and pain, so that he was plagued not only by the memory of the incident, but by the continuous desire for its repetition.[26]

Lawrence was caught in a vicious circle. The only punishment sufficiently severe to allay the guilt, according to Mack's interpretation, included the repetition of the experience itself—the pain of the beatings. However, this in turn required a repetition of the sexual aspect of the experience, thereby deepening the guilt.[27]

As in the case of Gandhi, Lawrence was continually "testing" himself, attempting to purify himself. As with Gandhi, his tests were self-imposed and highly ritualistic, and he identified with patriarchally constructed feminine roles. In Gandhi's case, the role was "motherliness"; for Lawrence, the role was that of rape victim who feels trapped in a sense of defilement and false guilt.

Gandhi's circle was less self-destructive. He psychically raped women, many of whom addressed him as "Mother." At the same time he conned them into behaving toward him in a "maternal" way. He got the best of both deals, receiving not only the respect due to a male "mother" but also the mothering—i.e., the spiritual nurturance, the energy injections—which he recognized women alone as capable of bestowing. Millions adored this imposter "Mother," an image which has survived even the scandal of the brahmacharya experiments.

Lawrence fared differently. He also was legendary and his fame was not destroyed by the revelations in the *Sunday Times* of his peculiar ascetic practices, but his life ended in self-destruction. A crucial difference relevant to this outcome came from the fact that Lawrence was not sexually attracted to women. Mack writes:

I believe Lawrence could not have allowed himself to be beaten by a woman (the masochism of many men does take this form), for the beatings, perverse, brutal and pathetic as they seem, are nevertheless a form of closeness, selected for the fusion of intimacy and simultaneous desecration they represent. . . . Lawrence was generally more comfortable with closeness among men, and could tolerate perhaps a perverse form of intimacy with certain men in a way that he could never have tolerated with a woman.[28]

Unlike the male who pays prostitutes to beat him, Lawrence was not able to drain energy so directly from females who could recycle his psychic waste. His paid torturer lacked this capacity. He found himself trapped in the male-created image of the rape victim who is driven to come back for more—which is classic patriarchal femininity. Mack suggests that "perhaps . . . he was forced in dealing with [his conflicts] to squander a certain amount of psychic energy." Thus, "his horizons were specifically limited by his personal conflicts." [29]

Both Gandhi and Lawrence lived out their lust-filled flights from lust in male-made feminine roles. The hindu "Mother" is generally praised and his shortcomings overlooked. The christian male rape victim, who strangely resembled a nun in his white Arab robes, is perceived by his biographers as unquestionably "great," but also as "pathetic." He is seen as a tragic victim of a "disorder" which, according to Mack, was due largely to his powerful identification with his mother, who used to beat him.[30]

It is perfectly consistent with the phallocratic ethic that men who lived through to the utmost limit of their capability the feminine roles which men have created should be honored as slightly flawed divinities. Gandhi was a "Mother" who did not succeed in his efforts to be Mother of a united India, but he was revered as no genuine mother was ever revered during her lifetime in patriarchal history, and certainly honored as no Self-identified creative woman has ever been honored. As for Lawrence, this "Prince" of "our" disorder is eulogized as tragic for falling into an imitation of the vicious circle which has been the common fate of countless women. This is the circle of those victims of rape who never break out because their spirits as well as their bodies have been torn apart, and the only "healing" offered has been a hideous "welding of pleasure and pain." Of course, the fate of Lawrence is mourned as "tragic" while a far more hopeless fate is accepted and legitimized by the psychiatrists and priests of sadospirituality as the "natural" and divinely ordained fate of women.

Untold numbers of women have suffered unnatural welding of pleasure and pain without any of the compensations of recognized achievement and adventure. Within the sadosociety, most women—unlike Lawrence—can hardly be described as actively choosing to "squander psychic energy." Rather, this precious life force is leeched before it can be actively assumed by the Self for her own process. The horizons of women thus trapped/sapped are limited not merely by "personal conflicts," but by a massive social conspiracy.

The many layers of destruction of women are especially crushing in Third World countries and in the severely depressed ghettoes of industrialized nations. Crones are especially aware of the manifold oppression of our sisters in Appalachia, Native American Indian reservations, the Roxburys and Harlems of any major American city, the Palestinian refugee camps in the Middle East, the reservations for Aboriginal people in Australia. All of these women are victims of the exploitation and imperialism that are logical extensions of phallic lust.

Female victims of phallic lust seldom have the chance to become "great," and later "tragic." Thus the true obscenity of the sadospiritual flight from lechery into phallic asceticism—the obscenity of its malignant deceptiveness, its masking/mocking of male destruction *of women*—is reflected in the careers of such ascetic "heroes," who function as distorted mirrors of the tragedy of women under phallocracy.

Dag Hammarskjöld. The ideas and behavior displayed in the documents of phallic asceticism do not always fixate explicitly upon sexual obsessions. In some cases, the asceticism gives the appearance of functioning for its own sake. This can sometimes be seen in the writings/lives of patriarchy's compulsive professionals, such as statesman Dag Hammarskjöld, famed secretary-general of the United Nations from 1953 until his death in 1961, whose ascetic ponderings are recounted in his well-known book of meditations, *Markings.* As the book jacket accurately asserts, this work is "a record that reveals the extent of his commitment to the Way of the Cross." Among his remarks to himself—in the manuscript intended for publication after his death—are the following:

Your life is without a foundation if, in any matter, you choose on your own behalf.[31]

And there is more of the same:

"Thine . . ." A sacrifice—and a liberation—to obey a will for which "I" is in no respect a goal! [32]

Masochistically:

Do you still need to evoke memories of a self-imposed humiliation in order to extinguish a smoldering self-admiration? [33]

Boringly:

The greatest creation of mankind, in which it is the noblest dream of the individual—to lose himself.[34]

Self-flagellatingly:

Destruction! What fury in your attack, how cruel your victory over this poor old body! You razed everything, you plunged a mind into abysses of anguish—and released this smile of ultimate joy.[35]

And onward . . . to explicit negation of Self as *telos:*

You will know Life and be acknowledged by it according to your degree of transparency, your capacity, that is, to vanish as an end, and remain purely as a means.[36]

In his foreword to this sadospiritual classic, W. H. Auden makes some telling comments, indicating, for example, that "the thought of suicide was not strange to Hammarskjöld." Indeed, he was fascinated by suicide:

When he has an automobile accident, his last thought before losing consciousness is, he tells us, a happy thought: "Well, *my* job's done." [37]

Auden informs the reader that Hammarskjöld "knew exactly what his problem was—if he was not to go under, he must learn how to forget himself and find a calling in which he could forget himself." [38] Explaining, or perhaps apologizing for, the repetitiousness of *Markings,* Auden suggests that many of the entries "must have been written by a man at the extreme limits of mental and physical exhaustion," as a result of constant nervous strain and overwork.[39]

Despite his self-flagellating attitudes, or, rather, consistent with them, was the enduring fact of Hammarskjöld's tedious narcissistic fascination with himself. He once jokingly told Auden that being secretary-general of the U.N. was "like being a secular

Pope, and the Papal throne is a lonely eminence." [40] Of course, *Markings* appears to be a virtual rhapsody to the merits of self-annihilation. In a 1957 entry, Hammarskjöld admonished himself:

And nothing for your future comfort or the future of your good name.[41]

Nevertheless, the book jacket informs us that he left behind the manuscript of this unctuous book to be published after his death.

Few women can afford the luxury of such lugubriousness. The common lot of women under patriarchy has been the sacrificing of personal needs and ambitions for the sake of children, husbands, aged parents, brothers, and just about everyone else. Women, particularly when poor, Black, and/or members of "minority" ethnic groups, suffer the enforced status of those who "remain purely as a means."

Robert Oppenheimer. Another ascetic professional, Robert Oppenheimer, "the father of the atomic bomb," * can be said to merit special attention here. For in his life and writings he demonstrates quite graphically the direction and logical outcome of phallic asceticism. In 1932, in a letter to his brother Frank, Oppenheimer wrote:

Therefore I think that all things which evoke discipline: study, and our duties to men and to the commonwealth, *war,* and personal hardship, and even the need for subsistence, ought to be greeted by us with profound gratitude; for only through them can we attain to the least detachment; and only so can we know *peace* [emphases mine].[42]

In Oppenheimer's worldview, then, war is justifiable on the grounds that it evokes discipline. In Oppenheimer's "vision," as in George Orwell's savage satire, *1984,* there is displayed the in-

---

* After the "successful" explosion of the first atomic bomb, in 1945, the National Baby Association made Oppenheimer its "Father of the Year." See Lansing Lamont, *Day of Trinity* (New York: Atheneum, 1965), p. 285. It is telling also to read that Edward Teller, known as the "father" of the hydrogen bomb, was said to have referred to that bomb as "my baby." See Robert J. Lifton, *The Broken Connection* (New York: Simon and Schuster, 1979), p. 422.

sane logic epitomized in the slogan: "WAR IS PEACE." Since Oppenheimer was able to justify war on the grounds that through it, "we" can know peace, it is not surprising to read his thoughts about the building of the first atomic bombs in the 1940s. Concerning this, several years later he wrote:

It is my judgment in these things that when you see something that is technically sweet, you go ahead and do it, and you argue about what to do about it only after you have had your technical success. That is the way it was with the atomic bomb. I don't think anybody opposed making it; there was some doubt about what to do with it after it was made.[43]

This consummately destructive ideology is phallic asceticism, which is to say it is a consequence of the obsession/aggression which is phallic lust. Thinking of this mental state as analogous to physical disease, we might describe it as something like *telic decentralization*—a phrase used to describe the condition of an organism that has been turned against its own purposes, becoming unhealthy, disordered, autoallergic.[44] Such a phrase is inadequate, however. For the word *telic* suggests that there *had been present* a sense of biophilic purpose (telos) that could be lost, and *decentralization* implies that there *had been* a focus, a center. Sadospiritual asceticism is the ideology and behavior of those who show no evidence of ever having experienced biophilic Elemental purpose or center. The problem of describing this condition is the problem of naming the deep mystery of evil. For words name what *is*. Here we are faced with the perversion of spirit, which is antispirit/antimatter, nonbe-ing.

Sadospiritual legitimation of this lust and its technological ejaculations is illustrated not only by Oppenheimer's choice of the code name "Trinity" for the 1945 atomic test that took place at Alamogordo, New Mexico, but especially by his explanation of this choice. "Oppie," as he was known by his colleagues, recalled that he was influenced by a devotional poem by John Donne, which opened with the words: "Batter my heart, three person'd God." [45] The battering of the Earth and of her creatures is the consequence of this disordered sentiment.

Reactions of statesmen to the "Trinity" report were consistent with the spirit of the scientists. We are told of Winston Churchill's reaction when Stimson called with a copy of the report:

Churchill, who was relaxing in his zippered siren suit, read the report, then waved his cigar with a flourish. "Stimson," he rumbled, "What was gunpowder? Trivial. What was electricity? Meaningless. This atomic bomb is the Second Coming in Wrath." [46]

Examples of such snoolishness can be multiplied *ad infinitum*. All illustrate that impotence to reach beyond appearances that characterizes phallic lust. Unable to be whole, those driven by phallic lust attempt to find holes everywhere, to penetrate, to pierce into an inner reality which they yearn to destroy but cannot even find.

Many effects of sado-asceticism shape the foreground conditions through which Wanderlusting women must pass. These are conditions of *imposed* asceticism, in which millions of lives are "lived" out, drained out. They include the massacres of war, racism, imposed economic poverty and famine, environmentally caused ill-health, the subtly spreading drabness, banality, ugliness of the man-made environment, the all-pervasive lies that deaden minds under the reign of the sadostate.

Women in the Third World, especially, are exploited to such an extent that imposed asceticism amounts to serious physical damage. Multinational corporations employ young women in jobs that destroy their eyesight and expose them to dangerous chemicals. Barbara Ehrenreich and Annette Fuentes describe a typical job in such a factory as involving "peering all day through a microscope, bonding hair-thin gold wires to a silicon chip." [47]

According to these authors, starting wages in the U.S.-owned electronics plants in the Philippines are between thirty-four and forty-six dollars a month, compared to the cost of living of thirty-seven dollars a month. In Indonesia the starting wages are about seven dollars a month less than the cost of living. Typically, workers in such places live in barracks, often rotating beds with workers on other shifts. Eighty to ninety percent of the workers employed in such sub-survival-level, life-destroying jobs are women. [48]

Exploitation of women's labor is hardly new in patriarchy, of course. In early times women were blinded doing close needlework for minimal wages. The history of sweatshops is well known. What might appear surprising is the fact that modern "advanced technology" still "requires" such body-and-soul-destroying labor.

Under the reign of the sadostate, imposed asceticism is The Rule; this continuing pattern should not be surprising, however. It will continue without serious opposition unless we manage to See through its legitimators' lies.

Mental Deprivation: Lies

I shall focus here upon the mental/spiritual deprivation inflicted upon women in sadosociety, for this form of imposed asceticism *fixes* women, stifling our Elemental ability to know, sense, feel, act on behalf of the Race of Women.

Within the sadosociety women are tracked and trained by male mediation of experience—a mediation which fixes the flow of female thought and passion. Women are held back from re-membering consciousness which is thus dismembered by phallo-crats, who fashion and promote the Biggest Lies, the cruelest degradations, deadening deep intuitive powers over and over again, forcing women repeatedly to re-invent the wheel. Indeed, the tactic of employing Biggest Lies to accomplish psychic dis-memberment is an essential feature of all sado-ideology, includ-ing science, theology, psychology, biology, pornography.*

It might seem, at first thought, that theological dogmas are not directly relevant to the destruction of female consciousness and confidence. At second thought, it becomes evident that dogmas of a male god and his incarnate son, combined with an all-pervasive myth of female evil, are only too relevant. Nag-Gnostic investi-gators turn our attention even beyond this to the effects of less obviously sex-related dogmas which have undermined psychic integrity.

Within christendom, a major theological tenet which illustrates

---

* The strategy of Biggest Lies is understood by many men as essential for maintaining the state of oppression. In his critical study of Marx, Ralf Dahrendorf writes: "But Marx overlooked what Tocqueville (whose work he probably knew) had observed before him, namely, that equality is a highly dynamic force, and that men [*sic*], once they are equal in some respects, 'must come in the end to be equal upon all.'" See Ralf Dahren-dorf, *Class and Class Conflict in Industrial Society* (Stanford, California: Stanford University Press, 1959), p. 61. This is why oppressors often say, "Give them an inch and they'll take a mile." Applied to women, the most lied to and lied about "group" in patriarchy, it means: "Give them a glimmer of truth and they'll want it all."

such undermining has been the doctrine of transubstantiation, according to which the substances of bread and wine are changed into the body and blood of Christ. In the course of this "change," only the "appearances" of bread and wine are said to remain the same. Popes and theologians through the centuries have proclaimed this to be the greatest of all changes, greater even than substantial change. They have taught that as a consequence of transubstantiation, the body and blood, soul and divinity of Christ are "really present." [49] The swallowing of this dogma, the denial of one's own sense and senses, prepares the way for acceptance of further deceptions. This is especially the case because of the brazenness of the deception.

Nag-Gnostic Elemental thinkers will note the significance of the fact that the bread and wine of the "Eucharist" are called "elements." In traditional catholicism, communicants must will to believe that they are not eating and drinking bread and wine, and thus acquire the habit of self-deception about the Elemental acts of taking food and drink. Such authoritatively required self-deception can happen only in a context of father-fostered false consciousness, and it reinforces such "consciousness."

The eucharistic dogma has affected not only hundreds of millions of believers, but also, in a more subliminal way, the whole of Western society. For training in doublethink and doubt of one's own perceptions is psychically contagious.*

The dogma has prepared the way for acceptance of such phenomena as "transsexualism." In recent years, propaganda promoting what feminist ethicist Jan Raymond has Named "The Transsexual Empire" has managed to persuade many people that a "real woman" actually can exist under the appearances of a

---

* Readers of George Orwell's *1984* (New York: New American Library, 1949) will recall illustrations of doublethink, for example:

[The frail slip of paper] was vanishing in a flash of flame. O'Brien turned away from the wall.

"Ashes," he said. "Not even identifiable ashes. Dust. It does not exist. It never existed."

"But it did exist! It does exist! It exists in memory. I remember it. You remember it."

"I do not remember it," said O'Brien.

Winston's heart sank. That was doublethink. . . . Perhaps that lunatic dislocation in the mind could really happen: that was the thought that defeated him. (p. 204)

male body—implying the "need" for a transsexual operation to make the body/appearance correspond to the "reality." The "transsexed" tennis pro Renée Richards, for example, is officially and legally a "woman" who can play "women's tennis." Richards is an illustration of what Raymond calls "the making of the she-male." [50]

This sort of warped interpretation of the idea that "appearances are deceiving" is manifested also in the jargon of anti-abortion "pro-lifers" who will refer to the abortion of an embryo after four weeks' gestation as the "murder" of a "baby." Indeed, these fanatics refer to cellular development from the moment of conception as "babies."

The imagery connected with the eucharistic dogma must color the perceptions of all who live within range of its cultural fallout. Thus all who hear on television or read on billboards that Coca Cola is "the real thing," and all who reside in or even have heard about Corpus Christi, Texas, are subliminally affected/infected.

This subliminal influence was dramatically demonstrated on April 25, 1981, when a fast attack nuclear-powered submarine called *USS Corpus Christi* was launched. According to an Associated Press report:

As 600 protesters denounced the launching of the USS Corpus Christi yesterday as a blasphemous instrument of death, Navy Secretary John F. Lehman Jr. praised the nuclear-powered submarine as "an instrument of peace, of justice, and of freedom. . . ."

The issue of the church became the focal point of this antiwar protest because of the name of the submarine. While Corpus Christi is a city in Texas with a large Naval Air Station, it is also Latin for the body of Christ. Several Roman Catholic leaders in Connecticut condemned the use of the name on a "hunter-killer sub." [51]

The protesters did not understand that the description of a fast attack submarine as "an instrument of peace, of justice, and of freedom" was consistent with the tradition of doublethink that is legitimated by the eucharistic dogma itself. For the viewers of the launching were being asked to deny the evidence of their own senses, to negate their capacity for logic, to *forget* that a fast attack submarine is an instrument of war, of unjust massacre, of enslavement.

The protesters' confusion was manifested in the style of the protest itself, as reported by Associated Press. The group—some of whom wore religious vestments and one of whom carried a ten-foot-tall cross—poured blood over the sidewalk and knelt in the street.[52] Although they intended to protest the "blasphemy" and alleged contradiction in the name of the submarine, they had "forgotten" the sadomasochistic associations of the cross as well as the history of christian holocausts which preceded those projected by the high priests of nuclearism.

The traditional theology of the "Real Presence" of Christ in the eucharist, then, is a particularly graphic example of sado-spiritual indoctrination into "swallowing the lie." [53] Under the guise of offering spiritual food and drink, the christian church for many centuries has starved the souls of women, stuffing minds with false food, with unreal absence, making the Real Presence of truth, of Elemental knowing and sensing, less and less accessible.

The imposed asceticism of spiritual/intellectual starvation— in the name of communion/communication—is all-pervasive in the sadostate. This indoctrination into compulsory/compulsive lie-swallowing—from the ingestion of artificially colored and flavored carcinogenic foods to the consumption of ABC Nightly News—depends for its efficacy upon the strategy of force-feeding the victims with Biggest Lies. It is for this reason that the eucharistic example is so enlightening.*

---

* A particularly horrifying example of Biggest Lies is the exploitation of millions of Third World women by the Nestlé Corporation, whose "Nestlé Infant Formula" is, according to a recent estimate, responsible for the deaths of as many as four million babies a year. Nestlé's aggressive advertising campaigns have convinced millions of Third World women that their product is better for their babies than breast milk. Not able to afford the formula, these women—convinced by propaganda that breast feeding is not the "modern" way—try to stretch their supply of Nestlé's by thinning it down. Trying to make a three-day supply last three weeks, they are driven to stretch it with unsanitary water, tea, or soda pop. According to recent accounts, Nestlé's budget for advertising alone was more than the total yearly budget of the World Health Organization. A sizable proportion of this goes into advertising of Nestlé Infant Formula. This campaign involves the use of hired "milk-nurses" to peddle their products and the use of hospitals as promotion centers. To entice physicians to cooperate in their program, Nestlé contributes equipment to hospitals, sponsors medical conventions, and provides lavish entertainment for physicians. Since their female victims are not in a position to

The technique of employing Biggest Lies is fundamental to the entire edifice of deception. For the function of Biggest Lies is the torture, by maiming and starvation, of the victim's intellect and senses, the weakening of these faculties, so that these always need a fix, even crave a fix, consisting of more deception in continuous smaller dosages.

Women whose minds and senses have been thus fixed exhibit the classic symptom of the tortured—gratitude for any semblance of leniency on the part of the torturers (even though the situation of torture is not recognized as such). Like the tortured political prisoner who has been denied liquids and is grateful for a modicum of water, so the victim of the sexual politics of lying is thankful for a modicum of reasonableness, of truth. Such partial reasonableness, however, is not reasonable/truthful at all. In the State of Boredom, such pseudo-reasonableness is much in demand, for the hacks/hucksters of this state have manufactured a market for mini-truths. Entombed/consumed in this state, women are thankful for menial jobs, moronizing education and entertainment, the right to vote for men.

Essential to the bore-ocratic strategy of deception is the labeling of modest reforms as "radical" and "extreme." Within this context women are informed that proponents of the ERA are wild radicals, and are boringly instructed by William Safire of the *New York Times* that the use of the title "Ms." is extremist and irrelevant. The psychic and physical violence inflicted by means of such mind-shrinking strategies causes women to scramble for crumbs; the slightest pretense of sense is hailed as the hallmark of great "progress." Chained to this wheel of absurdity, the victim does not even guess the extent of her victimhood.

Pornography

It is within this context of imposed intellectual deprivation—the infliction of Biggest Lies—that a feminist analysis of such gynocidal phenomena as pornography should be situated. Indeed, por-

---

refute the propaganda (many are illiterate) that this is The Modern Way to feed their babies and that breast feeding is wrong, they are forced to swallow the Lie, becoming token torturers/murderers of their own children, who are forced to swallow nonnutritious, poisonous food. Nestlé Infant Formula, then, is a eucharistic phenomenon.

nography (as well as the behavior which it reflects and perpetuates) cannot really be understood if it is construed as a separate and distinct phenomenon from other expressions of sado-ideology. Thus, for example, pornography, nuclear ideology, and theology are in many ways the same.

A key link between patriarchal theology and pornography, then, is total arrogance in the promulgation of deception. Andrea Dworkin has discussed the pornographic Lie:

The pornographic conceit is that the normal female demands the force, the violence, the pain. . . . This pornographic conceit accounts for the fact that men in general do not believe that rape or battery are violations of female will.[54]

Moreover, women in general do not know that men in general believe and sustain this Lie. Thus women are force-fed the Lie concerning this Lie. Nevertheless, the pornographic Lie is at least subliminally conveyed to all women in the culture even as it is being overtly denied. Given these conditions, it is not surprising that even young girls who are raped generally feel guilt and defilement as well as rage. Every woman is affected by the basic pornographic message that "women want it."

Having been forced to swallow this Biggest Lie, the victims of such mental torture continue to argue for justice, rationality, and human liberation and to be grateful for the slightest concessions, while remaining unable to see that their basic right to be-ing is denied by the sadosociety. Indeed, in this reversal world women who would claim this basic right are considered arrogant. In her discussion of the Marquis de Sade, Dworkin states:

The arrogance of women in claiming any rights over their own bodies is particularly offensive to Sade. Any uppity pretense to bodily integrity on a woman's part must be fiercely and horribly punished.[55]

Sade, of course, does not stand undefended. He has been applauded for his "genius" by countless "radical" biographers and admirers.

Papal Pornography

The fact that theological pornography uses similar strategies, entrapping women into fixed behavior, was illustrated by a November 7, 1980, declaration of pope John Paul II attacking the women's liberation movement as contrary to women's vocation to motherhood. It is not astonishing that such arrogance comes from this source. It is noteworthy, however, that christian women reacted with the knee-jerk response of the tortured when confronted with Biggest Lies—begging for crumbs of reasonableness. Thus women theologians circulated a petition timidly stating:

We believe that the woman's liberation movement, in its primary purposes, is a just and necessary corrective to the long centuries of subjugation of women to secondary participation in human development. We call upon the Pope to better acquaint himself with the actual concerns of this movement and to enter into dialogue with the women themselves who are members of this movement.[56]

By reducing the women's movement to a "corrective," by seeming to believe that the pope is capable of acquainting himself with the actual concerns of this movement, by suggesting that radical women would "enter into dialogue" with him, the petition writers/signers were attempting to appear "reasonable" in order to obtain a modicum of rationality in return. Their mistake lies in failing to confront the fact that they are dealing with dealers of Biggest Lies, from whom there is no hope of rationality. Such genuflecting gestures (begging for minitruths, or moderated lies) are exercises in self-abasement and absurdity, and can be compared to petitioning hard-core porn peddlers to acquaint themselves with the actual concerns of the women's movement and enter into dialogue about the ethics of their multi-billion-dollar gynocidal industry. The end result of such politics of prostration is frustration, and the reinforcement of Biggest Lies.

Scientific Pornography Concerning Nature

The sado-ideology that thrives on female degradation extends itself to destruction of nature, enforcing a kind of involuntary asceticism upon other species. Not surprisingly the strategy of spreading Biggest Lies is used to legitimate this torture. J. E. Lovelock, in his work *Gaia: A New Look at Life on Earth,* exemplifies the bore-ocratic view of nature, personified as "Gaia." He writes:

. . . the evolution of homo sapiens, with his technological inventiveness and his increasingly subtle communications network, has vastly increased Gaia's range of perception. She is now through us awake and aware of herself. She has seen the reflection of her fair face through the eyes of astronauts and the television cameras of orbiting spacecraft. Our sensations of wonder and pleasure, our capacity for conscious thought and speculation, our restless curiosity and drive are hers to share.[57]

This cockocratic assessment of Earth's need for *homo sapiens* (read: men) in order to be awake and aware of herself, to see her own "fair face," and to have any sensations or drive would be even more obviously obscene if Lovelock's readers had not been pre-schooled by the language of True Romance. Lovelock's expression of lust for Gaia (the Earth Goddess) is obscene in the traditional way. It fixes the stage for the more moderate droning of René Dubos, author of *The Wooing of Earth,* who writes:

. . . the phrase "wooing of the earth" suggests that the relationship between humankind and Nature should be one of respect and love rather than domination. Among people the outcome of wooing can be rich, satisfying, and lastingly successful only if both partners are modified by their association so as to become better adapted to each other. Furthermore, the outcome is more interesting when both partners retain elements of their individuality—of their own wildness.[58]

The reader of this pathetically fallacious passage may be wooed/ lulled into overlooking what wooing is all about, into forgetting which "partner" is modified and is reduced to retaining only (broken) elements of her own individuality and wildness. Dubos' euphemistic exhortation to exploitation sounds like a liberal treatise on christian marriage. Readers who have been fixed by sadospiritual propaganda that women and men are "partners" in christian marriage could be seduced by the analogy, for within the Lecherous State lies mirror lies, reproducing each other endlessly. Women who ingest this deceptive droning, legitimating the rape of nature, become even more susceptible when "nature" analogies are used to seduce women into the victim role.

Women as Mirrors of Sado-asceticism

Women have ingested negative and masochistic self-images implanted by the snoolish rulers—images that have spawned self-loathing, a need for punishment, hatred of other women which results in horizontal violence. Within the christian tradition, one consequence has been saintly masochism. Simone de Beauvoir discussed this several decades ago:

St. Angela of Foligno tells us that she drank with delight the water in which she had just washed lepers' hands and feet. . . . We know that Marie Alacoque cleaned up vomit of a patient with her tongue; in her biography she describes the joy she felt when she filled her mouth with the excrement of a man sick with diarrhea; Jesus rewarded her when she held her lips pressed against his Sacred Heart for three hours.[59]

As de Beauvoir concisely explains:

She [Marie Alacoque] was the one who offered to the adoration of the faithful the great red clot, surrounded with the flaming darts of love.[60]

There is also ample evidence of the masochistic fantasies of female mystics brooding over the lacerated body of Christ.[61]

It should be noted that the self-defiling acts of these feminine saintly masochists are acts of Self-denying flight, not from their own desire, but from natural disgust. They are attempts at self-purification as the saints perceived this to be required of them by a male god.* Moreover, these women were accurate in their assessment of the male god's demands. It is significant that the god-man Jesus is believed to have rewarded Alacoque immediately for swallowing the male patient's excrement. It is equally significant that the church legitimated this behavior and this fantasy by officially promoting the veneration of the sacred heart. Nags will not avoid noting that in the history of patriarchal symbolism, *heart* is frequently substituted for *phallus*. Given this background, the encoded message of Alacoque's vision is evident —and astonishing.

There can be no doubt that the societal embedding of false

---

* Religious asceticism practiced by females is not an exclusively christian phenomenon, of course. In his discussion of hindu ascetics, Barrington Moore writes: "Female ascetics are also quite common, though the sources have much less to say about them. Examples of extreme self-torture appear to be confined to males." See *Injustice: The Social Bases of Obedience and Revolt* (White Plains, N.Y.: M.E. Sharpe, Inc., 1978), p. 51.

guilt has had a major role in the manufacture of such feminine masochism. As Barrington Moore remarks:

Over the centuries the Catholic Church has had considerable success in expropriating guilt. It has achieved this by helping to create the sense of guilt and then providing the bureaucratic mechanisms for alleviating it. As an economist might put the point, the Catholic Church managed to create much of the demand and most of the supply.[62]

While Moore's criticism of the catholic church's breeding of guilt is applicable to the cases of female saints described above, his analysis in fact does not do "justice" to other religions and ideologies of phallicism, for *all* phallic religion and ideology directly or indirectly instill guilt in women.

Moreover, there is more to the problem than false guilt. Within the sadostate women are *ontologically* undermined, for the sado-intent is the conversion of female participation in Be-ing into mere being, that is, the conversion of women into things, and into complicity in thinghood. To the extent that phallic lust succeeds, women are reduced to nonbe-ing. Insights concerning how this ontological reduction relates to sadomasochism in women can be gained from Ernest Becker's analysis of sadomasochism. He writes:

The sadomasochist is someone who has trouble believing in the validity and sanctity of people's insides—their spirit, personality, or self. These insides could be his [*sic*] own or others'; if they are his own he tends to be masochistic: if they are others' he tends to be called a sadist.[63]

Women who have been thingified, deprived of conscious participation in Be-ing, have trouble believing in the sanctity of women's "insides"—both their own and those of other women. This doubt extends to spirit, personality, Self. Within sadosociety this doubt applies first to a woman's own participation in Be-ing. It extends to the be-ing of all women. Thus the disorder which I shall call *masosadism* is injected into women.* To the extent that this in-

---

* *Masosadism* is intended to Name the dynamics of the disorder injected into women in the sadostate, which begins with doubting the validity of one's own be-ing—a doubt experienced as Self-hatred—and extends

jection "takes," a woman is rendered incapable of moral outrage on her own behalf *as a woman* and on behalf of the Race of Women. Her outrage has been expropriated. She may experience and be informed about atrocities against women, and yet she is unable to feel sustained rage against the perpetrators of the atrocities, and incapable of acting against the men who are the originators, rulers, and controlling legitimators of the sadostate. Masosadism, then, fixes women. This injected variation of phallic sadomasochism is totally antipathetic to feminism. It is utterly inimical to the living of feminism, to the Race/Racing of women. For this reason the phallocratic war against women requires continual injections of masosadism. The instruments of these injections (fairy tales, fashions, theology, psychology, romance, "literature," et cetera) are tools of snools.

Masosadism as Eucharistic

The passage cited above from Ernest Becker unwittingly illustrates a phenomenon which I shall call the eucharistic syndrome* of the sadosociety. The passage describes the sadomasochist's inability to believe in the "insides" of himself or of the other. To translate this into ontological terms, he cannot get beyond appearances to be-ing. To put it into Aristotelian technical philosophical terms, he cannot get beyond accidents to substance. Thus sense-perceptible expressions, such as speech, visible and tangible physical gestures of affection, are to be discounted—unless these involve pain and/or humiliation. All intercourse, ranging from the most impassioned philosophic, poetic, and musical language to

---

to doubting the validity of other women's be-ing. This doubt is expressed in horizontal violence. Masosadism can manifest itself simply in radical passivity, an inability and unwillingness to resist one's own oppression and/or that of other women. It can also be acted out with varying degrees of intensity, awareness, and destructiveness. In contrast to this, I interpret *sadomasochism* to be essentially a phallic phenomenon, inherently directed toward the destruction of the other. The male's flight from his own aggression/obsession, his masochistic phallic asceticism is a consequence of his experience of his aggression/lust.

* I trust that it is clear that I am at this point using the term eucharistic in a metaphorical sense; that is, I am employing the word which is usually restricted to one phenomenon to describe other phenomena in order to unmask similarities.

the most intimate physical embrace, is to be disbelieved; it is not to be trusted to disclose what is substantial "underneath." This pattern is consistent with the pattern of eucharistic belief/disbelief which requires unquestioning acceptance of mediated "information" concerning what is "behind" or under the so-called accidents or appearances.

Such intellectual Self-denial is ontologically obscene, for it subverts basic confidence of that natural, Elemental knowing which is participation in Metabeing. It converts the Naming of natural, Elemental acts into stunted, possessed symbols, tracking and inhibiting the capacity of believers to ride Metaphors spontaneously as vehicles to/from Metabeing. When faculties are thus trained into Self-blockage, it becomes difficult to believe in the "insides" of oneself or others.

The role assigned to women within such a set-up is archetypally masosadistic. Since women are not the myth-makers, theologians, priests, distributors within such a system, but rather the passive recipients (communicants), the feminine role (shared, of course, by some males) is that of the blocked, rather than the blockers. Of course, some women are instruments of spreading the blockage of Metabeing. Although they are not the originators of this syndrome they are blockers by derivation (that is, token torturers) and thus participate in the destruction through masosadism.

It is instructive to read further in Becker's analysis of sadomasochism:

When one does not believe in the validity of one's own inner being and powers, and when one cannot relate to others as integral and unified persons, then the private self, the inner mystery, becomes a threat. Therefore, the mystery that others conceal in their inner selves must be brought to light by whatever means at one's disposal: in this way it can be rendered safe, or it can be justly exposed as the fraud that it is.[64]

The fact that this passage appears to be gender-free disguises the real situation which is sadosociety. Women are constantly bombarded with propaganda intended to force acceptance of eucharistic obscenity (denial of our own Elemental sensory and intellectual powers, which inhibits conscious participation in Metabeing). The fact is that the one who "does not believe in the validity of one's own inner being and powers" (the male) would logically be "the one" who manufactures and requires belief in such dogmas as the eucharist, such ideologies as the pornographic conceit, and such technological manifestations of this mentality as the nuclear attack submarine "Corpus Christi." Clearly, women are not the fabricators of these phenomena. It is not difficult to know the gender of the one who "cannot relate to others as integral and unified persons" or to know, genderwise, *who* is threatened by *whose* "private self" and "inner mystery." Within the sadostate women are always regarded as "mysterious." And, of course, women are the essential targets of the pornography and sadistic behavior that seeks to "bring to light" this "mystery," so that it can be rendered safe and exposed as a fraud. That is the purpose of rape, woman-battering, the sexual abuse of female children, the multi-billion-dollar porn industry.

Yet physical violence and violation are not sufficient to render female be-ing unthreatening to males. The whole program requires that women become collaborators in being "exposed" as frauds. This enforced collaboration requires that women be inducted into the State of Masosadism, that they be rendered incapable of *Knowing* and *Naming* the fact of this induction/indoctrination. That is, the sadosociety requires that the hooking of women into masosadism be eucharistic. Thus conditioned, women will conform behaviorally, participating in the verification process which "proves" female integrity to be "the fraud that it is."

The secondary aspect of masosadism, that is, the sadism and horizontal violence toward other women that results from implanted masochism/self-hatred, converts women who have been hooked by the sadomasochistic society into hookers of other women. In this deceptive chain of psychic vampirism, the Master Vampire—the sadistic fixer/framer—is lost sight of, and the masosadistic hookers/drainers are rendered more and more visible, and less and less comprehensible. The dependent, derivative, drained and draining victims function to protect and disguise Dracula himself.

Complicity in The Act

Elemental philosophers can be aided in dis-closing the fraud involved in the syndrome of the sadosociety through application of the metaphysical concepts of *potency* and *act*.[65] * As a technical term, *potency* usually has been understood in a passive sense, referring to the capacity to be acted upon. *Potency* (*potentia* in Latin), however, also has an active meaning, that is, capacity to act: power. "God" is said to have potency only in this second sense, for he is said to be "pure act," having no passive potency (which would imply limitations), and omnipotent, having totally active power. The sadospiritual male (who equates himself with "God") attempts to cover his sense of impotence (lack of sense of inner be-ing and powers) by his erection of the eucharistic pornographic conceit. As reversal king he plays god, the "pure act," becoming purely an actor, lusting for the reduction of everything else to purely an act, to fraud.

The lust to reduce everything to fraud is not simply a desire to fool others. The lecher desires to force them into complicity in The Act, to break the inner core of integrity so that there is no longer any threatening inner "mystery." In this broken-down state, the victims know the falseness and adore it, elect it. The election of actor-president Ronald Reagan and the massive uncritical adulation of the conservative "pop" pope John Paul II illustrate this phenomenon of mental degradation. Female complicity in The Act is masosadism.

Sensory Deprivation

The continued complicity of women in The Act is further insured by the imposed asceticism of sensory deprivation (often combined with sensory overload). Increasingly pervasive, sensory deprivation is particularly lethal because, while largely unnoticed, it paralyzes its victims, destroying the capacity to feel/know deeply, passionately, and therefore to act authentically. Most inhabitants of towns and cities are forced to exist in sensory-deprivation environments, which are mediated environments. As Jerry Mander has suggested, the modern office building is the archetypal example of the mediated environment.[66] It contains small, square, flat spaces; its decor is rigidly uniform; it has hermetically sealed windows; its sound environment is homogenized; its light is constant. The end result is that all of the senses are dulled. To glimpse the

* A fuller discussion of the metaphysical concepts of potency and act is pursued in Chapter Four of this book.

scope of this Wasteland of Boredom, one need only think of modern supermarkets, department stores, hospitals, universities, apartment buildings, sterile and uniform suburban neighborhoods. As we have seen, conditions in the factories in which working class women toil sometimes carry sensory deprivation to the extreme of damaging and even destroying the sensory capacities exploited by the work.

Some of the consequences of sensory deprivation are noted by Mander:

What we see, hear, touch, taste, smell, feel and understand about the world has been processed for us. Our experiences of the world can no longer be called direct or primary. They are secondary, mediated experiences.[67]

One consequence of this mediation is the enforcement/re-enforcement of fixocracy. With senses thus fixed, women must struggle to *feel* Elemental connections. Mander observes:

When we [*sic*] reduce an aspect of environment from varied and multidimensional to fixed, we [*sic*] also change the human being who lives within it. . . . The human being then becomes a creature with a narrower range of abilities and fewer feelings about the loss. We become grosser, simpler, less varied, like the environment.[68]

Nags will notice that the use of the pronoun *we* makes this statement deceptive (as are countless common expressions such as "when *we* decide to stockpile nuclear weapons," or "when *we* destroyed Vietnam"). The agent is misnamed, falsely including readers who have not chosen this pathological reduction/destruction of the environment. Unfortunately, it is not within Mander's range of intellectual/emotional vision to notice that his uncritical use of conventional grammar contributes to the smog of sensory deprivation and therefore is consonant with the mediated environment he criticizes. Nags note that as a result of such phallogrammar and other tools of snooldom—including, of course, phallo-technology—women and others are deprived into becoming "grosser, simpler, less varied, like the environment."

Sadosexual Politics

To the extent that she is reduced to becoming grosser, simpler, less varied, a woman is a ready target of sadosexual politics. These are the politics of the effacement of women. John Stoltenberg (who by reason of gender privilege has had access to information not directly available to women) describes a major contemporary manifestation of this phenomenon:

Culturally, the emergence of male homosexual sadomasochism from underground has coincided with a burgeoning of overt sadism against women in all the communications media. This coincidence has not been by chance. . . . While gay activists were campaigning against stereotypical images of "gay people" in the media, male homosexuals who have direct access to media have been promoting with a vengeance all the stereotypes of female masochism. We are witnessing the convergence of what was once deemed a "gay sensibility" with what was once deemed a "heterosexual sensibility." That convergence is conspicuously a male sensibility, and it now reveals itself fully as thriving on female degradation.[69]

The division of "gay sensibility" and "heterosexual sensibility" is, of course, a delusionary dichotomy. Male-mating has always manifested itself under the guise of heterosexuality throughout the sadosociety.

As I have already pointed out, the imprinting of images of female masochism is paralytic to women. These amount, in fact, to injections of masosadism, which is the most essential weapon in the phallocratic war against women, the most basic tool in the blockage of the Race of Women. Phallocratic male sensibility indeed "reveals itself as thriving on female degradation."

It would appear almost too obvious to mention the fact that women do *not* thrive on degradation. Yet the culture of Biggest Lies has succeeded in obscuring even that blatant fact, suggesting that it is fulfilling. Some women, from Alacoque to freudian Helene Deutsch to some contemporary sexually "liberated" women, have swallowed this ideological excrement, acted it out, and distributed it further. Stoltenberg's analysis yields further insights relevant to this disturbing behavior. Discussing male homosexual sadomasochism, he points out that the assumed masochism of gay males differs significantly from female masochism, because

. . . the male homosexual's drive to incorporate manliness functions as a means of dissociating himself from the inferior status of the female —whereas the masochism of a woman functions to fix her in that state.[70]

In fact, sadomasochistic acts between two males are ritualized games between phallic peers. Thus:

In any erotic encounter between two homosexual males, there really are two male sexual identities at stake. But the sexuality appropriate to male-sexual-identity reification is derived from a heterosexual model based on blotting out "the other." . . . True to their privileged status as genital males in society, the partners are at liberty to trade roles in private without jeopardizing their status in the culture in any way. . . . A crucial emotional adjunct to that agreement is their mutual derision of genital females, whose actual powerlessness they are at liberty to mock.[71]

The pathetic attempts of some women to mimic this role-playing feeds into the phallic fixation factories of snooldom. Apparently unable to experience the Elemental zest of *be-ing* spiritually, passionately, sexually, intellectually, they seek instead the drab "excitement" of bored boys, joining jockocracy, disseminating Boredom. Stoltenberg accurately names the game:

In order to believe that relationships between sadists and masochists are "liberated," one would have to believe that contempt is caring, that humiliation is respect, that brutality is affection, and that bondage is freedom. The fact that many women do so believe is a measure of the extent to which men have destroyed women's consciousness.[72]

Sexual Masosadism

When women, whether heterosexual or lesbian, whose consciousness has been thus destroyed proclaim themselves pro-sadomasochism, pro-pornography, and hail *The Story of O* as "our pornography," they may be exercising "free speech," but they are speaking neither *as* feminists nor *for* feminists. Since the inherent logic of their position is simply anti-feminist, they do not represent a "split" or a "struggle" *within* the feminist movement. Rather, they have become tools of the sadosociety in its continuing effort to destroy female consciousness.*

In order to understand the role of pseudofeminist sexual masosadism of the eighties in the destruction of woman-identified consciousness, I will briefly note here some aspects of the "wider" society, the snooldom which such pseudoradicalism mirrors.

First, the increasing conservatism of the society generates a

---

* Feminists can never forget that the actual battering of women by men is standard role behavior in patriarchy.

syndrome which Andrea Dworkin has identified as characterizing women of the Right, namely, an obsessive need for "safety, shelter, rules, form and love." [73] Unwittingly, masosadistic women are playing, in "chic" contemporary style, very old games expressing self-hatred and horizontal violence. The prizes for playing the game are safety and shelter (from reality), rules and form (in place of Pure Lust). Rather than threatening the gynocidal establishment, masosadists support it.

Second, it follows that contemporary pseudoradical masosadism mirrors that characteristic of the sadosociety which I have identified as *reversal*. Appearing to be "feminist," it is, in fact, inimical to feminism. It is man-made, delusory "sexual liberation," and to describe it and other such travesties I invoke the expression *foreground feminism*.

Third, masosadism mirrors the triumph of the therapeutic, which prevails in sadosociety. Absorbed in self-indulgent "acting-out," the "feminist" practitioners of sexual masosadism have little energy for knowing/acting in a radically creative way.

Masosadistic Politics and Horizontal Violence

It is within the context of creeping pseudofeminist masosadism in the eighties and of the sado-asceticism which this mirrors that the issue of horizontal violence among women who have chosen to name themselves feminists and/or lesbians can be understood. I refer specifically to the irrational and mindbinding conversion of terms such as *racist, classist,* and *elitist* into labels that function to hinder rather than foster the Movement/Race of Women.

First, it is important to see some points of commonality between such verbal abuse/stigmatizing and the masosadistic/sexual practices which are expressions of the destruction of women's consciousness and the perversion of women's energies. Just as masosadistic sexual practices reflect compulsive needs for "safety, shelter, rules, form" (not totally unlike those of extremely conservative women) so also the masosadistic politics of horizontally violent labeling reflect such obsessions. Rather than threatening the phallocentric establishment, women who practice such politics support this State by diverting energy into female self-destruction and by blocking woman-identified creativity.

Moreover, the practitioners of horizontal violence also mirror that strategy of the sadosociety which I have called *reversal,* for instead of Naming the *active perpetrators* of the social evils they claim to oppose, they choose the cowardly device of scapegoating women. Rather than confronting real danger, they promote among women the very atmosphere of irrationality, stigmatization, and hatred which endanger all women.

In addition, like the practitioners of masosadistic sexual obsession, the promoters of scapegoating and stigmatization mirror the Therapeutic Society. Absorbed in self-indulgent acting of such roles as judge, penitent, and judge-penitent, they distract from the fact that *women* are raped, beaten, maimed, killed, and dismembered by *males* of all nations, classes, races, in all times and places, on a planet dominated by phallocracy.

The hidden agenda of these politics is male-identification, which is malidentification. Some of the reported events at the U.N. Conference on Women held in Copenhagen in July 1980 illustrated this phenomenon, which has titillated the media-masters. An article in the *Boston Globe,* gleefully entitled "Beyond International Sisterhood," described the events of the conference:

They [the delegates] debated whether the conference should condemn female circumcision. Some feared that such a condemnation would reflect unfavorably on the African and Arab countries where the barbaric custom is still practiced. Some felt it would look as though industrialized nations were imposing their values on the Third World.

Many have expressed surprise that a women's conference, especially an international women's conference, could be torn apart in such a fashion on so many levels. . . . Surely, the UN conference challenges the naive assumption that women exist in a political vacuum where some kind of international sisterhood takes precedence over national self-interest.[74]

Licking their chops over female Self-betrayal, the editors then finish their meal with a sermon on perfection, droning that in a "perfect world" women

. . . would have pledged to work together to fight sexism and religious fanaticism and political ideologies that keep women down. But this is not a perfect world and women are, after all, only human.

Covering the same conference, the Associated Press reported:

While paying lip service to improving the lot of women, many speakers appeared to be using the conference as a platform to promote national political viewpoints on the world's problems.[75]

And *Time* gloated:

So many of the women so slavishly followed the dictates of their male-dominated foreign offices that a Danish journalist dubbed the convocation "the men's conference of women." [76]

The Time-men are specific:

Even the issue of female circumcision, which some feminists thought might unite the gathering, was caught up in Third World politics.

Although more happened at the U.N. Conference on Women than the journalists understood, the description "the men's conference of women" is realistic. The delegates were confessing their faith in phallic structures. Moreover, many other, less official and officious gatherings of women who identify as feminists could also be dubbed "men's conferences," insofar as male-identified concerns predominate over the cause of women. In such gatherings, the spirit—or rather the antispirit—of masosadistic politics is always manifested/man-infested[77] by horizontal violence and the manipulation of displaced guilt. In order to analyze this phenomenon, I will apply my seven-point analysis of the Sado-Ritual Syndrome, which in *Gyn/Ecology* was used to detect patterns in gynocidal atrocities.[78]

First, in the Sado-Ritual we find an obsession with purity. This is reflected in the obsession with confession that afflicts many women who have begun to have consciousness of oppression.

Hannah Arendt precisely describes this sort of dislocation in her discussion of the self-blame of young Germans in the 1960s for the Nazi atrocities perpetrated by their parents' generation. She wrote:

It is quite gratifying to feel guilty if you haven't done anything wrong: how noble! Whereas it is rather hard and certainly depressing to admit guilt and to repent. The youth of Germany is surrounded, on all sides and in all walks of life, by men in positions of authority and in public office who are very guilty indeed but who *feel* nothing of the sort. The normal reaction to this state of affairs should be indignation, but indignation would be quite risky—not a danger to life and limb but definitely a handicap in a career.[79]

Clearly, Arendt is making the point that the spurious and displaced guilt functioned as a substitute for the courage to challenge the generation in power. Instead of threatening the real criminals, this displaced self-blame helped them to dismiss their guilt by misnaming it as "collective." "Collective guilt," the idea that all members of a social construction, such as the nation, are guilty, erases guilt by its implicit message that if all are guilty, none are guilty.

Arendt's analysis is helpful in understanding the foreground conditions of consciousness/conscience in women. Frozen in unacknowledged fear, women, whether identifying themselves as feminists or not, often assume the guilt which the fathers and sons fail to feel. By so doing, they avoid confronting men in authority (and *all* males are by institutional sexual definition *in authority* over certain women), which would indeed "be quite risky," and in fact not only a handicap in a career. For, unlike the young Germans (males) of the sixties, women in all the patriarchal states do live in "danger of life and limb," whether or not this is overtly acknowledged. In this way, women perform the role of misfocusing attention away from those who have institutional power in the structures of oppression, unrealistically assuming a sort of "equal share" of responsibility for economic and racial oppression, for the rape of nature, and even for the oppression of women. Having never learned, or having fearfully forgotten, to Name the masters/mutilators/murderers who rule the sadostate, women who are locked into the Foreground fail to go to the heart of the problem. Displaced rage and myopic vision are rewarded by "protection" by liberal, leftist, and minority males, and gain approval from establishment males, who sense accurately enough that the only Dreadful Danger derives from the emergence of Revolting Lusty women.*

Second, in the Sado-Ritual Syndrome there is total erasure of

---

* Horizontally violent foreground feminism, or *plastic feminism,* feeds upon the *plastic passions* of guilt and anxiety, which will be discussed in the Second Realm of this book. This plastic passion syndrome spreads as the society becomes more conservative and as Naming the institutionally powerful agents of oppression becomes more dangerous for women.

responsibility for the atrocities performed through such rituals. The atrocities of horizontal violence within women's groups are horrors for which "no one" is held responsible. Some light on this phenomenon can be obtained from reading R. J. Lifton's analysis of the cult of confession:

But as totalist pressures turn confession into recurrent command performances, the element of histrionic public display takes precedence over genuine inner experience. Each man [*sic*] becomes concerned over the effectiveness of his personal performance, and this performance sometimes comes to serve the function of evading the very emotions and ideas about which one feels most guilty.[80]

As Lifton shows, within such a climate enthusiastic and aggressive confessors thrive, for they know that "the more I accuse myself, the more I have the right to judge you."

The identity of the "judge-penitent" thus becomes a vehicle for taking on some of the environment's arrogance and sense of omnipotence.[81]

Like the foreground female "sadist" who pretends in private to have power publicly denied to her in the sadosociety, the foreground feminist who plays the confessionalist games tries to participate in phallic "omnipotence" and arrogance by assuming the role of judge-penitent. As a consequence of their penitent-role, the "judges" of masosadistic politics accomplish total erasure of responsibility for the atrocities they perform against the women they judge.

The third aspect of Sado-Ritual practices is their inherent tendency to "catch on" and spread. It is clear that the masosadistic politics of foreground feminism follow this pattern. For each penitent has "earned" the right to be a judge, and her mandate is to manufacture more penitents, who then can judge *ad infinitum.*

The fourth aspect of Sado-Rituals is the fact that women are used as scapegoats and token torturers. When this is dis-covered as operative in foreground feminist circles, it is important to remember that such women are *token* torturers, serving the interests of fixers, framers, rakes and rippers, drones, and snools who applaud and promote such scenarios, such scapegoating.

Fifth, we find compulsive orderliness, obsessive repetitiveness, and fixation upon minute details, which divert attention from the horror. This description precisely applies to the phenomenon of confessionalism among women, which diverts attention away from the horror of gynocide.

Sixth, behavior which at other times and places is unacceptable becomes acceptable and even normative as a consequence of conditioning through the ritual atrocity. As a result of "recurrent command performances," foreground feminist horizontal violence becomes acceptable and normative among those who at other times and places have enthusiastically celebrated sisterhood.

The seventh point—legitimation of the Sado-Ritual by the rituals of "objective" scholarship—can be observed in reporting, interviews, and studies reflecting the masosadistic confessionalist phenomenon. For the most part these fail to identify the fact that women obsessed with confessionalism are working to destroy each other and thus serving the interests of patriarchy.

SADOSPIRITUALITY II: PHALLIC FLIGHT FROM LUST INTO "TRANSFORMED" LECHERY, IN THE NAME OF THE SUBLIME, OF SUBLIMATION AND OF SUBLIMINATION

Throughout this Foreground, Wanderlusters have confronted the first aspect of the Sadospiritual Syndrome, namely, sadospirituality as phallic flight from lust into lust-full asceticism. This aspect of the syndrome, as I have tried to show, forms/fixes the conditions/conditioning which Lusty women must move through/transcend as we enter the First Realm.

The second aspect of sadospirituality must also be faced. This is flight from lust into purified/putrified/refined products of phallic lust. Such transformation takes a trinitarian shape, manifesting itself in the seductions of the sado-sublime, in the prosthetic products of sado-sublimation, and in the ghostly, Self-destructive messages of sado-sublimination. By means of these transformations of phallic lust, the sadosociety robs women of our ancestral memory, blocking our capacity to conceive, utter, and act upon our own Original/Elemental Words. It is necessary that Wanderlusters face this trinity, as precondition for entering the Realm of Archespheres.

The Sado-Sublime

The idea of the "sublime" has been used in connection with piety and art, sometimes combining the two, as describing pious art. Among the definitions of *sublime* as an adjective we find "lofty in conception or expression," and "tending to inspire awe or uplifting emotion." * As a verb, *sublime* has a definition that is especially important for Nag-Gnostic analysis. It means "to cause to pass from the solid to the vapor state by the action of heat and again condense to solid form (many chemicals . . . are *sublimed* to rid them of impurities)."

Males have tried to rid themselves of their impurities by subliming themselves into "God," who is "sublime," and who is so lofty that he really is nowhere and thus can be said to be everywhere. The earthly/unearthly males have vaporized and then condensed/reified their self-images into the sublime product, god, and they use this condensed and purified product as a mask to engender *awe*. The mask of the sublime "heavenly father" is trotted out whenever males perceive the need to pretend to be what they are not, which, under the present societal arrangements, is almost all of the time. Of course, Ronald Reagan has constantly used the mask of "heavenly father," as did Carter, Ford, Nixon et al. before him. Not only do priests, rabbis, and ministers employ this device, but also "nonreligious" and even atheist psychiatrists, physicians, lawyers, scientists, and businessmen tap into this image (whether "consciously" or subliminally is not the point) to elicit the awe of patients, clients, "subjects," and other subordinates of all kinds.

Not only the "heavenly father," sublimed by males and employed as symbol of omnipotent, omnipresent masculinity, is called "sublime." Within christianity, the term is applied to god the son and god the holy ghost, who are believed to be "coequal" with the father. The term is also used to describe images of total subservience, such as the christian image of Mary, the dethroned and sapped Goddess, who was converted into a vessel chosen to be filled with an allegedly divine male offspring. Religious music and art devoted to the saga of these "persons" are deemed sub-

---

*As I have explained in the Introduction, all definitions, unless otherwise indicated, are from *Webster's Third New International Dictionary of the English Language.*

lime. So also are works of art which exalt the victimization of females by the secular institutions of patriarchy. Thus the paintings of Raphael and Goya are sublime; the lyric poetry of the Romantic and Victorian poets is sublime. For by idealizing the feminine, these glorify the divine father. "Nature" too is called sublime, insofar as this is captured in art and depicted as worshipping the father.

Nag-Gnostic subverters of the sublime recognize that the male myth-makers have been able to manufacture and promote their sublimed products only at the expense of female transcendence. Indeed, they have stolen women's Original Words, converting images of female transcendence into Godfather, Son, and Company. Unnaming/denying female participation in Be-ing, then, has been a basic maneuver in the sadospiritual flight from lust into transformed/refined lechery.

Disguising male lust has been essential to the ruse. In creating sadospiritual religion, men have fled into pseudo-purified and disguised lust In the Name of the Sublime. Phallic lust—christened *religion, mysticism, duty, charity, patriotism, romantic love*—is not only all right, but the height of virile virtue. Indeed, male rape fantasies become high theology and elicit religious rapture when these are vaporized and condensed, elevated and converted, into dogma and art concerning the "Virgin Birth." In the "Annunciation" the male-angel Gabriel brings poor Mary the news that she is to be impregnated by and with god. Like all rape victims in male myth she submits joyously to this unspeakable degradation.

Other sublime christian symbols function as reifications of sublimed lust. As a consequence of subliming, the believer can enjoy symbolic eating and drinking of human flesh and blood without consciously feeling like a cannibal. The crucifix can be adored without conscious indulgence in sadomasochistic fantasies. Worshippers can stare at the image of a dead body nailed to dead wood without consciousness of the fact that the living tree was/is a symbol of the Goddess. Priests can hear "true confessions" without feeling responsible for voyeurism. In the Name of the Sublime, the objects of phallic lust may be enjoyed without the burden of conscious guilt which weighed down ascetics such as saint Jerome, with his bevy of imaginary girls in the desert. However, the fixations are the same and the consequences for women are the same. Female victimization is glorified in sublime religion and art, but the victim does not experience this as glory, for the sado-sublime implies refined, perfected, heightened victimization. It is heightened lechery.

Sado-Sublimation

To *sublimate* is "to direct the energy of (an impulse) from a primitive aim to one that is higher on the cultural scale, especially in the course of psychoanalysis." *Sublimation* is defined as "discharge of instinctual energy . . . through socially approved activities." The christian dogma of "The Incarnation" is not only sublime; it is a paradigm of male sublimation. Indeed it is the supremely sublimated male sexual fantasy, assuming fantastic proportions. It is mythic Super-Rape.

Since the Virgin Mother mythically represents all matter to the sublimers/sublimators, the myth of "The Incarnation" symbolically legitimates the rape of all matter as well as all women—a project which has been a goal of patriarchal civilization for millennia, but which has been speeded up immeasurably in the age of computerized technology. Nuclearism, chemical contamination of the earth, planned famine, torture of political prisoners, torture of laboratory animals, obscene medical experimentation—all are discharges of male instinctual energy through activities that are socially approved by males.

Moreover, the culture of phallicism, which is the offspring of such forcible rape, is the increasingly artificial environment which blocks Elemental/Wild memory, knowing, and creation. This is the culture of warped words/ideas made "flesh"—the culture of sado-sublimation.

Sado-Sublimination

The adjective *subliminal* means "existing or functioning outside the area of conscious awareness: influencing thought, feeling, or behavior in a manner unperceived by personal or subjective consciousness." Moreover, *subliminal* means "designed to influence the mind on levels other than that of conscious awareness and especially by presentation too brief to be consciously perceived (subliminal techniques in TV advertising)." The widespread manipulation of minds by techniques that are *subliminal* in the last sense has resulted in the coinage of the noun *sublimination,* meaning "the use of subliminal techniques (as in advertising)."

The fact that subliminal perceptions *exist* is not contrary to Elemental knowing/perceiving. Indeed, concentration and focus require that we turn our attention to some aspects of experience, while others are only subliminally perceived. Quite distinct from this natural subliminal perceiving, however, is the manipulation of these levels—the use of "subliminal techniques." The latter, clearly, is destructive.[82]

Mind management through subliminal manipulation did not begin with modern advertising, however. The use of the symbol of Mary by christian missionaries as a tool for the conversion of "pagans" in Europe, for example, involved the manipulation of subliminal perceptions. Thus the presentation of Mary and Christ as a sort of "package deal" was expedient for the conversion of the Celts, who were not habituated to being deprived of female divinity. Although the converts were taught that Mary is "only human," and not divine, their subliminal perception and identification of Mary with the Goddess were used to seduce them into the christian church.[83] Moreover, the residue of apparently female qualities in the figure of Jesus (the "androgynous" product of pseudo-parthenogenesis) plays/preys upon subliminal perceptions of and desires for female images of divinity.

Mental manipulation, then, involves deliberate perversion of the natural phenomenon of subliminal perception, so that it becomes a tool of the sadostate, whose rulers have used techniques of sublimination for centuries before the advent of technological sublimination. One need only visit a court of law or a physician's office to find evidence of the role of subliminal messages in maintaining the power dynamics of the professions.*

The omnipresent subliminal messages of the sadostate block/ hide access to the Realm of Archespheres. They incapacitate/

* Courtroom mystique is conveyed by such items as the long black robe of the judge, the requirement that everyone stand when the judge enters, the raised bench of the judge, the ritualized formal language of lawyers and court officers. In a physician's office, the "patient" is conditioned to anxious passivity by the standard interminable wait to be "seen" by the doctor, by the subordinate behavior of the doctor's assistants, by the mystifying technical jargon used in "answering" the patient's questions. See Denise Donnell Connors, "Sickness unto Death: Medicine as Mythic, Necrophilic, and Iatrogenic," *Advances in Nursing Science*, vol. 2, no. 3 (April 1980), pp. 39–51.

castrate women on deep psychic levels by their ghostly presences. They undermine women's powers to Realize our powers.

Movement Beyond Sadospirituality

By Knowing and Naming the destructive demons of sadospirituality Nags gnaw our way through their blocks/blockades, entering Archespheres. In this Knowing/Naming/Gnawing we have already encountered primal emanations of phallic lust. It would be dangerously delusory to imagine that this is over and done with, as we approach the deep dimensions of Archespheres. Indeed, the process of exorcism continues in heightened degrees, incorporated into the ecstatic process of releasing our Elemental/Original Words. Entering Archespheres involves expelling/dispelling the lethal products of sadospirituality, the alien archetypes that imprison minds/passions of Witches, Weirds, Websters, Wild women who long to be free. Ecstatic movement through this Realm requires continuing expulsion of the pseudospirits/sado-spirits—the spooks spawned by the subliming, sublimating, sub-liminating sages and saints of snooldom.

Expelling these predatory presences, we move beyond the archetypes of the sado-sublime, evoking the Archimage, the Original Witch. Racing through, beyond the incarnations of sado-sublimation, we dis-cover Real Presence. Weaving through/past the mind-mines of sado-sublimination we Realize, and thus un-leash, our Elemental Powers.

CHAPTER TWO

BEYOND THE SADO-SUBLIME:
EXORCISING ARCHETYPES,
EVOKING THE ARCHIMAGE

Eyebite:	"Obsolete, rare: to bewitch with the eye."
	Oxford English Dictionary
Eyebite/I-Bite:	"to Be-Witch with the Eye/I."
	Websters' First New Intergalactic Wickedary of the English Language

Weaving past the Foreground of this Realm, Websters entering Archespheres sense our vision and our breathing being blocked. We must pass through the Vapor State, dis-spelling the gases of the sado-sublimers. Our tactic is to Name these vapors, not ignore them.

In its archaic sense, the noun *vapor* means "something unsubstantial or transitory: PHANTASM." Pursuing this clue, we find that the word *phantasm* helps us understand still more about the vapors. For it means "delusive appearance: ILLUSION, DECEPTION," and "GHOST, SPECTER, SPIRIT."

Looking at the vapors that impede us, we see that these definitions Name the game. The phantoms, specters, shadowy shapes are archetypes emitted by sublimers. The function of these archetypes is aptly expressed by one archaic definition of the verb *vapor,* which is "DEPRESS, BORE." Confused, asphyxiated by the sado-sublimers' mass production of archetypes, women are depressed and bored.

Engaged in expulsion/exorcism of the ghostly sublime illusions, women wield our Labryses to split open the word *archetype,* dis-covering clues to the nature of our victimization by the Vapor State. It is derived from the Greek *archetypos,* meaning "molded first as a model." This word, in turn, is derived from *arche*, meaning original, and *typos*, meaning impression of a seal, mold, replica. We note that it is mind-boggling to attempt to conceive of a replica which is at the same time original. Yet the common definitions of *archetype* attempt to weld these contradictory meanings. Thus it is said to mean "the original model, form, or pattern from which something is made or from which something develops." While on a surface level this might appear reasonable, the fact is, that which is truly original cannot be reduced to a model, form, or pattern without serious distortion. For one who is Original is a verb, always be-ing, changing. It is inherent in archetypes that they crush this biophilic lust for be-ing.

The horror of the life-crushing function of archetypes is exposed in the etymology of the second part of the word: *type*, which is derived from the Greek *typtein*, meaning "to strike, beat," and which is akin to the Latin *stuprum*, meaning "defilement, dishonor," and to the Sanskrit *tupati*, *tumpati*, meaning "he hurts." The sublimed archetypes are designed to beat, defile, dishonor, and hurt original female Elemental powers, the Archaic powers of Lusty women.

ARCHAIC ORIGINS AND PHYSICAL ULTIMACY

The process of unmasking the inherent evil of archetypes requires further examination of the word *arche* (plural: *archai*). This means "something that was in the beginning: a first principle: a) *in early Greek philosophy:* a substance or primal element b) *in Aristotle:* an actuating principle (as a cause)." One can pursue the history of this word through volumes of history of philosophy. Its basic meaning is always beginning or origin.[1]

The pre-Socratic Greek philosopher Anaximander identified *arche* with "the unlimited" (*apeiron*). By using these words he appears to have suggested that the beginning of the world should be understood in a sense other than temporal. As one authority puts it, he seems to imply "extratemporal priority and physical ultimacy." [2]

Elemental Searchers can identify with the idea of "extratemporal priority," for we have a sense of connectedness with deep origins, with ancient memories of the Elemental Race—memories which are not confined to the realm of linear time, memories which are uncovered and expanded in our participation in the unfolding of Be-ing.

Elemental women will also be at home with the idea of "physical ultimacy," finding this a refreshing change of focus away from the prevailing obsessions with "physical intimacy" within the culture of phallic lust. Physical ultimacy suggests the possibility of relations with others as well as with one's Self that are far-reaching, demanding that we stretch our physical, imaginative, psychic powers beyond the limitations that have been imposed upon them. *Ultimate* means "FARTHEST, EARLIEST." It also means "EXTREME, UTMOST." Our connections, the rhythms of our bodies/minds, are —like those of the tides—not only with the sun and moon but also with the farthest stars, whose light reaches us after traveling countless millions of light-years.

Since these connections are in the realm of participation in Be-ing, which is always unfolding, they involve continuing expansion of Elemental Powers, the breaking of barriers of space and time, the spanning of geographical and temporal distance. They therefore increase our powers of intimacy, reaching and replenishing innermost Sources. The physical ultimacy of those who choose biophilic be-ing is demanding in a manner totally unlike the casual or pseudo-intense "relationships" that are fostered/ fathered by the patriarchal setting/set-up—connections that arise mainly from such circumstances as geographical proximity and which depend upon such circumstances. Truly Archaic/Original relations among women demand ultimacy.

This is not the "ultimacy" circumscribed by the walls of patriarchal philosophy. The limitations of that thought are illustrated in descriptions of Anaximander's concept of *arche* as "an immense abstractive step away from the purely sensory." [3] A basic inadequacy of this way of naming knowledge of origins lies/Lies with the assumption that the senses need be as constricted as they have become under the domain of patriarchy. As we become more aware of the range of our subtle, complex sensory powers we hear "Purely Sensory" as descriptive not of limitations but of deep/rich perceptions of be-ing. Indeed, the expression takes on Musical dimensions, Naming our Metaphoric powers of Musing into Metabeing. As Nags/Hags awaken to our Lusty powers of perceiving/sensing we break dichotomies between the sense perceptible and the supposedly suprasensible, exposing these as senseless.

Western philosophy, of course, does hold forth hints that *arche* transcends matter-spirit dualism. For instance, as Walter Pagel writes:

In Stoicism . . . emphasis had been laid on the ambivalent—neither corporeal nor spiritual—character of "Prime Matter." This, to the stoic philosophers, was not "matter" in the ordinary sense, but an "Arche" or "Ousia." . . . It is matter that is alive and at the same time it is spirit that is of finest corporeality.[4]

Nag-Gnostic women, breaking free from the mentors' mind-tracks, begin to experience our Selves as Prime Matter—original matter that is alive and that is also spirit of the finest corporeality. In this sense we become Archaic, breaking the seals/molds/replicas which are archetypes designed to seal off the sources of that deep, original intuition which Jan Raymond has called the intuition of integrity.[5]

RECOGNIZING ARCHETYPES

Archetypes are devoid of living content. Even Jung acknowledged this, writing:

It is necessary to point out once more that archetypes are not determined as regards their content, but only as regards their form and then only to a very limited degree. . . . The archetype in itself is empty and purely formal.[6]

Archetypes indeed are vague/vaporous. A central figure/figment of this sado-sublime projection is the "Great Mother," who/which assumes many forms to which other so-called archetypes are attached. A typical list of "her" most obvious forms is offered by Erich Neumann:

To the left, there is ranged a negative series of symbols—Deadly Mother, Great Whore of Babylon, Witch, Dragon, Moloch; to the right, a positive series in which we find the Good Mother, who as Sophia or Virgin, brings forth and nourishes, and leads the way to rebirth and salvation. Here Lilith, there Mary; here the toad, there the goddess; here a morass of blood; there the Eternal Feminine.[7]

This litany, with its peculiar patriarchal reversals, is vaporously unspecific. Unaddressed are such questions as "Deadly to whom?" and "Good by whose standards?" Neumann and the other archetype-pedlars assume that the "values" of phallicism can go unchallenged. Of course, Deadly Witches and Dragons gladly assume the Negative—Naming our Selves No-Sayers to the Negators. Refusing to shrink into mummified marys, goody goddesses, eternally feminine toadies, we join with Lilith and with the Holy Toad, Naming the man-made massacres of Sister-Women, the morasses of murdered women's blood.

Jung himself produced a listing of great-mother-types, including paradise, the kingdom of god, the heavenly jerusalem, the church, the university, the city, the cow, the grave, the sarcophagus. . . .[8] Clearly, these are all "good" insofar as they serve and are possessed by men. In an obfuscated way, Neumann discusses the downfall of the Great Mother to this condition:

We have seen that virginity was an essential aspect of the Great Mother, of her creative power, which is not dependent on any personal mate. . . . Finally, in the patriarchal world, she is dethroned by her prince consort and is herself subordinated. But she always retains her archetypal effectiveness.[9]

The reader of this passage is mystified concerning the meaning of the "archetypal effectiveness" which "she retains." Clearly, the subordinated Great Mother is not effective in the same way as the original parthenogenetic Goddess. Nor can the effectiveness of the original Goddess symbols be classified as merely "archetypal." For this adjective describes the condition of patriarchally possessed female images, which are beaten into male-identified shape. So male-identified, indeed, is the patriarchal Great Mother that her vaporous outlines can condense to the "solid form" of a male. This is only fitting. Since males have sublimed "her" they are compelled to mime "her." "She" is, after all, a man-made product.

The Papal Great Mother: John Paul, Too

A contemporary graphic example of the male as great mother is pope John Paul Two ("he loves you"), the granite-jawed, white-robed superstar who has charmed hundreds of millions of TV viewers and live audiences as well, particularly since his 1979 debut as visiting Queen of Heaven descending upon continent after continent in a special airplane. Championing many of the values of the vacuous eighties, such as imprisonment in the family, fetal rights, and discreet christian gynocide, this pope could be nominated Male Mother of the Decade.

John Paul Two is without doubt the most pop patriarch of the eighties, using the electronic media to proclaim his love for souls. In his splendidly feminine robes, pope John Paul Two has been a darling archetype of the media, an electronically programmed and updated version of the Galli, the priests of the Great Mother in ancient Syria, Crete, and Ephesus. Like them, he has been representative of the patriarchal Great Mother (now commonly called Mother Church). Known as "the missionary pope," he has taken missionary positions appropriate to the age of nuclear missions. The papal mother functions to legitimate the age of nuclearism, not by favoring nuclear holocaust, but by fostering woman-hating ideologies, myths, roles, rules which undermine respect for life (while assuming the title "pro-life").

The papal position permits certain ancillary associations with women who endorse this Queenly role. The Associated Press report of his 1981 visit to the Philippines included the following information:

On the fourth day of his six-day tour of the Philippines, the Pope shared the limelight with the powerful first lady Imelda Marcos.

Traveling ahead of the Pope in her own jet, Mrs. Marcos greeted John Paul at each stop, kissing his ring as he arrived at each airport.[10]

Con-descending at each airport, the Jet Age Heavenly Queen could tolerate pursuit by the "powerful" lady-in-waiting provided that she arrived in time to kiss the papal ring. This widely publicized scenario displays the real position of "powerful" patriarchal women under archetypal phallic rule. It is consistent with this scenario that John Paul Two expresses ardent devotion to the christian mother Mary. This was particularly in evidence in his 1983 visit to Poland. Shrewd observers noted the ambiguity involved in his appearing to champion freedom while urging Polish women into the same old role of raising sons for sacrifice.

Forever Fetal: The Hostages and the "Great Mother"

The Great Mother can be sublimed by men to contain them as fetuses. In the 1980–81 Spectacular Soap Opera of "The American Hostages in Iran," the heroes of the saga—like the astronaut heroes of the previous decade—were spectacularly fetal. This theme was at least subliminally perceived by many. The *Boston Globe,* for example, reported the reaction of a twin brother of one of the hostages upon his release:

I want to say thank you to the world. Man, what a relief: it's like you gave birth to 52.[11]

The subliminal message of the hostages' fetal identification could be absorbed by the millions whose psyches have been softened by "prolife" propaganda. A letter published in the *Worcester* (Mass.) *Telegram* under the caption "Former Hostages and the Unborn" illustrates this point:

To the Editor:
   I just have to ask this question: How can we Americans feel so much joy at the saving of the precious lives of only 52 Americans and at the same time condone and even encourage the slaughter of innocent unborn babies in the millions?
   I can't help but wonder what if the mother of that valiant and brave young American, James Lopez, had decided she could not raise another child, that it was her right to do what she wanted with her body. Perhaps all those precious 52 hostages and the others that escaped would have died that day.[12]

Obviously, one does not look for logic in the state of possession by archetypes. The archetypes do have an inherent ill-logic of their own, however, as they blend and re-form themselves, reinforcing the Vapor State.
   The Saga of the Fetal Hostages was in fact a media-staged Odyssey, re-enacting the myth of separation and return—separation from the womb of the good mother (America), containment in the womb of the terrible mother (Iran), and return to the good mother's womb. The melodrama portrayed a struggle between alleged forces of good and evil, between heaven and hell, and the message was duly/dully absorbed. As the *Boston Globe* reported:

So profound was the effect of it all that one father said it was like seeing his son emerge from hell and going into heaven.[13]

This theme was reiterated on television, elaborated with gory details of torture and beatings in Iran and total love in America.

The force of the archetype's form as Good Mother depends upon the recurrence of its image as Terrible Mother. Unable to live outside a womb, The Hostages must reside either in the hellish or the heavenly womb. The message is that liberation consists in return to the good womb, from which the fetal hero has been separated. This is the true redemption, which bonds together the chosen ones. Filene's Department Store expressed this theme in an ad in the *Boston Globe:*

> Their bondage has been our bondage.
> Their freedom is now our freedom
> And we rejoice in their return.[14]

It is unimportant to the saga whether or not women feel like identifying with the fetal heroes. Clearly, this is not the intended basic feminine role. Rather, women "here at home" are the multiple nurturing wombs welcoming home The Hostages who have escaped from the bad surrogate mother—comforting, serving, caring for them. The greater the archetypal power that is aggrandized by the patriarchal Great Mother in any of her forms, the more degrading and absolute is the servitude of actual living women. Wherever this Alien/Alienating Archetype reigns, the parasitic paradise of fetalhood is secured. Under this rule, women's bodies/spirits/energies are endlessly converted into placenta—into living food for the fatal fetal fraternity. Subjected to the sado-sublime, then, women are reduced to the status of placental beings.[15]

DIS-COVERING THE ARCHIMAGE

The process of *anamnesia*—of Unforgetting our Elemental connections—is a process thwarted by the blinding, suffocating archetypes. This Unforgetting might well be called archelogy. *Archelogy,* as I have suggested in the Introduction, is "the science of first principles." It is about recalling our first questions, our native powers—the Original lustrous radiant sunrise of our be-ing. As Archelogians, women augur pasts and futures veiled by archetypes. Our method is intensely be-ing/knowing in the present. Our Present/Presence, as affected/effected by the past, unveils the past, since an effect resembles and dis-closes its causes. Moreover, the present, as cause of the future, dis-closes the future, for an effect is known in part from understanding its causes.

In order to reach our deep empowering memories, Archelogians must not only recognize the archetypes of the sado-sublime; we must also exorcise them. Our exorcising of these distorted/distorting molds involves/requires dis-covering the Archimage, who is hidden behind the archetypes.

The word *Archimage** is radiant with hidden Pristine Powers. The meanings, then, must be unfolded. The definition of *Archimage,* as given in the dictionary, is "a great magician, wizard, or enchanter." It is derived from the Greek *archi-* (which is akin to *arche-*), a prefix meaning principal, original, primary, plus *magos,* which is said to mean magus, wizard. A *magus* is "an adept in occult arts: MAGICIAN, SORCERER." This, of course, is the singular of *Magi,* the three wise "men" of christian folklore. It is derived from the Indo-European root *magh-,* meaning "to be able, to have power." [16]

The fact that the masculine form is used exclusively in these definitions suggests what sort of magic is involved in the masterminding of the archetypes, which are the masters' miming of the *arche.* It suggests that there are indeed master male magicians, manufacturers and manipulators of illusions, who are *behind* the archetypes in the sense that they project these everywhere, with the magic lanterns of their media. Moreover, the masculine definition of *archimage* suggests that the trick of *reversal* has been played upon/within this word itself. For the tricksters' power has consisted in the ability to steal and simulate Original Female Powers and Words.

Having perceived and Named the omnipresence of the trick of reversal in the sadosociety, Hags/Nags can Name this archi-trick, dis-covering that the true *Archimage behind* the simulators/reversers (whom I shall call archi-magi†), is the Great Original *Witch,* who is *in* women and all Elemental creatures. As an Original Act of Exorcism, of dis-spelling the archi-magi's bad magic, Lusty women can reclaim the name *Archimage,* Naming the fact that she is the Witch within our Selves. She is a verb, and she is

---

* This word is pronounced är kə̄ mäj (rhyming with *rage*).

† *Archimago* is used by Spenser in his *Faerie Queene* as the name of his personification of hypocrisy. I am coining the term *archi-magi* to Name the patriarchal tricksters/hypocrites who manufacture and manipulate archetypes and who impersonate the Elemental Source of power within, the Witch within, whom I am calling *Archimage.*

verbal—a Namer, a Speaker—the Power within who can Name away the archetypes that block the ways/words of Metabeing.

Archimage is a Metaphoric form of Naming the one and the many. She is power/powers of be-ing within women and all biophilic creatures. She points toward Metabeing, in which all Witches/Hags/Weirds participate, and in which we live, move, and have our be-ing. She is Active Potency of Hags, totally Other than mere "pure act" (god), her transsexed counterfeit. She is shimmering Substance—Real Presence—that shines through appearances. She is root of connectedness in the female Elemental Race. In mythic terms, *Archimage* Names the Triple Goddess. This image is not reducible to mathematical equations. Rather, she signifies unity and harmony in Diversity—as suggested also by the images of the Norns, the Muses, the Graces, the Fates. She spins the threads of life, the Stamina uniting all moving, singing Spinster-Witches across time and space in cosmic concordance.

THE MAGI: THREE WISE "MEN" FROM THE EAST

Every christmas season christians sing about and erect images of the Magi, understood to be three wise men from the East who, according to the gospel of Matthew, paid homage to the infant Jesus. They are often popularly described as "kings." These three wise men are described as following their star to the crib of the newborn Jesus. Christian preachers have interpreted the story to signify the universality of the kingdom of Jesus. (There is often a token Black in popular depictions and crèches.) Indeed, this message seems to be conveyed in christian music and art depicting the wise men as kneeling before the baby Jesus and offering him gifts.*

Among the popular descriptions of the three "kings" are some depicting them as throwing down their crowns before the infant. Such embellishments reinforce the popular image of the renunci-

---

* The story of the "three kings" so obviously belongs to the realm of popular legend that it has been something of an embarrassment to biblical scholars and theologians. The point is that it continues to function as an integral part of the imagery of the christmas story for hundreds of millions of people, and the symbol is embedded in the imaginations of believers (and nonbelievers).

ation of power by these wise and powerful rulers before the baby-god.

Nag-Gnostic star-gazers have reason to be fascinated by this story. One Nagging question that often re-occurs is "Why are there three?" Since we are by now familiar with innumerable myths of the Triple Goddess, many of which originated in the Middle East, the thought that in a religion of reversals the Triple Goddess would be presented disguised as three wise kings is indeed a Nagging thought. Also interesting is the fact that stars are closely associated with the Goddess. As Cooper points out:

> Stars are attributes of all Queens of Heaven, who are often star-crowned. The star is pre-eminently the symbol of Ishtar, or Venus, as morning and evening star.[17]

All of this suggests that if the subliminal message in the story is that the Goddess was brought to her knees before Jesus, the implications are indeed vast. If, symbolically speaking, Goddesses and no mere kings were throwing down their crowns, then star-crowns were thrown down, indicating a surrender of the whole cosmos. Even if the more conservative image of these dignitaries as merely kneeling and bowing their crowned heads is retained, the symbolism is essentially the same. Moreover, in traditional symbolism: "The radiate crown represents the energy and power contained in the head, which was regarded as the seat of the life-soul." [18] The message of surrender of mind/spirit to the incarnate boygod is obvious.*

Gnawing through the surface level of the "three king" symbol to the subliminal suggestion of the Triple Goddess surrendering to patriarchal religion, Nags note that the story thus unraveled is indeed an eye-opener. That is, it is an *epiphany,* in the sense of "sudden manifestation or perception of the essential nature or meaning of something . . . an intuitive grasp of reality through something usually simple and striking."

---

* Perhaps the three royal visitors were hoping to have the last laugh. At any rate, the symbolic significance of their gifts would seem to suggest a rather morbid attitude toward a baby shower. *Myrrh,* for example, signifies suffering and sorrow. See J. C. Cooper, *An Illustrated Encyclopedia of Traditional Symbols* (London: Thames and Hudson, 1978), p. 110. Frankincense was used not only in worship but also for embalming and fumigation.

The spectacle of the patriarchal symbolic conquest of Female/Elemental divinity is perceptible here, as in other patriarchal myth, and it is "simple and striking." Shrewd Shrews will be interested in finding further clues, however. These are to be found, of course, in words. As we have seen, the word *Magi* is derived from the Indo-European root *magh-*, meaning "to be able, to have power." Clearly, the empowering act for women will be to stop kneeling, collect our star-crowns and gold, and resume the Journey. This is, of course, a journey of star-lust.[19]

THE ACTIVE POTENCY OF THE ARCHIMAGE

Some clues concerning the Active Potency of the Archimage, as this expressed itself in the Middle Ages, can be gleaned from Paracelsus, the sixteenth century alchemist, physician, philosopher, who is known to have learned a great deal from the Witches, particularly in the realm of healing.[20] As preparation for discussing his words, Nags Nag our Selves to recall that one definition of the verb *heal* is "to restore to original purity or integrity: to make . . . spiritually whole: to restore from evil." The Archimage as healer, then, inspires Pure Lust for Archaic spiritual wholeness, rescuing those who acknowledge her from the evil of possession by patriarchal scholarship as well as by archetypes. Thus inspired, Searchers for Sources use such useful re-sources as Paracelsus,* untwisting their twisted tales to find our own First Principles.

Paracelsus links magic (which he writes in the feminine form, *Magica*) with the *Magus* (masculine form, meaning sorcerer). To decipher his tale of magic, then, Weavers will begin by unsnarling it. The feminine form for *magic* suggests that this is an instrument of the male sorcerer (Magus). This is particularly perverse, since he knew very well, from his countless conversations with healers, that most of the sorcerers/healers were women. That is, they were Witches. Bearing this distortion in mind, it is possible to dis-close some insights in his theory.

Paracelsus observed that what the saint is in the "Realm of

---

* The full name of this peculiar personage, by which he preferred to be addressed, was Philippus Aureolus Theophrastus Bombastus Paracelsus von Hohenheim.

God," the "Magus" [read: *Witch*] is in the "Realm of Nature," for the saint works through God, the "Magus" through Nature.[21] Deciphered, the essential point here is the distinction between the Witches and the christian "saints." The Witch exercises Active Potency in the Realm of *Nature*. Her Powers are natural.

One quality of this Active Potency is conveyed by Paracelsus when he explains that the "Magus" brings celestial forces to earth.[22] Gyn/Ecologically speaking, this means that insofar as we are Witches, women are in harmony with the rhythms of the universe. As participating in the work of the Archimage, our task is the re-establishing of connections with natural rhythms that have been severed. A powerful means for re-establishing this harmony and for healing the fragmentation is suggested in the idea that through the "Magus" symbols and words acquire forces like those of Arcana.[23] One definition of *arcanum* is "an extract of the vital nature of something: a powerful natural agent: ELIXIR." The power of the Archimage within is the capacity to extract the vital nature, the Elemental force in symbols and words, so that they regain their original meanings and act as powerful natural agents. The Archimage within Lusty women detects and communicates the *elixir* of words, that is, their quintessential transforming powers and life-fostering force.

The Active Potency of the Archimage, then, is transformative Power. This faculty, through which she "brings celestial forces to earth," is the power of healing broken connections. One way through which this is communicated is the transmission of Metaphoric words that transverse/pass across the fathers' archetypes, awakening the stifled *archai* with word-waves/wand-waves. The words/wands of Weird women also transverse the archetypes in the sense that they overturn and reverse them, reversing their reversals. For words are weapons, Labryses of Archimagical Amazons. Women participating in the biophilic powers of the Archimage also transverse in the "obsolete" sense of the term, which is "alter, transform," as we change our lives in the process of dis-spelling the archetypes.

The most joyful aspect of the powers of Archimagical word-wands is conveyed by yet another meaning of the verb *transverse:* "to turn or render into verse: VERSIFY." In her essence/quintessence the Archimage is the Muse within. As she muses, she re-minds her Self, dis-covering, creating, chanting new and ancient rhythms, in tenses that transverse present, past, and future.

Transversing unmasks memories of the Archaic, unsealing secrets by the magic of creation.

Thus understood, the Archimage is She Who Spirates. In christian doctrine of the triune god, the father "generates" the son, while both together "spirate," through their mutual love, the holy spirit. This spirit is the bond between the father and the son, his word. While women have been forcibly invited to participate in the generation of sons, we have been cut off from our powers of spiration/creation. As one woman has suggested, the concept of spiration provides a "missing link" for understanding the connection between women and creation.[24] Indeed, enslavement to patriarchal reproduction is a primary obstacle to *spiration,* which in its obsolete sense means "the action of breathing as a creative or life-giving function of the Deity." Confined by patriarchal motherhood, women are deprived of breathing space, basic to the process of creation.[25]

Muses breathe forth musings, transversing rhythms of spiration. This involves freeing words from bondage in the prisons of the omnipresent scripts of fatherland, where all are cast into roles of actors reading scripts, disconnected from the meanings of the words they are speaking.[26]

The spiration of the Archimage within Lusty women, who speak women's words, heals broken connections between words and their Sources, reconnecting speakers with their original words. Archimagical women, spinning/spirating Elemental connections between words and their Sources, transverse the verbicide of the ages. Women breathing forth healing words confront the agents of gynocide by re-membering the Archaic lore and Lusty logic of Racing women.

THE ARCH-IMAGE

Many Hags have studied the history and significance of the European Witchcraze, in the course of which hundreds of thousands of women (some estimate that the numbers reached millions) were tortured and burned alive. Although many women were killed as Witches before and after the three centuries of the Witchcraze, this period itself (late fifteenth to mid-eighteenth century) was a time of heightened, frenzied gynocide.*

* It was also a period of frenzied genocide, particularly under the Spanish Inquisition. The torture and massacre of Jews by the church is another manifestation of the sado-ideology of patriarchy.

Crone-logical thinkers can see that it was no coincidence that this age coincides with the rise of protestantism. For protestantism is characterized by its erasure of Mary, that vestige of the Goddess symbol that has been preserved in christianity as a hook for the heathen masses. It would appear that the multitudes had not been "ready," before the sixteenth century, for the total obliteration of female symbols of Archaic participation in Powers of Be-ing. During the earlier centuries of christendom, Mary as tamed Goddess had been an essential tool for the taming/training and conversion of the "pagans."

It has been noted that during the Witchcraze, particularly as it approached its most heinous heights, protestants and catholics killed women with relatively equal malice and "success." [27] On the symbolic level, however, their gynocidal tactics accompanying the physical massacre took different forms. Searchers might wonder why the catholic church did not follow the protestant lead and eliminate Mary simultaneously with the Witches. An obvious explanation would be that this symbol was still required by the "conservative" central trunk line of christianity to maintain its stranglehold upon the masses. While this is true, there is more for Gnostic Nags to think about.

In Europe during the Middle Ages Mary had been incredibly powerful as a symbol, as channel to the Archimage, who was not entirely concealed—or con-sealed.[28] Indeed, one could say that this image was powerful to an insufferable degree within a phallic society. Most of the major cathedrals were built to the "Mother of God," the Source who gave birth to god. No matter how lengthily the theologians protested, or how subtle their droning distinctions and discussions, it is obvious that she outranked male images of divinity.[29] Instead of functioning to conceal the Background memory of the Archimage, she was at times translucent, transparent, functioning to dis-close this Archaic Active Potency in women and nature.

A study of theology, piety, art shows that indeed the Archimage was shining through this attempt at manipulation and concealment. To describe this phenomenon I have invented the word *Arch-Image* to Name the Mary image. The Archimage threatened to explode through the Arch-Image, and indeed volcanic eruptions of consciousness/memory in women did take place.[30] In short, Mary malfunctioned as an archetype; the situation was intolerable to the mind-molders.

The protestant solution was substitution. Androgynous, sweet Jesus, the misbegotten and transsexed parthenogenetic daughter who incorporated both masculine and feminine roles, being lord, savior, and sacrificial victim, was the logical surrogate for the female principle.* Being plastic, Jesus was pliable enough to serve as stop-gap, filling the molds required for phallic anthropomorphic symbolization.

The catholic solution to the impending threat of explosion has been the retention of Mary, who was required by popular demand, while dogmatically draining this symbol of her residual vibrancy, slowly remolding and re-finishing her back into archetypal shape. The project of the papal puppeteers has been to make this fembot function as a decoy, distracting those who sense the presence of the Archimage—in their Selves, in their sisters, and in all Elemental reality. Thus catholicism worked on the symbolic level in a drawn-out process of psychic manipulation which has never been completely explored. During the centuries following the Witchcraze it has strived to drain, contain, pervert, and freeze this Arch-Image—the one who has been troublesomely translucent, dis-closing rays of Elemental Be-ing, casting shadows and reflecting shimmerings of the Archimage.

This slow vampirism is a tactic which complements the protestant total erasure of the Arch-Image. This dual strategy on the symbolic level mirrors the "real" political double strategy, employed by both sides of christianity, of murdering some women while maintaining others in the state of living death which is patriarchal womanhood. It is important now to pursue further our analysis of sado-sublime vampirism of Mary, the purpose of which is destruction of the Active Potency of the Archimage.

Since the Archimage is She Who cannot be defiled or broken down, the attacks are successful only on the foreground level.[31] Foreground images of women become increasingly defiled and defiling, and for this reason the breakdown of the Arch-Image is of direct relevance to such phenomena as the burgeoning of the multi-billion-dollar pornography industry and the increase of rape. The warfare against the deep Powers of women is in large

* It is no coincidence that while this symbolic transformation was being wrought through the alchemy of protestant theology, the re-formers were also obliterating female monasteries, forcing nuns to leave their autonomous condition and be assimilated into marriage.

measure on the level of the sado-subliming of male-identified feminine images—the vaporous archetypes—whore, victim virgin, et cetera—which are "condensed into solid form" in the sense that they are ingested and lived out/died out by women.*

The appropriate counter-strategy to the breakdown of the Arch-Image is certainly not the reinstatement of christian Mary but radical reconnection with the Archimage. This requires reconnection of women with our *own* Words. Women have been severed from our own Words, from our powers of spiration/creation. The interruption and distorted simulation of our Words is *verbicide*, that is, "deliberate distortion or destruction of the sense of a word." As a consequence of verbicide, words have become mere noises echoing each other in the fathers' flatland, Foreground, which is the place of babblespheres. The babble is *verbigeration*, which is "continuous repetition of stereotyped phrases."

One result of verbicide—this splitting of speaking from the Self's Elemental core—is a sense of shakiness in women who have heard the Call of the Wild, the Word of the Weird within, but feel overwhelmed by the omnipresent disharmonious vibrations of verbiage. Unable to recall the Source within, women become amnesic; unable to make verbal connections, women become aphasic. Sometimes able to speak, but not trusting words enough to act on them, women become apraxic—as Louky Bersianik has brilliantly explained.[32]

The closer a woman is to the hearing/speaking of the Archimage, the more acutely she senses the shakiness of the sublimed identities foisted upon her. *Shaky* means "marked by insecurity or instability: likely to fall or be overthrown: PRECARIOUS." It means "lacking in firmness of beliefs, principles or allegiance: UNSETTLED." It means "somewhat unsound in health." When in touch with the Source of stability within, women recognize that

---

* It is for this reason that a purely economic analysis cannot ultimately inspire women to revolt. This subliming programming is the key to the paralysis of middle class and upper class women who do have at least the minimal economic leverage necessary to break free. While economic impoverishment is an enormous factor in holding women down, it is not a complete explanation of female oppression, for women's *minds* are possessed. It is crucial that feminists contructing economic analyses of the condition of women focus attention on making these interconnections between deep psychic oppression and economic oppression.

symptoms of shakiness are caused by the archetypal assaults. The remedy is unrelenting understanding that Stamina is stronger than the verbiage of the re-verberators, and that breathing/speaking forth Elemental words/actions is itself the creation and communication of Stamina, which is the living thread of conversation spun by Fates. Since *fate* is derived from *fari* (Latin), meaning to speak, the very name *Fates* says "speakers." Naming our way beyond verbicide (which is deeply connected with gynocide) we are creators of our own fates—becoming Fates.

The Arch-Image as Metaphor

I have said that in the Middle Ages the symbol of Mary was highly charged—to such an extent that she represented an extreme, though veiled, as it were, threat to maledom. To some extent translucent, allowing the light of the Archimage to shine through into women's consciousness, this image not only malfunctioned as archetype but even functioned as Arch-Image of Elemental powers. At this point, it is important to reflect upon the meaning and role of images. Images cannot be understood merely as static, reified *things*. In the case of powerful images the reverse is quite true. Thus the image of Mary is an *operational* image.[33]

This means that the function of the Arch-Image as conduit of Archimagical powers was to inspire in women *acts* of knowing and passion, causing women to participate in such powers. That is, she has functioned as Metaphor, connecting women to some extent with ancient Racial memories. Nevertheless, I would call the Arch-Image a faded and *broken* metaphor, for she has been opaque as well as translucent, distorting as well as illuminating. As tamed and possessed Goddess she could not elicit exuberant Wonderlust as could an Untamed Metaphor of Metabeing. Rather, her messages have been covert, like hidden agendas. They have been conveyed stealthily, as in coded whisperings. Her tattered remainders of divinity have been glimpsed, as it were, by peripheral vision. Indeed, the more she has been officially "exalted," the more muted has been her message as Metaphor/carrier of Metabeing. Cloaked and veiled in sublimed splendor, she has served the sadostate as decoy, distracting women from our own true be-ing, while at the same time conveying subliminal messages of our Archimagical origins.

Like messages transmitted by the countless mothers possessed by patriarchy, who have given "double messages" of encouragement toward autonomy and discouragement to their daughters,* the Arch-Image has been charged with Metaphoric force and at the same time she has been frustratingly faded. Nevertheless, for many hundreds of years in Western culture this faded and broken image has been for women the primary conduit to Powers of Being. In the cultural wasteland of the sado-sublime, in which women have been subsisting spiritually on starvation rations, this Arch-Image was the only signal of hope. This cultural phenomenon has affected, at least indirectly, all women in Western society. For this reason it is of inestimable importance that we try to understand it.

The Arch-Image and the Hate of the Impotent Priests

The cognitive/emotional charge of the Arch-Image can be understood only if she is seen as connected with the Elemental Knowledge/Passion of real women. If there had not been Lusty women who were surviving even under the horrors of christian rule, women gifted with psychic and healing powers, living in harmony with the Elements, the charge would have faded completely. If there had not been women who were in touch with deep ancestral memories and therefore with expectations of a Fated/Fatal† re-awakening of Female Powers, the Arch-Image would have failed entirely to reflect the Archimage.

All of this has been problematic for the paternal puppeteers, for the Arch-Image would be of no use to them if she retained no charge at all. At the same time, she was potentially inflammatory and dangerous—like a tokenized woman who still has sparks of her Self. The dynamics inherent in the fathers' dilemma deserve some Shrewish attention here, for the present tokenization of women in some ways reflects the same paternal dilemma and the same strategies designed to maintain control.

To understand these patriarchal strategies, it is important to see something of the content of the charge of the Mary image, which is multidimensional. She is cosmic—the "woman clothed

---

* As in the popular parody of contradictory advice: "Mother, may I go to swim?" "Yes, my darling daughter, but don't go near the water."

† The word *fatal,* which has purely negative connotations for the fathers, can become an affirming word for women who can experience and acknowledge the Original Female Force of the Fates in our lives.

with the sun, and the moon under her feet, and upon her head a crown of twelve stars" (Rev. 12:1[R.S.V.]). As Marina Warner has observed, the descriptions of Mary are similar to those of Isis, who in Hellenistic Egypt was an astral divinity and who by the second century B.C. "had acquired characteristics that associated her with Diana and other classical sky goddesses." [34] This planetary symbolism was devoured by the church. The moon was first identified with the church and then by analogy with the Virgin Mary. By the Middle Ages the Virgin had acquired the lunar imagery previously applied to the church.

Mary was also associated with the Element Water. Warner writes:

In the thought of late antiquity, the light of the moon not only dispelled the shadows of night, but also had all-important life-giving powers. The grace of God, mediated through Mary, as the light of the sun reflects off the disc of the moon, also gives life and quickens and nourishes and purifies, like water. Thus the imagery of light was intimately associated with the imagery of water, itself the foremost image of grace.[35]

Thus Mary, as christian reflection of the lunar deity, is mistress of the waters.

But Mary is associated not only with the moon, but also with other heavenly bodies. Known as the Star of the Sea, she is a Light-Bearer. She is not only the pole star, the Gate of Heaven, but also the Morning Star, which the Babylonians associated with the sky goddess Ishtar.[36] As Star, she burns and burns but is never consumed. She is thus associated with Elemental Fire.

Since, in addition, the Virgin Mary is Mother, she also represents Earth, the universal genetrix. Clearly, then, the Arch-Image is connected with all of the elements. Her charge is cosmic and Elemental, though muted. Thus the Metaphoric words "Gate of Heaven," as applied to Mary, cannot carry the female speaker/listener through the "Gate," which of course is guarded by the male sublimers of this convoluted scenario.

To understand the weakened charge of the Arch-Image, it is helpful to think of the magic of christmas trees as remnants of the Elemental power of living trees. The symbolism of christmas trees is derived from the ancient "Tree of Life," the Sacred Tree, symbol of the Goddess. Christmas trees, however, which are used to celebrate the birth of the babygod, are *dead*. Indeed, they have been killed—millions of them—precisely in order to serve as christmas trees.* Even after having been cut down, dragged indoors, and decorated, they still have a certain "magic," and this is derived from the fact that they *were* alive and still look, feel, and even *smell* alive.† They are not mere copies of real trees; rather, they have been living trees, and their charge is related to the fact that they carry the past (when they were alive) into the present. That is, they evoke *memories* of living trees. As in the case of christmas trees, then, the Arch-Image has had metaphoric power because she is not merely a copy but rather a remnant of what once was alive and thus evokes memories of what had been alive, that is, the Goddess symbol in women's consciousness. The Arch-Image, then, can evoke memories of Self-affirming be-ing of women.

Both the dilemma and the strategy of the patriarchs, then, have to do with the maintenance and control of women's Elemental memories—our deep memories that connect us with the elements and with our own Elemental force. In order to destroy both women and wild nature (the elements), patriarchal males have chosen the strategy of maintaining these as "the living dead." In order to maintain life even in this degraded and comatose state, they have used the strategy of maintaining an officially approved and controllable conduit to Elemental memory.

Of course, if a significant cognitive minority of women ever should re-member Elemental powers and our connections with the elements, the most powerful threat to the patriarchal system and to its nature-killing offshoots, such as the build-up of nuclear weapons, would be unleashed. Therefore, the fathers have recognized Memory as their enemy, and they have worked to destroy its vestiges in women.

* And the killing and use of them each year is a ritual repetition of Goddess-murder—a ritual appropriately incorporated into the celebration of the "joyous" christmas season.

† As Ernest Schachtel points out, the faculty of smell is particularly crucial for evoking deep early memories, "sometimes merely in the vivid feeling that this is exactly the 'smell' of a childhood Sunday afternoon, or of a garment worn by one's mother, or of father's study. . . ." See Ernest G. Schachtel, *Metamorphosis* (New York: Basic Books, 1959), pp. 160–61. The analogy between killed and "dolled up" christmas trees and the killing and simulation of female divinity was suggested by Jane Caputi, during a conversation in Boston in 1977.

In a fascinating analysis of memory and childhood amnesia, Ernest Schachtel observes that an ambivalent attitude toward memory has accompanied "the history of man." He observes the "profound fascination of memory of past experience and the double aspect of this fascination—its irresistible lure into the past with its promise of happiness and pleasure, and its threat to the kind of activity, planning, and purposeful thought and behavior encouraged by modern Western civilization." [37] Schachtel does not consider the possibility that Gynocentric Memory, pre-patriarchal Memory, is at issue. Nor does he note that the "purposeful thought and behavior encouraged by Western civilization," which leads directly to nuclear holocaust, is purpose-less. Nevertheless, the threat posed by deep Memory is at least acknowledged.

Now the question arises: Just *who could* awaken these fascinating memories that are so threatening to the activity and planning of gynocidal, genocidal, biocidal Western civilization? I suggest that these potential catalysts are strong, woman-identified women, and that patriarchy requires that these be tokenized, as the catholic fathers have tokenized the Arch-Image, or that they be killed, as the protestant fathers have killed the Arch-Image. Or, of course, both (in due time).

For those who are still alive, the issue now is to focus upon our memory as it relates to the dilemma and the strategy of the fathers. There is good reason to think that in the Middle Ages and during the period of the protestant "reformation" the Arch-Image continued to stir up dangerously deep memories in women of primal powers—memories resulting in defiant, deviant actions. Without the real existence of such women, the Witchcraze would be inexplicable. Some strong women were tokenized, at least after their deaths.* Others were burned at the stake (or, if they lived in the British Isles, hanged).

The psychic and healing powers of these women, the Witches

* Hildegarde of Bingen (1098–1179), the Abbess of Rupertsberg, is an example of a deviant genius who succeeded in christian "history." She produced mystical writings glorifying the christian god. However, even christian scholars are obliged to admit that she also produced two books of medicine and natural history, that she created a language of her own composed of 900 words and an alphabet consisting of 23 letters. Hags may well speculate about this language and alphabet which have been lost to us. See "Hildegarde, St.," *New Catholic Encyclopedia*, 1967, VI, 1117.

—their active understanding of the elements which made them Potent as scholars, advisors, and healers—would have increased the translucency of the Arch-Image. This spiraling of Elemental Active Potency was a menace to the priestly caste. For surely the members of that caste have been on some level aware of their own derivative identity (from priestesses) and of the derivative identity of their god (from the Goddess). Depending upon drained female energy and upon the ruses that hid/hide this dependency, the priests were/are essentially impotent.* Disconnected from nature and obviously unable to heal, that is, to regenerate physical/spiritual wholeness, they have been capable only of causing further fragmentation. It was therefore natural, that is, fittingly unnatural, that they created the Witchcraze, in a blaze of archetypal patriarchal "creativity." Their reactive battle and babble against female power has continued to this day.

The rancor of impotent priests has been analyzed by Nietzsche. Of course, that philosopher did not Name the targets of priestly rancor (which he called *ressentiment*), namely women and nature—the true enemies of the priestly caste. For Nietzsche himself, despite his deviance, participated by reason of his sex in the privileges of the priests. Yet his insights are worth pondering. He wrote:

As is well known, the priests are the *most evil enemies*—but why? Because they are the most impotent. It is because of their impotence that in them hatred grows to monstrous and uncanny proportions, to the most spiritual and poisonous kind of hatred. The truly great haters in world history have always been priests; likewise the most ingenious haters: other kinds of spirit hardly come into consideration when compared with the spirit of priestly vengefulness.[38] †

* I am not restricting the use of the word *priest* here to christian priests in the service of the official church. The term extends here to include priests of all patriarchal religions, such as buddhism, hinduism, et cetera. Moreover, since patriarchy is the religion imposed upon the entire planet, the term *priest* is here applied to those males who are officially authorized members of all male-made hierarchies, with Holy Orders to perform the sacrificial, ritualistic, mediatorial, interpretative, or ministerial functions of the professions of patriarchy, for example, medicine, war, politics, law, nuclear science.

† Clearly, I am not endorsing Nietzsche's anti-semitism. I am using his partial insights concerning priesthoods in *my* context of understanding,

Nietzsche is accurate in his description of priestly hatred and impotence. He simply fails to know not only the identity of the targets of priestly hatred, but also the reason for this selection of targets. For Nietzsche himself, mired in priestly misogynism, could not acknowledge that it is the Active Potency of Elemental women that arouses such monstrous and uncanny proportions of hatred in the ontologically impotent drainers. That is, Nietzsche had merely foreground knowledge of priestly hate and impotence. Yet his words are often thought-provoking—for example, when he writes of "the intestinal morbidity and neurasthenia which has afflicted priests at all times," and adds:

but as to that which they themselves devised as a remedy for this morbidity—must one not assert that it has ultimately proved itself a hundred times more dangerous in its effects than the sickness it was supposed to cure? Mankind itself is still ill with the effects of this priestly naiveté in medicine! [39]

Nietzsche understood something of iatrogenic (physician-caused) disease and was able to identify the modern profession of medicine with the impotent priestly caste. He could not have known the extent of the morbidity of the nuclear scientific and political priests, who are ready to "cure" the world of its problems by means of annihilation.

Prudes pursuing the subject of priestly impotence will be interested in the etymology of the word *priest,* which is derived from the Greek *presbyteros,* meaning priest, elder, older, comparative of *presbys*—old man. The patriarchal priesthoods/professions characteristically are controlled by old men. These dictate the beliefs and rules of conduct for younger men—from whose ranks the rankest, the most ruthless, and the most robotized are recruited as replacements for their senile superiors. These in turn will join the select society of lecherous old men driven by impotence to ever viler forms of rapism, maiming, gynocide. The violations and massacres master-minded by these elders assume increasingly sublime dimensions as their target broadens to include the totality of life. The universality of their lethal intent

not his. Jewish and christian priesthoods, buddhist and hindu priesthoods, medical and military priesthoods, and all priesthoods in the service of phallocracy are variant forms of the same fraternity.

can be Named by the word *biocide*.[40] Indeed, the aging and deterioration of patriarchy itself into ever more vile/violent manifestations of senility follows the pattern of the lives of individual males who are the directors of the Sublimed Cinematic Sadosociety—where lechery is continually purified of its previous, puerile limitations and is extended to the violation of all living beings.

These degenerative and life-violating tendencies of patriarchy, which is essentially the State ruled by old men/priests, are the context within which the recent history of the Arch-Image can be understood, and within which the recent tokenizing of strong women can be recognized and comprehended. Since these phenomena are interrelated, it behooves Lusty women to turn attention to recent developments of Marian dogma, bearing in mind the fact that symbolic manipulation manifests a great deal about the political strategies of the manipulators.*

THE IMMACULATE CONCEPTION

It is Crone-logically significant that although belief in the "Immaculate Conception" of Mary was part of popular piety for centuries, it was not made an official dogma of catholic faith until 1854. For this coincides with the period when the so-called "first wave" of feminism was beginning to crest. The year 1848 marked the first Women's Rights convention in America, in Seneca Falls, New York. From 1848 on, American feminists increasingly voiced their grievances. Susan B. Anthony, Matilda Joslyn Gage, Angelina and Sarah Grimké, Elizabeth Oakes Smith, Elizabeth Cady Stanton, Sojourner Truth, and Emma Willard—to name a few—were beginning to find their voices.

Moreover, the killer instinct of the patriarchal males responded immediately. The impotent priests of the medical profession aimed their weapons directly at the female genital area, creating the gynocidal field of gynecology.[41]

The rise of feminism and the anti-feminist backlash were occurring more or less simultaneously in Europe.[42] Throughout

* The history of Marian dogmas is of crucial importance to women of every "background" (Foreground). As the priestly Carl Jung knew, these developments are of great significance in the history of Western mythology. For Nag-Gnostics they are a source of important information concerning mythic paradigms for the tokenization of women—a problem of crucial importance for our Movement.

Europe, ministers and journalists as well as politicians denounced female independence. In England, distinguished male writers in the late 1840s were protesting against the exercise of intellect in women—for example, Benjamin Disraeli in *Sybil* (1845) and William Thackeray in *Pendennis* (1848–50). It is within this context that Crone-ologists should analyze the proclamation in 1854 of the dogma of the "Immaculate Conception" by pope Pius IX, in the Bull *Ineffabilis Deus*. This bull signaled an advanced stage of chicanery, beautifully parodied in the title of Suzanne Arms' book on childbirth, *Immaculate Deception*.[43]

This dogma is a baffling phenomenon. It presents for belief a concept which is quite inconceivable, as we shall presently see. According to the dogma, Mary was conceived in her mother's womb without "original sin." Of course, it might seem that there is really nothing remarkable about such a conception, especially if one does not accept the concept of "original sin." * Thus the very fact that such a conception would be proclaimed, and proclaimed as unique, is already mind-boggling. This, however, is only the beginning of the boggle.

The doctrine of the "Virgin Birth" of Jesus—a doctrine that should not be confused with the "Immaculate Conception"—is also subversive of ancient myths of the parthenogenetic goddess.[44] Since parthenogenesis would produce only female offspring, the story of the "Virgin Birth" of a male savior should be eminently suspect. Or, to put it another way, the birth of Jesus was *indeed* a miracle, as Martha Yates has pointed out.[45] However, in comparison with the immaculate conception, the virgin-birth-of-Jesus story is but a pale perversion. The greater deception, the deeper mythic undermining of the Originally Parthenogenetic Goddess required the erasure of her own Self, prior to her role as mother-of-god.

Such mythic erasure of Mary's Self was attempted through the

---

* "Original sin" refers to a condition believed to be inherited by all descendents of the "first parents." According to catholic doctrine, no one can be saved except through the infusion of supernatural grace, which removes "original sin" as well as actual, personal sins. However, the "remains" of original sin stay in the soul, namely a darkening of the intellect, a weakening of the will, and an inclination to concupiscence. According to catholic doctrine, only Mary was spared this inheritance. In "poetic" language, she became "our tainted nature's solitary boast."

immaculate conception doctrine. According to this inconceivable doctrine, Mary was "preserved" from original sin by the grace of her son immediately at the moment of her conception—not only in advance of *his* birth, but also in advance of her own. Nor was she merely "purified" as an embryo in the womb of her mother.[46] Indeed, according to this astonishing doctrine, Mary never had a moment of life, even of embryonic life, without being "full" of the "grace" merited by her son through his death on the cross. Thus she was purified of autonomous be-ing before ever experiencing even an instant of this.

The doctrine certainly can be read as an expression of the impotent priests' hatred of Female Power. Indeed it represents their attempt at ontological castration of the Arch-Image, and, through her, of the Archimage.* Mary is so "full of grace" that she is de-natured, destined to become the mother of a god-son who bestows upon her his pseudo-nature, this "grace." In this pornographic mythic mirror-world, the son totals his virgin-mother-victim. The immaculate conception is the ultimate depiction of (pre-natal) woman-battering, a mythic model of incestuous assault. It is the primal rape of the Arch-Image. Within the mad ill-logic of dogmatic constructs, it is logically prior to the rape of the Virgin that takes place at "The Annunciation," when the adolescent Mary is told by the angel Gabriel that she is to be the mother-of-god and gives her fictitious assent. To put it in other words, as a consequence of her initial rape ("grace") Mary has been totaled, made totally unable to resist divine aggression/lust/rape. At "The Annunciation," then, the already raped Mary "consents" to further rape.

In the world of christian symbols, then, the immaculate conception exhibits a kind of ultimacy in undermining women—going far beyond the rape, killing, and dismemberment of the full-grown parthenogenetically conceived Goddess. Its target is her parthenogenetic (woman-identified) origin, and thus it undermines her original Power of Self-Naming, and Creation.† Since

* Again, it may be necessary to emphasize that whether or not this intent was/is fully "conscious" and explicit is not the issue. My point is that there is an inherent program/message in this revision of Goddess myth, and that it functions to serve the interests of the dogma dealers.

† The idea that there are some women so oppressed that "they have never had a Self" is widespread among women concerned with the hor-

the Original Source, the Archimage, cannot be defiled, she has been symbolically simulated and this simulation has been defiled and therefore called "Immaculate." Such rape of Female Archaic Power is appropriately named the "Immaculate Conception" since it is a purely phallic (mis)conception, a purification/purge of conceptions/memories of Elemental female be-ing. As Anne Dellenbaugh has remarked, this resonates with women's common experience of rape—one effect of which is the blockage of thoughts, the breaking/interruption of the thinking process.[47] Rape "purifies" women's conceptions, making these conform to phallic norms. Thus the doctrine is a mythic model for the thought/memory-stopping dimensions of rape.

Through its subliminal messages, then, the doctrine of the "Immaculate Conception" sets forth the image of Mary as model rape victim. From the moment of her conception she is ineffably undermined by this sublime spiritual rape. Later, by her inevitable acceptance of Gabriel's message, she seeks salvation by the rap-

rors of oppression. Some activists who totally repudiate christian myth on an overt, conscious level express this idea. In fact, on a subliminal level they are buying into the partriarchal/hierarchical belief system that is so blatantly illustrated in the doctrine of the "Immaculate Conception," and unwittingly propagating this belief system. Women who believe that they are totally beyond the influence of such christian doctrines and that discussion of such material is "irrelevant," could profit from a re-examination of this opinion, for the influence of such seemingly confined beliefs is vast and subterranean. To suggest that Third World women and others who are extremely oppressed "never have been allowed to have a Self" is a way of saying that such women were immaculately conceived. Such a view of severely oppressed women is grossly—indeed, ontologically—insulting. Moreover, the logical conclusion to be drawn from such a view of any woman would be that oppression is justified by the fact that she has no Self. This, of course, is exactly the "reasoning" of patriarchal oppressors, such as the executives of the multinational corporations that exploit female workers, to legitimate their exploitation. As Emily Culpepper points out: "To base self-definition on our oppressed state of affairs is the essence of perpetuating a derivative, secondary and oppressive definition. . . . Indeed, the oppressive conditions are a shock, a weight, a drain, precisely because they are a shock to something, a weight on something, a drain of something. That something is the sense of integrity of Self—a Self that may only or mostly exist as potential— but that potential is real." See Emily Culpepper, "Philosophia in a Feminist Key: Revolt of the Symbols" (unpublished Th.D. dissertation, Harvard University, 1983), pp. 107–08.

ist. In "real life," it is also often the case that once raped, a woman finds it difficult to forget the horrible event; she is continually trying to undo it. Conditioned to believe that she is to blame for the rape, she seeks to undo it by seeking male approval, for she no longer trusts the power of her own judgment. Believing that, through her own fault, a male has succeeded in degrading/defiling her, she concludes that only a male can save her. Thus rape implies the need of a male savior. This is one reason for the hold of christian myth upon women's raped psyches. The myth itself, of course, reinforces the self-blame of victimized women.

The immaculate conception thus illustrates and legitimates the ineffable circularity of rapism. Already violated at her conception, Mary affirms at the annunciation her need of male acceptance. Her initial violation made the later one—when "she conceived of the Holy Ghost" in order to become the mother-of-god —unavoidable. Pure rapism is inconceivably circular.

Mary's victimization is astonishing. She was totaled across time. Anne Dellenbaugh has remarked that as "Virgin" she is a reminder to women of their destiny to be raped, for in the patriarchal system, a virgin is a future rape victim.[48] * Since she is "forever virgin" (despite her maternity), she is forever future rape victim. The message is even exacerbated by the extremity of her tantalizing purity. Moreover, as archetypal "Mother," she is past rape victim. Encompassing all time, her rape is the perpetual entombment of her life-time.

By their subliming of this monstrous mythic disguise for the Archimage, the impotent priests produced an archetype who could not have had a Divine Daughter because she had been purified of her Self, and indeed never had been herSelf. Such a being would be inconceivable to herself. Totally de-natured of her Powers as parthenogenetic Goddess, she was set up as model for patriarchal women. And indeed patriarchally possessed women cannot have Daughters, although they may have female offspring. Patriarchal women cannot create, for they have been made unable to conceive of themselves—of their Selves. Thus an Elemental Female tradition within patriarchal structures is inconceivable.

Faced with this mythic and lived out boggle/baffle, Musing

* The use of the word *virgin*, then, in this context, is a particularly horrifying example of a faded and broken metaphor.

women can choose to exorcize the patriarchal myth through Naming and Living our own lives—which is to breathe forth the Archimage within. Only women who choose to participate in the Archimage can conceive of our Selves, creating our Selves and our tradition.* As more Websters find the Original Witch within, we obliterate the raped replacement and make ancestral Memories more available. It is by Self-identified creating that women can crack the archetypal mirrors, finding Archai/Beginnings, becoming Verbs, unleashing our Powers.

The "Immaculate Conception" and the Strategies of Tokenism

We have seen that the doctrine of the immaculate conception appeared much later in christian myth and theology than did the virgin birth. Many centuries of preparation were required for acceptance of *this* belief.

To put the matter bluntly, symbolically speaking the Goddess had to be totally done in, in order to be an appropriate mother-of-god. The fact that the church could not get around to this tidying up of the Goddess-murder program until recently would seem to have been a matter of political strategy. For, as we have seen, the power of the Arch-Image had been needed in order to convert the "pagans," even at the risk that this power might get out of hand. Moreover, it is Crone-logically significant that the proclamation of this dogma followed the European Witchcraze, for the mass murder of women and its deep psychic impact paved the way for the deceptively degrading dogma.

The promulgation of the dogma was equivalent to an advanced refining/subliming of the Arch-Image—a further battering of Female Power into archetypal shape—purifying the intuition of Elemental female be-ing to such a degree that this became inconceivable, inaccessible, while pretending that under christianity women are "on a pedestal," and, of course, Sublime.†

---

* I am not saying that women have to use this terminology, of course. Nor are any words for this process really adequate. The point is that metapatriarchal consciousness needs somehow to be expressed.

† The reader who wants to see this maneuver in mythic-historical perspective should recall that the transsexing of the Goddess had been accomplished thousands of years before through the conversion of the Goddess (Iahu) into Jahweh—a phenomenon which I have discussed in *Gyn/Ecology* (chapter 2). In christianity the triplicity of the Goddess

Shrewds who reflect upon this phenomenon will be able to see some interesting clues concerning the strategies of tokenism. Since the tokenizing of strong women is a primary feature of anti-feminist politics at this time, it is useful to consider in what ways the dogma may throw light upon the dilemmas posed by such politics. Bearing in mind that myths often function as self-fulfilling prophecies, we might well ponder the message of this mythic development. I suggest that the "news" is not cheering, but that the worst mistake would be refusal to know it.

We have seen that on the symbolic level the immaculate conception fosters a delusion of advancement of women's position while it undermines the possibility of conceiving any image of autonomous female transcendence. In this respect it resembles tokenism. Indeed, the case can be made that the proclamation of this dogma in 1854 ushered in the Age of Female Tokenism and subliminally contained prophetic messages concerning the ways in which the tactics of tokenism would be developed.

Since women have been incorporated (in limited numbers) into the professions in the nineteenth and twentieth centuries, the phenomenon of tokenism warrants close attention.* Hags might

---

is re-covered in the all-male trinity, in which the "feminine" aspect is relegated to the holy ghost. "His" impregnation of Mary, who is also a remnant of the Goddess, can be seen as a parody of parthenogenesis, since the Goddess appears to be impregnating herself. The holy ghost in this scenario is a caricature of her will and Mary is her body, broken off from spirit/will. The union accomplished when "he" impregnates "her" is not at all a re-membering of original integrity. It is merely an integration/impregnation which further estranges the mythic Mary from her Source.

Seen in this context, the dogma of the "Immaculate Conception" might appear to be a sort of overkill. What more could be done to the symbol of female divinity? It may be helpful to see that theology resembles pornography, that a good deal of the time it functions as sublimed pornography. Like pornographers, theologians exercise "creativity" by inventing variations on the same theme and sometimes by manufacturing heightened horrors. Just as pornography overtly promotes unimaginable sadism against women's bodies, a great deal of theology covertly promotes mutilation and dismemberment of women's psyches. The latter is sublimed sadism. Its strategy of overkill is not essentially dissimilar to such propensities in pornography.

* Modern tokenizing of women in the professions is a recent and refined adaptation of the very old patriarchal strategy of tokenism. In

ask our Selves forthright questions, for example: Will there be a second Witchcraze? If so, what form will it take? There is, of course, a perpetual Witchcraze in patriarchy, and I have discussed some of its forms elsewhere. For example, gynecology and psychotherapy are gynocidal weapons of the patriarchs. My precise concern here, however, is to find the most deceptive and Modern Mode of gynocide, succeeding the European Witchcraze (which terminated in the mid-eighteenth century), in Western industrialized society. My method is to look at the recent Marian dogmas (the Assumption will be treated in the next chapter) as mythic paradigms disclosing and foretelling social reality.

There are clues in the fact that the Witchcraze in Western Europe was fostered and fueled by the rising professional power block. Not only priests and ministers, but members of the legal and medical professions had an active role and vested interest in the killing of the Witches. Looking at the professions today, we can see a continuation of this vested interest and overt violence against women, for example, by the medical profession. The phenomenon that I intend to focus on here, however, is the false inclusion of women within the professions as a means of destroying female integrity and powers. There are several points to be considered.

First, looking at the immaculate conception and at the tokenizing of women—in the professions and, by extension, in various men's/boys' clubs, such as male-led political groups—we find that both promote an *illusion of progress.* Both Mary and tokens are "raised up." What is obliterated from memory is the knowledge of *who put them down* in the first place. The fact of the sexual caste system is disguised, or at least the impression is created that if it ever existed, it has now been overcome—or is well on the way to being overcome. Of course, nothing could be further from the truth. The immaculately conceived/deceived woman is being prepared for the ultimate Self-destruction—the selling out of her Self and of her sisters. As Judith Long Laws

---

its cruder forms, it involves the use of women as token torturers of other women (and girls). A classic example is the footbinding (footmaiming) of daughters by their mothers in China—an atrocity that prevailed in Chinese society for almost a thousand years and that was terminated only a few decades ago.

points out, she is appointed to the role of hatchetman to her sisters.[49] Like Mary, she has been prepared to assent to the spiritual rape that will reproduce the myth of male divinity.

This delusion of progress inhibits radicalism. Some insight concerning the strategy operative in this production of delusion can be gleaned from Ralf Dahrendorf's critique of Marxian theory. He makes the following point:

A class composed of individuals whose social position is not an inherited and inescapable fate, but merely one of a plurality of social roles, is not likely to be as powerful a historical force as the closed class Marx had in mind. Where mobility . . . is a regular occurrence, and therefore a legitimate expectation of many people, conflict groups are not likely to have either the permanence or the dead seriousness of caste-like classes composed of hopelessly alienated men [sic].[50]

The point is that the appearance of social mobility, or progress, squelches the instinct to revolt and create radical change. Tokenism provides this appearance/illusion for women (and all oppressed groups), taming the radical impulse with false hope.

A *second* point of comparison between the dogma and the strategy of tokenizing women is the employment of the *delusion of exceptionalism*. The immaculate conception worked a symbolic transformation, rendering Mary an exception, free of "original sin." As Laws shows, "the self-attribute of exceptionalism . . . is central to the psychology of the Token." [51] If we ask: "Exception to what?" the answer is clear. The token woman believes herself to be an exception to the alleged incompetency and array of weaknesses ascribed to women in general, that is, to the "original sin" of being a woman. If the tokenized woman in this situation is a woman of color, or Jewish, or lesbian, or elderly, or of working class background, or belongs to any other stigmatized group, her self-attribution of exceptionalism is, of course, multiplied.

Third, Mary is exceptional because she is full of grace, that is, full of male-identification, bestowed by her son, who is her "Savior." Likewise, the token is in a *role partnership with a male sponsor/savior* who legitimates her male-identification. However, as Judith Long Laws points out:

Once the Token is confirmed in her role, her interaction with the larger group is facilitated and need not be mediated by the Sponsor.[52]

Like a brain surgeon after performing a lobotomy, the sponsor knows when his work is done. The token has lost a great deal of her capacity to cause trouble. She has been groomed to deny her autonomous Self.

Fourth, the immaculately conceived Mary is immaculately deceived—*emptied of autonomous intellect and will.* She can have no memory of woman-identified consciousness. Her mind is, as it were, a clean slate. Similarly, the token "is more unaware of her stigma [of being a woman] than any member of the dominant class." [53]

What does all of this tell us about the strategies of the contemporary Witch-killers? Following through on the mythic paradigm employed here, I suggest that the strategy of tokenizing women is ultimate purification from society, or, more precisely, from women's consciousness, of woman-identified Elemental/Original thinking and passion. The perfect token is the perfect traitor, betraying her Self and womankind. She gives her assent to rapism. The spectacle of her betrayal feeds the patriarchally embedded hatred of women in women.

I suggest that the mythic paradigm of the immaculate conception carries the war against female Elemental be-ing beyond earlier stages. This is not simply physical massacre of women. It is killing of consciousness and integrity in women. In this Second Coming of the Witchcraze, the chief character of the story is missing. There is no Witch to be crazed/razed. Moreover, this mythic model goes far beyond the symbol of the twice-born Athena, who was born, male-identified, from the head of Zeus. For a born-again might have some memory of her previous life. After all, Athena's mother, with Athena in her womb, was swallowed by father Zeus. Athena is tokenized and she betrays women, but the myth itself reminds us of her original parthenogenetic mother, Metis, the Goddess of Wisdom. In contrast to this, the immaculately conceived Mary has no memory of a Divine Mother. She is not a Daughter. In the age of the second Witchcraze, Memory of Gynocentric Origins is obliterated. Tokens, having memorized male words and uncritically copied male texts, become complicit in the destruction of Memory. The token, detached from her Self, filled with gratitude to her sponsors, destroys the Source, which would have been her only recourse. Moreover, she knows not what she does. The Pure Token is an

Immaculate Conception, freed from all knowledge of the stain of Original Female Nature, freed from consciousness of stigma.

To put it starkly and simply, the Second Coming of the Witchcraze will employ different methods. This time, women are trained and legitimated to do it to each other. Women have been coached by the impotent priests to destroy each other.

A particularly lethal instrument of this training is man-made and male-controlled pseudofeminism. One of the most deadly effects of pseudofeminism is the manufacture and spread of disillusion among women, who have been tricked into believing that the "illusion" is feminism itself. Thus the illusion-makers create the illusion that feminism is an illusion. Since this causes deceived and discouraged women to turn to the phallic sponsors for support in their crisis of feminist faith, the further spread of tokenism is achieved.

In the process of embedding this confusion, the master tricksters rely upon the unexorcised mechanisms of horizontal violence. Their success is measured by the degree to which they are able to erase women's Archaic Elemental Memory. Since men cannot by themselves completely erase Memory from women, they must channel women into effecting the erasure ourselves, of our Selves. The most effective means employed by males to induce women to perform this dirtywork has been and continues to be the manufacture of illusions which trigger the mechanisms of Self-hate and horizontal violence among women. Thus programmed and activated in the direction of Self-destruction, women actively will *not* to re-member deep Memory, for woman-identified knowledge has been made to seem repugnant. Fixed by the pushers of pseudofeminism, women are "purified" of even the desire to re-member. Filled with the "grace" of false knowledge of "feminism," women turn to their saviors/sponsors, cooing, "Let it be done to me according to your will." Thanks to the purifying effects of phallic lust, this immaculate conception is achieved. Bored by the stimulations of female be-ing, women retreat further into the amnesic state of totaled tokens. Complicit in their own brainwashing, women thus totaled become intellectual scrubwomen, fanatically cleansing the minds of others. The fanaticism reaches fantastic proportions, especially when a woman is consumed with the Need not to know her Self. Immaculately conceived, women often have a zeal that can only rarely be ascribed to males—for this is Elemental vigor turned against its Source.

The only hope for Overcoming this Second Coming of the Witchcraze is to risk be-ing the Crazed Witch, re-calling Rays of Elemental Memory. This involves facing the blinding light of the mythic paradigm of female assimilation/tokenism—seeing through the conception of deception, Undeceiving ourselves, Believing our Selves.

Translucent Transcendence of the Immaculate Conception

The heading of this section is double-edged. It means, *first,* that women, insofar as we are translucent to deep Memory within, can transcend the trickery of dogmatic deception. It means, *second,* that the symbol itself of the "Immaculate Conception" functions as a broken metaphor of Translucent Transcendence. These meanings, clearly, are interrelated. Amazons wield our Labryses to cut through the illusions/deceptions, dis-closing transcendence.

In this case, what we are cutting/smashing is a distorting mirror of Memory dis-closing the prisms in which women can recognize the Radiance of our own Origins. Since the "Immaculate Conception" is an especially powerful, though distorted, mirror, the Arch-Image under this aspect provides reflections of that which we seek—the Primal Parthenogenetic Sources/Forces within female Elemental be-ing.

Precisely because it was designed to undermine that which is most Archaic/Elemental, this dogma can function as a Metaphor evoking Parthenogenetic Powers in women who choose to be Translucent, transcending trickery. Turning this alienating dogma to good use—as telescope for viewing Archaic Memory—we participate in knowledge of its radical Origins. These Origins the would-be destroyers cannot destroy, but only caricature and cover over, attempting to distract. Recalling the insight that evil is that which distracts, we are enabled to focus with intensified intent upon the hidden messages of this Metaphor. Nag-Gnostic Searchers can unmask such hidden messages, dis-closing those Elemental Powers which, by the mechanism of reversal, the dogma attempts to hide—the multidimensional Powers of Parthenogenesis.*

---

* Veiled suggestions that the "Immaculate Conception" masks and dis-closes Mary's parthenogenetic origins can be found in art. Marina Warner describes a sixteenth century illustration: "In more imposing canvases of the same period [early sixteenth century] the propaganda crystallizes around an image of a second trinity. Like the three ages of man, St. Anne looms, a towering matriarch, over both her daughter Mary

The word *parthenogenesis* is derived from the Greek *parthenos,* meaning virgin, and from *genesis,* which means origins, and which stems from the verb *gignesthai,* meaning to be born. The *fact* of biological parthenogenesis in some species has been demonstrated. However, *parthenogenesis* means more than reproduction or procreation. Anne Dellenbaugh has shown that this can be heard as a New Word:

Within a phallocentric semantic context, parthenogenesis is a method of reproduction. But wrenched from this context and heard with a radical feminist consciousness, *Parthenogenesis* names a wholly different phenomenon. Hearing it in this new way requires a qualitative leap into Self-consciousness, for Parthenogenesis names nothing less than the process of a woman creating her Self.[54]

And of course this extends to all forms of Spinning female creativity.

One essential feature of Virginal Scolding/Scalding creativity is the fact that no father is required for this creation. Indeed, the works of Weirds are Wild/Wayward, born out of Wedlock, having been conceived in Sinful Originality. Foretellings of Fates are unfathered/unfettered.

Freed from the fathers, Virgins/Viragos reclaim our connection with the elements. Dis-illusioned Labrys-wielders break the barriers between our Selves and the natural world. Thus reconnected with the forces of nature, women dis-cover our Mantic Powers. *Mantic* means "of or relating to the faculty of divination: PROPHETIC." Parthenogenetically creating Crones are Mantic in multiform Elemental Ways.* Gnomic Nags practice Geo-

---

and a smaller Christ child in Mary's lap. The triad asserts the sanctity of Christ's lineage, and by eliminating Joachim, implies the unsullied purity of Mary's conception. Leonardo treated this trinity three times." See Marina Warner, *Alone of All Her Sex* (New York: Alfred A. Knopf, 1976; Simon and Schuster, Wallaby Books, 1976), p. 243. Of course the church never maintained that Mary was the product of a virgin birth, although it was commonly believed that she was born to her parents in their old age by a direct and miraculous intervention. But images work in ways that doctrinal verbiage cannot control. The fact is that in the sort of painting described above, Mary's "father" is missing.

* The noun *mantis* means "prophet, diviner" (*O.E.D.*). It is synonymous with soothsayer.

mancy, or "the art of divination by means of signs derived from the earth" (*O.E.D.*). This is sometimes accomplished by the observation of crevices, mountain chains and in general of the configuration of the earth's surface. Sylphic Soothsayers specialize in Aeromancy, or "divination from the state of the air or from atmospheric substances." Imbued with Undine Understanding, women undertake Hydromancy, or "divination by means of signs derived from water, its tides and ebbs, or the . . . appearance of sprites therein" (*O.E.D.*). This divination is based on the observation of whirlpools, springs, lakes, or smooth brilliant surfaces of water. Finally, Salamandrous Shrews practice Pyromancy, or "divination by means of fire or flames"—re-calling the Forecrones, the Witches.

Such prophecies do not exclude rigorous reasoning. Nor does the absence of fathers exclude the use of male-authored texts as secondary re-sources. These authors are not parents of parthenogenetic works, but are conduits to the knowledge that has been controlled and contaminated within tombs/tomes of sado-schooling. In fact, vigorous, independent creativity commands the use of such re-source materials. Shrews do not shrink from the task of assessing and assuming material that is related, even in a distorted way, to our own heritage. The theology of the "Immaculate Conception" is itself an example of this kind of material, as I have shown. The process of reversing the reversals of male-authored pronouncements and theories is an important work of parthenogenetic creativity. For this process dispels the sublimed vapors that depress and bore women.* It releases the elements of our dismembered past, so that these again become tangible, audible, visible, ready to be rewoven in tapestries of images, sounds

---

* The relation of patriarchal re-sources to the Parthenogenetic creator is one of that-which-must-be-seen-through to the Seer. To illustrate the necessity of such See-ing, I suggest that the reader who lives in the Western world reflect upon the experience of psychically surviving each year the christmas season. Every woman who enters the supermarket or turns on the radio is bombarded with sublimed invitations to "come let us adore him." This overt omnipresence of mind-raping messages—combined with countless covert and subliminal communications of the same "lesson," drains gynergy, which goes into fighting it off or "ignoring," that is, repressing, the horror. But to See Through the lies to that which has been reversed, that is, to Gynocentric Sources, is empowering.

that are alive and rhythmic with the pulsing of Passionate Searching.

Such study requires Stamina, staying power, which is also Straying Power—ability to Stray off the tracks of traditions that betray women and nature. Straying is sparked by E-motion, that is, passion that moves women to thinking and acting The Way Out. E-motion is ecstatic, delirious. *Delirium* is derived from the Latin *de* (from, off) plus *lira* (track). Deliberate delirium keeps us off the tracks of trained responses, traditional expectations. Since the word *learn* is also derived from *lira,* it is clear that Lusty women's delirium should be a matter of Studied Unlearning. The word *studied* is important here, for one must know the tracks well in order to break out of them, without sliding back into them. To be truly truant requires study/training and untiring untraining. The process is unnarrowing, harrowing. Ultimately, its motivating E-motion is Wonderlust/Wanderlust. Its scope is vast, visionary, planetary. The wonderings/wanderings of Straying women are wayward, earthward, skyward. Witches long and learn to fly.

Flying with free-wheeling symbols—symbols whose Metaphoric powers have been released—requires deep rootedness in women's own Elemental Race, from which the phallic fathers try to uproot us.[55] Our ability to *know* this has been blocked, however. Regaining this knowledge and the Self-confidence that accompanies it is the key to creation, for this Pyromantic knowledge burns through the coverings that conceal the Arche/Archai. The radiant gynergy that women experience when deeply focused pulses in harmony with the rhythms of the cosmos—rhythms masked by the archetypes but also throbbing through these. Focusing through is not a once and for all matter, of course. It is creative process of dis-covering Who we are.

THE ELEMENTAL BACKGROUND OF MARY AND THE BLACK MADONNAS

It is well known that throughout Europe the Black Madonnas are considered especially wonder-working, and that they are associated with mysterious knowledge and power. These images are to be found in many shrines, for example at Montserrat, at Chartres, and at Einsiedeln, Switzerland. Discussing her experiences during a tour of the Marian shrines in Europe, a feminist scholar spoke of the fact that there was, for her, a particular sense of presence and power surrounding the Black Madonna at Montserrat.[56] Many Hags have responded to these images as viewers into the Background. It is worth Nag-Noting scholarly studies of these, in order to pursue our own analysis.

Scholars have made a three-fold classification of types of black representations of Mary. First, there are the dark brown or Black Madonnas "with physiognomy and skin pigmentation matching those of the indigenous population." These include Nuestra Señora de Guadalupe in Mexico City and various Black Madonnas in Africa, which reflect efforts to assimilate indigenous traditions of female power and divinity. Second, there are art forms that have turned black as a result of physical factors, such as deterioration of lead-based pigments, accumulated smoke from the use of votive candles or other smoke damage, oxidation of silver, accumulation of grime. Finally, there are Black Madonnas found in Europe (where the natives are Caucasoid) which are black originally and there are some that turned black as a result of physical damage and later were repainted black.[57]

Some scholars have connected the Black Madonnas of the third category with ancient earth goddesses. Offering this hypothesis, two scholars suggest:

. . . the black madonnas are Christian borrowings from earlier pagan art forms that depicted Ceres, Demeter Melaina, Diana, Isis, Cybele, Artemis, or Rhea as black, the color characteristic of goddesses of the earth's fertility.[58]

These scholars affirm that Demeter Melaina, or the Black Demeter, as distinct from the sorrowful Eleusinian mother, is a more powerful figure and is associated with the fertility of black earth.[59] Crone-ologists take the argument a Leap further, and go on to Wonder about Egyptian/African Sources for these images of female divinity.

Nag-Gnostic Searchers can see in these images glimmerings of our Archaic Elemental heritage. These stir deep Memory, enabling Hags to ride the Metaphors of the Black Madonnas to spheres of imagination that transcend insipid caucasian cookie-cutter depictions of the Arch-Image. Having glimpsed the Arch-image as black earth, we are prepared to see her associations with the other elements.

STAR OF THE SEA

Descriptions of Mary were assumed from those of Sky Goddesses, including Ishtar and especially the great astral divinity, the Triple Moon Goddess, Isis.* Archimagical Powers that are both veiled and partially disclosed in the Image of Mary are suggested in descriptions of Isis.† She was said to be a potent "magician" (even the gods were not immune to her sorcery). She is "star of the sea and patron divinity of travellers." [60] Moreover, she is a word-worker:

> ... for I am Isis the goddess, and I am the lady of words of power, and I know how to work with words of power, and most mighty are my words! [61]

* It is clear that Isis is an important key to the Background of Elemental be-ing. "Her cult continued to grow in importance until it ultimately absorbed that of nearly all the other goddesses. It even crossed the frontiers of Egypt; seamen and merchants in the Graeco-Roman era carried her worship as far as the banks of the Rhine. . . . In the Nile valley she kept her worshippers until well into Christian times." See *New Larousse Encyclopedia of Mythology,* trans. from the French by Richard Aldington and Delano Ames (New York: The Hamlyn Publishing Group Limited, 1959), p. 19. Clearly, the christian conquerors knew about Isis. One author writes: "We need not doubt that Paul had taken the measure of the female deities of whose influence he had had long experience, especially Artemis and Isis. . . . Paul could tell that here was a dangerous rival." See R. E. Witt, *Isis in the Graeco-Roman World* (Ithaca, N.Y.: Cornell University Press, 1971), p. 261. The christian method of dealing with this rival has been assimilation and use/abuse of her image.

† Merlin Stone reminds us that Isis is merely the Greek translation of the Egyptian name Au Set, meaning "Exceeding Queen" in the Egyptian language. According to Egyptian religion she was revered "as a great healer and physician and as the one who first established the laws of justice in the land." See Merlin Stone, *When God Was a Woman* (New York: Harcourt Brace Jovanovich, Harvest Books, 1976), p. 36. Clearly, this Goddess image was also possessed, diminished, distorted by phallic religion after the patriarchal take-over. In dis-covering her, however, we uncover further layers of our stolen tradition. There are many, many manifestations of Female Divinity in all cultures. Among her names are Artemis, Bridget, Cerridwen, Coatlicue, Danu, Hecate, Hepat, Hsi Ho, Jezanna, Ishtar, Ix Chel, Lia, Lilith, Maeve, Mawu, Nu Kwa, Pele, Rhiannon, Shekhina, Songi, Spider Woman, Teteu Innan, Tiamat. See Merlin Stone, *Ancient Mirrors of Womanhood* (New York: Beacon Press, 1979). See also Patricia Monaghan, *The Book of Goddesses and Heroines* (New York: E. P. Dutton, Dutton Paperbacks, 1981).

In addition, the Lady of Words is cosmic writer and librarian. She (Isis) has been identified with Sekha(u)it, who is:

... the "goddess of writings," or Fate, whose pen directs the course of all the world. She is termed "the one before the divine place of books," i.e. the librarian of the gods [*sic*].[62]

Moreover:

As a goddess of fate Sekhait [*sic*] sits at the foot of the cosmic tree, or, in other words, in the nethermost (southern) depths of the sky or at the meeting-place of the upper and lower sky; and there she not only writes upon this tree or on its leaves all future events, such as length of life ... but also records great events for the knowledge of future generations, since everything, past and future ... is written in the stars.[63]

These words suggest a Power to speak/write Words that evoke deep memories. The Spiration of these Words connects the speaker and the hearer with the stars, with the elements, and calls us to travel further in the Realm of Archespheres.

Intuitions about the cosmic writer and library are by no means limited to women who explicitly identify as feminists. In an astonishing book, *Psychic Politics,* Jane Roberts describes an experience in the course of which she "saw" the image of a library transposed over the southeast corner of her living room, and her own image within this library. She also experienced then the inspiration to write a new book. Roberts quotes from notes that she wrote to herself during that experience:

The image of the library may be symbolic, of course, yet on another level I can see myself standing there by those volumes, nearly weeping, thinking that I've finally come home. I feel that my destiny is to transcribe these invisible books, sifting them through my psyche as it lives in our time, and therefore re-creating the books by imbuing them once more with life.... And I feel that the books and my life will interweave, so that each adds to the other.[64]

Jane Roberts goes on to explain that her feeling then was that at some "other level" she had entered a college or a community of scholars. She states that it is possible that someone else might experience the other-dimensional environment in a different way, for example, seeing flashes of light instead of books. She re-iterates, however, that for *her* from the beginning there was a li-brary at another level of experience, "and that while I went about my work here, I'd be making my way there at the same time." [65]

It is by no means my contention that the task of feminist writ-ers, or of any writer, is literally to "transcribe" books that exist elsewhere. However, the intuition of a library and a community of scholars in another dimension seems to me inspired. For in true acts of creation one does participate in Other dimensions.* More-over, it is true that as we go about our work "here" we are making our way "there." For in honest acts of creation deep Be-ing is dis-closed. Such acts are carriers/Metaphors of Metabeing.

The tradition of the Cosmic Librarian/Writer is one of Learning/Speaking/Spirating in harmony with the moon, sun, stars. Elemental writing is a means of voyaging into time past and future. Writing, Websters call forth secrets of our depths, becom-ing Soothsayers, voyaging Weirdward. Webstery connects women with Gnomic Wisdom of the Ages, Nagging us into the time/space of this knowing.

The Wording of Websters gives vent to the Rage of the Ages, for our Words, having been stolen, are coming home to us. The Cosmic Writer is any Lusty woman who speaks the Words of her own be-ing. This Speaking takes many forms, including printed books, pots, paintings, consciousness-raising sessions, work in battered women's shelters, Take Back the Night marches, rituals, concerts, scholarly conferences, anti-pornography protests. Each woman's focus is a matter of circumstances, necessities, tastes, and talents. The point is that all these Spirations are Books of Lusty Lives.†

The schoolboys of snooldom have named themselves authors and their ideas "seminal." Reflecting this situation, the dictionary

---

* In this sense, the much longed for Feminist University already does exist.

† Sojourner Truth's use of the title *Book of Life* to Name her personal archives manifests a deep intuitive understanding of Webstery. This col-lection includes correspondence, newspaper interviews and accounts of her speeches, autographs of famous people she met, notices of her speeches, and other memorabilia. See *Narrative of Sojourner Truth* (Chi-cago: Johnson Publishing Company, Inc., Ebony Classics, 1970). The work contains a "History of Her Labors and Correspondence Drawn from Her *Book of Life*."

gives as first definition of *author* "one that fathers: PROCREATOR, PARENT, ANCESTOR." Having assumed authorship, they claim authority, using the divine author (their fiction) as authority legitimating their atrocities.

Having penned women into the mirror world of their archetypes, the authorized authors have refused women the right to write, saying to Wayward women that to publish is to perish.[66] They have inscribed the word CAUTION over the gateway to our psychic creative depths. Cautious cowardice is then perceived as virtue, labeled "courage," and timidity is the rule for writing. Self-censorship serves the institutions of intimidation.

As Wild women hear inner Words, we face the task of Wording the way out. Our Stellar journeys beyond incarceration by and in patriarchal pens require transcendence of authorized incarnations—the warped words, twisted texts, and tortured civilization which are products of phallic sublimation. This is the subject of the following chapter.

CHAPTER THREE

BEYOND SADO-SUBLIMATION:
REAL PRESENCE

Real Presence: "the doctrine that Christ is actually present in the Eucharist."

Webster's Third New International Dictionary of the English Language

Real Presence: "Female Elemental participation in Powers of Be-ing, which implies Realizing as present our past and future Selves."

Websters' First New Intergalactic Wickedary of the English Language

In the preceding chapter I have discussed archetypes as perversions of Original Words, of Archai. These constitute the patriarchal sublime, the sado-sublime. In this chapter I will analyze sado-sublimation, the "discharge" of allegedly instinctual energy through activities that are socially approved within patriarchy—activities resulting in multiple incarnations of the alienating archetypes as cultural forms that kill women and nature. The Sublimated Society is constituted of Warped Words Made Flesh. On the foreground level women and the elements are possessed, domesticated, deprived of our Elemental Divine Daughterhood. Animals, plants, minerals are possessed. The sublimers intend that all be relegated to the role of breeders, vessels, vehicles of the repetitive discharges that produce phallic culture.

One way of Naming the re-productions/incarnations of archetypes that constitute this culture is to call them *stereotypes*. This word is derived from the Greek *stereo,* meaning solid, plus *typos,* meaning impression of a seal, mold, replica. To aid us in the process of understanding stereotypes, Archelogians recall that the archetypes are arch-efforts to beat and defile the Arche/ Archai. Archetypes are like ghosts/gases/vapors that are particularly deceptive, since one can imagine that she "sees through" a vapor when in fact her vision is distorted. Since archetypes continually change form, just when a woman has exorcised one of its manifestations, she is in danger of becoming entrapped in another —and yet another. We have seen also that in the sado-subliming process, archetypes are "condensed," that is, projected onto persons, institutions, things—assuming "solid" forms.

Among the solid wastes that result from this entrapment of gynergy and projection of archetypes are wasted lives of women, lives that are slowed down, hardened, deadened. Such lives become more and more stereotypical, modeled on stereotyped images that are dispensed through sado-religion, psychology, pornography, fashions, films, and that are ever more intensively disseminated through television commercials/news/dramas—forms which are increasingly indistinguishable from each other. These images are designed to keep women typed, that is, beaten and defiled, in our own minds. The object of this mass production is the beating of women into *solids* in the most horrifying sense, making us "entirely of one substance, kind, or character."

Indeed, it is chilling to read definitions of the noun *stereotype*. It means "something repeated or reproduced without variation: something conforming to a fixed or general pattern and lacking individual distinguishing marks or qualities." Among the definitions of the verb *stereotype* are "to fix in a lasting and usually rigidly precise form," and "to make standardized or hackneyed."

Cut off from the flow of the Arche/Archai and from the Divining Powers of the Archimage within, women who are potential Hags become hackneyed, lacking individual qualities, fixed in rigidly precise forms. Thus solidified, stultified, con-fused, women are confused and confusing to each other. Moreover, as Andrée Collard has shown, animals and all of nature are stereotyped within patriarchy, perceived and treated in such a standardized, deadening way that torture and massacre pass uncriticized and unnoticed.[1] This oversimplified, depraved typing legitimates the violation of all animal and vegetative life. Collard points out that perceptions have been so dulled by stereotypes—reflected in such expressions as "dumb brute," "beastly," "only an animal," and "vegetate"—that even the well-intentioned participate in atrocities.[2] When the images of women and of all natural creatures are thus frozen and degraded, we can be deemed fit subjects for experimentation and massacre, which are manifestations of sado-sublimation. We are set up to be victims, caught in a maze of false assumptions.

FALSE ASSUMPTIONS AND THE ASSUMPTION

Among the definitions of the verb *assume* are "to take as one's right or possession: ARROGATE, SEIZE, USURP," and "to take in appearance only: pretend to have or be: FEIGN." These definitions combined describe the manner in which women and all Elemental beings are possessed in phallocracy. For our rights are arrogated, seized, usurped. Yet the usurpers cannot seize Elemental powers. They do this "in appearance only," by masking our origins with archetypes and perpetuating these symbols through the production of stereotypes, pretending to have power over female Elemental powers.

Thus the Androcratic Assumers fill minds with false assumptions. Women are tricked into assuming that these assumers have/ are the reality they feign to have/be. Since their program of usurpation of minds has been hugely successful, they appear to go unchallenged in their rampant destruction of the planet. The Program of Assumption is total. It moved into a period of climax with the building of the first atomic bombs in the 1940s, ushering in the Age of Nuclearism. The fitting slogan for this Age, a line from the *Bhagavad-Gita,* was uttered by Robert Oppenheimer, "father of the atomic bomb," at the time of the first atomic explosions: "I am become Death, the shatterer of worlds." [3]

It was altogether appropriate that just a few years after the beginning of this Age of Nuclear Assumptions the catholic church officially proclaimed the dogma of the Assumption of the Blessed Virgin Mary. In 1950 pope Pius XII officially proclaimed that "Mary . . . was taken up body and soul into the glory of heaven." The idea of the "Assumption" had been around for centuries, as had been the case with the "Immaculate Conception." What is Crone-logically significant is the time at which the church got around to making it official dogma.

It can be seen that in important ways the "Assumption" and the explosion of atomic and nuclear bombs are symbolic parallels. As Marina Warner states: "The assumed Virgin is clothed with the undying and golden sun, which in paintings envelops her as if in a gilded shell." [4] The first atomic explosion, which was at Trinity Site, was described by Oppenheimer in his recollection of lines from the *Bhagavad-Gita*:

> If the radiance of a thousand suns
> Were to burst at once into the sky
> That would be like the splendor of the Mighty One.[5]

Brigadier General Thomas Farrell, who was second in command at Alamogordo, used the following words in describing the scene:

No man-made phenomenon of such tremendous power had ever occurred before. The lighting effects beggared description. The whole country was lighted by a searing light with the intensity many times that of the midday sun.[6]

Like the explosion of the bomb, the dogma of the assumption of Mary is a phenomenon that "beggars description," that has unnatural power and that is an assumed/usurped destructive simulation of something deeply powerful, natural. The artificiality of both of these products of phallic civilization is captured in Farrell's expression "lighting effects."

Warner suggests, moreover, that, as a consequence of the "Assumption," Mary acquires ubiquitousness—"she can appear on earth to visionaries in any place at any time." [7] Of course, there were reported apparitions for centuries before the dogma was proclaimed. The dogma simply adds further legitimation and solidity, as it were, to these claims. Likewise the testimonies of scientific and political priests concerning the beauty and wonderfulness of the initial atomic explosions legitimated the proliferation, the ubiquitousness of biocidal weapons.

It is important to keep in mind also the fact that the "Assumption" is about death. The body of the Virgin is said to experience death but does not decay. The dogma is about triumph over death.* The Virgin dies and is instantly restored to "life." So also

---

* Having been set up by the fathers in a situation of man-made enmity with the snake, the Assumed Mary is placed in conflict with Elemental powers of renewal, symbolized by the snake. The snake, whose periodic shedding has always connected her Metaphorically with triumph over death, has been separated from females by the phallic myth-molders who,

"the bomb" is about death and triumph over death.* Unbeliev-
ably, its legitimators have seen in it a shelter against annihilation,
a restoration of hope for life. William Lawrence, the science
writer who recorded many of the comments of scientists and
statesmen about the first atomic explosion, exemplifies this doublethink:

This great iridescent cloud and its mushroom top, I found myself
thinking as I watched, is actually a protective umbrella that will forever shield mankind everywhere against threat of annihilation in any
atomic war. This rising supersun seemed to me the symbol of the dawn
of a new era in which any sizable war had become impossible; for no
aggressor could now start a war without the certainty of absolute and
swift annihilation.[8]

Lawrence's ability to persuade himself that the bomb is itself protection against annihilation by the bomb is all-pervasive in the
priesthood of nuclearism. It is reflected in Pentagon policies, for
example, in the "M.A.D." (Mutually Assured Destruction) Pentagon policy that prevailed in the seventies and it underlies more
recent tactics and strategies.
   This protection racket mentality is and has always been pervasive in the Lecherous State. Feminists are aware of it as a basic
pattern in rapist society, in which women are forced to seek from
allegedly nonrapist males protection against rapists. On one level,
this can be seen as operative in the sense that men can pretend
that they are protecting their nation, family, or some other form
of the "Great Mother" archetype that suits their purposes, from
"the enemy"—the men who wield nuclear power on "the other

_____

in gazing at the serpent, have been able only to project onto her the
image of the penis—their obsession. Thus the superficial meaning of the
snake as "phallic symbol" conditions responses to this Wild, Elemental
creature. Gorgons/Dragons/Maenads/Furies are reclaiming our Archaic
connection with the serpent. Overcoming the phallic assumptions, we are
coming into contact with our Original powers of renewal/restoration,
which are mimicked by the impotent renewers/restorers.
   * Crone-ologists will note the significance of the date of the proclamation of the dogma of the Assumption—1950. The advent of "the bomb"
had stimulated the apocalyptic fears and desires of the catholic hierarchy,
and the emphasis upon the "fact" that Mary is "intact" (coupled with
traditional belief in Christ's Ascension) suggests that the church was
getting ready for the long anticipated "end of the world."

side." On a deeper level, the nuclear madmen can be seen as "protecting" themselves, by this ultimate destruction, against the Elemental forces of nature that terrify them—for life is more horrifying to them than is unnatural death of themselves and of the planet caused by their own berserk technology. On this level, the protection racket works in a comparable way in the doctrine of the Assumption. For by constructing a tamed simulation of the Archimage—a simulation whose physical presence is essentially elsewhere than on this earth, and who cannot *ascend* into heaven of her own volition but has to be assumed by the male god—the myth-masters attempt to protect themselves against the terrifying knowledge of creative biophilic female power. Like the bomb, Mary is lifted up by phallic sublimations/machinations.

Thus atomic and nuclear weapons and the myth of the Assumption are expressions of the lethal split/fission in phallic culture and of the false fusions consequent upon these. They are supreme manifestations of sado-sublimation, technological and doctrinal discharges that reflect and perpetuate divisions and dualisms antithetical to life. The real target of attack is Elemental be-ing. The priests of nuclearism seek to destroy the integrity of spirit/matter that is negated mythically and ideologically by the priests of phallic religion. This integrity is the biophilic power that the assumers pretend to have. Their arrogance is longstanding. We should recall again the words of the second epistle of Peter:

But the day of the Lord will come like a thief, and then the heavens will pass away with a loud noise, and the elements will be dissolved with fire, and the earth and the works that are upon it will be burned up. (2 Pet. 3:10 [R.S.V.])

Moreover, as we have seen, they experience themselves as already dead.

In fact, the assumers, like Dracula, could more accurately be described as "undead"—neither really alive nor dead, feeding on living spirit/matter. Their undeadness is perpetuated in their products. It is exemplified on the mythic level by the nonbiodegradable assumed virgin and, on the material plane, by man-made radioactive plutonium, which, once produced, remains poisonous for at least half a million years.[9] Devoid of life, the products of sado-sublimation—from the immaculately conceived-and-assumed-virgin to the clean neutron bomb—are perfectly pure.

Moreover, Crone-logical thinkers should not overlook what was happening to women in America and Europe around the time of the official proclamation of the dogma of the Assumption, in 1950. In the forties in America women had obtained substantial jobs while "the boys" were busy with World War II. "Society" had needed women's higher capacities—higher than the ability to wash dishes, at any rate. Since "boys" were recruited into the armed forces, women also gained admission in greater numbers to colleges. Women were beginning to taste something like freedom and an illusion of institutional power. When the war was over, so were female gains. The massive brain-scrubbing campaign of the later forties and fifties had as its goal the firm establishment of "The Feminine Mystique." [10] Women were battered by propaganda from all sides, badgered into housewifery.*

The "Assumption" emerged during this time of backlash. It is sensible to see it as part of this picture. As Mary went "up," women went down, without realizing it. The familiar tactic of reversal was in operation, and as women gazed heavenward at the feminine mystique personified—Mary the happy housewife, gone home to heaven—they were in reality being herded into the womb-tomb, The Home.

---

* The process of pressurizing into feminization was repeated for Black women in the sixties and seventies. Ironically and tragically this coincided with the Civil Rights Movement. In a brilliant analysis, a young Black writer, Michele Wallace, shows that Black leadership made the deadly mistake of defining itself in sexual terms, equating power with manhood. She explains that the living of the Black macho myth has been disastrous for Black women, forcing them into feminine roles largely imitative of while femininity. Wallace explains the confusion and guilt of these women, who have been crushed by the reversal-ideology of the "Black Matriarch." She writes: "During the sixties it was not unusual for a successful black woman in a profession to feel extremely guilty, even to the point of sabotaging her own career or of pursuing a male to replace her. Some just simply quit their jobs and had babies. Black males thought nothing of saying, in reference to a black woman's job, 'A brother should have that.' " See Michele Wallace, *Black Macho and the Myth of the Superwoman* (New York: The Dial Press, 1978, 1979), p. 116. This situation has not greatly improved. Wallace points out: "Obsession with the lynching of the black man seems to leave no room in the black male consciousness for any awareness of the oppression of black women. ... As far as I have been able to tell, black women have no status at all in the black community, particularly since the sixties" (ibid., p. 120).

Another possibility, not to be dismissed lightly, is that the catholic assumers sent Mary "up" in preparation for annihilating her earthly presence and for joining the protestant annihilators in ecumenical brotherhood.* It would have been necessary to give her a glorious send-off, guised as a heavenly homecoming. And of course they reserved to themselves the option to bring her back whenever she might be needed for an important job.

Translucent Transcendence of the Assumption

Whatever the intent of the assumers, the Assumed Virgin of course can function as a freewheeling Metaphor of Elemental reality, so that in this image can be glimpsed traces of the Sky-Goddesses from whom she was derived—and behind these can be sensed cosmic, Elemental forces/sources. For the Sky-Goddesses re-mind us of the *stoicheia*—the spirits, life forces, of the sun, moon, and stars. They point to cosmic connections. The image of the Virgin rising can become a Metaphor for Muses who fly beyond the "Assumption" and the assumers, roaring at their asinine assumptions. Thus in the "Assumption" the Arch-Image is not only a tool for intercepting of messages of Wild be-ing. She is also a subliminal transmitter of these messages. For in her Metaphoric dimensions, the Rising Virgin is out of the control of the patriarchal propagandists and is lustrous with Archaic Radiance. As Metaphor of Metabeing, she is indeed Mediatrix of the Graces.

The cannibalism of the christian assumers is suggested by their choice of the date of the Feast of the Assumption, August 15. For they have attempted to assume/consume Lammas, one of the four great feasts of the Old Religion of the Witches. Although originally Lammas, the harvest feast, was celebrated on August 1, the closeness of the dates makes the association probable.[11]

An interesting fact is recorded by Marina Warner:

As early as the tenth century, the intimate association between the aromas of herbs and flowers and the victory of Mary over death was celebrated in the ritual of the feast of the Assumption. Medicinal herbs and plants were brought to church on that day. Periwinkle, verbena,

---

* I am talking about the dynamism inherent in their myth-making, not with the intention of ascribing "conscious" political evil genius to their propagation of fantasies, but with the purpose of describing some legitimating functions of these images.

thyme, and many other ingredients of the herbalist's art were laid on the altar, to be incensed and blessed. Then they were bound into a sheaf and kept all year to ward off illness and disaster and death. But the ceremony was abolished in England at the Reformation, and is extinct everywhere now except in some towns of northern Italy.[12]

Warner does not indicate that she sees any connection between the practices she describes here and the traditional wisdom of the Witches—the herbalists/healers/wise women of whom the church was so terrified. Moreover, Warner does not note any significance in the fact that the ceremony is now extinct and that it was abolished in England "at the Reformation." For Crone-logical thinkers it is noteworthy that the sixteenth century phenomenon of the Reformation coincided with the beginnings of the Witchcraze. Since the protestant churchmen were bent upon discrediting and destroying the Arch-Image as well as the healers/Witches themselves, who participated in Archimagical powers, it is quite logical that they would abolish this ceremony. For it displayed/dis-closed too much.

INCARNATIONS, RESTORATIONS, RENEWALS

To understand the workings of the assumers in the course of modern sadosocietal events, it is important to study the syndrome of "restoration." The all-pervasive obsession with restoration (spiritual, cultural, medical) implies the necessity and desirability of a breakdown of Elemental nature, preparing the way for this omnipresent process of restoration/rehabilitation, which is, in essence, sado-sublimation. Within the society of restorationism, almost total debilitation is the optimum condition for acceptance of the phallic priesthood's gruesome grace.

Restorationism should be seen within the context contrived by the sadospiritual myth-reversers/restorers. The sadosocietal sovereigns' will to warp Original Words requires sublimated incarnations—warped words/ideas made flesh. In the world of pornographic theological myth this involves an archetypal rape. The christian incarnation myth fulfills this requirement on a grand scale. The transsexed, broken spirit of the Goddess, guised as the holy ghost, rapes the broken and dis-spirited matter of the Goddess (Mary). Thus the myth-molding voyeurs have produced what could be designated the Purest Peep Show of the millennia, a male-identified counterfeit lesbian love scene, issuing in male off-spring. The product of this fantastic feat is Jesus. This spectacle of the transsexed, divided goddess raping herself is the ultimate in sadospiritual speculation. It is an idiot's re-vision of partheno-genesis, converted into rape. The myth of The Incarnation, then, logically implies the usurpation of female power. Moreover, since the Virgin Mother symbolizes matter to the myth-masters, the myth legitimates the rape of all matter.

The Incarnation depicts the material re-production of a male pseudogoddess, Jesus, who is a plastic goddess, in several senses.* First, he is an unnatural imitation of the typical effect of partheno-genesis, which would be a daughter. Second, he is easily molded to serve the purposes of his manufacturers in different cultural situations. Third, like nonbiodegradable plastics, he is difficult, almost impossible, to dispose of. In modern technology the sado-sublimated "incarnations" legitimated by The Incarnation are also plastic, resulting in the destruction and simulation of nature, the replacement of all that is natural and organic.

Since sado-subliming involves stealing—in the sense of con-cealing—Original Elemental knowledge/words and their replace-ment by warped words, it follows that the incarnations of these warped words will be deadly distortions and simulations of Ele-mental reality. Moreover, since the mechanisms of sado-sublim-ing involve exquisite deception, which is the torture/twisting of minds/spirits, it follows that the incarnations of these deceptive ideas/words—that is, the products of sado-sublimation—will per-petuate this torture and de-form matter as well. That is, verbicide implies biocide. In a special way, verbicide implies gynocide. The figure hanging on the christian cross is subliminally female and a model for females.[13] The crucifixion of the "Incarnate Word" is really the crucifixion of female meanings/words.

In christian mythology, the Word became incarnate in order to suffer and die for the sins of "men." It is unthinkable that he was

---

* Crones will recall the popular sing-along song "Plastic Jesus":
    I don't care if it rains or freezes
    Long as I got my plastic Jesus
    Sittin' on the dashboard of my car.
    Virgin Mary's got to go.
    She's fouling up my radio,
    Sittin' on the dashboard of my car.

"born" in order to be joyous and to live because life is good, since unfortunately he was a twisted thought/word to begin with. This sort of distorted, blunted purpose/final causality is so ingrained in patriarchal thought patterns that it is rarely perceived as twisted. Rather, suffering is god's will. A myth of "Incarnation of the Biophilic Word" would fail to "catch on" in the mainstream of sadosociety and could not legitimate such a structure. For the rulers of these sadospheres require that sickness, suffering, poverty, depression, immobility, guilt and basic breakdown of integrity be the norm.[14] Furious women break that norm in the process of Naming it. Naming is battling against verbicide, cutting through closures that conceal the biophilic words.

Naming, unlike mere labeling, is ongoing E-motional analysis, ontological knowing/gnawing the way through incarceration by lethal incarnations. An aid in this knowing process is Robert J. Lifton's concept of "restorationist totalism." [15] This involves three stages: (1) annihilation, (2) renewal, (3) embrace and dependent worship. Apparently without consciously knowing it, Lifton has described the manifestations of phallic trinitarianism. In christian terms, "creation" is appropriated to the father, "restoration/ renewal" is associated with the incarnate word, and "love" (embrace and consequent dependency) is a name of the holy ghost.[16] In the reversal world legitimated by this threesome, "creation" clearly means annihilation, "renewal" means imitation and replacement, and "embrace/love" means suffocation. Moreover, these correspond to amnesia (annihilation of memory), aphasia (enforced substitution of verbiage for truly spirated words), and apraxia (disoriented acts such as embrace and dependent worship of the wrong things).[17]

As Muses re-calling our Selves and the elements, women can use this threesome as a take-off point. We have seen that the fathers' abortive attempts at annihilation (which they call creation) result in breakdown, the separation of "matter" from Elemental spirit. This ineffably dis-spiriting, discouraging, disheartening ploy results in fabricated needs for restoration/renewal/rehabilitation. The world is, as it were, brought to its knees, and this condition is called "the fullness of time." This state is brought about through a process of breakdown/battering, requiring a lengthy period of preparation between the "sin of Adam," and the first "coming" of Christ. Aquinas describes this aptly:

. . . Man was to be liberated in such a manner that he [*sic*] might be humbled, and see how he stood in need of a deliverer.

Aquinas adds as a reason for this "humbling" of man the idea that "having recognized his infirmity he might cry out for a physician, and beseech the aid of grace." [18] Having been sufficiently humbled and having suffered almost total breakdown of inner communication with the Original Self, the victim is ready for renewal by the savior/physician and for the third stage, which is dependency upon the embrace of these wholly ghastly ghosts.

This restorationist syndrome, so perfectly described by Aquinas, is executed in a variety of professions including modern medicine and psychology. It is precisely illustrated, for example, in the manfacture, management of, and ministry to mastectomy victims.* In an article entitled "Psychoemotional Aspects of Mastectomy," Michael J. Asken exposes the psycho/emotional state of his profession. He writes:

While mastectomy performs a gratifying service by saving a woman's life, her appreciation is muted by the price she must pay for that service—the loss of a breast and permanent disfigurement. Within the value system of American society, that price is a considerable one.[19]

With no sense of irony nor any acknowledgment of such phenomena as iatrogenesis (doctor-caused disease), the carcinogenic environment, and the less than gratifying long-term survival rate after mastectomies, this "authority" on women's bodies and emotions can call mastectomies a "gratifying service." The question Gratifying to whom? does not arise. While obliterating such realities as pain and anxiety, he insinuates that the "price" of loss of a breast and permanent disfigurement is a considerable one only "within the value system of American society." The obvious implication is that women are mere products of society whose bodily integrity is not in itself very important, even to themselves. Having been annihilated psychically, they have no personal right to mute their "appreciation" for such gratifying restoration and renewal.

---

* I use the term *manufacture* to name the fact that cancer is in large measure a man-made disease and also to name the fact that some mastectomies are performed unnecessarily.

The obscene attitude of this typical professional is further displayed in the following passage from the same article:

Millard and associates and Freeman suggested that offering the chance for breast reconstruction even before the breast is removed can be of great comfort to the patient. Of course, any safe procedures that limit the destruction of the breast are desirable; to accomplish this, Millard and associates offered a procedure for saving the uninvolved nipple. The nipple-banking procedure consists of temporary grafting of the nipple until it can be replaced onto the reconstructed breast. The authors found this procedure to be a great morale-booster, giving the woman something to look forward to and serving as a token of the doctor's faith in her recovery.[20]

A sense of grief mutes female fury at this absurd "reasoning." The expressions "offering the chance," "morale-booster," and "something to look forward to" suggest the horror of the restorationist syndrome. To paraphrase the words of Aquinas cited above:

Woman was to be liberated in such a manner that she might be humbled, and see how she stood in need of a deliverer, so that having recognized her infirmity she might cry out for a physician, and beseech the aid of surgery and psychotherapy.

Moreover, even when she "cries out," the nature and motive of her request has been predetermined by the professional. Writing in the *Journal of Rehabilitation*, Harold J. May intones:

Whether or not breast reconstruction is considered, the major task facing the mastectomee is to regain any personal loss of both femininity and sexual desirability.[21]

With this defined as her "major task," the woman labeled and categorized as "mastectomee" might well conclude that continued existence as a "desirable" object is hardly worth the effort.

As these mastectomy managers disclose, therefore, the restorers are also the assumers, peddling false assumptions, assuming the right to define the very reason for existence of these patients/victims. They also assume the right to cause the breakdowns which are the prerequisites for restoration and renewal. Howard A. Rusk, M.D., in a textbook entitled *Rehabilitation Medicine*, is quite explicit and unabashed:

Contrary to opinions expressed by some, the growing incidence of chronic disability in the United States is a tribute to American medicine rather than an indictment. But since the physician has been largely responsible for this development, he must assume leadership in its solution.[22]

Having doublethought himself and others into accepting this "tribute," the physician does indeed assume leadership—arrogating, seizing, and usurping institutional power. Yet in large measure this is healing power in appearance only. It is assumed power to heal and to exercise "leadership" in the solution of problems created by the medical profession itself. Such medical restorationism typifies sadosocietal incarnations of restorationist myth.

Jesus is one model for victims of the restorationist syndrome, who are destined for crucifixion and death (in various forms), followed by resurrection and ascension into heaven. Mythically speaking, however, the restorationist vision is incomplete without the assumption of Mary. For although the androgynous feminized Jesus is in some sense a compound resulting from the combination of the severed halves of the Goddess, it is important to the myth-masters that this reunification be presented also in female form. This is accomplished through the doctrine of the Assumption of the Virgin Mary, in which the dead Virgin is instantly re-inspirited and taken up. The Goddess in female form is thus rehabilitated. The Queen of Heaven for all eternity will kneel before her own son. As Simone de Beauvoir has written:

For the first time in human history the mother kneels before her son; she freely accepts her inferiority. This is the supreme masculine victory, consummated in the cult of the Virgin—it is the rehabilitation of woman through the accomplishment of her defeat.[23]

Moreover, the assumers extend the chance of "rehabilitation through defeat" to all of the elements. They arrogantly attempt/pretend to give back "life" to the matter they themselves have broken down and deadened. They do this in their customary way, by further violation of all the elements. The reason for their incapacity to heal or to restore in any real sense is unwittingly implied in the words of René Dubos, who writes:

Paraphrasing Paul of Tarsus, it can be said that humankind is *in* Nature but no longer quite *of* Nature.[24]

Appropriately, this sentence appears in the book entitled *The Wooing of Earth,* for, quite simply, restorationists relate to all of nature in the same unnatural, rapist way they relate to women. This unnaturalness is christened "supernatural," and indeed it is in line with christian tradition. As John J. Vincent writes in *Christ in a Nuclear World*:

The Christian believes that God has revealed the wonders of atomic and nuclear energy in order that man might accomplish His will upon earth.[25]

Vincent does glimpse a few problems with nuclearism, but as a true restorationist he looks forward to salvation in the form of further breakdown. As he writes:

It seems that we have been allowed to come to this situation in order that we can see Christ again.[26]

Thus the wheel of "renewal" turns full circle. Those caught in its spokes, broken and "restored," re-turn to embrace the cause of their breakdown. For these restored-again victims, Elemental being is buried and forgotten.

RESTORATION AND THE PROBLEM OF MEMORY

Restoration, the product of sado-sublimation, conceals the real nature of the breakdown it pretends to mend and thus distracts women's minds/hearts from the quest to know Elemental integrity. It does this in part by misnaming the dis-ease inflicted upon women and nature. To tell a woman who has been sickened and mutilated that her major task is to regain "femininity and desirability" is to distract her from her deep Self's search, her final causality. It distracts her from re-membering her powers. In order to comprehend her breakdown and therefore be enabled to heal her Self, she would have to intuit what a woman *can be*. The problem is how to be in touch with such intuitions, when they have been obscured by restorationist ideology.

So colossal has been this concealment that even the French feminist philosopher Simone de Beauvoir, in her monumental work, *The Second Sex,* actually reaffirms the discouraging assumption that underscores all of the other assumptions of androcracy, namely, that women have always been "second." This is suggested in the title of her book. One could, of course, argue that the title is factually accurate since women have been relegated to the status of "the second sex." However, de Beauvoir is more patriarchal in her assumptions than that.* In the Introduction, she writes:

Throughout history they [women] have always been subordinated to men, and hence their dependency is not the result of a historical event or a social change—it was not something that *occurred*. The reason why otherness in this case seems to be an absolute is in part that it lacks the contingent or incidental nature of historical facts.[27]

This premise is repeated in the book. De Beauvoir introduces her chapter on the nomads, for example, with the cliché that "this has always been a man's world." [28] And again in the following chapter she repeats this assumption:

From humanity's beginnings, their biological advantage has enabled the males to affirm their status as sole and sovereign subjects.[29]

Many feminists today find it hard to believe that de Beauvoir could have written of women:

They have no past, no history, no religion of their own; and they have no such solidarity of work and interest as that of the proletariat.[30] †

It is not unusual, of course, to hear such assumptions/clichés from the mouths of women's erasers. That the author of such an important feminist work as *The Second Sex*—first published in

* In criticizing de Beauvoir or any feminist it is important to keep in mind the extreme isolation and the harsh sanctions endured by such prophets. From the perspective of the 1980s it is possible to see some limitations that were impossible to perceive when de Beauvoir was writing in the 1940s. This point was emphasized in a conversation with Marisa Zavalloni and Nicole Brossard, Montreal, August 1983.

† Emily Culpepper suggests that "it is a measure of how far we have come that within her own lifetime, de Beauvoir has lived to see feminists cast doubt on all of these assertions." She also suggests that de Beauvoir can be read as "accepting 'the worst possible case' and going on to claim that—even if thus it has always been—it need not remain so." Emily Culpepper, "Philosophia in a Feminist Key: Revolt of the Symbols" (unpublished Th.D. dissertation, Harvard University, 1983), p. 111–13.

1949—accepted them so uncritically is evidence of the memory-covering effects of restorationist "knowledge." *

Within the context of such unexamined assumptions it is extremely difficult to guess what a woman *can be*. Within such a context personal hope is muted, undermined. Despite all the positive values of de Beauvoir's work, the woman who accepts this context is mired in the suspicion that the situation is immutable.

Of course, other feminist scholars writing before and after the publication of *The Second Sex* have brought forth mountains of evidence to support the idea/intuition that this has *not* always been "a man's world." These scholars include Matilda Joslyn Gage in *Woman, Church and State* (1893) and Elizabeth Gould Davis in *The First Sex* (1971).[31] Women who have not read such books but have maintained a sense of Self have done so because on some level we have known with profound certainty that this has not always been "a man's world," and that reality in the deep sense—Elemental be-ing—has never been such. For the man's world, patriarchy, is the Foreground, which, since it is derivative, contains countless subliminal messages about the deep spheres of meaning—Archespheres—which its myths are intended to mask. The power to decode its myths is the natural power of Lusty women to hear the messages of the elements, the Elemental Words—to recognize these and re-member them.

One suggestive term which we might use to name the incarnations that constitute the Foreground, the "this" world that has "always been" patriarchy is a word used by Paracelsus: *elementary*. According to his theory:

. . . the elementary is an artificial being, created in the invisible worlds by man himself. . . . Most elementaries seem to be of an evil or destructive nature. They are generated from the excesses of human thought and emotion, the corruption of character, or the degeneration of faculties and powers which should be used in other, more constructive ways.[32]

I will use the term *elementary* here to Name a number of phenomena which mediate/distort our experience of elements, and which are largely invisible by reason of being all-pervasive. Ele-

* Restorationist "knowledge" is to Elemental knowing as a dysfunctional prosthesis is to a natural part of the body.

mentaries include not only the poisonous fumes and radioactive emissions of phallic technology, but also the popular media and the specialized fields (the -ologies that mediate knowledge), as well as traditional assumptions, spoken or unspoken. All of these artificial beings are filled with fallacies invisible to those manipulated by means of them. In mediating experience they modify memory; they mummify memory.*

It is through acts of Elemental creation that Lusty women unblock/unlock our deep memories. Therefore, in sado-sublimated society, women must be prevented from such acts, not only by the embedding in the female psyche of elementary images and words of which women are unwitting recipients, but especially by the cooptation of women into elementary speech and action. Insight can be gained from knowledge of the fact that according to traditional christian theology the image of the (all-male) trinity is to be found especially in the acts of the soul.[33] In keeping with this tradition, possessed women are converted into images of artificial beings by being trained to act/operate like elementaries even on the level of internal thoughts and desires. Pre-occupied with elementary concerns, a woman becomes a memory-blocker.

In order to understand how women are caught on the wheel of elementary thinking and acting, it is important to face the fears and embedded sense of vulnerability which are the foreground conditions of phallocracy afflicting all women—since all are threatened perpetually by the phallic lust that rapes, kills, and dismembers women and nature. There can be no genuine doubt about this situation, which has been demonstrated and documented in many books and in the individual histories of women. So terrible is the lust, the intent, to destroy female nature, that women commonly attempt to erase their Selves in order to be spared.

SELF-ANNIHILATION AND CONFESSIONALISM

The attempted Self-annihilation of wives and mothers, of "old maid" aunts, of "dedicated" volunteers and professional women is well known. In various ways, women caught in this syndrome

---

* As Emily Culpepper has remarked, it is ironically true that our first major institutional training in patriarchal roles is "elementary school." Conversation, Leverett, Mass., April 1983.

hope for the reward of male protection and approval, for the restoration and lethal embrace that is misnamed "love." Moreover, there is realistic terror of recrimination for any refusal to comply to the stereotype.

Women breaking out of these tracks can remain partially tracked, terrorized, since there are many deep levels of tracks and terrors. As long as these remain unexorcised, women's "liberation" is at least partially just restoration, hiding a secret settling for the reward of male protection. That is, it remains elementary. Then women remain in the posture of the veiled virgin mother kneeling before the son who has derived everything from her, begging his aid. It is helpful to recall that the word *protection* is derived from the Latin *protegere,* meaning "to cover in front," which is literally the condition of a woman with a veil over her head and face. That is, she is hindered and blindfolded—which is the intent of the male protection racketeers, who require such Self-hindrance. It is noteworthy that *blindfold* is derived from the Middle English *blind* plus *fellen,* meaning "to strike down," "to fell." Restored, veiled women have been struck down/felled to their knees (as the christmas carols and crèches, the bridal veils and the chadors all proclaim) and they have been blinded to the fact of their fall. In the sadoworld legitimated by The Incarnation and its satellite myths, moreover, the Fraternity of Phallic Fellers attempts to bring down all of nature together with the virgin-mothers. All the victims are subjected to the rituals of restoration.

Felled to their knees, restored women are in the correct position for confession. Having been veiled/blindfolded, and knocked down, women find it difficult to say what they mean. Aphasic, they utter/mutter the assumers' formulae. Each act of saying what the Self cannot really mean causes restoration of memory, that is, the further hiding of deep Memory. Confession becomes a preoccupation, preventing acts that are rooted in ancestral Memory. Each act of confession is a construct of elementary consciousness and a construction of further elementary consciousness, causing contagion of corruption.

In the reversal world of restoration, confession is hailed as an act of courage, rather than confronted as an act of cowardice. Women are "encouraged" to confess, which is to perform repeated acts of attempted linguistic Self-annihilation and reconstruction. The phenomenon is omnipresent. It is important, in understanding confessionalism, to remember that *confession* means not only "acknowledgment of sins," but also "acknowledgment of belief or profession of faith." Moreover, since the mythic, doctrinal, and ideological belief systems that legitimate the Lecherous State necessarily include and imply the belief that Elemental women are sinful, wrong, and a threat to the established order, both meanings of *confession* usually apply to the same behavior. Thus women's confessions of faith in the prevailing ideologies and practices, such as phallic religion, romance, politics, therapy, etiquette, fashions,* imply confessions of sin, inadequacy, sickness, ineptitude, failure. The confessions required by the Restorationist State are multiple and commonplace, perversely permeating everyday behavior. Consequently, they are largely invisible to the penitents/believers.

As a consequence of confessionalism, then, not only a woman's conversation but also her body-language becomes aphasic. Moreover, such unnatural, disjointed expressions of repression are reproduced without genuine variation, fixed according to prescribed patterns, standardized, beaten into Self-denying stereotypical shape.

CONFESSIONALISM AND SEPARATION

The entire lifetime of a patriarchal woman is a series of confessions. This syndrome does not automatically disappear once a woman becomes a feminist. Even in the process of breaking away from the tracks and terrors of the Lecherous State unwary women can be caught in parodies of movement. Mesmerized by visions of "liberation" that are elementary, rather than Elemental, women are stopped dead, while apparently active. This happens when the forces that oppress women as women—the fathers who have fabricated phallocracy and who maintain its reign—are not Named. One consequence—and cause—of not-Naming is immersion in the muck of confessionalism.

Many women's projects, conferences, workshops have been blighted by this phenomenon and therefore have remained restorationist and elementary, confusing the participants rather than

* A woman tottering on spike heels is a living, walking, or rather wobbling, confession of acceptance of phallic loathing and disdain for women's minds/bodies.

unmasking the masters. Since, in the reversal world of restorationism, confession is hailed as courage, both the denial of one's own perceptions (Self-censorship) and refusal to Name the Enemy of the cause of women can sometimes masquerade as feminist and woman-identified behavior. Horizontally violent behavior is labeled "brilliance" and Self-denunciation that wins instant gratification is called "bravery."

As I have indicated in the Foreground, Hannah Arendt analyzes this kind of distortion in her discussion of the self-blame of some young Germans in the 1960s for the atrocities of the Nazis.[34] Wallowing in "collective guilt," they avoided confronting institutionally powerful males and genuinely risking their careers. In the conservative 1980s women have fear of men in authority, and the temptation to deflect rage against the sado-rulers, turning it against women, is strong not only among women of the right, but also all too frequently among those who have experienced a passion for justice. Protection by "radical" males, liberal males, establishment males is the reward for refusal to give priority to the cause of women.

This reward, however, is elementary, illusory. In contrast to the German youths who used "collective guilt" to avoid responsibility for confronting their elders, and to escape the ensuing penalties, women *as women* are not destined to become the future Ruling Caste within the patriarchal system, but to be victimized by this caste. The reward for false consciousness/conscience—for putting other causes before our own—is fixation in the State of Sublimated Servitude. This could also be called stasis in the Stereotypic State.

Stereotypic consciousness can invade and prevail even in groups of women who have in many ways separated themselves from the mainstream of straight society, but who lack ongoing, passionate analysis of phallocracy. This condition is marked by refusal to acknowledge the meaning and even the existence in oneself of phallocentric myths and ideologies, and of the conditioned responses embedded in women's psyches and incarnated in the institutions of gynocide. Such denial of the fact of patriarchal male presence in one's own psyche is substituted for courageous acts of denying such presences access to one's psyche. In other words, the terrifying risks involved in the process of exorcism are avoided at the cost of maintaining a destroyed and restored semblance of female consciousness that has been rehabilitated in the image of its makers.

Moreover, women who settle for a partial break from patriarchy while failing to sustain and further the feminist vision—for example, by combining nontraditional life styles with male-identified activism or tokenized professionalism—may be "liberated" from the onus of the incarnate male presence just sufficiently to lose touch with the real horrors of patriarchy. Thus even the conditions of physical separation/freedom, which are so important for the development of a radical feminist analysis, are—in the absence of rigorous Elemental thinking—converted into servitude to the patriarchal system. Mere social club, sexually liberated lesbianism, for example, serves the fathers and sons—the ones on the left as well as those on the right—feeding into the mechanisms of institutionalized repressive desublimation of which Marcuse wrote, years ago.[35] That is, women are kept "happy" with truncated, unrebellious existence.[36] As an offshoot of the "sexual revolution" and permissive paternalism, tamed/contained lesbianism is a by-product of phallicism.

What is forgotten in this tamed state is the radical, Elemental meaning of woman-identified, Self-identified separation. In *Gyn/Ecology* I described radical separation:

It is Crone-logical to conclude that internal separation or separatism, that is, paring away, burning away the false selves encasing the Self, is the core of all authentic separations and thus is normative for all personal/political decisions about acts/forms of separatism. It is axiomatic for Amazons that all external/internalized influences, such as myths, names, ideologies, social structures, which cut off the flow of the Self's original movement should be pared away.[37]

Without this internal burning away of false selves, which is radical separatism, and which requires clear analysis, women in all-female gatherings and communities uncritically fall into the role of mirroring male-ordered society.

It is important to remember that in patriarchy women are vehicles that incarnate the male presence. This is an essential mode of male incarnation. The mother who constantly reminds her children that she will "tell Daddy when he comes home" is a classic example. Upon examination, however, it becomes clear that the chief torturers in patriarchy are the invisible fathers, for example, the scientists, bureaucrats, generals, physicians, psychiatrists who invent and employ lethal weapons, pesticides, pollutants, medicines, treatments.

The *visible* executors of the fathers' orders are often female. There are, for example, the "pro-nuke" women who hand out propaganda in American airports. In the novel and movie *One Flew Over the Cuckoo's Nest,* the character of "Big Nurse" is presented as the powerful ogre, masking the fact that such females are vehicles and not truly "in charge." Most spectacularly, women are used to render god (the father, son, and holy ghost) "omnipresent." This is quite a feat, for god is omniabsent. Indeed, according to christian doctrine he is not sense perceptible, not knowable in himself by natural reason. In fact, it requires unnatural reason, labeled as "supernatural" to "know" adequately about his attributes and to "know" anything at all about his triunity.[38] Traditionally, mothers of families, nuns, wives of ministers and wives of rabbis have been the common vehicles of his presence. (Priests, ministers, and rabbis are of course mostly absent from the everyday, commonplace scenes in which religious beliefs are unofficially preached and perpetuated.)

Even "women's communities" sometimes perform this traditional function of perpetuating the patriarchal presence. This has sometimes been manifested in "women only" events, especially when these events have lent themselves to ritualistic behavior. Lacking an adequate understanding of the sadosociety and its effects upon their own consciousness and behavior, women in these situations have sometimes responded to the condition of *physical* absence of males by assuming the traditional feminine function of incarnating the male presence, described above. The gathering then becomes divided into "sides": Some assume the male role and put other women down into a victim role; others accept or have forced upon them the victimized stance. The male-role players frequently have used such tactics as accusation of a serious fault, for example, some political incorrectness concerning racism, classism, or oppression of the handicapped. The accused must then choose whether to fight back, withdraw, or give the desired response: self-accusation.

Groups in which such behavior predominates are pseudo-cognitive minorities of women. In fact, they are doing exactly what is prescribed by the "moral majority" of maledom in the Society of Sado-Sublimation. The participators in this phenomenon have compliantly reproduced mirror reflections of omnipresent patriarchal totalism. Such unreflective reflections have served patriarchal purposes only too well. Dis-couraged by horizontal violence, many women have lost sight of the validity and importance of creative Women's Space.

As I have shown in the Foreground, the phenomenon of the totalistic environment was analyzed by Robert J. Lifton in the early sixties, in his study of "thought reform" in China. Although Lifton does not identify this phenomenon as an essential feature of *patriarchy,* some of his points are applicable to the infestation of totalism that functions to dismember the feminist movement from without and from within. Lifton writes of the cult of confession as characteristic of the totalistic thought-reform environment:

The assumption underlying total exposure . . . is the environment's claim to total ownership of each individual self within it. Private ownership of the mind and its products—of imagination or of memory—becomes highly immoral.[39]

This could be reworded as follows:

The assumption underlying the demand that women totally expose themselves (confess) is the Lecherous State's claim to total ownership of each individual woman within it. Private ownership by a woman of her mind and its creations—of imagination or of memory—becomes highly immoral.

This is the world described in George Orwell's *1984* in which "nobody ever failed to confess" [40] and in which "there was fear, hatred, and pain, but no dignity of emotion, or deep or complex sorrows." [41]

In the State of Lechery, in which women are the property of males, women's bodies and minds are allowed no other acts than acts of confession—confession in phallocratic beliefs and confession of self-loathing. Universally, the confessionalism imposed upon women takes the form of prostitution on all levels. Within christendom, the cult of confession took the form of a sacrament which required that women bare their souls to a male priest, accusing themselves of male-defined "sins." In the course of the

Witchcraze in Western Europe (occasioned in part by the rise of professionalism in the early modern period) untold numbers of women were forced by means of torture to confess to the "crime" of practicing Witchcraft (that is, natural religion and healing). The modern professions have included enforced female confession as a primary tool. Total exposure is the rule, illustrated in the questioning of rape victims in court, of patients in hospitals and in psychiatric clinics, and in the exposure of women's bodies to experimentation of all kinds. Such total exposure means in reality total closure/hiding of a woman's Elemental Self and the breakdown and restoration of that which is accessible to the professional rehabilitators.

Given these conditions, it is not surprising that women's communities or groups sometimes reflect the professional rituals of the cult of confession. Those who succumb to the cultic demands deny themselves and each other private ownership of their own minds and creations. The reward for this behavior is in part described by Lifton: "the continuing opportunity for emotional catharsis and for relief of suppressed guilt feelings." [42] In addition:

. . . the sharing of confession enthusiasms can create an orgiastic sense of "oneness," of the most intense intimacy with fellow confessors, and of the dissolution of self into the great flow of the Movement.[43]

When this behavior takes over among women, an occasion is provided for denial of the fact of subliminal phallic presence and for failure to exorcise phallocentric beliefs and behavior. In this case, women's groups/gatherings are totaled by the tactics of totalism, man-ipulated and man-infested.[44]

PHALLIC POWER OF ABSENCE

Since patriarchal male omnipresence is in reality an omniabsence that depends upon women for its incarnations, it is totally unlike the power of Presence of Elemental women. In *Beyond God the Father* I have discussed this Presence:

The power of presence that is experienced by those who have begun to live in the new space radiates outward, attracting others. . . . For those who are . . . threatened, the presence of women to each other is experienced as an absence.[45]

Such power of Presence is individual, original, creative. It is participation in Powers of Be-ing. In contrast to this, patriarchal power of presence is institutional power. This power requires absence of genuine individuality, of true deviance. Whereas Elemental female power of Absence is a consequence of our Presence, the patriarchal male's (or female's) institutional presence is derived from ontological absence; it is elementary presence.

When this elementary presence is not denied access to our psyches by women—when it is allowed to insinuate itself in the form of myths, ideologies, or emotional responses—women become its vessels, vehicles, carriers. Pregnant with it, women perpetuate its incarnations. Vampiristic, the elementary patriarchal presence is forever fetal. Women who are pre-occupied by it are not only de-energized; they are spooked. For this is both *presence of absence* and *absence of Presence.*

Phallic *presence of absence* is experienced by women as a growth of nothingness, an expansion of emptiness that fills the mind. The meaninglessness of male-centered myths and ideologies is experienced as mental/spiritual bloat. It is "stuff" that packs the mind, which becomes a garbage heap of details without a focus. The glut of non-sense can be experienced watching television, reading newspapers, or attending an ordinary university. It is decentralized mass without organic purpose; it expands like a tumor of the soul. It is a parade of images and "facts" that are not facts because the context is a lie. The emotional responses that it elicits also pre-occupy the mind, weighing it down with guilt, anxiety, despair. Its victim becomes absent to her Self.

Phallic *absence of Presence* is lack of content and purpose. It is negation of meaning in a conversation, lack of affection or of intelligence in a face, nonresponse to a question, to an act of love. It is absence of soul.

This double-edged absence has power insofar as it prevents women from being Really Present. It accomplishes this through the double method of deception and discouragement. For it is nonbe-ing that poses as Presence, and that blunts the hope of dis-covering Presence. Therefore, Wonderlusters should consider further the meaning of Real Presence.

REAL PRESENCE

First of all, Gnomic Nags should note that Real Presence implies being presentient—"feeling or perceiving beforehand."

When a woman's consciousness is captured and filled with phallic absence, to be presentient is to be filled with foreboding about a coming ill or misfortune, that is, to have anxiety. When women are Present to our Selves, however, to be presentient is to be animated with hope. This presentient Presence is Positively Powerful, for it implies our capacity to *presentiate,* that is "to make or render present in place or time; to cause to be perceived or realized as present" (*O.E.D.*). Real Presence of the Self, then, which is participation in Powers of Be-ing, implies powers to Realize as present our past and future Selves. Augurs, Sibyls, Soothsayers, Muses, Actualize/Realize these powers.*

* It can still be distressing even to an experienced Searcher, when a scholar such as Julian Jaynes sweeps over significant information as if it were barely worth noting, when such information relates to powers of women. He writes: "And a comment can be added here about sexual differences. It is now well known that women are biologically somewhat *less lateralized* in brain function than men. This means simply that psychological functions in women are not localized into one or the other hemisphere of the brain to the same degree as in men. Mental abilities in women are more spread over both hemispheres. . . . And it is common knowledge that elderly men with a stroke or hemorrhage in the left hemisphere are *more speechless* than elderly women with a similar diagnosis. Accordingly we might expect more residual language function in the right hemisphere of women, *making it easier for women to learn to be oracles.* And indeed the majority of oracles and Sibyls, at least in European cultures, were women" [all emphases mine]. See *The Origin of Consciousness in the Breakdown of the Bicameral Mind* (Boston: Houghton Mifflin Company, 1976), pp. 343–44. This fascinating point is mentioned in only one other place in the book, and there even more scantily (p. 350). Shrewd Shrews will notice that Jaynes' language is deceptive and patronizing to women. For by his syntax he manages to belittle the oracular gifts of women and the Elemental integrity of female mental faculties, while at the same time obscuring the negative implications of overly localized psychological functions in males. For example, in this passage "less lateralized" and "more speechless" illustrate this bias.

Male terror of such Elemental integrity in women is directly related to many of the phenomena discussed by Jaynes, although he fails to make this connection. For example, his split awareness is manifested in his discussion of the christian doctrine of the "hypostatic union"—the union of the divine and human natures in Christ. Referring to this doctrine as the "Bicameral Word Made Flesh," he fails to raise the question of why male theologians felt the need to insist dogmatically upon a miraculous union of two natures in a *god-man* (divine male). Jaynes does not sug-

The primary meaning of the verb *realize* is "to make real: change from what is imaginary or fictitious into what is actual: bring into concrete existence: ACTUALIZE." The Real Presence of Lusty women is Realizing Presence. It is active potency/power to create and to transform, to render present in place and time.

The elementary omnipresence/omniabsence of phallocracy obstructs Elemental Realizing Presence. Therefore, a Lusty woman uses her Labrys, her double ax of exorcism and ecstasy to extricate her Self from its ghostly manifestations. These are the *presence of absence* and *absence of Presence* that frustrate her Lust, distracting her from her deep *telos,* her purpose.

The elementary *presence of absence* that blunts and bloats our minds with messages of unreality requires expulsion, exorcism. Elemental women expel such pseudopresence, achieving the *Absence of absence*. By acts of daring, Prudes prune away this pseudospirit/pseudomatter. We know that *exorcism* traditionally means "to drive out or drive away (an evil spirit) by adjuration, especially by use of a holy name or magic rites." As Dragons/Dryads women drive away the phallic presence of absence, not by use of a holy name/noun, but by Wholly Naming actions, ideas, symbols, feelings, that is, by Naming these events in Gyn/Ecological context. We do this in Archimagical Rites that include clear reasoning rooted in deep intuition and verified by direct experience. Prudish, Shrewish reason burns away the expanded vapors of non-sense, freeing the places, spaces, that have been occupied, possessed.

The elementary *absence of Presence* that is the normal nothingness of bore-ocracy, the routinized rule in snooldom, is expelled through the expansion of our own reality. Yet this absence is difficult to face and Name. As Orwell expressed the problem in *1984*:

The only evidence to the contrary was the mute protest in your own bones, the instinctive feeling that the conditions you lived in were intolerable and that at some other time they must have been different.[46]

---

gest the possibility (so obvious to any Nag-Gnostic) that the reification of oracular powers as the "Bicameral Word Made [Male] Flesh" is a dogmatic cover-up designed to distract from his own admission that oracular powers have been more widespread among women than among males.

Since all women born and bred in the Restored Society that is patriarchy have spent most of our lives in conditions of overt and/or subliminal states of intellectual, emotional, and sensory deprivation, it requires Amazonian Acts of imagination and courage to continue feeling the mute protest, and to attend to the signals of Real Presence. Indeed, many women coming to real consciousness can identify with the experience of Winston as described in *1984*:

He was a lonely ghost uttering a truth that nobody would ever hear.[47]

The truth is that there are millions of women who feel like "lonely ghosts" in the endless "1984" that is phallocracy. Imagining that nobody will ever hear her truth, a woman can feel the elementary absence of Presence and feel helpless. Yet the fact of feeling it is, of course, a signal of potentiality for something more. When this signal is heard, a woman has the chance to begin Realizing/Actualizing her potentiality. Her Realizing Presence radiates to other "lonely ghosts" who recognize their own truth in her expression/expansion. This *Presence of Presence* is increasingly contagious. It is ecstasy. *Ecstasy* is derived from the Greek *existanai*, meaning "to put out of place." Realizing Presence puts/pulls Wild women out of the places/times of absence, releasing our be-ing. Refusing false assumptions, unassumed and unassuming Elemental women are of the Earth, Earthy. Together with winds, seas, trees, sands, fires, rains, thunder, moon, sun, stars, we are Present. Unfathered/Unfettered, we are Sisters and Daughters of the Radiant Array of the Elements.*

PRESENTIATING OUR SELVES: THE COURAGE TO SIN

When Prudish/Shrewish women first uncover our presentient and presentiating powers, our unleashed Sparking, Spinning speech and action may appear to those possessed by restored reason as pixilated, that is, "BEMUSED, under or seeming to be under a magic spell: ENCHANTED, BEWITCHED." In fact, the ontological,

* *Daughter* is the term chosen by scientists to mean "the immediate product of radioactive decay of an element such as uranium; also known as decay product or radioactive decay product." (*McGraw-Hill Dictionary of Scientific and Technical Terms* [New York: McGraw-Hill Publishing Co., 1974, 1981].)

presentiating powers of Elemental women make us BE-MUSED, BE-WITCHED, casters of Archimagical spells from our depths of be-ing. Small wonder that we also appear to be *Pixie-led,* that is "led astray by Pixies" (*O.E.D.*). The term *astray* is derived from a Middle French word (*estraier*) meaning to roam about without a master. The *Pixie-led,* then, would seem to be moving in a promising direction. This insight is confirmed by the following definition of *astray:* "into a wrong or mistaken way of thinking or acting: in or into error: WRONG: away from a proper or desirable course of development." As women roam about without masters, breaking the rules of snools, the statutes of studs, the decrees of drones, the canons of cocks, the precepts of prickers, we are indeed "in error: WRONG." Wandering away from "a proper or desirable course or development," we presentiate our Selves.

Self-presentiating women—being WRONG according to the prevailing assumptions—may be said to Sin. It is pixilating to find that the word *sin* is probably etymologically akin to the Latin *est,* meaning (s)he *is,* and that it is derived from the Indo-European root *es-,* meaning *to be* (*American Heritage Dictionary*). Clearly, our ontological courage, our courage to be, implies the courage to be WRONG. Elemental be-ing is Sinning; it requires the Courage to Sin.

Rather than confessing the creeds of cockocracy, which implies eternal confessions of guilt, Lusty women Sin in the most major way, by be-ing Really Present and presentient. This implies becoming Soothsayers. As Soothsayers we presentiate, making our future *be* present, as we prognosticate, presage, portend. Moreover, as we foreshow the future we are mindful of the past.

The word *sooth* (which means truth)—like the word *sin*—is derived from the Indo-European root *es-.* Ironically, so also is the word *suttee.* As one authority has put it, *suttee* (from the Sanskrit *satī*) means "a true or virtuous wife, a term applied to a widow who immolates herself on the funeral pile of her husband. . . . Sanskrit *satī* is the feminine of *sant:* being, existing, true, right, virtuous; present participle of *as,* to be." [48] Joseph Campbell, then, was etymologically correct when, apparently with no sense of irony, he wrote:

Satī . . . is the female who really *is* something inasmuch as she is truly and properly a player of the female part: she is not only good and true in the ethical sense but true and real ontologically. In her faithful death, she is at one with her own true being.[49]

Nag-Gnostic Soothsayers will not forget this and other massive crimes against female be-ing. The memory is embedded in the history of the very words we use to speak of truth and be-ing.

The Courage to Sin, to be Elemental through and beyond the horrors of The Obscene Society, is precisely about being true and real ontologically, about refusing to be "a player of the [patriarchal] female part." It is about moving away from elementary pseudoreasoning to Elemental reason. To Sin against the society of sado-sublimation is to be intellectual in the most direct and daring way, claiming and trusting the deep correspondence between the structures/processes of one's own mind and the structures/processes of reality. To Sin is to trust intuitions and the reasoning rooted in them. To Sin is to come into the fullness of our powers, confronting now newly understood dimensions of the Battles of Principalities and Powers. To Sin is to move deeper into the Archespheres, overcoming the ghosts of sado-sublimation, Realizing Elemental potency.

CHAPTER FOUR

BEYOND SADO-SUBLIMINATION: REALIZING ELEMENTAL POTENCY

Realize:

"to make real . . . bring into concrete existence: ACCOMPLISH."
"to bring from potentiality into actuality: ACTUALIZE."
"to conceive vividly as real: be fully aware of."

Webster's Third New International Dictionary of the English Language

Real Eyes:

"the Authentic, Elemental, Wild Capacity to Realize." [1]

Websters' First New Intergalactic Wickedary of the English Language

Given the conditions of the Snoolish State, whose subjects are haunted by archetypes (the products of sado-subliming) and blocked by elementary incarnations (the discharges of sado-sublimation), it is inevitable that this artificial atmosphere be filled with subliminal messages intended to incapacitate on deep psychic levels. These messages are designed to prevent women from Realizing our Elemental potency. They are the ghostly products of sado-sublimination.

Since sado-subliminal messages are omnipresent in bore-ocracy, they are at first difficult to see (hear, taste, smell, feel). It is common knowledge that they are all-pervasive in modern advertising.[2] Clearly, such messages permeate patriarchal myth.[3] In yet more subtle ways, sado-sublimination perverts abstract thought, so that this becomes an instrument for causing the thinker to be more and more absent from her Self, consequently castrating her will to use her powers, to act.

Nag-Gnostics must now confront the phenomenon of sado-sublimination as it affects reason. For, moving more deeply into

Archespheres, we become more presentient. Living in the Gnomic Present, we begin to Realize the future, the past. Sinning, Spinning radically, we touch the depths of Elemental reason, desiring to know more.

THE BURIAL OF ELEMENTAL REASON

Among the ancient Greek philosophers the word for deep reason was *logos*. Wanton women wielding this word wrench it from that context, unveiling Elemental reason. Crone-logically it is clear that the breakdown of Elemental reason is connected with the breakdown/cover-up of female Presence. Elemental awareness was still expressed by philosophers in the Middle Ages and faded noticeably in the "renaissance." It is largely absent from modern philosophy.

The dying of consciousness of Elemental reason among professional philosophers, or rather their attempted murder of it, coincided to a rather impressive extent with the European Witchcraze. To the Crone-logical mind it is no mere coincidence that Francis Bacon and René Descartes constructed sterile systems while women burned.

Moreover it is not an accident that philosophy and theology were severed from each other during this age of holocaust.[4] For dismemberment of wisdom logically correlates with the dismemberment of the Goddess, that is ritually carried out in the dismemberment and massacre of women. It is understandable that philosophers wanted to get out from under the "queenship" of theology (i.e., theologians), but much was lost in the process of escape. Obviously I am not proposing a return to the medieval synthesis, which, of course, was itself sadospiritual theory. I am suggesting, however, that that synthesis reflected, dimly and distortedly, an original integrity in questing wisdom—just as Mary partially and distortedly reflected the spark of female Elemental be-ing.

Although the separation of philosophy from theology had obvious positive aspects, it had negative effects which are seldom acknowledged. For one thing, this functioned to "liberate" philosophy from some of the personal intensity of concern which motivated the medieval philosopher-theologians. Implied in this "liberation" is the fact that philosophy was denuded of interest in final causality—a violation comparable to lobotomy.[5]

Another misfortune accompanying the severance of philosophy

from theology was the perishing of philosophical discourse about the "separate intelligences," identified by christian philosophers as angels. Post-medieval Western philosophy nearly abandoned its speculation about the meaning of "pure spirits"—their mode of knowing, their choices, their movement, their mode of duration, their communication. If such issues sound to the reader like appropriate subject matter for fairy tales or for science fiction—alien and perhaps entertaining but "irrelevant"—I suggest that the relevance of "relevance" be reconsidered. Fixation on superficial notions of relevance hinder the philosophical quest, for creativity implies the seeing of connections among seemingly disparate realities. Thus the philosophy of the angels has had power to inspire the philosophical imagination, raising questions about the nature of knowledge, will, change, be-ing in time and space, and intuitive communication.[6]

This removal from the philosophical enterprise of intuitive/imaginative reasoning about angels (which some identify as "Elemental Spirits") is associated with the bore-ocratization of philosophy. It is connected also with the "philosophical" discrediting and erasure of "final causality" (purpose)* and with reduction of the profound meaning of final causality—which I would describe as unfolding of be-ing—to mere reified "goals" and "objectives." The inspiring, moving reality of final causality—the centralizing force/focus within the Self and within all be-ing—is spirit-force. This becomes inaccessible, or "out of sight," when the spiritual/philosophical imagination is dried up and reasoning banalized, routinized, reduced to the elementary realm. Under such conditions, Elemental reason is deeply buried. The sado-subliminal message is that such reason does not exist.

PAUL TILLICH REVISITED, OR, ELEMENTARY, MY DEAR TILLICH

Theologians, who did not exactly lose the final cause but merely mummified it, have never hesitated to point out the limitations of philosophy. The most rigorous, useful, and systematic among these critics was undoubtedly Paul Tillich, who noticed the materialization/fragmentation that prevails in modern philoso-

---

* This concept, together with theorizing about the angels, was relegated to the domain of theology, which was being dethroned from "her" previous role as "queen of the sciences."

phy, attributing this to a split between ontological and technical reason. He writes:

While reason in the sense of Logos determines the ends and only in the second place the means, reason in the technical sense determines the means while accepting the ends from "somewhere else." There is no danger in this situation as long as technical reason is the *companion* of ontological reason and "reasoning" is used to *fulfill the demands* of reason. This situation prevailed in most pre-philosophical as well as philosophical periods of human history, although there always was the threat that "reasoning" might *separate* itself from reason. Since the middle of the nineteenth century this threat has become a dominating reality. The consequence is that the ends are provided by *nonrational forces,* either by positive traditions, or by arbitrary decisions serving the *will to power* [emphases mine].[7]

This passage is a typically Tillichean blend of important insights, confusions, and astonishing subliminal embeds. One would not wish to disagree offhand with the idea that technical reason ("reasoning") should receive its ends from ontological reason. But Tillich's use of language—of symbols—carries the reader to strange conclusions/confusions. Referring to technical reason as the "companion" of ontological reason, he is appalled that the former has separated itself (herself?) from the latter, rather than fulfilling "its" (his?) demands—a situation which it (she?) had threatened to bring about for many centuries. Tillich thus depicts technical reason as a sort of wayward wife who refused to meet the demands of her lord and master and finally not only threatened but actually obtained a divorce—in the middle of the nineteenth century. Now, the mid-nineteenth century would seem a somewhat puzzling time to specify as the date of the divorce. Unless, perhaps, some Crone ventures to point out that this was the moment of cresting of the so-called "first wave" of feminism.*

* Tillich, of course, gives his reasons for his chronology, maintaining that ontological reason "is predominant in the classical tradition from Parmenides to Hegel," while the technical concept of reason "though always present in pre-philosophical and philosophical thought, has become predominant since the breakdown of German classical idealism and in the wake of English empiricism." See *Systematic Theology,* 3 vols. (Chicago: University of Chicago Press, 1951–63), I, 72. In fact, the "split" was already evident after the breakdown of the medieval synthesis and with the rise of nominalism, and it is grotesquely manifested in the writings of Descartes in the early seventeenth century.

I am not saying, of course, that Tillich was *thinking* of any such thing. However, words, sentences, paragraphs *carry* meaning(s). Tillich's use of language conveys that he does not understand reason as having its own integrity and original unity but rather as being a tenuous and unequal union of "companions" in a typical patriarchal marriage, in which the unruly wife/subordinate has a disconcerting ability to disobey and run away. The (probably unintended) subliminal symbolism may at first be difficult to detect—not only because the reader may not be accustomed to look for subliminals, but also because intuition is supposedly associated with women and technology with males.* However, as depicted in a servant role, "technical reason" is feminine. The hidden symbolism is consistent with the usual patriarchal images of battleships, tanks, spacecraft, and other vessels and tools as females who are always threatening to disobey and go berserk.

Tillich thus describes a split of reason into two "halves"—a condition which then continually poses the problem that the subservient half will break away and become the servant of "nonrational forces." He fails in this context to acknowledge reason's essential unity. This bifurcated vision is consistent with other cognitive distortions of the sadostate. In that state, for example, the elements (matter) are unnaturally separated from (Elemental) spirit. Such assumptions of unnatural separations as "natural" constitute the subliminal underpinnings of enforced unnatural combinations (which, naturally, are called "natural"), such as patriarchal marriage, nonbiodegradable earth-destroying chemicals, and, of course, the Assumed Virgin Mother Mary, the dismembered Goddess patched together again. Within such a state of enforced separation and contrived combinations, "technical reason," the functionary concerned with "means," that is, the wife in the saga, of course had to do what she was perceived as threatening to do, that is, flee from her domineering mate, "ontological reason," who provided her with her purposes, ends. One might well wonder what are the "nonrational forces" which Tillich dislikes to see providing technical reason with ends. Does he refer to other male constructs, for example, the demanding agendas of

* "Technical reason" in Tillich's context is not reducible to technological reasoning, but the association is obvious enough.

the technocrats? Or does he somehow vaguely have in mind the most terrifying of "nonrational forces," that is, the Principalities and Powers with which Wild reason and Wild women are connected and which exceed the comprehension of phallocentric rationality?

The limitations of such elementary rationality are unwittingly displayed by Tillich in his definition and explanation of "ontological reason." He states:

Ontological reason can be defined as the structure of the mind which enables it to *grasp and to shape reality* [emphasis mine]. From the time of Parmenides it has been a common assumption of all philosophers that the *logos,* the word which grasps and shapes reality, can do so only because reality itself has a *logos* character. There have been widely differing explanations of the relation between the *logos* structure of the grasping-and-shaping-self and the *logos* structure of the grasped-and-shaped-world. But the necessity of an explanation has been acknowledged almost unanimously.[8]

Tillich here proposes as normative a "grasping-and-shaping-self." He also presents what might be called the "hairy claw" view of ontological reason. While it is not the case that this "common assumption of all philosophers" of patriarchy is expressed so directly by all as by Tillich, Shrewds should perhaps be thankful that he makes this assumption so explicit.* Here indeed is a not entirely subliminal premise of an aggressive/invasive "rationality" of metaphysical proportions. Shrewds also note that in the definition of *ontological reason,* Tillich conveys very little about the contemplative, intuitive, speculative, aesthetic activities of the mind that ineffably escape his "grasp" in this crucial context.

Wild, Elemental reality is absent from this rather lecherous scenario. Indeed, Tillich's tamed "reality" would appear to be hopelessly elementary. Not only this: he actually says that all this grasping and shaping is possible "only because reality itself has a *logos* character." Having just learned what logos "characters" are

---

* Tillich explains that " 'grasping' . . . has the connotation of *penetrating into the depth,* into the essential nature of a thing or an event, of understanding and expressing it" [emphasis mine]. See Paul Tillich, *Systematic Theology,* 3 vols. (Chicago: University of Chicago Press, 1951–63), I, 76.

like, the reader might conclude that "reality" also is obsessively grabby. But no, Tillich is thinking here in terms of bi-polar opposites. Clearly, the character of reality is to-be-grabbed. "Reality" appears to be doomed to the role of recipient of "reason's" unsolicited attentions.

This could be seen as a scenario of "blaming the victim" that is carried to ontological extremes. From this vantage point it is philosophical/theological pornography; it is elementary ontology. The very intelligibility of be-ing is reduced to capacity-to-be-grasped. The secret of phallic philosophy is thus unmasked. Tillich has managed to give the show away.

Indeed, Tillich has accomplished a gargantuan task, one requiring the skills of a philosophical theologian—the reduction of reality to the elementary realm. The Fire of Heraclitus is now reformulated: an impulse to grasp.* In the light of this revelation we can better understand Tillich's views on being, a topic which fascinated him. He proclaims:

Mythology, cosmogony, and metaphysics have asked the question of being both implicitly and explicitly and have tried to answer it. It is the ultimate question, although fundamentally it is the expression of a state of existence rather than a formulated question. Whenever this state is experienced and this question is asked, everything disappears in the abyss of possible nonbeing; even a god would disappear if he were not being-itself.[9]

* The pre-Socratic philosopher Heraclitus thought of reason as a material force akin to Fire. *Logos* for Heraclitus had multifold meanings: thought about the universe, the rational structure of the universe, and the source of this structure. See Michael C. Stokes, "Heraclitus of Ephesus," *The Encyclopedia of Philosophy*, ed. by Paul Edwards, Editor-in-Chief (New York: Macmillan Publishing Co. and the Free Press, 1967), III, 477–81. See C. B. Kerferd, "Logos," *The Encyclopedia of Philosophy*, V, 83–84. Tillich was not unaware of these meanings, of course. Indeed, one would have to say that they are present in his work. My point is that his language-as-symbolic as it is used to explain these concepts carries its own meanings and that this subliminal flow of images "grasps and shapes" the reader's mind on levels of which the reader is not usually aware. My method is to suggest some of these images, making them explicit. This kind of analysis is crucial for Elemental philosophers who recognize the value of the monumental work of such a philosopher/theologian as Tillich and therefore choose to use such work as a springboard for our own original gynocentric thought.

Indeed, everything would "disappear in the abyss" if we were surrounded by a "grasped-and-shaped-world." In such a non-Elemental, artifactual world, we would be constantly in a state of " 'metaphysical shock'—the shock of possible nonbeing." [10] For this is the elementary world of phallic assumptions, of restoration and replacement of Wild reality.

The shock of recognizing this world is the Shock of Sham. Those who adapt to it and pass as "normal" remain trapped in the elementary state. Those who break under its horror are often labeled "schizophrenic." In a journal article published in the 1960s, typical statements of psychiatric patients are cited. For example, one is reported to have said: "It's all a stage production. Everyone is acting and using stage names." Another "spoke of herself as a doll and even moved like a mechanical toy." [11] In the 1980s, in the country which elected Ronald Reagan president, it would seem that the gap between "schizophrenic" and "normal" speech and behavior is becoming less apparent.

Beyond numbed normality and psychotic breakdown there is another option for presentient Prudes. I suggest that this is to presentiate Elemental reason by Realizing its presence. This process is Wildly natural. It moves us further Weirdward.

REALIZING REASON

In the classical philosophical tradition, reason (logos) has multi-dimensional meanings and implications: thought about the universe; the rational structure of the universe, that is, its intelligibility; and the source of this structure. The question of *how* these aspects are related, especially the question of how minds are related to that which they know, or can know, has preoccupied philosophers in the West for thousands of years, and the varying responses to the questions are well known.

The "answer" or approach known as "realism" formerly referred to the doctrine that universals have a real existence outside the mind. According to Platonic realism, this meant that universal ideas exist prior to things. The mind remembers these pre-existent forms (ideas). Memory is stirred by experiences of the material world, which is made up of mere reflections of the ideas. According to Aristotelian realism, universals exist in things (treeness is in the tree). All knowledge comes through the senses, and the intellect attains a knowledge of universals through the process of abstracting these from the "phantasms" perceived through the senses.*

The doctrine of nominalism stands in sharp contrast to classical realism. A common dictionary definition of *nominalism* conveys its deficiencies quite adequately: "a theory . . . that universal terms such as indicate genus or species and all general collective words or terms such as *animal, man, tree, air, city, nation, wagon* have no objective real existence corresponding to them but are mere words, names, or terms or mere vocal utterances and that only particular individual things and events exist." As one author put it, "nominalism empties out the big words." [12] As Orwell has shown, the world of *1984* (which Crones recognize as having been around for a long time) *requires* the destruction of words.

Elemental philosophy is not compatible with nominalism and its claim that only the individual has reality, for this negates participation. Tillich accurately criticizes the nominalist rejection of participation. He writes:

But pure nominalism is untenable. Even the empiricist must acknowledge that everything approachable by knowledge must have the structure of "being knowable." And this structure includes by definition a mutual participation of the knower and the known. Radical nominalism is unable to make the process of knowledge understandable.[13]

I would add that it also renders incomprehensible the sense of Wonderlust, the desire that is Wanderlust, the Journey through

* In modern philosophy, *realism* means that material objects exist externally to us and independently of our sense experience. Modern realism takes a number of conflicting forms, including the new realism, perspective realism, common-sense realism, representative realism, critical realism. See R. J. Hirst, "Realism," *The Encyclopedia of Philosophy*, ed. by Paul Edwards, Editor-in-Chief (New York: Macmillan Publishing Co. and the Free Press, 1967), VII, 77–83. Tillich is probably right in his assessment of the situation when he states: "The word 'realism' means today almost what 'nominalism' meant in the Middle Ages, while the 'realism' of the Middle Ages expresses almost exactly what we call 'idealism' today. It might be suggested that, whenever one speaks of classical realism, one should call it 'mystical realism.' " See Paul Tillich, *Systematic Theology*, 3 vols. (Chicago: University of Chicago Press, 1951–63), I, 178, note. I suggest that it be called *classical realism*, which is what it is.

Archespheres, the ontological bonding that is female friendship, the connection with elements that is at the heart of Gyn/Ecological, Elemental be-ing and thinking.

The negation of any deep ontological Elemental sense of creative participation of the knower and of the known in Be-ing, whether this negation is called "nominalism" or "modern realism" or simply "science," is indeed an emptying out of big—that is, meaning-full—words. It is verbicide/logocide in the fundamental sense that it is an expression of the will to stop reasoning. In this Stopped State words are reified, disconnected things, reproducing themselves endlessly. Their Metaphoric powers, which characterize them as Messengers of Metabeing, are suffocated. They become embodiments of that glut which we recognize as *presence of absence*. They also become vessels of the sado-subliminal messages which massage our minds into deeper and deeper amnesia.

Lusty women Realizing our Presence reclaim the original force of words. For presentiating our Selves requires Self-conscious participation in ontological Elemental reason. By living our Real Presence beyond the confines of the State of Lechery, then, Wonderlusting women Realize reason. This is not simply "taking a philosophical position," such as classical realism (although studying such a "position" can be invigorating and enlightening). Rather, the living of our Real Presence is the *process* of Realizing the meaning that is behind the prevailing meaninglessness by thinking and acting passionately out of Lust for Wild Wisdom. Realizing reason is both dis-covering and participating in the unfolding, the Self-creation, of reason.

Many times, women coming to consciousness of reason that transcends the elementary assumptions introduce discussions of their previous condition with remarks such as: "I just didn't realize . . ." The statements are often more accurate than the speaker realizes. For elementary thinking, feeling, acting does not Realize, that is, actualize understanding which is latent, potential. The speaker is of course also expressing astonishment that what she now sees as self-evident was not previously obvious, but somehow masked. It is important at this point that she know clearly that Realizing reason is not a supernatural revelation, but an Elementally natural process/unfolding that will continue.*

---

* The expression "Realizing reason" is double-edged. It is even multiple-edged. On the one hand, it Names the *act* of Realizing (actualizing) reason. It also Names the *power* which Realizes, that is, reason itself.

The correspondence between her mind and deep reason has always been there. It has not been "there" merely as a thing fits into a place, however.

To understand this dynamic connection, it is helpful to think of the word *correspond,* derived from the Latin *con-,* meaning together, and *respondere,* meaning to answer, which in turn is from *spondere,* meaning to promise. The correspondence between the minds of Musing women and the intelligible structures of reality is rooted in our *promise,* that is, our potential and commitment to evolve, unfold "together," in harmony with each other and with all Elemental reality. This promise is answered/echoed in the promise of others. This is why the experience of Realizing reason, after what seems to have been aeons of amnesia, often feels like coming home.

In the process of Realizing reason, women realize that the restored world is an artificial product resulting from the forced compliance of "reality" to the patriarchal male's perception of and designs upon "reality." [14] This "creativity" of restoration results in the embedding of layers of unreality in minds and over the surfaces of things which, like plastic coatings, insulate/isolate minds from Elemental reality, breaking the threads of connectedness, and requiring attitudes of "grasping-and-shaping." In contrast to sado-pseudocreativity, Realizing reason elicits the natural Wild correspondences among minds and other realities. This Realizing, which is active participation in Wild reality, makes possible the deep connections among Realizing women.

When analyzing conflicts and misunderstandings in women's relationships/friendships with each other, it helps to know that Realizing does not happen "all at once," for Realizing is a verb. No woman is/has completely Realized. So long as the sadostate is supported and legitimated by the (unreal) world-building activities of subliming, sublimation and sublimination, generating the elementary covers/veils that disconnect our minds from Elemental reality, and so long as women's minds/passions are still contaminated/laminated with these coatings, we will continue to be

---

In the second case, "Realizing" functions adjectivally, to describe the power of reason. As a consequence of Realizing her *realizing reason,* a woman participates in the actualization of the structure of the universe, and she participates ever more fully in the source of this structure—Powers of Be-ing.

haunted by mixed messages, false feelings, aphasic namings, apraxic actions. All of these are forms of possession paralyzing the Archimage.* Pure Lust, then, is not a suddenly arrived at state; it is unfolding, questing, Realizing.

Women who are risking Realizing soon realize that this event is not at all a passive reception of a revelation. The latter is inevitably a re-veiling, for active participation is essential to true dis-covering. Realizing is a "creative political ontophany." [15] It is continuing manifestation of be-ing; it is participation in creation, overcoming the reason-blocking elementary constructs, unfolding the potentialities of be-ing.

Women are universally trained not to Realize, especially in those institutions that proclaim that they are offering a "higher education." Andrea Dworkin describes this phenomenon as she experienced it when a student in the sixties at academically prestigious Bennington College (which at that time was still a college for women). She conveys a sense of rage and irony as she recalls that the students did not know they had been "consigned from birth to that living legal and social death called marriage." Moreover:

We imagined, in our ignorance, that we might be novelists and philosophers. . . . We did not know that our professors had a system of beliefs and convictions that designated us as an *inferior gender class,* and that that system of beliefs and convictions was virtually universal —the cherished assumption of most of the writers, philosophers, and historians we were so ardently studying.[16]

Despite the two-decade interval, during which the feminist movement has flourished, the situation described above still pre-

---

* I am *not* saying that when/if the patriarchal sadosociety is exorcised from our existence the mystery of evil will disappear. I am developing the thesis that phallocracy is the most basic, radical, and universal societal manifestation of evil, underlying not only gynocide but also genocide, not only rapism but also racism, not only nuclear and chemical contamination but also spiritual pollution. I am further developing my thesis, first presented in *Beyond God the Father,* that "a declaration of identity beyond the good and evil of patriarchy's world. . . . [is] a massive exorcism. Repudiation of the scapegoat role and the myth of the Fall by the primordial scapegoats may be the dawn of real confrontation with the mystery of evil" ([Boston: Beacon Press, 1973], p. 66).

vails. The "cherished assumptions" of the sixties were subliminal, undermining the unsuspecting students. In the 1980s, despite the large body of feminist writings and the re-emergence of the feminist movement, and despite the presence of a few genuinely feminist women on faculties, the sado-sublimination continues, incorporating into its multiple multifarious messages distorted ideas about feminism—for example, the lie that the goals of the movement have been achieved, and the depiction of feminists of the seventies as bitter, "old" women.

Since the lecherous "cherished assumptions" are subliminal, they constitute an elementary presence of absence, and they are also experienced as absence of Presence. The presence of Mark Twain and the absence of Harriet Beecher Stowe—or again the presence of James Joyce and the absence of Gertrude Stein—in literature courses typify this presence of absence and absence of Presence. So also does the presence of the christian triune god and the absence of the Triple Goddess in religion courses. Since the "inferior gender class" assumptions, or what I call the Touchable Caste assumptions, are subliminal, so also under these conditions female Presence is rendered subliminal. Only the process of Realizing Elemental ontological reason can break through the smog of sado-sublimination, actualizing the natural, Elemental relation between women's minds and the structures of our own reality.

The training of a woman not to Realize begins, of course, many years before she reaches the age when, if she is among the "privileged," she can receive the advanced subliminal indoctrination of a Bennington College, a Vassar College, UCLA, or the University of Notre Dame. From her earliest years, a woman is dependent for elementary information upon the assumers, who engender lack of confidence in her own perceptions. The cliché "Women (or girls) are not logical" is an assumed "truth." When properly programmed, a woman becomes an avid consumer of mediated "knowledge." She becomes herself a propagator of mediated "knowledge," a male-ordered missionary fueled by the zeal that characterizes the "selfless." In short, she becomes a walking, talking subliminal message, cajoling women to accept defeat. Psychically castrated, she is a master-minded medium for male presence of absence. Fortunately, *perfect* programming is rare. There is always the hope that women will Realize. In order to understand this process better, it is helpful to consider the meanings of *potency* and of *act*.

POTENCY AND ACT: REALIZING POTENCY

In Aristotelian and medieval philosophy, *potency* can mean either passive potency, or capacity to receive a perfection (called "act"), that is, capacity to be acted upon, or it can mean active potency, meaning capacity to act. To put it another way, whereas passive potency is a capacity to receive something from something else, active potency is the ability to effect change. It is power.[17] Clearly, phallic lust assigns/confines women to the arena of passive potency, as vessels/vehicles for males, who have reserved what they believe to be active potency for themselves. Moreover, its intent is the castration of women both on the level of passive potency and of active potency.

The reversal involved in the epithet "castrating bitch" has been recognized, at least in its more obvious dimensions, by feminists for years. The physical castration of women has taken place on a vast scale through genital mutilation of millions of women, especially in African countries and through modern gynecology. One of the dictionary definitions of the verb castrate is worth re-viewing: "to deprive of vigor or vitality (intelligence is *castrated*—John Dewey): weaken by removal of the most effective or forceful elements: EMASCULATE (the bill was castrated by removal of the enforcement provisions)." Although *Webster's* does grant (in another definition) that *castrate* can also mean "to deprive of the ovaries" (while ignoring clitoridectomy), it is significant that this definition is confined to the purely physical level. *Webster's* does not connect female physical castration with "to deprive of vigor or vitality," and "weaken by removal of effective or forceful elements." The subliminal message is that vigor, vitality, and effective or forceful elements are "masculine." Thus the very definition functions to castrate the minds of women, who are thus conned once again into a negative self-image, injected with the assumption that effective and forceful elements are not female.

The castration of women's reason is a collective and not merely an individual phenomenon. One definition of the noun *castration* is "a depriving of vigor: WEAKENING (mass persecution of most eminent scientists, a castration of science—A. G. Mazour)."

Never has any dictionary acknowledged and legitimated the fact that the mass persecution of women, for example through the European Witchcraze, Chinese footbinding, American and European gynecology, has been a castration of female reason. For, first of all, these historical facts are not acknowledged as atrocities. Second, it is not admitted that female reason—the minds of women and the memories, ideas, products engendered by our minds—even has an identity, to say nothing of vigor and vitality, that is capable of being castrated. The assumption is that there are no "effective or forceful elements" to be removed.

Moreover, if one substitutes "feminist scholars" for "eminent scientists," the conditions of women's culture can be moved from a subliminal to an overt state in the reader's mind. Thus, we might read *Webster's* chosen example as follows: "mass persecution of most feminist scholars, a castration of women's studies." The first phrase immediately seems absurd, because, unlike the quantity of (male) scientists, the number of feminist scholars has not been allowed to reach "mass" proportions. Indeed the persecution of feminist scholars happens on a level of "Immaculate Conception." It is done to women from earliest infancy, so that girl children's minds are purified of positive conceptions of "feminist" and "female scholar," and certainly of "feminist scholar" before these can be conceived as possible. That is, the persecution/execution takes place on the level of potency/potentiality before this can begin, in most cases, to be actualized. Thus persecution is on the level of passive potency—on the basic level of capacity to receive information/inspiration that would move the female Self to active potency. It is therefore persecution that is difficult to perceive; it is subliminal persecution.

The problems inherent in the expression "castration of women's studies" are less obvious, more subliminal. For many women assume that "women's studies" is a "field" that freely thrives in universities and that is already vigorous, unhindered, strong. If one's analysis is at this stage, it could seem plausible that "women's studies," big and strong, is already "all there," capable of being castrated. However, the fact is that it, too, is often destroyed/persecuted in the stage of early infancy, on the level of passive potency—on the basic level of the students' and teachers' capacity to receive the information and inspiration that would move them to active potency. Thus women's studies, not allowed truly to develop, has become in some situations "immaculately conceived." * Here too, the purification/persecution is difficult to perceive. It is subliminal persecution/castration.

Lusty Searchers should reflect also upon the following definition of *castration:* "the deletion of a part of (a text) especially for purposes of expurgation: *also,* a part deleted." If we apply this definition to the majority of women's texts, we again find that the word *castrate* just barely begins to name the horror of the violence against women's potency. For it is hardly adequate to say that a "part" of the texts of women has been deleted by primal sado-silencing. Nor does the term "deleted" fully describe what has been done. *Delete* means "to reduce to nullity as (a) *archaic:* DESTROY, ANNIHILATE; (b) to reject by physically obscuring (as by blotting out, scratching out, or cutting out) or by excluding or marking for exclusion during further processing." This is indeed a sufficiently powerful word to name some of the everyday atrocities perpetrated against women's writings, and, indeed, against women's active potency in all spheres. However, to be deleted, something has to have some actual existence. It is true that in countless cases the actual texts of women have been deleted, and this has discouraged both the deleted writers and other women, who are then deprived of our tradition, of historical memory, of knowledge that women can and did produce important works. But the *primal* deletion is the blotting out of what might have been, of the texts—philosophical, theological, literary, scientific—that were *not* conceived, composed. It is the cutting out of the potency/capacity to receive inspiration and therefore of the active potency to create.

The purpose of this kind of castration/deletion is named in the

* Clearly, I am not saying that no Women's Studies courses are successful. Some, indeed, are excellent, given the conditions under which they are conceived and taught. I am saying that in a society that castrates female reason in such a primal way, women are impeded from imagining freely what such courses of study could be. Frequently this blunting of imagination is achieved through reducing Women's Studies to courses obsessively fixated upon details of the past, in the name of Academic Credibility, thus serving the interests of bore-ocracy and making feminism seem irrelevant and boring. The challenge facing Wise Women/Prudes who are struggling to create Women's Studies "on the boundary of androcratic academia is to trust our Selves and break the mindbindings that still impede us from Realizing freely our Elemental powers of intellect and imagination.

last part of the definition: "for purposes of expurgation." *Expurgation* means "purification from something morally harmful, offensive, sinful or erroneous." Knowing the intent of patriarchal morality, and being familiar with its strategy of reversal, Nags know that the "morally harmful, offensive, sinful, and erroneous" object of its acts of castration is our biophilic potency.

Phallicism, then, inherently tends to the destruction of Elemental female passive potency—our capacity to receive inspiration, truth from the elements of the natural world, the Wild, to which our Wild reason corresponds. This, obviously, is not the passive false potency of the female vessel who transmits elementary beliefs and norms and who corresponds merely to the stereotypes of the sadosociety. In the case of women confined to the role of "vessel" of male ideas and values, this passivity/receptivity to and carrying on of elementary belief systems is simulated active potency. This simulated active potency can be seen in women writers, teachers, artists, activists, and professionals of all kinds who simply function as conduits for phallic presence of absence. Elemental passive potency, in contrast to this, is receptivity to the Call of the Wild, the Word of the Weird. It is inseparable from Elemental active potency, which is creation in interaction with the Elemental Wild.

Realizing potency, then, is interacting with the Elemental world, and not merely re-acting/re-enacting in the elementary "world." Ontological interacting is participation in Be-ing. Insofar as women's interacting is still contaminated with elementary re-acting/re-flecting, this participation is diluted, weakened. This is not to say that fighting in the Foreground is unnecessary. It is to say that the motivation of such fighting must come from remembering levels that are deeper than the attack itself. It is deep Elemental rootedness/connectedness that wards off the elementary invasions. In order to Realize potency in truly radical participatory ways, then, and to get through and beyond the subliminal sidetracks and set-ups that distract women from Realizing, it is necessary to encounter the meaning of memory, both elementary and Elemental.

POTENCY AND MEMORY

As Louky Bersianik has pointed out, the memory of a woman within patriarchy is such that "she can't see the first in the second." [18] That is to say, she usually does not see the cause of her suffering. She forgets the identity of her torturer—and often the fact that there was/is a torturer—who gave her the problem she now seeks to solve. For example, as Denise Connors has demonstrated, many women cannot remember that physicians have caused the complications, the unnecessary mutilations, and the diseases from which they now seek relief.[19] Women often deeply forget who they were before the destruction inflicted upon them in rapist society and they forget the destruction. This forgetting, interlaced with partial memory, debilitates, and it is rooted in fear.

Clearly, both the forgetting and the memory of atrocities against women function to debilitate, to castrate. The forgetting makes one powerless to develop a liberating analysis. The merely foreground memory, in the context of which a woman forgets the identity of the primary agents of her affliction—remembering only the instruments, such as token torturers—is false because it is partial, because it is out of context, because it is the part taken for the whole. Moreover, it is the kind of partial truth that functions to seal off deep ancestral Memory that liberates.

Similarly, the merely foreground memory of a symbol, in the context of which a woman forgets the deep mythic Background —remembering only the residue—for example the Virgin Mary or the twice-born Athena—is false because it is partial, because it is severed from its roots, because it is the reflection mistaken for the Original. And this is the kind of masked/masking memory that seals off deep ancestral Memory.

Such memories that seal off Memory, however, insofar as they are partially true, can also function as vents through which the Background breathes forth Memory. The destruction of foreground memories, therefore, can be a lethal blow to women, for it closes the vents. As we have seen, this occurred on a massive mythic scale with the protestant obliteration of Mary, the Arch-Image. On an individual level, in this century, this closing of Memory's vents is often achieved through psychotherapy, in the course of which a woman is dis-couraged by agents of the snoolish system to give up her *own* memories, to be falsified/framed by the therapeutic assumers. Women whose memories have thus been destroyed become converted into walking, talking subliminal messages/messengers of the phallocratic belief system—instruments for the concealing of Memory.

In contrast to all of this, there are explosions of foreground/ elementary memories that originate in stirrings of deep, internal potency. This is sometimes experienced as comparable to the eruption of a volcano. Recalling the definition of the word *volcano* can be helpful here: "a vent in the earth's crust from which molten or hot rock and steam issue." Volcanic eruptions and women's deep re-memberings are Elemental, breaking through vents in the crust. Although they may be experienced as sudden, their Elemental force has been brewing in deep, natural cauldrons. All Lusty women are Brewsters, actively potent. One meaning of the verb *brew* is "to bring about (something troublesome or woeful) as if by brewing magical potions or spells (brewing mischief)." The bringing forth of Original Memory by Brewsters is indeed troublesome to the torturers of women. It also *troubles* Brewsters, especially in the sense "to put into confused motion: cause to become turbulent or turbid through moving." For Elemental Memory stirs deep Passion. It is E-motional, generating movement out of the Foreground.

Virginia Woolf knew about E-motional Memory. She wrote:

In certain favorable moods, memories—what one has forgotten— come to the top. . . . Will it not be possible, in time, that some device will be invented by which we can tap them? I see it—the past—as an avenue lying behind; a long ribbon of scenes, emotions. . . . I feel that strong emotion must leave its trace; and it is only a question of discovering how we can get ourselves again attached to it, so that we shall be able to live our lives through from the start.[20]

Other women have had a sense of what Virginia Woolf here describes, have known moments when memories "come to the top." An old Jewish woman, quoted by Barbara Myerhoff, described this experience after participating in a storytelling session:

But finally, this group brought out such beautiful memories, not always so beautiful, but still, all the pictures came up. It touched the layers of the kind that it was on those dead people already. It was laying on them like layers, separate layers of earth, and all of a sudden in this class I feel it coming up like lava. It just melted away the earth from all those people. It melted away, and they became alive. And then to me it looked like they were never dead. . . .

The memories come up in me like lava. So I felt I enriched myself.

And I am hoping maybe I enriched somebody else. All this, it's not only for us. It's for the generations.[21]

Yet in pondering "how we can get ourselves again attached to it" (past strong emotion), many women would empathize with the question posed by Frances Theoret: "How can this (explosion of memories) happen without destroying the woman?" [22] For memories do come in ribbons/chains and, as we have seen, many of these—if a woman allows herself to really feel them—are excruciating. As Muriel Rukeyser has written:

What would happen if one woman told the truth about her life?
The world would split open[23]

Many women are consciously afraid that if they tell themselves the truth about their lives they themselves will split open. Within the sadostate then, elementary memory functions as eraser and censor, preventing deep E-motional Memory from "coming to the top."

In the passage cited above, Virginia Woolf wonders whether it is possible that "some device will be invented by which we can tap them [deep memories]." She is being whimsical, perhaps. She knows very well that her own "device" is writing. The profound importance of writing to Virginia Woolf for "getting ourselves again attached" to what I choose to call E-motional Memory has to be understood in relation to her re-membered experiences of "sudden violent shock." Most of these initially engendered a feeling of powerlessness:

I only know that many of these exceptional moments brought with them a peculiar horror and a physical collapse; they seemed dominant; myself passive.[24]

She explains, however, that this was not always the case, describing her experience of an intuition, a shock, when she suddenly perceived a flower and understood that the flower itself was part of the earth, "and that was the real flower, part earth, part flower." The intuition was expressed in the words "That is the whole." This was a different experience from the others, in which the horror held her powerless, as when she discovered that people hurt each other. In the moment of experiencing the flower she was not powerless, for, as she writes, "I had found a reason."

She goes on to suggest that as one gets older one has a greater power to provide explanations through reason. Virginia Woolf understood that there is a design behind the "cotton wool of everyday life." For her, these "moments of being," as she calls them, or "shocks," were "scaffolding in the background . . . the invisible and silent part of my life as a child." [25]

This Great Shrewd had a particularly acute "shock-receiving capacity," which was essential to her greatness as a writer. Since the way of access to the Background was very explicit for her, she was able to provide passages to deep Memory. It is clear from the sections I have cited that she understood profoundly the experience of powerlessness and the empowerment that comes through reason, through what I am identifying here as Realizing reason—and which is re-membering reason.* Having experienced volcanic explosions, and having learned the connecting power of reason as Memory, she was a Brewster. Needing to know connections, she was a Gnostic Nagster, Nagging her Self, and consequently others toward the knowledge of deep re-membering. Intuitively, she knew that the shocks from the Background which she had felt as a child were ontological. Their Elemental force singled them out as "moments of being . . . embedded in many more moments of non-being." [26] She was a Webster, dis-covering the hidden connections and weaving them into audibility, visibility, with words. She was/is a Muse, singing other women into conscious Memory, a Soothsayer whose creative pursuit of the past overcame impotence and paralysis, actualizing potency. Intuitively she knew that the passive potency to hear/see/receive knowledge of the Background is interconnected with active potency to Name, for "it is only by putting it into words that I make it [reality] whole." [27]

Writing actualizes Memory in an especially potent way. The process of writing, and of seeing/hearing the words come forth on the page, is journeying. The dis-covering of one connection, this lifting it out, lifts out others. A complex tapestry is found, woven. The writer becomes more energized as the process continues, as she seeks, says, and finds more. As Woolf wrote: "The pen gets on the scent." [28]

---

* The expression "re-membering reason"—like "Realizing reason"—is double-edged, multiple-edged.

One might turn into an "objection" the obvious fact that Virginia Woolf was a professional writer, and claim that such a "device" is inaccessible to most women. There can be no question that in addition to courage and genius she had privilege. But the fact is that nearly all women have the potency to "put it into words," in their own unique ways. It is possible to write letters, journals, notes. Women can talk to each other, sharing stories, dis-covering through Spinning conversations, beginning "to put the severed parts together." [29]

To affirm this possibility is not to underestimate the enormous difficulties—the unspeakable oppression—of countless women, especially women of color and all poor women. Alice Walker writes:

How was the creativity of the Black woman kept alive, year after year and century after century, when for most of the years Black people have been in America, it was a punishable crime for a Black person to read or write? And the freedom to paint, to sculpt, to expand the mind with action, did not exist. Consider, if you can bear to imagine it, what might have been the result if singing, too, had been forbidden by law. Listen to the voices of Bessie Smith, Billie Holiday, Nina Simone, Roberta Flack, and Aretha Franklin, among others, and imagine those voices muzzled for life. Then you may begin to comprehend the lives of our "crazy," "Sainted" mothers and grandmothers. The agony of the lives of women who might have been Poets, Novelists, Essayists, and Short Story Writers (over a period of centuries), who died with their real gifts stifled within them. [30]

Knowledge of this horror, rather than stopping the possibility for creativity, must be channeled—together with Unrelenting Rage, into creation *now,* whenever, wherever, this is possible. Gloria Anzaldúa has written of the struggle of women of color to write:

The problems seem insurmountable and they are, but they cease being insurmountable once we make up our mind that whether married or childrened or working outside jobs we are going to make time for the writing.

Forget the room of one's own—write in the kitchen, lock yourself up in the bathroom. Write on the bus or the welfare line, on the job or during meals, between sleeping and waking. I write while sitting on the john. No long stretches at the typewriter unless you're wealthy or have a patron—you may not even own a typewriter. [31]

Women, particularly those who are multiply oppressed, are silenced.[32] The struggle to break the silence can call forth further possibilities. The chains of silencing are broken by continuing acts of creativity, inspired by Pure Lust.

What women find by Naming—through writing, speech, all forms of art—is something like a stream that runs deep within the soul. Its sounds are musical, rhythmic. Significantly, the word *stream* is etymologically connected with *rhythm*. Both are rooted in the Greek *rhein,* meaning "to flow." Underneath the elementary unrhythm of mediated, master-full memories flow rhythms of empowering Memory. One meaning of *rhythm* is "an ordered recurrent alternation of strong and weak elements in the flow of sound and silence in speech." Although women who are Muses for our Selves do not measure "strong" and "weak" elements by the rules of the masters, there is definite Diversity among experiences re-membered, and among Nagsters re-membering. Diversity is essential to proud and positive Potency.

The rhythms of Naming deep Memory are quite unlike the tidy, tedious tick-tock of patriarchal clocks and watches. The rhythms of re-membering are Tidal. They are in harmony with the elements within and around us, and they are expressed in Elemental sounds. The complexity of these rhythms can be intuited when we think of tides. Rachel Carson explains:

The tides present a striking paradox, and the essence of it is this: the force that sets them in motion is cosmic, lying wholly outside the earth and presumably acting impartially on all parts of the globe, but the nature of the tide at any particular place is a local matter, with astonishing differences occurring within a very short geographic distance.[33]

When Muses re-membering enter the rhythms of Tidal Memory we experience a connectedness with the cosmos that had been broken. Our reason/passion connects with the most distant of the stars, yet the astonishing differences within short distances make re-membering difficult. Although Crones do experience synchronicity, there is also the sense of being broken-hearted/broken-souled as we break from the mazes of delusion. As Gnostic Nags break from the stable-world of pseudo-memory, we become Unstabled. This is pixilating at first—the striving for new and ancient equilibrium.

A Nag who races with the rhythms of Tidal Memory is also a

Stiff. One meaning of the noun *stiff* is "a horse not intended to win or certain not to win a race." Stiffs intend and are certain *not* to win in patriarchy's tidy racetracks, for to be *stiff* is to be "characterized by moral courage: FIRM, RESOLUTE," and "characterized by obstinacy: STUBBORN, UNYIELDING," and "characterized by independence or self-esteem: PROUD."

When racing with the rhythms of Tidal Memory, women are focused. *Focus,* of course, means: "a point at which rays (as of light, heat, sound) converge or from which they diverge or appear to diverge." As a verb it means "to bring (as light rays) to a focus: CONCENTRATE." Concentrating, re-membering, women bring light, heat, and sounds together and send them forth again with intensified intent. Empowered by Memory to concentrate, women are enabled to *consent,* which, in an "archaic" sense, means "to be in harmony or concord especially in opinion, statement, or sentiment." It also means "the being of one mind: ACCORD, UNANIMITY." This accord (being of one heart) and unanimity (being of one mind/soul) can be genuine only when Dreadful and Daring Diversity is recognized. When women break into Naming this concord and this difference, the consequence can be a cosmic *concento,* the Crone-logically simultaneous sounding of the tones of a chord.

Certainly this dream of a gynaesthetic concert/concordance often can seem "far out." It is. As Jan Raymond has movingly written:

It is not enough for feminists to dissect the corpse of patriarchal pathologies. Women have not always been for men. We need to know the genealogy of women who did not and who do not exist for men or in pivotal relation to them. And we need to create a vision of the future of Gyn/affection. What women search for can be as important as what we find.[34]

The search itself is part of the process of presentiating our past and future concordance.

When feeling unfocused, out of contact with the rhythms of Tidal Memory, it is important to realize that this Memory *is,* needing only to be Realized. Perhaps we can take heart from Rachel Carson's description of a very small green worm known to marine biologists as *Convoluta roscoffensis,* who lives in the sea sand, rising when the tide has ebbed and sinking into the sand when the tide returns. Sometimes scientists transfer a whole colony of these worms into an aquarium, where there are no tides. Rachel Carson writes:

But twice each day Convoluta rises out of the sand on the bottom of the aquarium, into the light of the sun. And twice each day it sinks again into the sand. Without a brain, or what we would call a memory, or even any very clear perception, Convoluta continues to live out its life in this alien place, remembering, in every fiber of its small green body, the tidal rhythm of the distant sea.[35]

For women, who do have "what we would call a memory," the situation is more complex than that of Convoluta, however. Monique Wittig and Sande Zeig wittily describe the problem of "leaks":

There are leaks comparable to water leaks in the consciousness of every person. Many companion lovers begin to fast when confronted with this drain in their memories, their information, their knowledge. Others take baths of volcanic mud or clay. In vain. "When the memory leaks, it's forever," says an old song from the Concrete Age. There are also leaks in interest, leaks in feelings, leaks in energy, leaks in imagination. There is still another kind of leak called a "galloping leak" which helps one forget all the others.[36]

Lusty women can be glad if there are some "galloping leaks" of elementary/foreground memories, information, interest. The drain of Elemental Memory is something else, however, for it falls, it seems, to an almost inaccessible part of the mind. Yet it *can* be Realized. Our efforts need *not* be "in vain."

Frequently, though, the conditions for this Realization seem to be absent. Virginia Woolf writes:

The past only comes back when the present runs so smoothly that it is like the sliding surface of a deep river. Then one sees through the surface to the depths. . . . But to feel the present sliding over the depths of the past, peace is necessary. The present must be smooth, habitual. For this reason—that it destroys the fullness of life—any break—like that of house moving—causes me extreme distress; it breaks; it shallows; it turns the depth into hard thin splinters.[37]

Many women can read this with a sense of bitterness. For how often, one might ask, do the lives of most women "run so smoothly"? How often is the necessary peace experienced? Women suffer the devastation of constant interruption—doubly, multiply when this is combined with the oppressions of class and race—and always, by reason of sexual caste.[38] Yet the point is to seize the present moment, to turn even the "breaks" into opportunities. Realizing potency requires acknowledging the atrocities, without turning these into excuses. In the cosmic concento, a woman who Names deep Memory—any part of it that she can catch—makes the hope of Memory more accessible to other women, for, as we have seen, memories are connected. A woman who re-members actualizes her own potency, and the active potency of any woman is en-couraging, contagious. This remembering is the most radical, the most necessary activism. In *1984,* Winston believed that he was uttering a truth nobody would ever hear. But:

. . . so long as he uttered it, in some obscure way the continuity was not broken. It was not by making yourself heard but by staying sane that you carried on the human heritage.[39]

Women consenting can sense that be-ing sane *is* making our Selves heard in the only way that matters. Be-ing of sound mind, a woman participates in the flow of sound and silence that is the Tidal Rhythm of Empowering Memory. Actively potent, she makes sense of things, inspiring her sisters to trust their own senses. Putting her memories into words, she Nags others to find and weave their wholeness, to Race with Tidal rhythms and to know in the Gnomic Present—the present that is experienced when one is backed and moved by the past, by E-motional Memory, and therefore presentient. Thus she comes to understand more about principalities and powers.

PRINCIPALITIES AND POWERS: ANGELS OF THE ELEMENTS

I have noted in the Introduction that the apostle Paul, arch-hater of women and of the elements, used Greek terms commonly translated as "principalities" and "powers" to stand for all of the "classes" of angels, or Elemental spirits (*stoicheia*).* That is,

---

* We have seen that *stoicheia* has four basic meanings: (1) the spoken letters of the alphabet; (2) the fire, air, earth, and water of which the world was thought to be constituted; (3) the elements of the uni-

"two of the classes of *stoicheia* are put for the whole array in all its gradations." [40]

Pauline animosity toward these spirits is evident. In the Epistle to the Colossians, for example, we read:

He [Christ] disarmed the principalities and powers and made a public example of them, triumphing over them in him. (Col. 2:15 [R.S.V.])

Principality is a translation of the Greek *arche* (plural: *archai*). Biblical commentators maintain that the plural form, *principalities* (*archai*), when used by Paul refers to the organized cosmological powers of the angels and represents a group of spirits which may interfere with and hinder "salvation in Christ." [41] Nag-Gnostic Searchers note that *archai* would indeed hinder such "salvation," for they are understood to be Elemental, *of this world*.

Moreover, we have seen the meanings of *arche* in Greek philosophy, which include beginning, first principle, cause. It points to transcendence of matter-spirit dualisms, and the word's history allows it to imply original unbrokenness of matter/spirit.

Considering all of these senses of *archai*, Searchers perceive that *principalities*, used in our own Nag-Gnostic context, can have Metaphoric dimensions, conveying ideas/images of actively potent Elemental spirits —*stoicheia* in the sense of spirits/angels ensouling the heavenly bodies and enspiriting fire, air, earth, water, and all Elemental sounds/words. This word, then, can function to Name Elemental dimensions in which Wild women participate.

The word *power* is also important. It is used to translate the Greek *exousia* (plural: *exousiai*), among whose meanings are right, power, liberty, free will, authority, magistrate, abundance. It is derived from a verb meaning to have power or authority. Like principalities, powers represent Elemental forces—actively potent reality that is hard to control—which necrophilic lust attempts to destroy, not merely in the sense of annihilation, but

---

verse, the larger cosmos, including the sun, moon, planets and stars; (4) "the spirits, angels, and demons which are believed to ensoul the heavenly bodies, traverse all space, and inhabit every nook and cranny of earth, particularly tombs, desert places, and demented persons." See Raymond T. Stamm, Exegesis of the Epistle to the Galatians 4:3, in *The Interpreter's Bible*, 12 vols. (New York: Abingdon-Cokesbury Press, 1952–57), X, 521. The fourth meaning is especially relevant here.

in the sense of conversion and oppression without end. The lust for destruction of potent Elemental spirits is blatantly expressed:

Then comes the end, when he [Christ] delivers the kingdom to God the Father after destroying every rule [*arche*] and every authority and power. (1 Cor. 15:24 [R.S.V.])

Of course, the most "loving" form of destruction is conversion. Thus Paul could write:

To me, though I am the very least of all the saints, this grace was given, to preach to the Gentiles the unsearchable riches of Christ, and to make all men see what is the plan of the mystery hidden for ages in God who created all things; that through the church the manifold wisdom of God might now be made known to the principalities and powers in the heavenly places. (Eph. 3:8–10 [R.S.V.])

The lust expressed here is not simply for annihilation but for forcible external "enlightenment" and subjection of the enemy. Such desire is echoed in the first epistle of Peter, which speaks of the resurrection of Christ:

. . . who has gone into heaven and is at the right hand of God, with angels, authorities, and powers subject to him. (1 Pet. 3:22 [R.S.V.])

Such eternal ontological bondage is the doom intended by the sadorulers for all who actively seek the autonomy that is represented by the principalities and powers. It is obvious, then, that strong, threatening, Lusty women, who participate in such a quest, must be assimilated/subordinated.

Such, then, is the godfathers' goal: eternal subjection of the originally autonomous participants in the reality represented by the Elemental spirits—that is, condemnation to eternal living death. The magnitude of this lecherous ambition is mind-boggling. The aim of the apostolic aggressors is the subjection of all speech, of all energy/matter, of the cosmos. Since this aim is not for simple annihilation, but for establishment of the State of the Living Dead, the consequences are predictable: Words are converted into verbiage and speech into logorrhea; vital matter is degraded into nonbiodegradable plastic; and the cosmos becomes a stage for obscene "exploration"—at least to the extent that penile projectiles can penetrate.

The theme of destruction of autonomous strength by conversion is succinctly explained in Orwell's *1984* in the words of the torturer, O'Brien:

We do not destroy the heretic because he resists us; so long as he resists us we never destroy him. We convert him, we capture his inner mind, we reshape him. We burn all evil and all illusion out of him; we bring him over to our side, not in appearance, but genuinely heart and soul. We make him one of ourselves before we kill him.[42]

Such ontological possession is the destiny intended by the phallic lusters for those who participate creatively and autonomously in Be-ing—a Lusty Way of living that is Metaphorically represented by "principalities and powers." As the pauline text summarizes this intent:

And ye are complete in him, which is the head of all principality and power. (Col. 2:10 [K.J.V.])[43]

The Pauls, the O'Briens and other fanatic fans of Big Brother require that all strong, threatening Selves be subsumed under The Head.

Terrified of Elemental sensuality/spirituality, the "inspired" apostle sputtered:

Therefore let no one pass judgment on you in question of food and drink or with regard to a festival or a new moon or a sabbath. . . . Let no one disqualify you, insisting on self-abasement and worship of angels, taking his stand on visions, puffed up without reason by his sensuous mind, and not holding fast to the Head, from whom the whole body, nourished and knit together through its joints and ligaments, grows with a growth that is from God. (Col. 2:16–19 [R.S.V.])

Lusty women, who are a-mazingly aware of the new moon and who have learned to beware of Heads and the growths associated with these, judge our Selves able to judge for ourSelves. Clearly, it is important that we re-member the lore of principalities and powers—of Elemental spirits.

The activities ascribed to principalities and powers are vividly depicted in ancient writings, some of which are referred to by scholars as "Old Testament Apocrypha." One ancient text, the

Book of the Conflict of Adam, after discussing the lowest order
of angels (guardian angels) and the archangels, states:

> The third order is that of the Principalities, and their task is to hie
> themselves to the places where the clouds rise from the ends of the
> earth, according to the word of David, and to cause the rain to de-
> scend from thence upon the earth. All the changes in the air, rain and
> hail and snow and dust-storms and showers of blood are all produced
> by them, and to them also belong the storm-clouds and the lightning.
>   The fourth order is that of the Powers, and their task is the govern-
> ment of all light-giving bodies, such as the sun and the moon and the
> stars.[44]

It is clear that these angels are seen as spirits of the elements.
In other texts, although specific reference is not necessarily made
to principalities and powers, angels are clearly depicted as Elemental spirits. The Book of Enoch depicts angels as having
charge of specific Elemental forms. One sample gives the idea:

> And the spirit of the hoar-frost is his own angel, and the spirit of the
> hail is a good angel. And the spirit of the snow has forsaken his cham-
> bers on account of his strength—there is a special spirit therein, and
> that which ascends from it is like smoke, and its name is frost. . . .
> And when the spirit of the rain goes forth from its chamber, the an-
> gels come and open the chamber and lead it out.[45]

Despite the masculine pronouns and the obscurities, the Elemental role of angels is hardly in doubt. Moreover, in this same work
angels are said to have their own special pathways in heaven
(Enoch 18:5). This will remind Elemental women of the Pixie-
paths of women as Wayward spirits.

In the second chapter of the Book of Jubilees, the Elemental
connections of angels are very explicit. Reference is made to "the
angels of the spirit of fire, and the angels of the spirit of wind, and
the angels of the spirit of the clouds of darkness and of hail and
of hoarfrost, and the angels of the depths and of thunder and of
lightning, and the angels of the spirits of cold and of heat, of
winter and of spring, of autumn and of summer." [46]

The connections of angels with elements in the canonical
books of the Old Testament is significant. Motifs that are common in folklore and fairy tales (Märchen) can be seen to recur
in connection with angels (who are often like fairies or trolls).

These themes are often consistent with the tradition of Elementals as "administrators" of the processes of the elements. For example, the story in Genesis of Jacob wrestling all night with a spiritual being at the ford of Jabbok contains the motif of the traveler who must grapple with the genius of a river or a stream before being able to cross it (Genesis 32:23–32). Again, the story in Judges of the angel who appeared to Manoah and his wife and then disappeared in the flame of a sacrifice conjures the familiar theme of the genie who vanishes in smoke (Judges 13: 20). Such identification of angels with the controlling spirits of natural phenomena is a widespread theme and has parallels in Near Eastern folklore as well as many other traditions around the world.

In the New Testament, the connection of angels with the elements is particularly evident in Revelation. For example:

After this I saw four angels standing at the four corners of the earth, holding back the four winds of the earth, that no wind might blow on earth or sea or against any tree. (Rev. 7:1 [R.S.V.])

Again, in the same work, there are references to "the angel who has power over fire" (14:18) and to "the angel of the water" (16:5) and to "an angel standing in the sun" (19:17). In these instances, angelic spirits leap out from the Background of events and natural phenomena.

Particularly interesting for women Realizing our Background of Elemental potency is an understanding of the widespread—over space and over centuries—presence of the lore of angelic Elemental spirits. Jacob Grimm, among others, shows that the conception of *stoicheia,* which has its origins in remote antiquity, has survived in Europe in the ideas and vocabulary of the common people, often as images of "tutelary deities." [47] The word *tutelary,* as an adjective, means "having the guardianship or charge of protecting a person or a thing: GUARDIAN, PROTECTING (tutelary goddesses)." It is significant that *Webster's* names goddesses as examples of tutelary spirits. Indeed, there is every reason to see connections between *stoicheia* (Elemental spirits) and Goddesses. The Moon Goddess, for example, has been known as the "immortal element." [48]

I suggest that there is a subliminal connection in sadospiritual mythic tradition between the spirits represented by the names *principalities* and *powers*—as signifying the angels of the elements—and the spirits of Elemental, Untamed women. Hostile and hateful intent expressed in violent statements about the former are also directed against the latter. Thus portrayals of Christ as the one who "disarmed the principalities and powers and made a public example of them, triumphing over them in him" (Col. 2:15) can be decoded by Prudes as phallic descriptions of and justifications for male breaking, humiliating, and gloating over vanquished women.

Recognizing this link, we can also see in the "apocryphal" as well as in the biblical passages cited above, subliminal acknowledgment of awesome Elemental powers which are also in Wild women. I have suggested also that there are historical linkages between descriptions of Elemental spirits and tutelary deities, especially Goddesses. Phallic fear of the force represented by Wild women and the forces of Wild nature is embedded in these texts.

PSEUDO-DIVINATION: THE BREAKAGE OF ELEMENTAL CONNECTIONS

Wild, Weird women who sense and act in harmony with Elemental forces are commonly called Witches. Nag-Gnostics know that Witches have always been close to the elements. Witchburners have also known this. The *Malleus Maleficarum,* the textbook of demonology and handbook for Witch prickers published in 1486, contains a chapter entitled "How they Raise and Stir up Hailstorms and Tempests, and Cause Lightning to Blast both Men and Beasts." After a discussion of Aquinas' view that "with God's permission, the devils can disturb the air, raise up winds, and make fire fall from heaven," followed by material from confessions of women accused of Witchcraft, the authors/inquisitors conclude that as disciples of the devils (bad angels) women have such powers:

It has been found that witches have freely confessed that they have done such things, and there are various known instances of it, which could be mentioned, in addition to what has already been said. Therefore it is reasonable to conclude that, just as easily as they raise hailstorms, so can they cause lightning and storms at sea; and so no doubt at all remains on these points.[49]

The purpose of the Witchcraze was to destroy women's connections with the elements and with our Elementally Spirited Selves. Its aim, that is, was to destroy our ontological, Elemental powers. Since they themselves were incapable of being truly Mantic, of soothsaying/divining, the torturers lusted then, as they do now, to blunt and debase these powers. To this endless end, the inquisitors practiced perverted parodies of divination, attempting to draw upon such powers and turn them against their victims.*

Thus they cruelly caricatured *Geomancy,* which refers to the art of divination by means of signs derived from the earth. Professional Witch prickers performed perverse imitations of Geomancy by their obscene explorations of women's bodies, attempting to "divine" whether the object of their prurient interest was indeed a Witch. Matilda Joslyn Gage explains:

It was asserted that all who consorted with devils had some secret mark about them, in some hidden place of their bodies; as the inside of the lip, the hair of the eyebrows, inside of the thigh, the hollow of the arm or still more private parts, from which Satan drew nourishment. This originated a class of men known as "Witch Prickers" who divesting the supposed witch, whether maid, matron, or child, of all clothing minutely examined all parts of her body for the devil's sign.[50]

Since women's bodies are, in patriarchal symbolism, associated closely with the earth, it can be seen that these sadistic operations were subliminal travesties of Geomancy.

Moreover, we have witnessed a continuation of this hideous tradition in more recent times, in the physical "examinations," "exploratory" operations, and experimentation done on women's bodies by male physicians, particularly gynecologists. This prurient objectification is experienced by women with varying degrees of resignation, repugnance, and horror. Alice James expressed her experience in her diary:

---

* It does not matter whether these perverted forms of divination were "consciously" understood by the perverters as twisting of the powers. As in the case of rapists who do not "consciously" understand the mythic/ontological significance of their act of violation, so also with the Witch persecutors the point is that the violent acts were performed knowingly and *do in fact* have deep mythic meaning.

I suppose one has a greater sense of intellectual degradation after an interview with a doctor than from any human experience.[51]

Reading this, "one" knows that "interview" is a euphemism and that Alice James is referring to a female "one," that is, herSelf. Of course, some male patients may experience degradation. As Denise Connors has shown, however:

The role of patient is patterned after the role of woman; hence women patients are doubly cursed.[52]

The Witch prickers parodied *Hydromancy,* which is "divination by means of signs derived from water, its tides and ebbs." This was most obviously accomplished through "ordeal by water," or "swimming." The test required first restraining the accused by tying hands and feet together, often with "the right thumb on the left big toe, so that the witch was 'cross bound.' " [53] Then the accused woman was thrown into deep water, three times if necessary. If she floated she was guilty; if she sank, she was innocent. In the latter instance, she usually drowned, unless her torturers decided to rescue her. Here is a classic manifestation of the doublethink decreed by drones, which we can summarize in the maxim: If you win you lose, and if you lose you lose. The fallacies of their own ill-logic were lost upon the lechers who promoted such perverse divination by water. King James I pompously proclaimed:

So it appears that God hath appointed, for a supernatural sign of the monstrous impiety of witches, that the water shall refuse to receive them in her bosom, that have shaken off them the sacred water of baptism and willfully refused the benefit thereof.[54]

Although water is not commonly used by today's Witch prickers, psychiatric torturers do commonly use the "heads I win, tails you lose" approach in determining mental illness. In his classic comparison of modern psychiatry with Witch-finding, Thomas Szasz remarks that in all of his years in psychiatric work,

. . . I have never known a clinical psychologist to report, on the basis of a projective test, that the subject is a "normal, mentally healthy person." While some witches may have survived dunking, no "madman" survives psychological testing.[55]

On a wider scale, the therapeutic fathers and the women who follow this train of "thought" promote the ideology that views all women as psychologically defective. Since "defective" really means deviant, and since any woman with a spark of autonomy is deviant enough from bore-ocracy's regulations to have "shaken off [some of] the sacred water of [its] baptism" it is impossible to escape from this judgment. The sado-subliminal message of such testing is that "you can't win."

The inquisitors' perversion of *Aeromancy*—divination from the state of the air or from atmospheric substances—can be seen in their enforcement of confession. We have seen that symbolically air is associated with the creative breath of life, and hence speech. Once a woman accused of Witchcraft was in chains, she *had* to confess, for the inquisitors would feel disgraced if they acquitted a woman. The fact that the confession was obtained under torture caused no doubt or distress. In fact, this was considered right and just. The authors of the *Malleus Maleficarum* were indeed just men. They wrote:

Common justice demands that a witch should not be condemned to death unless she is convicted of her own confession.[56]

We have already seen that women under the sadostate are continually confessing guilt and begging forgiveness. Both the inquisitional methods and the confession itself are more subliminal under "liberal" rule. Yet submission to rules of grammar, rules of etiquette, rules of dress, "reasonable" expectations of agreement and approval—all cause a woman to be "convicted of her own confession."

Finally, the Witch killers sadistically mimicked *Pyromancy,* divination by means of fire or flames. Pyromancy has been practiced by women from time immemorial. The significance of fire as source of light and heat and as symbol of energy, passion, courage is deeply experienced by women. The inquisitors' primary and ultimate perversion of Pyromancy was their attempt to consume female potency by a crude and violent form of pyromachy —of fighting with fire. They tried to fight Elemental Female Fire with fire, and thus to put an end to *Pyrosophy,* our Impassioned Wisdom. They attempted to demolish, once and for all, female powers of divination, by burning women alive.

The European Witchcraze did not succeed in this endeavor, and modern methods of burning are used to further the "cause." Under the auspices of the medical establishment, women have been unnecessarily cauterized, subjected to electric shock treatments, irradiated, embedded with electrodes for behavior modification. The burning continues.

The destruction of women's connections with the elements requires also the destruction of the elements themselves. Recognizing, on some level, that threatening Wild women participate in the Elemental powers, the Witch burners have attempted to fix, contaminate, pervert the elements, preventing the possibility of female contact with them and divination by them. As Valerie Solanas stated with reason, "He has made of the world a shitpile." [57] Filling the earth and her waters with chemical pollutants and nuclear weapons/waste, contaminating the air and practicing "weather control," planning nuclear holocaust that will destroy the world with artificial fire, the killer male attempts to fix female Elemental potency forever by interposing his nondisposable self and his nonbiodegradable fabrications between women and the elements. In this divided state, with this plug-ugly obstacle between our Selves and our homeland, the Elemental world, women distrust our senses, our powers. Sado-sublimination is everywhere, massaging our minds with its messages that invite us to sleeping death.

The adequate response to this atrocity happens when women choose deeply to focus our Fire, our Elemental force, the gynergy of spirit/matter which naturally relates to its own kind. In order to do this, we must understand the problems posed by the prickers' perversion of female creative participation in Be-ing—their attack upon our Wild way of be-ing that is Metaphorically represented by "principalities and powers." We must confront their strategy of converting women into possessed principalities and powers, who are delegated to hold down Wild female powers in themselves and in other women—that is, to stop the Race of Women.

BATTLES OF PRINCIPALITIES AND POWERS

Women who are unveiling the Archimage, Realizing active potency, are unleashing Archaic powers. To be actively potent is to Realize/release that which is most Dreadful to the impotent priests, the prurient patriarchs—our participation in Be-ing. This is Dreadful also to women who have not yet Realized their own powers. Since no one has fully Realized her potency, emergence of our own powers is at times terrifying to all women. In this situation, it is predictable that the priestly predators will attempt to use fear-filled women as powers holding down Elemental female powers.

From the evidence I have already presented it is clear that the attempt at taming principalities and powers is not new. In fact, this *is* what the "battle of principalities and powers" is about: taming/draining of Elemental powers and resistance to this destruction by actualizing of powers. We have seen some important expressions of phallic hatred of the reality represented by the "angels of the elements" and the pauline intent that "through the church the manifold wisdom of God might now be made known to the principalities and powers in the heavenly places" (Eph. 3: 8–10). Behind this paternalistic wish to enlighten is the hate-full wish to bring all that is Elemental under subjection to the Big Brother figure, Christ, and to destroy Elemental be-ing.

Nag-Gnostics should bear in mind that within the anti-Elemental christian mythic world of reversals there are "good" angels—those who are subject to Christ—and "bad" ones, those who choose their own natural happiness and pridefully refuse such subjection. The male's fear of the spiritual strength of these "bad" angels who refuse subjection is connected with his own sense of impotence. The following text is revealing:

Finally, be strong in the Lord and in the strength of his might. Put on the whole armour of God, that you may be able to stand against the wiles of the devil. For we are not contending against flesh and blood, but against the principalities, against the powers, against the world rulers of this present darkness, against the spiritual hosts of wickedness in the heavenly places. (Eph. 6:10–12 [R.S.V.])

Obviously the apostolic author protested too much. He certainly felt the need of an armor and was indeed contending against flesh and blood, particularly the flesh and blood of women.

In the development of christian theology of the angels of the Middle Ages the nature of the "sin" of the "bad" angels becomes explicit. Thomas Aquinas writes of the sin of the chief fallen angel:

But he desired resemblance with God in this respect—by desiring, as his last end of beatitude, something which he could attain by the virtue of his own nature, turning his appetite away from supernatural beatitude, which is attained by God's grace. Or, if he desired as his last end that likeness of God which is bestowed by grace, he sought to have it by the power of his own nature; and not from Divine assistance according to God's ordering.[58]

Clearly, this "fallen" angel's problem was that "he" wanted to find happiness commensurate with his own natural ability, rather than remaining an eternal recipient of divine care packages. "He" was proud and independent, valuing "his" own nature—unlike the good apostle Paul, who could only be "strong in the Lord."

The pronouns used to represent the angels, whether "good" or "bad," despite the fact that they were/are considered to be sexless, are always masculine. Since they are believed to be naturally far superior to human beings, the patriarchal mind would find it most unfitting to designate them by the pronouns reserved for the "inferior" sex. It is thought-provoking to experiment with substituting the feminine pronouns for the masculine in the text cited above. The exercise can be even more enlightening if we substitute the word *men* for *God,* since within patriarchy "God" obviously is the projection of men, and signifies Super-Man/Men.* Thus we have:

But she desired resemblance to men in this respect—by desiring as her last end of beatitude, something which she could attain by virtue of her own nature, turning her appetite away from supernatural beatitude, which is attained by men's "grace." Or, if she desired as her last end that likeness of men which is bestowed by "grace," she sought to have it by the power of her own nature, and not from men's assistance according to men's ordering.

Elementally spirited women do not, of course, desire resemblance to men—except in the sense of desiring freedom from the

* The English language is particularly deceptive because it lacks a gender-specific article for "God" (as well as other nouns). Thus the term can appear neutral, and the masculine imagery is pushed to a subliminal level. In German, "God" is "der Gott," and therefore obviously masculine. In French, it is "le Dieu." And so forth. Although a German or a French person may argue the case that "der Gott" or "le Dieu" is a spirit and has no sex, the words themselves are laughing at the speaker, so to speak.

protection racket, the subjection, the artificially imposed dependencies that are inflicted upon women as victims of the sexual caste system. Elemental women want happiness attainable by virtue of our *own* nature, not as a "supernatural" dole, or a handout. "Good angels," however, settle for the protection racket and forgo their independent, Wild natures, their pride.

Keeping in mind the reversals I have discussed and the christian wish to believe that Elemental spirits are safely under subjection to Christ and no longer threatening, it is thought-provoking to read descriptions of principalities and of powers in the *Dictionary of Angels*. Of the former it is said:

The principalities are protectors of religion; they also, as Dionysius declares, "watch over the leaders of people" and presumably inspire them to make right decisions.[59]

Here we are obviously reading about "good," i.e., possessed principalities. One might think of the roles of ministers' wives and of nuns as "protectors of (male) religion," and of the innumerable political wives, mistresses, and secretaries who "watch over the leaders of the people." And, of course, prostituted principalities "inspire them to make the right decisions," that is, they accept the role of "power behind the throne."

In the entry under "Powers," the same author writes:

The principal task of the powers is to see to it that order is imposed on the heavenly pathways. "The powers," says Dionysius, "stop the efforts of demons who would overthrow the world." In Pope Gregory's view, the powers preside over demons.[60]

Here is the heart-rending fact. The prostituted powers have been assigned by the patriarchal "heads" to keep Elementally powerful, Wayward women in line. In other words, the role assigned to "good" patriarchally powerful women (tokens) is to track and confine those who are Realizing our powers. The possessed powers have been trained and delegated to "stop the efforts of demons who would overthrow the world." The "demons" are true Witches, Weirds, who are in touch with the powerful creative Demon/Genius/Muse within.*

* The word *demon* has positive as well as negative meanings. Indeed, the first definition of *demon* given in *Webster's* is "an attendant, ministering, or indwelling power or spirit: DAIMONION, GENIUS." The subject of demons will be pursued at length in Chapter Eight.

Wild women Realize powers that threaten to overthrow the patriarchal world. Not surprisingly, then, possessed powers are delegated to "preside" over such women. The Powers/Demons who will overthrow the patriarchal world, however, are not easily presided over, especially when Wild women are able to divine gynergetic genius.

EXORCISING POSSESSED POWERS

One such Power who divined her genius was Emily Brontë. As Sandra Gilbert and Susan Gubar have shown, Emily Brontë was a "practitioner of mystical politics," and *Wuthering Heights* is a "rebelliously topsy-turvy retelling of Milton's and Western culture's central tale of the fall of woman and her shadow self, Satan." [61] As they point out, she had "a tough, radically political commitment to the belief that the state of being patriarchal Christianity calls 'hell' is eternally, energetically delightful, whereas the state called 'heaven' is rigidly hierarchical, Urizenic, and 'kind' as a poison tree." [62] Emily Brontë understood the mechanisms of reversal that govern sadomyth and sadosociety. In *Wuthering Heights,* Catherine is imprisoned, tamed, and trained by prostituted powers at Thrushcross Grange, which represents patriarchal heaven and the state of grace into which Catherine falls after existing in the truly Wild and Graceful State which christians would call the state of sin. In the heaven of patriarchal society she is reduced to a role, a walking costume. That Wild Genius Emily Brontë comprehended deeply the horror of constriction of female powers to the imposed order of the "heavenly pathways" and described the processes by which this order is established. Moreover, she detected the sado-subliminal politics of patriarchal myth, decoded its messages, and reversed its reversals on the subliminal level itself. In so doing she Realized the potency of her genius and engaged actively, creatively in battles of principalities and powers.

In the tradition of the Brewster(s) Brontë, Virgin Woolf, Webster Gage et al., Wondering Wanton Women are Realizing, releasing Elemental powers. As we do so, we are forced to confront the fact that within phallocracy women are commanded to act as powers who hold down female Elemental powers. We are charged by the bore-ocrats with the responsibility of being our own worst enemies. The precepts of prickers prescribe that we preside over our own genius and that of other women, taming it, keeping it on the heavenly pathways, calling it evil, crushing, tracking, concealing it. We are under orders to rule the "evil spirits," our Selves. This is manifested within the sadosociety everywhere. Mothers have been delegated to maim the genitals of their daughters in Africa and the Arab world, to mentally mutilate their daughters in the United States and generally throughout the world. Women are used in pornography to degrade the image of women. Token women in the patriarchal professions are paid to hold down truly Original female powers, in themselves and others, imposing man-made order on the "heavenly pathways." The impotence of the patriarchs requires that they pervert the powers of women in these ways.

Within the feminist movement, women are obliged to confront this order of demonic Self-destruction, which is destruction of the Positively Demonic Self. Indeed, the pathology/evil is often experienced to an intensified degree within this context. Women becoming aware of the powers/genius within women, and of the threat this poses to the ontologically impotent patriarchs, often believe that danger is posed to themselves by the existence of Deviant/Defiant women who are Naming the enemy more and more clearly, more coherently, more contextually, and more uncompromisingly. Yet the real danger is the Self-censorship which is the mental knee-jerk response to a message subliminally embedded in our psyches by the fixers—the perverted master-minded message that tells us: "Hold Down Female Powers."

To the extent that she has failed to exorcise this power-punishing embedded reflex, a woman—even one who has become associated with feminism—can function as possessed power, censoring the Archimage within her Self, obstructing those more creative and daring than she feels able to be. In this way, women who have identified with feminism in a foreground fashion are delegated—seemingly self-appointed—to kill the Feminist Demons. In the society of sado-sublimination, pseudofeminism is also sadofeminism, the fathers' final solution to the problem of female be-ing.

The adequate response to this travesty is, on one level, simple to Name: it *is feminism*. In the patriarchal world there is an ineffably destructive dislocation of consciousness. As Emily Culpepper has stated, there is a "primal distortion at the heart of consciousness." [63] Since this dislocation depends upon keeping women as the primordial other, the model for all other "others," the transformation must come from women who radically reject this otherness, and who move on to knowing our Selves as truly Other and acting accordingly. Feminism in this radical sense *is* Realizing reason, and it is Realizing Elemental potency.

In this true and radical sense, feminism is a verb; it is female be-ing. Unlike sado-pseudofeminism fabricated by the fathers, which is a thing, a reified state, feminism as Realizing is constant unfolding process. It was/is inevitable that women who conceive of feminism as a thing, a state, would come at some point to believe themselves to have moved "beyond feminism." But if one understands feminism to mean the radical, ontological process of Realizing female Elemental potency, one does not move "beyond" it. One moves with it. *Feminism* is a Name for our moving/movement into Metabeing. Given the conditions of the sado-state, the Moving that is *feminism* requires overcoming the possessed powers—engaging in battles of principalities and powers. This Battling is our great exorcism, and it is also our ecstasy, for it is the claiming of our principalities, the Naming/Actualizing of our powers. That is, it is creation, and it brings us to the entrance of the Realm of Pyrospheres. For Womankind must once again dis-cover Fire.

THE SECOND REALM
PYROSPHERES

CHAPTER FIVE

FOREGROUND TO THE SECOND REALM: PLASTIC AND POTTED PASSIONS AND VIRTUES

Pyrosphere: "a hypothetical spherical zone of molten magma that is held to intervene between the crust of the earth and a solid nucleus and to supply lava to volcanoes."

Webster's Third New International Dictionary of the English Language

Pyrosphere: "A spiraling zone of molten Passions that permits passage between the surfaces of Elemental female be-ing and the inner cauldron/core, and that supplies E-motional energy to Brewsters."

Websters' First New Intergalactic Wickedary of the English Language

The foreground conditions that block the entrance to the Pyrospheres must now be faced, for these are intended to hamper the force of our Furious Fire. The dis-passionate aggressive tactics of phallic lust block ontological Passion and Virtue. This is achieved through religion, science, amusements, all of the professions, especially the therapeutic professions. Just as reason/memory is muted/mediated, so also are passions and virtues. Women Realizing reason need to develop a potent analysis, a vigorous exercise of reason concerning the meaning of passions and virtues.

PASSIONS

The perversion and dulling of women's passions by the fixers/flashers/framers/frauds of fatherland is a tactic accompanying the blocking of reason. I have chosen the word *passion* rather than the more modern term, *emotion,* to Name the movements within the soul that express deep Fire/Desire, as well as the counterfeits and stunted varieties of these. Moreover, I have chosen medieval naming of the passions as a springboard for Elemental Naming of them, for there is a refreshing vigor, clarity, bluntness, and complex simplicity in that analysis that is lacking in contemporary psychobabble. This translucency is helpful for rendering the Background of passions accessible, that is, for the dis-covering of deep Elemental Passion, which I will Name *E-motion.* E-motion designates that Fire which moves women out beyond the Foreground and its fatherly fixes, into Pyrogenetic ecstasy. To provide an aid for Furies unleashing this Fire, I shall outline briefly some aspects of the traditional theory of the passions.

First, passions were understood to be *movements* of a faculty known as the "sensitive appetite," which tends toward the good and shrinks from the evil as perceived by the senses.[1] Essential to this analysis is the idea that passions are *caused* by something that is perceived. They are movements rooted in knowledge and are not static, inexplicable blobs of "feeling."

Second, there are six basic passions, which are said to be movements of the "concupiscible part" of the sensitive appetite. The "concupiscible part" has as its object "sensible good or evil, simply apprehended as such, which causes pleasure or pain."[2] This is the more basic "part" of the sensitive appetite. It is the seat of the most fundamental inclinations "to seek what is suitable, according to the senses, and to fly from what is hurtful."[3] The passions of the concupiscible power are distinguished according to the opposition of good and evil. Thus *love, desire,* and *joy* tend to the good, whereas *hate, aversion,* and *sorrow* tend away from the evil. Love and hate are related as opposites inasmuch as they express the most basic harmony with what is perceived as good for the organism, and the most radical disharmony with that which is perceived as bad for the organism. Desire and aversion are a pair of opposites, since desire is a movement toward the absent good and aversion is a movement away from the absent but impending evil. Joy and sorrow, or sadness, are opposed, since they are responses to the good and the evil that are present.

Third, there are five passions that are said to be movements of the "irascible part" of the sensitive appetite. These are necessary "since the soul must . . . experience difficulty or struggle at times, in acquiring some such good, or in avoiding some such evil." [4] The irascible part has as its objects "good or bad as arduous, through being difficult to obtain or avoid." [5] Thus *hope* and *despair* are passions in opposition to each other, both being concerned with the good that is hard to obtain. As long as this is perceived as possible of attainment, there is a tendency/movement toward it, which is hope. When the good is perceived as too difficult, or impossible to attain, there is a shrinking from it, which is called despair. Similarly, *fear* and *daring* both are concerned with the "arduous" evil. Considered as evil, this has the aspect of something to be shunned and thus elicits fear, "but it also contains a reason for tending to it, as attempting something arduous, whereby to escape being subject to evil; and this tendency is called *daring*." [6] Finally, there is *anger,* which has no contrary passion:

For anger is caused by a difficult evil already present: and when such an evil is present, the appetite must needs either succumb, so that it does not go beyond the limits of sadness, which is a concupiscible passion; or else it has a movement of attack on the hurtful evil, which movement is that of anger. But it cannot have a movement of withdrawal: because the evil is supposed to be already present or past. Thus no passion is contrary to anger according to contrariety of approach and withdrawal.[7]

The medieval scholastic philosophers studied these eleven passions in some detail, as well as combinations and interconnections among them. The stark simplicity combined with logical complexity in their analysis offers the possibility of a fresh beginning, a leap behind and/or ahead of the mire of muddled therapeutic jargon into which nearly all contemporary discussions of "feelings" seem to sink. I am not saying that this analysis can simply be taken as it is and applied to women's situation. But the merit of this analysis is that it has sufficient clarity to make the Naming of agents possible if it is used as a tool by Shrewd women. Indeed, its own inherent logic requires the naming of agents and of objects.

Using this instrument, Pyrognomic thinkers can work to attain/regain Earthy/Elemental wisdom about the passions. At any rate we can aspire to breaking set, time-traveling, and seeking to formulate our own way of understanding the passions that is not tracked and trapped by the limiting parameters of popular and professional psychology. We can aspire, then, to the attainment of our own Pyrosophy—knowledge of the nature and properties of Fire.

Women are held back from the attainment of Pyrosophical wisdom not only by the withholding of information, but also by the stopping and stunting of our passions. We must understand this, for deep E-motion is needed for Realizing reason. Real passions are movements within us, and they move us. They are essential to be-ing as verbs. They are recognizable as having specific causes, or "objects." Thus *love, desire, joy, hate, aversion, sadness* are passions that have nameable causes. So also *hope, despair, fear, daring,* and *anger* are words that can Name true passions. This listing, derived, as we have seen, from medieval philosophy, is accurate enough to initiate an Amazonian exploration of Passion/E-motion, if we hear the words with our "third ear" and see them with our "third eye"—that is, in ways that apply to women and that surpass the intent and comprehension of the philosophers whose texts have incorporated/incarcerated these terms.

In contrast to such truly moving passions, which connect our process with the movements of the Elemental world, there are pseudopassions which are the products of patriarchy, which paralyze women, containing and concealing our Fires, our true desires. I have dis-covered two species of these. To Name the first species of pseudopassion I will coin the expression "plastic passions." The second species will be referred to here as "potted passions."

Plastic Passions

Plastic passions are those blobs in inner space which preoccupy and paralyze their victims—predominantly women—draining our energies, perverting us from the pursuit of Pure Lust. They are unlike real passions, described above, which are movements, verbs, and which are e-motions connecting one's psyche with others and with the external world. In contrast to real passions, plastic passions are free-floating feelings resulting in more and more disconnectedness/fragmentation. Since they are characterized by the lack of specific and nameable causes, or "objects," they must be "dealt with" endlessly in an acontextual way, or within a pseudocontext that is fabricated by the fathers of sadopsychology and other priestly professions.

The plastic passions, moreover, are endless in the sense that they cause those whom they infect/infest to feel deprived of purpose, end, final causality. Whereas genuine passions or e-motions move the woman experiencing them out of the fixed/framed state, plastic passions stop her dead. They function to hide the agents of her oppression/repression. Plastic passions are restored passions, which have been converted from verbs into things. They are thingified, reified passions. Since they have no perceivable causes, they function to serve the mechanisms of "blaming the victim."

The following list Names some of these unmoving, paralyzing feelings: *guilt, anxiety, depression, hostility, bitterness, resentment, frustration, boredom, resignation, fulfillment.* These feelings exist, of course; women do feel them. In this sense they can be called "real." Indeed, plastics exist and we can feel them. However, like plastics, these feelings lack natural Wildness. It is my contention that they are man-made, that they are products of fix-ocracy. I would sustain the thesis that they are sickening substitutes that poison our powers, preventing E-motion. They fail to connect our process with the context of Elemental reality. Those whom they infest can be nervously neurotic, but are hampered from be-ing potently Pyrotic—from burning down the bastions of bore-ocracy, flying free.

Plastic passions, then, have many names. Often, however, they have no name; they are then nameless to the woman who is experiencing them. This namelessness and apparent unnameableness function to prevent women from potently Naming and therefore changing their situation. This situation was acknowledged to some extent in the sixties by Betty Friedan when, in *The Feminine Mystique,* she discussed "the problem that has no name." [8] The housewives she interviewed—and the millions more whom they represented—believed that there must be "something more" to life than the supposedly "fulfilled" lives they were enduring in quiet desperation, but they had no idea what that might be. Instead of being able to move/act purposefully, they could only confusedly feel, and deny, their "nameless" problem floating within.

In the eighties, millions of women are in a similar situation, for the eighties are at least as repressive as the fifties and early sixties. However, there are differences. For now there is a recent tradition of feminist writing and activities—a feminist culture—that is largely, although not entirely, inaccessible to the majority of women in the United States and in other parts of the world. Even the advantage of partial accessibility of this tradition is blunted by the plasticization of the feminist movement, its reification into a "thing" controlled by the media-men and other professionals. The situation might be compared to the propagation of information concerning the need for natural foods, combined with the selling of unnatural foods, labeled "natural."

One consequence of this situation is that many women believe that they have had the "option" of feminism and that they have rejected it with full knowledge and consent. Another consequence is that some have bought the plasticized product, while believing that they have become feminists. In both instances plastic passions are reinforced within the deceived women's psyches. The possibility of Moving is blocked. Yet there are many other women for whom the memory, the hope, and the fact of real movement have not been destroyed, and in subterranean ways this movement has expanded and intensified.

The way out of the plasticization of feminism is identical with escape from possession by plastic passions. For true feminism is movement, just as true passions are movements. The process of Naming is essential to this breakthrough beyond problems that seemingly have no name. Such Naming is basic and at the same time it requires the most subtle and clearheaded analysis of which we are capable. For even women who, having seen through much of the master-minded mediation, continue courageously on the Journey of feminism, often become enmeshed in seemingly unnameable feelings. When one has avoided or managed to get beyond traditional roles and other pitfalls, it can be puzzling to encounter again—though in less familiar forms—the all too familiar internalized demons.

Plastic pseudopassions are the products of patriarchal processing. In the nineteenth century Matilda Joslyn Gage wrote of the "materialization of spiritual truth" by the christian church.[9] Analogous to this is the plasticization (unnatural materialization) of enspiriting passion by patriarchy through *all* of its institutions.

The plastic passions are unnatural knots—snarls—of the spirit. Just as the fathers' lies are mind-bindings, these feelings are will-bindings that twist the movements of women's appetites in upon themselves. Instead of spiraling outward, these snap backward, strangling the victim. Instead of experiencing e-motions that are her living threads of connectedness with external and internal reality, the paralyzed prey is fixed in the Foreground, dis-connected from Elemental movement. She experiences only elementary "emotions," those foreground feelings that she cannot really Name.

It might be objected that I do claim to Name some of the plastic passions in the listing printed above. My point is that these are by their nature, or rather, by their pseudonature, not adequately Nameable by their victim, for the woman possessed by a plastic passion cannot Name its agent or its object. Indeed, it does not have easily identifiable agents or objects, for it is a snarl of petrified passions. It stops the woman from e-motional breathing and ultimately can cause her spiritual and physical death. I am not saying that she cannot use the "right" labels, as labels go. She may say: "I feel depressed . . . anxious . . . frustrated . . . bored . . . ," et cetera. But this is not Naming. For Naming is a verb that evokes and that *is* a process of active Realizing. Since plastic passions are not ontologically/Elementally real, that is, since they are not movements of be-ing, they are not Realizable. Rather, a woman Realizes her true passions that are being choked by these synthetic substitutes, and this process frees her from the lethal fix that is freezing her. The vast difference between E-motion and pseudopassion then becomes tangibly understood.

A woman then recognizes that when she experiences real anger —that is, Rage—at her oppressor/suppressor she is moved to action by her Rage. She sees that in contrast to this, if she is merely frozen in states that can accurately be labeled "hostile," or "bitter," or "resentful," she is not moved to act. She sees also that the agents of snooldom are constantly trying to convert her Rage into plastic by labeling it as "hostility," "bitterness," et cetera. They work to label it out of existence, converting it into these plastic passions by the bad magic of verbigeration. She sees also that these sickening substitutes are blended with anxiety, depression, guilt, frustration. The furthest that she can "move" with this package deal is to resignation. And, as Simone de Beauvoir has written, "there is hardly a sadder virtue than resignation." [10]

I would suggest that there is possibly something sadder, however, that is, "fulfillment." "Fulfillment" is the therapeutized perversion of the passion of joy. A fulfilled woman is one who is filled full. She is a vessel, a stuffed container, her condition being comparable to that of a wild animal that has been shot and stuffed. *Fulfillment* is defined as "the act or process of fulfilling: EXECUTION." It also means "the quality or state of being fulfilled: COMPLETION." A fulfilled woman has been executed and is therefore completed; she is finished. Having spent her life in the fixers', flashers', framers' finishing schools, she has nowhere to go/grow. The image of the fulfilled, finished woman is fixocracy's final solution for the Wanderlusty Webster who pursues her final cause, her own deep purpose.

The full-filled woman cannot live the e-motion of joy, for this means moving. Nor is hers a clear case of sadness, for this also is movement—away from present evil. Rather she is, in fact, depressed—pressed down with the weight of what fills her, kills her. As one woman has remarked, a depressed woman is a perfect tool of the patriarchy. Because of her frustration and low self-image she craves romantic love and marriage, religion, professional help, alcohol and pills, and all kinds of man-made things. She lacks the energy to fight back or to move ahead and has an insatiable need for male approval. She is psychically impotent.

In her novel *The Story of an African Farm,* Olive Schreiner describes this full-filled condition through her character Lyndall:

We [as girls looking in the mirror] see the complexion we were not to spoil, and the white frock, and we look into our own great eyes. Then the curse begins to act on us. It finishes its work when we are grown women, who no more look out wistfully at a more healthy life; we are contented. We fit our sphere as a Chinese woman's foot fits her shoe, exactly, as though God had made both—and yet He knows nothing of either. In some of us the shaping to our end has been quite completed. The parts we are not to use have been quite atrophied, and have even dropped off. [11]

The analysis here of fulfillment/contentment is accurate, and hardly can be written off as applicable only to the nineteenth century. The inadequate alternative to this confined/resigned state is depicted as the passage continues:

But in others, and we are not less to be pitied, they [the parts] have been weakened and left. We wear the bandages, but our limbs have not grown to them; we know that we are compressed, and chafe against them.
But what does it help? A little bitterness, a little longing when we are young, a little futile searching for work, a little passionate striving for room for the exercise of our powers,—and then we go with the drove.[12]

Here Schreiner has summarized what might be called the plastic alternative to full-fillment. While only "bitterness" is named explicitly, also clearly implied are the whole demonic crowd: anxiety, depression, guilt, hostility, resentment, resignation, frustration, boredom, *ad infinitum*. Through Lyndall, however, Schreiner offers a vision of transcendence of the plastic alternatives through passionate analysis and action. This is perceived, though dimly, by her childhood friend Waldo:

Waldo looked in wonder at the little quivering face; it was a glimpse into the world of passion and feeling wholly new to him.[13]

It is a world of passion and feeling hardly new to feminists, for it is the seeing of and through this dilemma of impossible alternatives that *is* the very core of feminist movement. Cutting through both the myth of full-fillment and the plastic alternatives to this is basic work of Labrys-wielding Lusty Movers. The hope of healing lies in the Pyrogenetic Passion of Unfulfilled Women—women who are unexecuted, incomplete, and unfinished. As unfinished women unfulfill ourselves of pseudopassions, we find room of our own—room for movement, for passions that are contagious, that fuel the Fire of other Furies. Such Pyrogenetic, Pyromagnetic politics of passions are essential for passage into Pyrospheres.

In some areas, there appears to have been movement backward among feminists in the eighties. In the mid-seventies at a women's concert the performer's "rap" about alcoholism would have had some power of political analysis. The message would be: "Don't let the man drive you to drink." In the early eighties often this was replaced by therapeutic confessional rap sessions, in which the musician proclaimed: "I have a drinking problem." In these cases, no agent has been Named, and the ultimate in "daring" has been to proclaim oneself sick. Since women have always been discouraged by the fathers into such confessional self-descriptions, which hide the agents/causes of their situation, the predictable response elicited is bonding in victimhood—the glue that holds the victims together being a con-glomerate of plastic passions. This recipe is unlikely to produce Self-identified bonding. Just as Naming passions involves identifying the agent and object of this movement, so also an adequate Naming of feminism requires Naming the stoppers as well as the direction of this movement. All else is therapy, psychobabble, therapy, self-hatred, therapy, futility.

Potted Passions

The sadosociety also produces and reproduces what I shall call potted passions. *Potted* means "preserved in a closed pot, jar, or can." It means "planted or grown in a pot." It also means "made easily comprehensible or superficially attractive by abridgment or glamorization: CANNED." All of these definitions throw light on the potted passions, for these are preserved (mummified), enclosed, abridged, and thus made superficially attractive, glamorized. That is, they are stunted, artificially contained. In a word, they are canned. Consequently, they are twisted and warped versions of genuine passions. Like the nine-inch-high potted bonsai tree that could have grown eighty feet tall,[14] these passions are dwarfed; their roots are shallow. Moreover, since they are contorted, distorted, they bend in unnatural directions, stopping at the wrong objects.

Potted passions, then, are feelings that fragment and distort the psyche, masking Passion, making Pyrognostic Lust incomprehensible. Thus, in the Cockocratic State women are intimidated, tracked, and trained to love, desire, and rejoice in the wrong things, hate, have aversion to, and be sad over the wrong things, hope for and despair over the wrong things, fear and dare the wrong things, be angry over the wrong things. These passions are "real" in a sense (like the bonsai tree or canned orange juice) but they are less than they should be and therefore dysfunctional, potentially deadly (like an extremely low blood count, or hypothyroidism). They are incomplete, and, like lies which are partial truths parading as the whole, they are substitutes for genuine e-motions, deceiving their subjects and those with whom they are connected/disconnected in this deceptive way.

A common example illustrates this point: A woman often is therapeutically directed to express her anger toward her mother for events that transpired several decades ago, when the fact is right now that the sadosociety's plug-uglies and butchers are physically and/or psychically battering her. In some cases, her mother is the man-made target for displaced rage, even many years after her death, and without examination of the social context in which she acted. This canned anger, stunted and molded by the manufacturers of soap operas, "great literature," and therapy, prevents the expansion/expression of accurately directed Pyromantic Rage. The deflected anger never becomes the full-blown Fury that could *move* such a woman to understand her own oppression and that of her mother. Rather, her displaced, potted/rotted anger functions to perpetuate that oppression by contributing to an atmosphere of horizontal hatred and violence among women in which "blaming the victim" is the norm.

Media Potters/Plotters I: Tootsie

Clearly, the plastic and potted passions serve the purposes of the sadosociety, preventing the E-motion which makes possible women's entrance into Pyrospheres. It is hardly surprising, then, that the media-men work feverishly to promote these pseudopassions, injecting them regularly in the name of amusement which a-muses women, killing the passionate powers of Musing Muses.

Such onslaught upon women's psyches in the eighties has been extreme, both in overt and in subliminal forms. The film *Tootsie,* widely praised and viewed by millions in the early eighties, illustrates the phenomenon. It is understandable that men and women have found this film funny—men, because the last laugh is on women; women, because the last laugh is on women. It is an interesting exercise in detection of plastic and potted passions to notice what feelings are elicited in the course of viewing *Tootsie.*

One point that is quite overtly made is simply this: Little Dustin Hoffman, guised as "Dorothy," is better at being a woman than are any of the women in the film. Near the end of the movie, after his maleness has been dis-closed, he tells Julie: "I *am* Dorothy." The message clearly is one of cannibalistic androgynous maleness. Little Dustin, whom Julie had loved but rejected because she believed he was a woman, incorporates the best of womanhood—like Dionysus and Jesus before him.

According to the plot, Dustin could not find work as a male actor but when he dressed up as a woman and applied as "Dorothy" to play a hospital supervisor he was immediately accepted in preference to the real female candidates for the role/job. Dorothy was an instant success, admired by female soap opera fans for "her" courage and feminism, for "being her own person." Unlike the fans of Dorothy within the plot of the film, the actual viewers of *Tootsie* are in on the "feminist heroine's" sexual identity. This means that the movie viewer is invited to swallow the message that a male in drag is better at behaving as a feminist and as a friend than are real women. All of the unmemorable wimpy women in the film illustrate this point.

Of course, any thoughtful moviegoer can reflect upon the fact that "Dorothy" did not have years of feminine conditioning to overcome. Examining the list of plastic passions (to which any Prude can make her own additions), we see that the real females in the film were held back and to some extent paralyzed by lives filled with these pseudofeelings. Having none of this baggage of patriarchal female conditioning to contend with, Dustin/Dorothy Acted like a woman who has Self-respect—except for wearing the absurd drag outfits that fascist fashions require "professional women" to wear and that Dustin, of course, enjoyed. Unless the moviegoer's understanding of this set-up was very explicit, she came away from *Tootsie* filled with fresh subliminal injections of plastic feelings. She was dosed with anxiety, depression, guilt, bitterness, resentment, resignation, frustration over the "fact" that no real woman in the film—meaning no real woman in the world—could "be her own person" so easily and with such instant positive acclaim as could "Dorothy." The female viewer was also dosed with hostility toward the female fuck-ups in the film and with boredom at their insipidity. Together with Dustin/Dorothy, she could hardly help feeling frustration at their lack of authentic anger and their resignation to being mauled over by such lecherous creeps as the actor who played "doctor" on the TV show. Moreover, even if the female amusement-seeker watching *Tootsie* was able to carry through with a clear analysis on a cerebral level of just what the film was doing to her, *Tootsie* had/has negative power, since images have a life of their own—a mind-massaging capacity that defies reason.

A big serving of potted passions was also on the menu for *Tootsie* tasters. Women were invited to admire Dustin/Dorothy's "daring," which was false because there was no genuine fear to overcome. The film was a travesty and rip-off of female friendship, and the "lesbian" scene in which "Dorothy's" attempt to kiss Julie was met with Julie's aversion/disgust was a mindtwister. When Julie admits with self-loathing/hatred that "those [lesbian] instincts" are also in her and is answered by Dustin that "those instincts are natural," the audience is supposed to get the message that Julie's attraction to "Dorothy" is really based on the fact that on some (subliminal) level she perceives that she/he is male and that only heterosexuality is "natural." Thus before they can find free expression, lesbian love, desire, joy are negated/potted/converted into heterosexist hate, aversion, sorrow concerning lesbian instincts. The false hope for finding a man-who-incorporates-all-that-is-good-about-women-and-more is generated, and despair over the possibility of recognition/legitimation of woman-woman love is inculcated. Moreover, the female viewer's anger at this a-musing atrocity is mitigated by the "knowledge" that the whole thing is meant to be harmless entertainment and that criticism such as the one just presented proves that the critic lacks a "sense of humor." Can't she take a jock/joke?

Such a potpourri of plastic and potted feelings is a sample of the "prolefeed" described in *1984* as "the rubbishy entertainment and spurious news which the Party handed out to the masses." [15] The target "proles" are women. The intended result is prostitution of our passions, vitiation of our virtues, stealing of our Fire.

Media Potters/Plotters II: "News" Reports

In the early vacuous eighties, the decade of archetypal re-turns, the plotters/potters of *Time* crudely and emphatically enforced the trend of embedding pseudopassions. The theme of woman-as-baby-machine was the cover story of their February 22, 1982, issue. In keeping with the extreme paucity of women's faces on the covers of *Time*—its deliberate erasure of strong, creative women—was its cover photo emphasizing the belly of "expectant actress Jaclyn Smith." This picture, together with the slick pictures inside of prominently pregnant celebrities and the "news" story of "The New Baby Bloom," was obviously not news but rather propaganda intended to function as self-fulfilling prophecy. Full-fillment was crassly peddled in this piece, where the pitch was made for "career women" over thirty who wonder "Is this all there is?" Preying upon frustration and anxiety, the *Time*-men whispered that more and more career women "are choosing pregnancy before the clock strikes 12." [16]

Wedded to the archetypal baby machine is her alleged opposite, the archetypal whore. The embedding of the same plastic and potted feelings is a necessary strategy for the entrapment of women into both molds. As Kathleen Barry has shown, procurers of prostitutes use "love" to entrap their victims:

Procurers who employ the strategies of befriending or love and romance use both tactics together. They may begin by befriending a forlorn runaway and then calculate a romantic connection. . . . A procurer's goal is to find naive, needy teenage girls or young women, con them into dependency, season them to fear and submission, and turn them out into prostitution.[17]

The play upon the feeling of "love" is crucial. Barry explains:

Affection and love-making are meant to hook a woman, make her dependent emotionally and psychologically. Meanwhile she is thinking in terms of a mutually developing relationship.[18]

The eliciting of potted love is essential in the making of a whore by the pimp, the archetypal professional. Potted love, fostered/ festered by the myth of "romance," short-circuits the power of Pure Lust. When women trapped in the Foreground are still caught in the role of whore, they are infested/infected with the poison of pimps, smothered by potted needs for potted love. The fear that prostitutes feel for their pimps, who commonly beat and rape them, and who sometimes murder them, is real enough. For women whose prostitution/sexual slavery is less visible, more subliminal, fear is often potted, since the objects of realistic fear, the agents of violence, are less visible and are denied. The knowledge that is denied to and by women is the knowledge of uncontrollable male violence, physical and psychic, which is omnipresent and can surface at any moment. Given this ignorance, which is in part caused by the terror of knowledge itself, aborted terror is often converted into fear of the wrong things, for example, of not finding a husband or of losing an abusive one. It is converted into all of the plastic passions, most notably into anxiety, depression, and resignation. Moreover, it pots the other passions.

Sometimes women's passions are so potted that there appears to be an abyss of Self-lessness where passionate be-ing should be. This vacuum is illustrated in some of the statements of political wives such as Nancy Reagan, who vacuously stated in an interview:

Integrity has always been important to me because I know my husband means what he says and says what he means.[19]

This incapacity for anything other than indirect, vicarious feelings, flaunted before women as normal, as American as apple pie, and even ideal, is one of several plastic options.

Another sort of model is Helen Gurley Brown, who, unlike the political wives, is ambitious for her own career and can even name herself as subject of some sort of passion. Significantly, Brown has named fear as a motivating force in her life:

My ambitions are steeped in fear, anxiety. I'm afraid the hobgoblins will get me.[20]

And again in the same interview:

I told you, fear energizes me. Fear is part of the challenge of life, of living.

Although Helen Gurley Brown speaks of the "challenge of life," her ambitions seem securely fixed in the Foreground. Any Hag who even casually peruses *Cosmopolitan* and/or Brown's 1982 best seller, *Having It All,* can recognize the all-pervasive plasticity of her views and advice.[21]

In contrast to this sort of personal ambition that lacks woman-identified consciousness but also lacks overt malice toward women, there is the phenomenon of Athenic women who view women and nature with rancor and hatred. Phyllis Schlafly excels in this perversion. Since she is a stereotypic twice-born Athena who fights for men and apparently loathes women, it is not astonishing that "while women's issues have given her fame, defense issues have her heart." [22] The "women's issues" she defends are of course basically undermining of female independence and hope. As Andrea Dworkin suggests, "she seems to be able to manipulate the fears of women without experiencing them." [23] The "defense issues" are, of course, the proliferation of nuclear weapons and of the military-industrial complex. Years ago Schlafly made it known that she would like to be Secretary of Defense, and she has been cited as calling the nuclear bomb "a marvelous gift that was given to our country by a wise God." [24] As a sort of female Doctor Strangelove, Schlafly illustrates a consistency of pathology, combining machine-like callousness toward women with the same sort of indifference to all of Elemental nature and to all of life, except in fetal form.*

Women are constantly invited to betray their own sex as the price for advancement in a career—the object of their potted desires. Female physicians are often used in this way. When the news of "toxic shock syndrome" associated with the use of tampons hit the papers, spokeswomen represented the position of the tampon manufacturers, functioning to contain/pot women's fears. A female epidemiologist from the Centers for Disease Control in Atlanta was cited in the *New York Times*:

Because we expect only a small number of women to get the disease, we are suggesting that women not discontinue tampon use unless they have the toxic shock syndrome already. [25]

The "smallness" of the number—hardly relevant to the individual women poisoned—seems to justify everything, including the physician's lethal detachment and the apparent smallness of her moral capacity.

The pimping of women is not limited to the medical profession. One example from the early eighties cited by the media potters

---

* As a fan of nuclear technology, Schlafly could hardly be called a true friend of fetal life either. Even without nuclear holocaust, which means the end of all life, there is the fact of lethal radioactive contamination of the environment which is already having damaging effects upon future offspring, which is cumulative and irreversible, and which will increase immeasurably to the extent that Schlafly's views prevail.

of the *New York Times* occurred in an article about a four-day D. H. Lawrence festival honoring that misogynist:

Prof. Evelyn Hinz attempted to rescue Lawrence's work from the charge of misogynism that has recently plagued it. Professor Hinz, in a re-visionist paper, asserted that Lawrence did not despise women, but rather venerated them. It was agreed by all sides in the discussion that the fact that Lawrence used to beat his wife, Frieda, had nothing to do with the case, she was a singularly difficult woman.[26]

Indeed, the media-men use women from all "fields" in such contexts to such an extent that the phenomenon becomes almost invisible because omnipresent.

Emotional de-tachment from the plight of women on the part of women trying to attain recognition from the masters sometimes reaches such an extent that a woman claims the role of pimp for herself. Again, this attitude is promoted in the media. It is summarized in a *New York Times* article on women making it in the corporate world, in which a female vice-president-division-head of Chemical Bank is quoted as saying:

The key to success is to sell yourself. Be creative, make decisions, take chances, know you are marketable and walk out if things get too rough.[27]

Particularly mystifying is the mixture of daringly good advice—"be creative, make decisions, take chances"—with the counsel to "sell yourself." The statement aptly exemplifies the state of real but potted/stunted daring.

At the other end of the plastic/potted spectrum is the omnipresent masochistic model. The promotion of such figures as Mother Teresa by the media feeds the embedded guilt and self-hatred of women who feel that they cannot "live up" to such standards of self-sacrifice. This promotion/injection of pathology is reflected in the rash of self-flagellating "letters to the editor" which follows each time Mother Teresa and her views are featured. When, in December 1979, she was awarded the Nobel Peace Prize, she was reported to have condemned abortion as "the great destroyer of man in the world today." In an article in the *Boston Globe* entitled "Mother Teresa Hits Abortion," she is quoted as saying:

"To me, the nations which have legalized abortion, they are the poorest nations. They are afraid of little ones, they are afraid of the unborn child. And the child must die because they don't want to feed one more child, to educate one more child. So the child must die." [28]

The point here is not to question Mother Teresa's good intentions but to see how her well-meaning but inherently woman-destroying simple views are massively used against women, eliciting not only guilt but also despair that there might be another way of be-ing. Thus the publicly legitimated alternatives seem to be the pseudoself-serving, woman-betraying politics of a Schlafly on the one hand, and the self-sacrificing, unconsciously woman-betraying beliefs of a Mother Teresa on the other.

The media-featured stories succeed in making the self-sacrificing option less unattractive than the deeply hateful model of Schlafly et al. Typical of this tactic is the 1980 *Boston Globe* front-page story entitled "For Her, Happiness Is 11 Handicapped Kids," in which the mother of fourteen, eleven of whom are handicapped, is quoted as saying that although she is always tired she is so happy "that sometimes I feel guilty about it." [29] Indeed, in the paternally potted world, no degree of self-sacrifice is enough to erase female "guilt." In fact, the equation runs as follows: The more self-sacrifice, the more "happiness," and therefore the more "guilt." The extent of the emotional crippling of women by the incessant propaganda of prickery is incalculable.

It is not my intent to "attack" any of the women whose beliefs and politics are used in this way to serve the master-minded media. In fact, they have been converted into attackers of their Selves. My intent is to Name the foreground fixing of female Passion, the forces at work to freeze our Fire. For these mutilating messages infect *all* women, killing the possibility of Elemental E-motion.

Guilt, Betrayal, Unrealistic Expectations

The psychic dislocation which is at the very core of patriarchal consciousness is a dislocation of the passions as well as the thinking of all women insofar as we are still caught in the Foreground. Our purging of these poisoned feelings is a process that has to be lived through, and the living is not possible without Naming/Realizing.

Of all the damaging and continually embedded pseudopassions, the most poisonous probably is guilt. This—which spawns anxiety and falsely focused fear—is at the core of the undermining of feminist E-motion, of Pure Lust. It is at the source of the unspeakable betrayals and abandonments that women have endured from each other, and I suggest that it is also at the root of the unreasonable expectations which women sometimes have of each other, once feminist awareness has become somewhat accessible.

The betrayals, always deeply shocking, usually are not perceived as such by the betrayer. She, too, is struggling with seemingly unnameable emotions—at any rate they are inadequately named passions that block insight. If she is therapeutized, the chances are slim that she has escaped the victim-blaming psychobabble and the self-fixated solipsism of endless "dealing" that is part of the therapeutic syndrome. In any case, I suggest that when the phenomenon experienced as betrayal occurs, a woman look at the array of plastic and potted passions. It may help also to consider the word *betray*. One meaning is "to lead astray and abandon (a girl or woman): SEDUCE." It also means "to deliver into the hands of an enemy by treachery or fraud in violation of trust."

A woman who has been betrayed by another woman has been led astray and then abandoned. This implies that she had some sort of expectations of the other, the betrayer. The expectations may have been reasonable or they may have been utterly unrealistic. The phenomenon of real betrayal, the violation of reasonable expectations, as well as the phenomenon of unreal expectations are both rooted in embedded guilt.

Within a feminist context, women who really do betray other women, particularly when this involves delivery into the hands of an enemy by treachery, are acting out of false loyalties inculcated by patriarchy. Women succumb to such false loyalties that involve treachery largely out of fear and anxiety, of course. However, the power of such fears to twist a woman against her own kind comes from some place other than a realistic assessment of patriarchal retaliation for loyalty to women. It comes, I suggest, from the bottomless pit of man-made guilt for her very be-ing, which, so long as it infests a woman's psyche, prohibits her from deep and sustained loyalty to other women. The knee-jerk response to a push of what may be called her "guilt-button" is betrayal of the friend or comrade of the "guilty" woman to the "party"—whether this be the male Right or the male Left, and whether the Party representative pushing the button and demanding betrayal be male or female.

Unrealistic expectations, which result in feelings of having been betrayed or abandoned, are also traceable to man-made guilt in women. For the low degree and even the absence of Self-esteem—an absence which is women's "birthwrong" within the sado-society—is the socially inherited consequence of the "original sin" of having been born female. This patriarchally made pathology is dis-placement of responsibility for one's Self-esteem onto others. Unless she is able to be her own Source of Self-esteem, having high expectations of her Self, a woman is a bottomless pit of need, inviting, producing abandonment by other women, who cannot bear this intolerable burden. This exaggeration of expectations is sometimes heightened by feminist awareness at first, when unrealistic hopes are unleashed and projected onto feminists. Then sisterhood becomes a horrifying reversal of itself and a perfect set-up for justifying horizontal violence.

In an earlier chapter I maintained that women, in order to move, have to develop the Courage to Sin, burning away false guilt. At this point Furious women need to elaborate further upon this concept, and develop an analysis of the Courage to Sin Originally, that is, the Courage to commit an Original Sin. The Pyrogenetic Mover/Luster has to shed her inherited guilt attendant upon the "original sin" of being female—the guilt with which she has been cursed by priesthoods of cockocracy. Together with snool-imposed guilt she needs to shed the other demonic pseudopassions. This act of shedding/purging is an Original Sin, a Sinning/Spinning forth of a woman's own Originality. It is Pyrogenesis, the birthing/flaming of Female Fire. In order to arm our Selves to bring this about, Prudes must consider the meaning of Virtue.

VIRTUE

Not only passions but also virtues are counterfeited/plasticized and potted in the fatherland. I have chosen the Aristotelian/medieval naming and analysis of the virtues as a springboard for Naming Elemental Pyromantic Virtues. As with the passions, so also with the virtues the classical analysis has refreshing clarity and complex simplicity that can be helpful to Prudish Pyrographers burning through jockocratic "ethical" jargon. For this reason I will present briefly some aspects of that tradition's philosophy of virtues.

First, a virtue is understood to be a good operative habit that exists in a power of the soul. A virtue can reside in the intellect, in the will, or in the irascible or the concupiscible part of the sensitive appetite.[30] The virtues of the speculative intellect are wisdom, science, and understanding. There are two other intellectual virtues, art and prudence, which are in the practical intellect.[31] The chief "moral virtues" are justice, which is in the will, courage or fortitude, which is in the irascible power, and temperance, which is in the concupiscible power. These three, together with prudence, which is defined as "right reason about things to be done," are called "cardinal virtues." In addition to the chief "moral virtues" there are clusters of subordinate virtues, or "parts," connected with each. For example, according to Aquinas, virtues connected with fortitude are magnanimity, magnificence, patience, and perseverance.* [32]

Second, prudence and the moral virtues are connected in an organic way. Thus it is impossible to have moral virtues without also having prudence, since moral virtue requires good judgment in order to be virtue at all. One cannot act justly, for example, without the exercise of "right reason." Moreover, it is impossible to be prudent without possessing moral virtues, since reason about our actions is distorted by bad habits. One cannot act prudently, for example, if swayed by intemperance.[33]

Third, according to this philosophical tradition, moral virtues are deeply connected with the passions. Virtues are not identical with passions, however, for virtues are habits, not movements. They are "principles of movements."[34] The moral virtues, especially those "residing" in the concupiscible and irascible powers, "order" specific passions. For example, the virtue of courage especially and directly orders the passions of fear and daring. If

---

* For medieval theologians, in addition to the intellectual and moral virtues, which they studied and named in accordance with the classical philosophical tradition, there were three "theological virtues," faith, hope, and charity. These virtues were considered to be of supreme importance, supernaturally infused together with sanctifying grace, and absolutely necessary for salvation. As we shall see in transversing Pyrospheres, these concepts can also be used as springboards.

fear repeatedly controls one's actions, the vice of cowardice replaces the virtue of courage. If the passion of daring continually takes over, and is not "ordered" by the virtues of courage and prudence, the vice of rashness replaces the habit of courage. Clearly, a whole constellation of passions is connected with any moral virtue. Courage, for instance, is connected with love, desire, and hope, as well as hate, aversion, and despair. In order to act courageously, one must fight off unreasonable despair, although it might be reasonable to despair over certain things (for example, becoming wealthy), while hoping for better things.

Fourth, according to this tradition, prudence and the moral virtues are always striving for the mean between extremes. The mean, however, is not exactly in "the middle." Aristotle explained:

> To the mean in some cases the deficiency, in some the excess, is more opposed; e.g., it is not rashness, which is an excess, but cowardice, which is a deficiency, that is more opposed to courage, and not insensibility, which is a deficiency, but self-indulgence, which is an excess, that is more opposed to temperance.[35]

As we have seen in examining the traditional naming of passions, this tradition can provide elements useful for the sharpening of Labryses. Women thus sharpening become Shrewds, seeking the meanings of Pyromantic Virtues, discarding the masters' immoral morality, be-ing extreme.

Pseudovirtues

In the sadoworld, in which reason is un-Realized and passions plasticized, it is inevitable that the naming of virtues is vitiated, so that these are combined to form an ideology that legitimates the servitude of women. It is not only that the "names" (nouns) to designate virtues are in themselves "incorrect"; rather, the problem consists primarily in the use of these words for naming/describing the wrong actions. Thus acts performed out of fear are honored and called "prudent." Likewise, petitioning and gratitude for the slightest relief from oppression and degradation—begging for crumbs—is considered an aggressive sense of justice. Self-destructive acts performed by women are so consistently praised as "courageous" (often *by* women) that the reality of this virtue is almost totally obscured. "Temperance" is identified with compliant obedience to male-made rules for sexual behavior of "good" women. Of course, compliant obedience to male rules for the sexual behavior of "bad" women is labeled "intemperance." Typically neither the virtue nor the vice has anything to do with Elemental, Pyromantic Virtue and Vice. Indeed, these virtues and their "opposing" vices can aptly be called virile virtues and vices, for all are vitiating the vitality of Virgins, Viragos. As we have seen in the case of pseudopassions, pseudovirtues fall into two categories, or species. To Name the first species of pseudovirtue I am employing the expression "plastic virtues." The second species will be designated "potted virtues."

Pseudoprudence versus Pyrometric Prudence

Within the litany of plastic virile virtues, plastic "prudence" is a euphemism for craven cowardice, pusillanimity. It is a spiritually mercantile habit. The dictionary conveys this plasticity aptly. *Prudence* is said to mean "providence in the use of resources: ECONOMY, FRUGALITY (wealth due to prudence during prosperous times)" and "attentiveness to possible hazard or disadvantage: CIRCUMSPECTION, CAUTION (prudence not to go . . . unescorted —W. A. Swanberg) (conservative from prudence—T. S. Eliot)." In phallocentric lore it is feminine. William Blake blatantly summarizes the reversals implied in "prudence":

Prudence is a rich, ugly old maid courted by Incapacity.[36]

Spiritually rich, Ugly Old Maids, that is, Spinsters/Prudes, are enabled to ask questions that can crack these stereotypes. For example: *Whose* incapacity/impotence is threatened by Prudes? *Whose* courtship is rejected because of his radical incapacity? *Whose* rancor inspires the epithet "ugly old maid" which is so universally applied to Spinning Spinsters?

Plug-ugly pundits have accurately described the prevailing plastic "prudence." Mark Twain wrote:

It is by the goodness of God that in our country we have those three unspeakably precious things: freedom of speech, freedom of conscience, and the prudence never to practice either of them.[37]

The moral turpitude wittily identified here is more ponderously expressed by others, for example, the eighteenth century British statesman and orator Edmund Burke, who intoned the faith of the fathers:

All government, indeed every human benefit and enjoyment, every virtue and every prudent act, is founded on compromise and barter.[38]

While this does express the prevailing morality, it hardly describes Passionate, Pyromantic Prudence.

We have seen something of the condition of plastic prudence. The other form of pseudoprudence—potted prudence—is, like potted passion, stunted, enclosed, abridged, made superficially attractive. This exists when a woman's passions are potted. Thus a female executive, academic, politician who is possessed by potted desire (ambition) and controlled by potted fears (what will people think?) may transcend mere mercantile/plastic prudence, and yet she lacks the Fire of Pyrometric Practical Wisdom.

In the course of transversing Pyrospheres, Prudes/Shrewds will dis-cover and study our own Prudence, which, unlike the paternal, virile variety, is informed by deep Passion. Pyromantic Prudence reflects the situation of Pyrogenetic women. Unlike virile virtue, which consists in choosing the mean between "extremes," our Prudence reflects both our experience and our movement, which are Extreme. Both our exorcism and our ecstasy demand passionate choices that are Extreme. The Practical Wisdom that is our Prudence is Pyrosophy. Our judgments are Pyrometric, and they are steps in unfolding our skills in Pyrometry.

Certainly, Prudes, informed by our own Extreme Prudence, do strive to dis-cover the Pyrometric measure in Virtue—according to our own measurements. Thus a Prude would choose courageous acts that transcend the vices of cowardice and rashness. However, our Prudently chosen Courage, informed by Dreadful Daring, is very close to rashness, and *is* rash in the sense of "full of life and vigor: ENERGETIC," but not in the sense of "acting, done, or expressed with undue haste or disregard for consequences." Prudes carefully consider the consequences of our acts, and then act, Ragingly, Wildly.

The Task of Unmasking "Moral" Pseudovirtues

Of all the "moral virtues," none is more pompously advocated in platitudes and ponderous tomes than "justice." Yet the very idea that there could be justice within patriarchal society, sustained by phallic myths and ideologies, is a logical absurdity. In this asymmetric system there is oppression of women—and of all others who are treated *like women* by powerful males, such as Third World people and all poor people—and there is privilege. For some women there can be derivative privilege by reason of association with certain males, particularly if these women are upper or at least middle class, white, and Western, but this dependent and derivative status has nothing to do with justice.

The "justice" of the fathers' Foreground is false, elementary, plastic. This is not to say that women should not seek "equal pay" or the "Equal Rights Amendment." It is to say that one should not be misled by such misnomers. To believe that such changes will bring about real "equality," while failing to understand the need for almost ineffable changes at the very heart of consciousness, is to settle for potted "justice." Knowing that there will never be "equal rights" or full "civil rights" within a patriarchy, but that there can be some relief of oppression and improvement of some conditions, Nagsters righteously Nag for such political changes in the Foreground. As Nag-Gnostics, however, we know that our empowering and moving are essentially in the deeper Realms and that our real Journey is Weirdward.

Pyrognostic seekers seek *beyond* justice for Nemesis. This Goddess of Retribution is to be sought in Pyrospheres. Although she is commonly associated with revenge, Pyrologians passionately understand that her most gratifying acts are the rewarding of those who ardently seek her. Nemesis as divine vengeance has often been envisioned by pyrophobic male mythographers as a visitation in the form of Elemental phenomena. Nemesis as *rewarding* power is known to be Extremely Elemental by Pyrosophic women, whose quest for Nemesis within the Pyrospheres is passionate, virtuous.

Plastic "courage," also called "fortitude," is omnipresent in snooldom. It is thought-kindling to discover that in classical christian theology one of the principal acts of fortitude was believed to be martyrdom.[39] This is indeed the principal act required of women. It is ironic that the word *martyr* is etymologically associated with the Latin *memor,* meaning mindful, remembering. For the martyrdom of women issues in the fabrication of foreground memories that block out deep Memory. *Martyrdom,* which is "the suffering of death on account of adherence to one's religious faith or to any cause," has been the programmed punishment for Witches, who are faithful to the cause of women. The martyrdom/massacre of Witches (which happens in all places and times of patriarchy) wipes out Archaic Memory by wiping out women, and by manufacturing terror. The consequent fabricated foreground memories set the stage for the martyrdom of women in the usual sense of christian martyrdom—masochistic Self-sacrifice. In this second kind of martyrdom, women are complicit in their own Self-sacrifice for "causes" that are not our own, having become fixed with false loyalties to sado-pseudoreligions and other institutions that erase women and all of the Wild.

The plastic courage manifested in masochistic acts of martyrdom fixes women in a Static State, which is the State of Martyrdom. Within this State women are offered various models of suicide—the slow passive longsuffering forms being the most popular. There is also what I would call the "Athenic" form of plastic courage, the ultimate expression of which also is masochism/martyrdom. The twice-born Athena fighting the battles of the fathers and sons, lacks loyalty to her sisters. In this role, she is a practitioner and model of masochistic "courage," for her deep Self-interest is denied, defeated—often with the deluded belief that she is acting out of "enlightened self-interest." She is, in fact, acting for the interests of the foreground/fictional self, and she furthers/fosters this fiction. As fictional fighter, counterfeit Amazon, she dis-courages women into masochistic martyrdom in servitude to the sadostate. More deceptive than the overtly Self-sacrificing woman, she practices the sadosoldier's "virtue," willingly accepting the death of her Self in a battle that is not for her own cause, voluntarily serving in an army that intends the destruction of her Self, for that Self is the Ancient Enemy of the Lecherous State.

In addition to these plastic simulations of courage there are potted varieties of this virtue. Thus the courage to earn a degree, to become a good athlete, to succeed in a job, even to confront an "authority," all can be admirable and important, but if such acts of courage are a-contextual, that is, based on the belief that such mettle is enough, or as far as it is necessary to go, they remain acts of potted courage, stunted, enclosed, superficially attractive, and certain to be glamorized by the godfathers. A woman who is "outstanding" in specific achievements that require some daring but who fails to threaten the establishment serves the deceivers well.

Perhaps the most sophisticated form of potted courage is that promoted as existential courage, whether this is encapsulated within a christian theological context or within an atheistic philosophical perspective. Theologian Paul Tillich, for example, maintains that "the courage to be" transcends the fortitude which is concerned only with specific fears, and that it confronts existential anxiety of nonbeing.[40] However, patriarchal theological/philosophical analysis of anxiety has no way to Name adequately the specific structures of "nonbeing"—mythic, ideological, or societal. It therefore cannot fully Name the way past these, which is the Elemental Realizing of participation in Metabeing. In other words, patriarchally named existential courage is described as "affirming being over against nonbeing," and this is all it can do. It can only affirm one reified opposite over against another, but it cannot re-member the metapatriarchal Elemental intuition of be-ing. Thus the nebulous nothingness called "nonbeing" looms larger than life.

Elsewhere I have discussed the Courage to See, recognizing that the unseeing—indeed eyeless—existential courage of Tillich is also I-less for women.[41] In now Naming the Courage to Sin Originally, I mean to Name not only the daring defiance of Deviant women, but also our Pyro-ontological burning/be-ing—our Meta-Wise Wondering, Spiraling Starchase.

The third moral virtue of the Foreground is temperance—a notoriously tedious virtue. Like prudence (and unlike courage and justice) it is especially associated with women's behavior. One is conditioned to think of the man-made caricatures of the Women's Christian Temperance Union, for example, and of timid and/or fiercely fanatic but always grim insistence upon moderation, restraint, and self-control. Temperance is defined as "habitual moderation in the indulgence of the appetites or passions." In medieval christian doctrine temperance as a special and distinct virtue is concerned specifically with moderation of certain pleasures of touch. Clearly, or rather, unclearly, women are considered to be inherently intemperate in the sexual sphere, invariably erring either by "excess" (the whore) or by "defect" (the frigid woman, the old maid).

The problem for Pyrognostics is not simply with the classical abstract definitions themselves of temperance, for there is in fact a moderation and restraint of sexual impulses that is necessary for psychic balance and clarity of mind. The problem is that the rules of "moderation and restraint" are externally manufactured and imposed; they are male-made and, to use Jan Raymond's term, "hetero-relational." As applied to female sexuality, patriarchal "temperance" is a man-made, plastic virtue, for it implicitly imposes hetero-relational rules and standards, implying that heterosexuality is itself the norm. For example, this plastic temperance rears its ugly head when a woman desires that her friendship with another woman include sexual expression of affection but blocks this expression solely because she has accepted the bore-ocratic belief that this is morally wrong.

Potted temperance can also occur among lesbians insofar as hetero-relational "values" and norms are allowed to pot, abridge, mummify, enclose, superficially glamorize women's relationships with each other. An obvious manifestation of this would be restricting the meaning of affection and/or commitment to the realm of sex only, or even primarily, and then imposing "rules" and "roles" within this a-contextual, fetishistic, canned category.

In order to practice Pyrosophic Temperance, then, Shrewd Prudes break out of the context of male morality. Wild Temperance is Salamandrous—"living as it were in fire: fiery, hot, passionate" (*O.E.D.*). The radiant luster of Salamandrous Temperance is evoked by such Sister-Words as *temper, distemper,* and *distemperance*. This evocation will be heard/seen in Chapter Seven.

SURPASSING PSEUDOVIRTUE: ENTERING PYROSPHERES

Moving out of this fracturing/fragmenting Foreground into Pyrospheres is fueled by distemperate re-Naming/re-Claiming of passions and virtues. Since virtues, including the vicious pseudovirtues, are habits, Un-naming of foreground virtues necessitates breaking old habits, that is, the changing of behavior patterns formed through repeated acts. Naming forth Pyrosophic Virtues requires performing radically different acts which drive out the pseudopassions and pseudovirtues embedded in our psyches by the rulers of snoolish society and by the tokens/tools of snools.

Escaping from the Foreground into the Pyrospheres requires

eruptions of Prudish Passion and of Volcanic Virtue. This is at first difficult, since, as we have seen, plug-uglies have plugged themselves into women and nature, draining energy, closing female Elemental circuits, sapping the flow of gynergetic currents. But Brewsters should bear in mind another definition of *plug:* "the filling of the conduit leading to a volcanic vent." Discussing these natural plugs, experts in volcanology explain:

. . . in dormant volcanoes the solid plug may overlie a still-fluid column of magma. The explosions that mark the resumption of activity at such volcanoes commonly throw out numerous fragments of the solid plug.[42]

Volcanic Furies fuming over frustrations in the State of Fixation throw out fragments of our own natural spiritual "plugs," i.e., restraints, so that through such carefully timed Self-release the unnatural embeds can be expelled, in "explosions that mark the resumption of activity" that is Wild and Archaic. Venting Elemental E-motion, Pyrophiles connect with our sisters the Earth, Air, and Water, as well as with Fire. Viragos vent rage, sadness, aversion, hate, love, desire, fear, daring, despair, hope, joy. It may be that volcanic "plugs" have been necessary formations of women's auras, as well as of the Earth, that they have been natural Pyrometric instruments of Gnomic timing, enabling women to hold back the molten rock, the steam and ashes of our passions for the right moments of be-ing. In this case, not only explosions of E-motion but also withdrawals are expressions of Volcanic Wisdom.

An important project for Prudes, demanding Shrewish Shrewdness, is learning to distinguish between embedded unnatural plugs and our own Self-produced, Gnomic plugs. While the former keep women tame and tidy, enslaved to the schedules of snooldom, the latter are implements of our own devising—habits of restraint required for our practice of Tidal timing, which pulses in harmony with cosmic rhythms that are not perceptible to botchers and bores, to the bosses of bore-ocracy. This naturally attuned timing is essential for breaking past the Foreground of Pyrospheres, releasing imprisoned passions and confined virtues.

Gnomic knowledge of Pyromancy, of Divination through Passion, can be recalled. Those who are Divining through impassioned knowing become skilled in Pyrometry, the measurement of high temperatures. In Pyrognostic, Pyrognomic lore, these "temperatures" refer to degrees of gynergetic Fire, which vary under different sets of conditions. Accurate assessment of temperatures is necessary for Elemental timing of Volcanic eruptions. Pyrometry pertains to the Elemental Volcanology of Viragos. Simply stated, it is an E-motional acquired wisdom, helping us to judge when to act.

As Viragos/Brewsters stir the cauldrons of passions in preparation for breaking through the Foreground and clearing channels into Pyrospheres, it is predictable that jocks and bores as well as all the other demons of snooldom will accelerate their attacks, explaining that Viragos have missed "the thrust of the argument." Viragos do not stop to explain that we have successfully *dodged* this thrust. Increasingly the "geniuses" of jockdom jab and stab, prick and push, snook and snoop, hack and lunge, snitch and twitch, fabricating a world of Pure Thrust.[43] Incessantly twitching, they try to block Witching, all in the name of their lecherous, treacherous goal/goad, their god/rod. Theirs is the state of dis-passion, the sphere of intercepted Fire.

Moving through this Foreground into Fireground, Furies fight fixers with the Fire of our Passion and enter the Realm of Pyrospheres. Prancing into this Realm, Pyromantic Prudes unlock our treasures of Elemental E-motion, burning through the taboos that have kept us entombed as the touchable caste. Focusing our Fury, we join the Raging Race. Raging, Racing, we take on the task of Pyrognomic Naming of Virtues. Thus lighting, igniting the Fires of Impassioned Virtues, we sear, scorch, singe, char, burn away the demonic tidy ties that hold us down in the Domesticated State, releasing our own Daimons/Muses/Tidal Forces of Creation.

Thus released, Musing Maenads mutually agree to be MAD and consequently enjoy/employ our freedom to dis-cover Elemental, Female Fire. Volcanic powers are unplugged, venting Earth's Fury and ours, hurling forth Life-lust, like lava, reviving the wasteland, the World.

CHAPTER SIX

ELEMENTAL E-MOTION: FROM TOUCHABLE CASTE TO RAGING RACE

M.A.D.:	*Mutual Assured Destruction:* "A concept of reciprocal deterrence which rests on the ability of the two nuclear superpowers to inflict unacceptable damage on one another after surviving a nuclear first strike."
	A Glossary of Arms Control Terms, Prepared by the Arms Control Association
M.A.D.:	*Mutual Assured Deduction:* "A concept of Self-deduction/separation from the State of Boredom, which rests upon the ability of two or more enraged Female Powers to refuse further damage to our Selves and Sisters, after surviving innumerable phallic touches and strikes."
	Websters' First New Intergalactic Wickedary of the English Language

In order to understand and accomplish releasement of Elemental passions we must continue to be aware/beware of the conditions of the Boring State. One meaning of the verb *bore,* of course, is to penetrate or drill. Furies need only reflect upon the monotony of drills—school drills, military drills—to forge an analysis of the tactics of bore-ocracy. It may be helpful to recall fire drills, which give the illusion of relief from other drills, but are in fact more of the same. This severe limitation of experience and of expectations, relieved only by other forms of the same limitations, is standard bore-ocratic procedure.

One result of this procedure is total mediation of experience, causing extreme sensory deprivation. Jerry Mander offers a graphic description of his experience of the Deprived State that is "normal":

Leaning on the deck rail, it struck me that there was a film between me and all of that. I could "see" the spectacular views. . . . But the experience stopped at my eyes. I couldn't let it inside me. I felt nothing. Something had gone wrong with me. I remembered childhood moments when the mere sight of the sky or grass or trees would send waves of physical pleasure through me. Yet now on this deck, I felt dead. I had the impulse to repeat a phrase that was popular among friends of mine, "Nature is boring." What was terrifying even then was that I knew the problem was me, not nature. . . . Through mere lack of exposure and practice, I'd lost the ability to feel it, tune into it, or care about it.[1]

Clearly, the problem is not "mere lack of exposure and practice," as Mander himself demonstrates. There is, as he shows, a manipulative and deadening technology that reinforces Boredom. Mander specifically focuses upon television, which, for reasons demonstrated in his book, "is inherently boring." [2] The horror of the phenomenon lies in the fact that this inherently boring medium, which has only minimal content and which cannot convey/transmit the auras of living creatures, keeps viewers hooked and fixated. Mander quotes a friend's reactions:

"It's the most curious thing; when I watch television I'm bored and yet fixated at the same time. I hate what I'm watching and I feel deeply disinterested but I keep watching anyway." [3]

The hypnotic-addictive quality of television keeps the bored viewer fixated. This is achievable in part because of the unsatisfying artificial environment in which contemporary "civilized" people are imprisoned and which keeps the prisoners starved for excitement. In addition, this state of bored fixation is carefully cultivated by the technological fixers through technical tricks which keep the viewer unaware of the boredom. Conditioned to such vacuous "fast action" on the screen, to artificial stimulation, the victim is fixed in a state in which "life becomes boring, and television interesting." [4]

Television is just one technological instrument of the State of Boredom. The conditions in which it thrives and festers have existed for a very long time. Within Western culture this Boring

State has been symbolically ruled by a god who is said to be immutable, which is to say, boring. Another of the divine attributes, according to classical christian theology, is omnipotence. The hidden signification of this attribute also is "boring," for in the State of Reversal the all-potent father is the empty boast of impotent prickers, who must bore and goad to sustain this image of god (themselves), as the eternally erect rod, the Pure Act.

The society erected and sustained by worshippers of the goad-god is boring in many ways. The tedium of most work/jobs is well known: the architecture and furnishings as well as the pre-scribed roles in a modern office building exemplify this horror. Study, which should mean the excited pursuit of Wonderlust, is also made boring, as anyone should know who ever went to school. Consequently, conversations are boring. So-called escapes from tedium are also made boring, for example, travel. Certainly, genuine Journeying is adventurous, filled with surprises. In place of this, however, the Boring State offers guided tours and package vacations as extensions of tedious work and study. Alternatively, there are electronic "amusements" close to home. One major result is imposed passivity (which can take the form of hyper-"activity"). In reality there is narrowing of experience and blocking of creativity. Those who are bored, especially if they don't even know that this is the case, are penetrated and filled with alien and alienating images and impulses that paralyze.

Since connecting with nature, with Elemental be-ing, requires active participation, the sensory deprivation and the anti-creative imposed passivity of the State of Boredom, makes nature—the Wild—seem "boring." Images of the Wild are reduced to flattened foreground perceptions and women's impulses to Wander-lust and Wonderlust are stifled. This means that our auras or force-fields are stunted and dimmed, for auras are expanded essentially through acts of creation. Spiritually weakened and withered by bore-ocracy's infliction of passivity, women suffer from anxiety and depression and look to bores for relief and fulfillment. The nineteenth century writer Lilian Bell, wrote wittily of bores:

Women are too tender-hearted. A woman cannot bear to hurt a man's feelings by letting him know that he is killing her by his stupidity. And even if she did, in the noble spirit of altruism, rather than selfishness, the next woman, with one reproachful glance at her, would pick up the mutilated remains of the man's vanity and apply the splints of her respectful attention, and the balm of her admiration, partly to add a new scalp to her belt, and partly to show off the unamiability of her sister woman.

So it is of no use to kick against the pricks. Bores are in this world for a purpose—to chasten the proud spirit of women, who otherwise might become too indolent and ease-loving to be of any use—and they are here to stay. We have no conscience concerning women bores. We escape from them ruthlessly. And, perhaps, because women are quicker to take a hint is the reason there are fewer of them. It is only the men who are left helpless in their ignorance, because no woman has the courage to tell them.[5]

Lilian Bell's humorous description rings bells of recognition in the mind of the reader who has understood Boredom. Although Bell does not analyze *why* "women are too tender-hearted," or *why* "no woman has the courage to tell them," Websters are able to weave this missing context of feminist analysis into visibility. We see that the Self-defeating forms of tender-heartedness and lack of courage with which patriarchal women are afflicted arise from man-made fears that are converted into guilt, anxiety, and depression. We also see that the way out of this state is expansion of gynergy, which happens through ever new and varied acts of creation. But the natural impulse to such expansion is precisely what is blocked by the anxieties engendered in the State of Boredom. Instead of creating powerfully, women often adapt/shrink our creative powers to the depressing task of pleasing those who are boring us to death.

In this state of anxiety, of course, a woman cannot let herself know the deeper causes of this unjust situation. Thus her ways of trying to solve her problems are often dysfunctional. Feminist musician Willie Tyson, in her song "The Ballad of Merciful Mary," expresses awareness of one such dysfunctional attempt to set things right:

> To seek justice from those who put me there
> Has been my most foolish mistake.[6]

And women mistakenly seek more than justice from those who have "put us there." Patriarchal women pathetically seek love, joy, and, most tragically, happiness from the manufacturers of Boredom. Since genuine happiness is *not* simply a static state, but activity by which we expand our creative powers, the embedded idea that this could be achieved by sacrifice of Self-identified creativity is a cruel joke. Subliminal awareness of this jockocratic joke paralyzes women, who know that something is terribly wrong but still cannot focus upon it.

The need for an outlet for held-down fear and rage as well as displaced hope drives many women into fanatic devotion to male ideologies. In Orwell's *1984* Winston observes this behavior (but without assessing its sources):

He disliked nearly all women, especially the young and pretty ones. It was always the women, and above all the young ones, who were the most bigoted adherents of the Party, the swallowers of slogans, the amateur spies and nosers-out of unorthodoxy.[7]

Indeed, women often correspond to this description and subscribe to the prevailing orthodoxies. What Orwell fails to allow his central character, Winston, to observe, however, is the *cause* of this bigotry: the fact of women's oppression as a caste, their need for relief from anxiety and for channels for hate and rage. The most essential point—one that is entirely overlooked in *1984*—is the fact that women are terrified and tricked into becoming first and foremost swallowers of *woman-hating* slogans, and amateur spies and nosers-out of unorthodox ideas and activities that threaten patriarchy.

Women's lived experience of this fact of horizontal violence among women drives many to bed and board with bores, and—as general rule of conduct—to prefer the shelter and safety offered by snoolish "protectors" rather than face the dangers inherent in the choice to struggle for the cause of women, which is the cause of one's Self. This latter choice involves a living hope of breaking away from the State of Boredom. It also involves facing the conditions imposed within the Lecherous State.

Under these conditions women, animals, plants, and all of the elements are subjected to the tyranny of the Boring, that is, to the drilling, penetrating, invading touches of Boredom's privileged prickers. Under these conditions women and nature are cast as the touchable caste, vulnerable to vulgar and sublime pricking, prying, plugging, sniffing, snooking, snooping, snuffing by snools of all professions and persuasions. Pyrosophical purging of this caste system, then, is essential for Pyromancy. Women must allow our Selves to *know* how it is that we have been so lecherously touched.

THE TOUCHABLE CASTE

I have carefully chosen the word *caste* to name the framed condition of women. In *Beyond God the Father* I described this phenomenon:

This planetary sexual caste system involves birth-ascribed hierarchically ordered groups whose members have unequal access to goods, services, and prestige and to physical and mental well-being. Clearly I am not using the term *caste* in its most rigid sense, which would apply only to Brahmanic Indian society. . . .

It may be that the psychological root of selective nit-picking about the use of the term *caste* to describe women's situation is a desire *not* to be open to the insights made available by this comparison.[8]

One of the most important characteristics of caste systems is that they are extremely difficult, though not impossible, to change. In other words, caste systems are rigid, like plaster casts. Moreover, women are cast into fixed roles within the sexual caste system. Escape from these requires that we cast our Selves outward, inward, Weirdward, into other dimensions, refusing castration.

It is instructive to consider the roots of the word *caste*. It is derived from the Portuguese *casta,* meaning race, breed, lineage. This is traced to the Latin *castus,* meaning pure, chaste. Women are doomed by the patriarchs to be confined to the caste/breed/race of creatures who are "chaste" by male-ordered standards. While on the surface, "chaste" would appear to mean *untouchable* rather than *touchable,* in fact, phallic femininity, the norm imposed upon the caste of women (and all of nature), means precisely that members of this caste are touchable by those who are in possession of a penis. If there is an apparent dichotomy between touchable and untouchable this has to do only with property disputes among men—that is, this opposition is merely about which women can be touched by which men, and in which ways. The point is that all women in patriarchy are touchable by males and have no acknowledged right to refuse this role, for this is *the* role of women and nature within the phallocratic caste system. Female "chastity" within this system *is* acceptance of one's touchable essence, of one's duty to submit to the touches of men on all levels—physical, emotional, intellectual, spiritual.

The Latin word *castus,* moreover, is akin to the Latin *carere,* meaning to be without; to the Greek *keazein,* meaning to split; and to the Sanskrit *śasati,* meaning "he cuts to pieces." To the degree that women are confined by phallocentric "chastity"/ touchability we are doomed to be full-filled by the grim conditions suggested by these words. Thus women are split off from our process, from the cosmic harmony of Elemental be-ing. And, as the Sanskrit *śasati* suggests, the logical consequence for the patriarchal male is that "he cuts to pieces" women and other creatures, severing us from our autonomy and from our roots. The logical conclusion for every member of the touchable caste, then, is dismemberment. Reversal of this fragmentation imposed upon the chaste/touchable caste requires the Racing of Raging women to Original Integrity. To understand the possibilities of this Racing/Race, we must understand clearly the conditions of touchability.

Among the meanings of the verb *touch* are "to have sexual intercourse with," "to lay violent hands on," "to rob by swindling: CHEAT," "to reach the heart or secret of," "to hurt the feelings of: WOUND, STING." In all of these ways, women under patriarchy are touchable. Specifically, women—especially poor, Third World, and "minority" women—are touched by rape, battering, emotional manipulation, gynecology and other gynocidal professions, the perpetual stream of insults that constitutes "acceptable" discourse—whether that be under the guise/subject of religion, humor, history, science, science fiction or straight pornography. Lorraine Hansberry graphically described the pornographic dimensions of touchable caste status in the everyday experience of Black women:

Follow me sometimes and see if I lie. I can be coming from eight hours on an assembly line or fourteen hours in Mrs. Halsey's kitchen. I can be all filled up that day with three hundred years of rage so that my eyes are flashing and my flesh is trembling—and the white boys in the streets, they look at me and think of sex. They look at me and that's *all* they think. . . . Baby you could be Jesus in drag—but if you're brown they're sure you're selling! [9]

Beth Brant eloquently depicts the touchable conditions endured and fiercely resisted by Native American women, pointing to the vast dimensions of the touchable caste system:

We have a spirit of rage. We are angry women. Angry at white men and their perversions. Their excessive greed and abuse of the earth, sky, and water. Their techno-christian approach to anything that lives, including our children, our people. We are angry at Indian men for their refusals of us. For their limited vision of what constitutes a strong Nation. We are angry at a so-called "women's movement" that always seems to forget we exist. . . . *We are not victims*. We are organizers, we are freedom fighters, we are feminists, we are healers.[10]

Affirming spiritual powers beyond the conditions of touchability, Brant continues:

We made the fires. We are the fire-tenders. We are the ones who do not allow anyone to speak for us *but* us.
Spirit. Sisterhood. No longer can the two be separated.[11]

Touchability and Asceticism Compared

In the Foreground to the First Realm I have discussed freely chosen ostentatious asceticism as a phallic phenomenon in sado-society. Flamboyant asceticism is, for the most part, the prerogative of males. It is important to clearly distinguish this phenomenon from the suffering of the oppressed, of the touched, which is hardly ostentatious, hardly Self-chosen.* Very significant is the fact that the suffering of ascetics is not essentially psychic suffering. Barrington Moore writes:

It [asceticism] is definitely not psychic suffering in the form of degradation or damage to the individual's self-esteem, as can happen among the Hindu Untouchables. The practitioners of asceticism are the objects of veneration and curiosity, not to say notoriety.[12]

As members of the touchable caste, women suffer indescribably from degradation and damage to Self-esteem. This is the case not only for women who are "dishonored" within patriarchy, for example, whores and "old maids," but in a special way for women who are "honored" for their conformity, for example, as ideal housewives and mothers, as nuns, as career women who are male-identified and hateful of their female identity. The latter

---

* Obviously, members of oppressed groups, as well as others, sometimes seek to use asceticism as a sort of career. This does not vitiate the distinction between the state of oppression and the choice of asceticism.

may be feminine in the traditional and/or modern sense, in order to gain the approval of their colleagues/bosses, while at the same time playing boys' games as would-be members of boys' clubs. The price of such "honors" is damage to female Self-esteem in the deepest sense.

Clearly, members of the touchable caste also have been, and continue to be, subjected to extreme physical suffering as a result of caste status. In addition to the rape and battering of women in adulthood, one need only think of the frequent sexual molestation of female children throughout phallocracy. Atrocities against women on a massive scale are omnipresent in patriarchy. There is also the simple/complex fact that even "privileged" women who have escaped the more overt forms of destruction do suffer from the disease-inducing tortures inflicted upon all women —the stress, anxiety, depression manufactured in maledom.

Women have not freely chosen the spiritual and physical abuses inflicted within phallocracy. However, there is an appearance of choice. For example, some women appear to choose unnecessary mutilating surgery or to stay with husbands who beat them. Only in a very limited sense can these "decisions" be called "choices," for clearly they are not fully free. Yet it is true that most of the time most women do not openly revolt and apparently are resigned to degradation, often thinly disguised as "respect," without visible or audible protest. Therefore, Furies must face the fact of women's damaged Self-esteem, which, combined with terror of taboo-breaking, inhibits many from forming and expressing even an idea of revolt, and certainly inhibits the hope of developing a philosophical analysis of prevailing conditions and a political strategy for surmounting them.

The Braking of Self-Lust

As the universal low caste within all castes, classes, and races of patriarchy, women, the touchables, suffer almost indescribably from damage to Self-esteem, that is, from breaking of Self-love, braking of Self-Lust. Knowledge of this damage and the psychic suffering that accompanies the State of Degradation is subliminal, difficult to face. Even the most successful and self-confident women—in traditional terms—suffer from this largely unacknowledged knowledge. Yet this inchoate knowledge—akin to what Orwell called "the mute protest in your own bones"—is an

experience of nonbe-ing that implies be-ing.[13] Thus it is a signal
of hope, pointing to a vast reservoir of knowledge hidden in the
Self.

One problem, simply stated, is how to make this knowledge
accessible. In 1870 Susan B. Anthony ragingly pondered this
problem:

So while I do not pray for anybody or any party to commit outrages,
still I do pray, and that earnestly and constantly, for some terrific
shock to startle the women of this nation into a self-respect which will
compel them to see the abject degradation of their present position;
which will force them to break their yoke of bondage, and give them
faith in themselves; which will make them proclaim their allegiance
to women first; which will enable them to see that man can no more
feel, speak or act for woman than could the old slaveholder for his
slave. The fact is, women are in chains, and their servitude is all the
more debasing because they do not realize it. O, to compel them to
see and feel, and to give them the courage and conscience to speak and
act for their own freedom, though they face the scorn and contempt of
all the world for doing it! [14]

For each individual woman, the required "terrific shock"
awakens her not only to "information" coming from outside but
to the reservoir of previously inaccessible knowledge and passion
within. Sonia Johnson, author of *From Housewife to Heretic,* has
written of women's hidden knowledge as a subterranean file entitled "What it means to be female in a male world." Johnson
believes that for some women this file is readily accessible, while
for traditional patriarchal women it is buried deep and defenses
against knowing it are "inordinately powerful." She writes of the
"breaking open" process:

Finally, however, no matter how strong that file—and patriarchal
women have almost bionic files—there comes along the one piece of
data that breaks it wide open.

Not everyone responds identically to the bursting of the file. Women
who have no faith in themselves, who are totally dependent upon approval of both patriarchal men and women—as is classically the case in
fundamentalist church settings—and whose feelings of self-worth have
been almost totally crushed, these women must still deny what their
now open file tells them is the truth. But in order to deny now, in the
very face of the truth, they must distort reality so much that they
become ill: emotionally, physically, and morally.[15]

It is necessary to consider also the situation of women who appear to be at the other end of the spectrum from traditional women—those for whom the file seemingly has been or has become "readily accessible." For the fact is that *all* women under patriarchy are in a position which Anthony has Named "abject degradation." Moreover, all to some extent have had Self-Lust crushed and replaced by prosthetic "self-respect." All to some extent still lack faith in our Selves, a condition that is in some cases covered by faith in pseudoselves.

There are different degrees of access to the contents of the file. The contents that are "readily accessible" must be examined—a process which is long, complex, and dangerous. Even the most daring of women still has a vast reservoir/file of the Unknown, that is, of subterranean knowledge—not only of "what it means to be female in a male world" but also of what it can mean to be a passionate creative female in harmony with the cosmos. Since radical feminists do now have access to much that was previously unknown and unknowable, it is easy to forget the fact that there are vast depths in that labyrinthine file that are still unknown—which we must presentiate, make Present to our Selves and to each other.

Sonia Johnson writes:

The miraculous part of an epiphany is that when the file bursts, and all the file data flood into the conscious mind, they are perfectly organized; they present one with conclusions. I knew instantly what the women's movement was all about; I knew it in my very bones.[16]

This statement is accurate, although in apparent contradiction with what I have just written. For it is true that women who have experienced the epiphany have found that the previously subterranean data are perfectly organized, and have almost immediately known what the women's movement is "all about." This knowledge is intuitive and organic. However, the "all" that is known is a potential "all." Much of it is *in potentia.* Presentient women who have experienced the feminist epiphany must know our own E-motional knowing to be a verb. It could be compared to the seedling of a tree that will grow forever, if we choose this knowing/growing. To choose it is to choose participation in the Tree of Life, whose roots and branches can always expand, and will do so if not impeded. The biophilic will to know E-motionally is a will to impassioned expression of Original Integrity.

Women's complicity in the necrophilic anti-process of stunting female participation in the Tree of Life arises in part from and perpetuates low Self-esteem, breaking/braking Self-Lust. I do not refer to "self-esteem" in the usual sense, but rather esteem/value of the deep Original Self in women, the living spirit/matter, the psyche who participates in Be-ing. The blockage of this élan vital, of this expression/expansion of final causality constitutes women's entrapment in the touchable caste. Rather than expanding, roots and branches, as participant in the Tree of Life, a woman caught in this complicity remains nailed to crossbeams of dead wood, suffering, immobile, and double-crossed.

In order to analyze this damage to Self-esteem and the terror that is inseparable from it, I shall draw some analogies between the condition of women as touchables with that of hindu untouchables (not forgetting, of course, that roughly fifty percent of the latter are women).

Untouchables and Touchables Compared

Websters have become increasingly aware that the method of analogy is enlightening, for we have seen on many occasions that our creatively passionate understanding is enhanced through seeing connections among apparently disparate phenomena. Bearing in mind that the situations compared are comparable precisely because they are also different from each other, we can proceed to uncover several points of comparison and contrast between the situation of touchables and that of hindu untouchables.

First, a "choice" of our low caste status is ascribed to women as touchables as well as to the members of the untouchable caste. Women are said to have chosen this condition, and this ascribed pseudo-choice legitimates our touchable caste status, even in our own eyes. Hindu untouchables also have been "encouraged" to believe that their low caste status is the result of choice, in the sense that it is supposedly the consequence of transgressions committed in previous incarnations. Passive acceptance of their condition is thus fostered by the hindu doctrine of transmigration of souls. Barrington Moore writes:

Thus evil and misfortune in this life are due to transgressions, particularly transgressions against the Brahman, in the preceding life. If, on the other hand, according to these beliefs, the individual accepts fate patiently and fulfills the duties of caste, the reward will be to be born into a higher caste in the next reincarnation.[17]

If this rationalization appears totally unlike that proferred to women to legitimate our touchability, Furies should think twice. For women are taught to believe that female suffering is the result of the acts/sins of our mothers and foremothers. Indeed, this is a basic canon of cockocratic psychology. It implies that our oppressed condition was in some way chosen by these women, who can be seen as our previous "incarnations." And of course when women who have inherited such a "karma" become mothers, these in turn "choose" touchability for their daughters. What is rendered invisible by this ideology and its ensuing cyclic consequences is the fact that patriarchal mothers, forced to become token torturers, function as instruments of female touchability. They are moved by the Bosses of Boredom in ways not comprehensible to these instruments/victims.

The *second* point of comparison, implied in the first, is that both in the case of hindu untouchables and in that of women as touchables injustice is made to resemble justice. Thus, as we have seen, just as the doctrine of reincarnation functions to legitimate the degradation of untouchables, so also mother/victim blaming ideologies function as hidden reversals, legitimating the degradation of the touchable caste. In the case of the touchable caste, however, there is such a demonic degree of contrived ambiguity in the primary legitimating ideologies that the transformation of female ignorance requires a special analysis—one quite distinct from the usual sociological analyses of untouchables. Nags must take into account, for example, that mothers, although they are continually blamed for all of the ills of society, are often "honored" in Boredom. This maze of doubletalk/double images/double treatment can be broken only by the Labryses of Furiously Focused analysis. Such Amazonian analysis uncovers the duplicity disguising not only the fact of injustice but also the baffling complexity of the conditions of the universal low caste status of women.

The fact of women's low caste status is masked by *sex role segregation,* which is more subtle than spatial segregation, by women's *derivative status* resulting from connections with men, and by patriarchal ideologies.[18] Thus, since women are derivative beings by patriarchal standards, this fact obscures our low caste status within all castes, classes, races, nations, as well as subgroups such as professions and social "movements," including socialist, Third World, and gay rights movements. As derivative beings, women share in some of the privileges and many of the hardships of their male possessors. For example, as white, wealthy, or middle class, many women have advantages over many sisters in other echelons of the patriarchal world, as well as over many men of oppressed races, classes, nations, and other groups.

As the women's movement has grown more powerful, more global, this fact of derivative status has been used to serve the divide and conquer tactics of the patriarchy. It has been used by men to render the patriarchy itself invisible to women, to distract from the fact that we are the touchable caste within all classes and races. Obedient to the classic rules/roles for token torturers, some women predictably give knee-jerk responses to these tactics. The conversion of women into token targets of token torturers masks the inherent injustice of patriarchy itself and obliterates understanding of the universality of the sexual caste system. It is precisely because they can see that classism and racism are evil and oppressive that some women, frightened of seeing the universality of patriarchy, can be confused by shortsighted tactics. For it is terrifying to know that the evil triad of sexism, racism, classism is a manifestation of planetary phallicism.

Phallicism, defined euphemistically as "the worship of or reverence for the generative principle in nature as symbolized especially by the phallus" is in fact the ideology and practice consequent upon and reinforcing the belief that "God" is male and the male is "God." It is the negation of female potency. This universal religion of phallocracy is the basis of the sexual caste system, and under its rapist reign women of all nations, races, and classes on this planet are touchable. Only by understanding this context of universal gynocide can women begin to think, speak, and act beyond phallic "justice" and "injustice," and to bring forth the reign of Nemesis.

The *third* point of comparison and contrast between untouchables and touchables is the fact that loathing, disgust, and pollution are associated with these castes. This is true of women, but it is masked by such pseudo-dichotomies as "pure" versus "impure," "good" versus "bad," "healthy" versus "sick" women. It takes time to realize that the derivative status of women who have male protection does not change the basic status of all women as whores, as polluted. Bamboozlement characterizes female degradation.

The peculiar nature of the pollution ascribed to all women by the ideologies of phallicism may perhaps be perceived better by looking at specific prohibitions inflicted upon untouchables. I will consider three examples. *A:* In earlier times, in some parts of India, an untouchable had to shout warnings when entering a street so that higher caste persons could get out of the way of her/his contaminating shadow. *B:* In many parts of India, untouchables formerly had to carry brooms in order to brush away their footprints in the dirt behind them, if they entered streets used by other hindus. *C:* There were prohibitions against untouchables entering any hindu temple or higher caste hindu's house, and against using water from the common village well.[19]

There is a certain logic, albeit a horrifying logic, in these sanctions, viewed as practical conclusions drawn from the assumption that untouchables are polluted and polluting. If we consider the touchable caste, however, the situation is more complex. Although women throughout the planetary caste system are blamed for male lechery and thus considered "dirty," there is little reason to be alarmed that males will stay clear of our contaminating shadows. In fact, males shadow women, using obscene touches, obscene words—on the streets, in movie theaters, in bars, in churches, in the home, over the telephone—never allowing women to have our space, our shadows, for ourselves.

Carrying a broom to wipe out footprints is an apt Metaphoric illustration of a problem that women do *not* have in one sense, but *do* have in another sense. For the patriarchs have prevented us from making footprints/traces of our thoughts. When we have managed to leave such traces the phallocrats themselves have erased them. In their customary manner, however, they also have used women to do the dirty work, the sweeping away of our own footprints in the proverbial sands of time. Women as token erasers do this to each other and, most horribly, to our Selves—by erasing and hiding from our Selves our own experiences, perceptions, creative potential, and actual achievements. Women do this out of terror, and the result is continual diminishing of Self-esteem and, consequently, increasing terror.

As for prohibitions against entering the houses of the upper caste—clearly, the situation is reversed. For women are confined in the houses belonging to males and certainly do use water from the "common well" to cook and scrub for their masters. However, women are prohibited from male "houses" in the sense of Boys' Clubs/Men's Associations, and the undermining is all the more lethal because largely invisible to the victims.

A *fourth* point of comparison between touchables and untouchables is the fact that in both cases the underlings have absorbed the dominant beliefs of the higher caste. The oppressors are perceived as having moral authority. Moore attributes the almost total lack of open revolt among the untouchables to this "internalization." [20] Yet it would be simplistic and in fact false to see acceptance of oppression/possession as issuing solely from within the psyche of the victim. There are real and terrible sanctions against stepping out of line.

In the case of women, feminists have long understood that there is continual bombardment with messages, threats, and real punishments. Threats of rape and woman battering, for example, are omnipresent. Nancy Henley's discussion of "gestures of dominance" explains the omnipresence of these sanctions, which often rear their threatening heads in modes that are not obvious. [21] Henley cites Nicole Anthony's "Open Letter to Psychiatrists":

Sometimes, in the middle of a heated discussion with a man, a strong woman finds herself acting chimp-like [submitting]. I'm oppressing myself, she thinks. . . .

If we filmed the scene we would see that what really happened was that he gave a gesture of dominance and she submitted in fear.

There's no need to submit, the psychiatrists say. Another lie. If a woman refuses to respond to the gestures of dominance she is frequently physically attacked. A wife needs only to be hit by a husband larger and heavier than she. Thereafter the most fleeting subliminal gesture will serve to remind her of the costs of rebellion.

The moments of "internalization" are really the moments when we respond to gestures of dominance. They are not inside of our heads. [22]

Another woman makes the point concisely:

The forms of female behavior that our contemporary ideologues have called internalized self-hate or masochism are usually just a logical response to a man's gesture of dominance. Women have spent years on the psychiatric couch hunting down a nonexistent internal enemy.[23]

I would emphasize, however, that women *have* "internalized" their submissive role. Of course, this role is reinforced continually by external "gestures" that carry subliminal messages.

A *fifth* point concerns sharp divisions which set off subcastes among the untouchables. It actually has happened that in parts of India there are "pure untouchables" who consider themselves above "impure untouchables" (who still eat beef).[24] One can think also of the "pure" women of patriarchy who have been made to feel superior to "impure" women. Of course, both of these subcastes of women are touchable, but by different males, and sometimes in different ways. Even celibate women who have dedicated their lives to the male god and/or to careers in male-identified professions, however sexually "pure" they may be, are touchable and touched mentally and emotionally. Such women can be touchable physically as well, for many of the physical disorders commonly called "psychosomatic" are traceable to this disordered mental/emotional touchability.

This fifth point, which concerns what I would call division by delusion, Names an important aspect of the tragedy of women within patriarchy. For we are not simply divided into subcastes such as whores versus wives. Our peculiar caste status keeps us divided in the deepest way from our Selves and from each other. The endless touchability required by the lecherous controllers of the caste system has precisely the effect of making women unable to Touch our Selves and each other. While fixated in this state, we cannot move. We are unmovable.

TOUCHABILITY AND TABOO

It is Taboo for women Intimately/Ultimately to Touch each other. An ordinary encyclopedia gives the following explanation of *taboo:*

Polynesian word denoting persons, places, things, or acts which are to be shunned. In modern anthropology, it embraces all prohibitions enforced by magico-religious sanctions, fortified by fear of ill-luck, disease, or death. The primal taboos were totemic.
Taboo came to concern itself with vital crises, especially childbirth and death, and when kingship and priesthood emerged it was utilized

for protecting property and privilege. The violator of a taboo is himself [*sic*] taboo, lest his [*sic*] transgression should become contagious.[25]

For the touchable caste, *the* acts which we are required to shun are those which express, legitimate, and create deep, Elemental connections between and among women—connections which are intellectual, passionate, erotic, and psychic, and which imply deep respect, honor, caring, gratitude, and commitment. Seen/heard within the dimensions of psychic expansion beyond these conditions they are simply Natural Acts of Women, Wild and Weird.

The Taboo against these Natural Acts is enforced by magico-religious sanctions, and it is fortified by phallic injections of fear, so that women have realistic terror of ill-luck, disease, or death inflicted by men if we Touch and become Positively Touchable by each other. Taboo against our Most Natural Acts is the most primal Taboo. It is essential for protecting the male's property and privilege. For the sustaining of patriarchy it is prior in importance to taboos concerning other matters, for example, incest, which men impose upon themselves and regularly violate with impunity.

Focused and complete violation by women of the Most Unnatural Taboo would undermine/overturn phallic rule. Therefore, this Taboo against expression/expansion of Ontological Female Connectedness is totalitarian, total. The violator of this Taboo is herself Taboo, for her transgression is contagious. Since Wild, Natural Women are Taboo-Breakers of the millennia, we *are* Taboo and our transgressions are incalculably courageous, contagious.

Transgression is from the Latin *transgressio,* meaning "act of crossing, passing over." To *transgress* means "to go beyond limits set or prescribed by (law or command): BREAK, VIOLATE." And it means "to pass beyond or go over (a limit or boundary): CROSS (the adjacent seas transgressed almost all the coast . . .—J. B. Bird)." Transgressing women go beyond limits set/fixed by lechers' laws. We pass beyond bore-ocracy's boundaries. While in certain dimensions of our activities we live "on the boundaries" of patriarchal institutions, in our deepest dimensions of be-ing, we pass beyond these boundaries. We pass beyond our own former limits. We become and are Other. Finding our Original Otherness, we break the Terrible Taboo. We *become* Terrible, Taboo. By this crossing we are outrageous, contagious. Taboo, we are Tidal, transgressing coasts, coasting freely.

Truly Taboo women ride the Tides of connectedness. We have seen through the tricksters' attempts to stem our Tide by tying separate and partial transgressions into tidy boxes, labeled "trade-offs." They would have us preoccupied with breaking partial taboos, offering us the delusion that the part is The Whole. Thus they offer "Deviant Sexual Preference" as liberally acceptable "taboo-breaking" on the condition that the breaker/buyer swear intellectual/professional allegiance to the Men's Association. Accepting such snoolish compromise is labeled "bravery" and praised as "prudent." Or again they offer "Deviant Career Choice" as a reward for cementing connections with Old Boys in the customary manner of choosing bores as bedfellows.

A Terrible Woman earns this title by breaking the Whole Taboo, consistently performing Natural Acts, giving allegiance to her own kind. Her motive is not zeal for martyrdom, but zest for life. What she wants is nothing less than Original Wholeness. She Touches this in her Self, by the sense of *touch* that is defined as "to reach the heart or secret of: guess at correctly: FATHOM." In/by this sense she Touches other women, who themSelves awaken to Touch others into Otherness. Contagion spreads; the Touchers move.

Touching women See/Touch through the fallacious/phallic dichotomy implied in the misleading expression "only skin deep." Since males in the State of Obsession require penile penetration to believe that they have made "contact," the vast expanse of Surface knowledge, of Touching, is underestimated, unexplored, as Nicole Brossard has shown.[26] Wild Sensuousness/Sagacity is Skin Deep, which means it is sensitive to Others—spiraling to trees, winds, mountains, seas. It is Gyn/Ecological, Gyn/affectionate.[27]

The soul is on the Surface, as well as in the Depths. The soul that Touches, Breathes, Loves, Lusts, Explores is Surface Soul. It need not seek the false "depths" which phallic philosophy drones about, drowns out. The Surface Soul is in Touch with the Air, Earth, Fire, and Waters. She is in Contact, Communion. Her tactics are tactile; her triumphs and trials tangible. Her travels are Outward. She cannot be tracked down, trod upon, trained.

Her flights are etheric, aerial. She is aura, force-field, glowing with gynergy. Her expanses are astral, her contacts cosmic. The Female Soul is sensate, Lusty, inspired/fired. She is ethereal, material.

Concerning "the pattern of the surface" of the sea, Rachel Carson writes:

Nowhere in all the sea does life exist in such bewildering abundance as in the surface waters.[28]

Further on, she notes:

With these surface waters, through a series of delicately adjusted, interlocking relationships, the life of all parts of the sea is linked. What happens to a diatom in the upper, sunlit strata of the sea may well determine what happens to a cod lying on a ledge of some rocky canyon a hundred fathoms below, or to a bed of multicolored, gorgeously plumed seaworms carpeting an underlying shoal, or to a prawn creeping over the soft oozes of the sea floor in the blackness of mile-deep water.[29]

Cut off from our Surfaces, our Skins, women have been robbed of our lives' "bewildering abundance." We have been deprived of the delicately adjusted interlocking relationships with all parts of the Seas which are our Selves, our Souls, our Home. We have been robbed of the keys, the clues that link our lives in complex changing patterns.

Deprived of our powers of Touching, women have in fact been skinned alive. In order to reclaim our Skins, rename our Skins, we must think further about the frightening subject of taboo.

Untwisting the Terrible Taboo

Women seeking clues for untwisting the "facts" about taboo might as well go to the most convoluted re-source, father Freud. As Convolutas re-membering, we can untwist his tales, Touching truths. In *Totem and Taboo* Freud cites at length an article entitled "Taboo" in the 1910–11 edition of *Encyclopaedia Brittanica*. Part of this is worth re-citing:

"The objects of taboo are many: (i) direct taboos aim at (a) the protection of important persons—chiefs, priests, etc.—and things against harm; (b) the safeguarding of the weak—women, children and common people generally—from the powerful *mana* (magical influence) of chiefs and priests; (c) the provision against the dangers incurred by handling or coming in contact with corpses, by eating certain foods, etc.; (d) the guarding the chief acts of life—birth, initiation, marriage and sexual functions, etc., against interference; (e) the securing of human beings against the wrath or power of gods and spirits; (f) the securing of unborn infants and young children . . . from the consequences of certain actions, and more especially from the communication of qualities supposed to be derived from certain foods. (ii) Taboos are imposed in order to secure against thieves the property of an individual, his fields, tools, etc. . . ." [30]

Leaving aside the specific information/misinformation used by the re-cited anthropologist to back up his description, Taboo women can see how this description can usefully be applied (with alterations) to the universal patriarchal Taboo against Women-Touching women—the Terrible Taboo that is masked by myriad lesser taboos, which function to distract us from knowing *what* it is that is most seriously forbidden to us. I shall take in turn each point of this anthropological description of the objects of taboo, applying these points to the Real Taboo that governs cockocracy.

A: This universal Taboo against Women-Touching women does indeed aim at the protection of "important persons" such as chiefs and priests, since these are not "important" in the eyes and lives of Taboo-breaking women, and therefore sense themselves to be in danger of annihilation by simple neglect. *B:* The Terrible Taboo can be seen to aim at "the safeguarding of the weak [*sic*] —women, children, and common people generally," from the powerful positive *mana* (Archimagical influence) of Wild and Free women. *C:* The Total Taboo also aims to put a stop to the primary danger to chiefs and priests, which is the danger that Vital, Women-Touching women will see through the corpse-like, necrophilic "natures" of these men and therefore force them to acknowledge the horror of their own deadness. *D:* The Total Taboo aims to guard cockocratic control of such "chief acts of life" as "birth, initiation, marriage and sexual function etc. against interference" by autonomous women. *E:* This Universal Taboo aims for "the securing of human beings [males]" against the Wrath and Powers of Goddesses, especially Nemesis, and Elemental spirits. *F:* This Ultimate Taboo aims for "the securing of unborn infants and young children from the consequences" of

Wild Female Presence. Finally, the Great Taboo is imposed in order to protect the thieves who have stolen women's Rights/Rites of Touching—who have been shrinking and confining these within the rituals of phallicism, reducing the rightful owners of powers of Touching to the role of tools of our own destruction.

The encyclopedia article cited by Freud makes further important points. For example:

"Persons or things which are regarded as taboo may be compared to objects charged with electricity; they are the seat of a tremendous power which is transmissible by contact, and may be liberated with destructive effect if the organisms which provoke its discharge are too weak to resist it. . . ." [31]

Musing upon this passage, Muses can make the comparison of our Selves to "objects charged with electricity." For Women-Touching women are the seat of a tremendous power which is transmissible to other women by contact. The liberation of this power will indeed be perceived as "destructive" by the chiefs and priests of reversal, for as necrophilic organisms they recognize that they are too weak to resist such power, which has a gynergizing, creative effect upon inherently strong, biophilic organisms.

It is clear that an adequate understanding of the true sources of the Total Taboo must go much deeper than mere class analysis that focuses upon the interests of privileged classes as the alleged origin of oppressive taboos. Wilhelm Wundt, as cited by Freud, wrote:

Taboo is originally nothing other than the objectified fear of the "demonic" power which is believed to lie hidden in a tabooed object.[32]

Wundt adds that the unspoken command underlying all the prohibitions of taboo with their numberless variations is one only: "Beware of the wrath of demons!" [33] This analysis can be applied to the Total Taboo. The male terror of demons—of principalities and powers—is bored into the psyches of women, who thus become possessed by fears of our own Touching Elemental powers. In this way, women under the reign of phallocracy are thwarted by the Total Taboo.

It is important to examine this phenomenon further, with helpful hints from Freud and Wundt. Freud writes:

According to Wundt, this original characteristic of taboo—the belief in a "demonic" power which lies hidden in an object and which, if the object is touched or used unlawfully, takes its vengeance by casting a spell over the wrong-doer—is still wholly and solely "objectified fear." That fear has not yet split up into the two forms into which it later develops: veneration and horror.[34]

Women are terrorized by phallocentric Taboo and thus are kept back from Touching the "object"—our Selves—in which the demonic powers (our own Elemental powers which are disguised by the Possessors) lie hidden. Women are paralyzed by this injected fear that our own powers, if we Touch them or use them "unlawfully," that is, in ways contrary to the laws of the Lecherous State, will take vengeance by casting a spell over us as "wrong-doers." In other words, the Taboo against Touching makes women afraid of our Selves, of our powers, terrified of the vengeance that will be wrought against us by our own Selves, terrified that our Selves will cast a spell over us.

It is important to notice that the spell already has been cast over women under patriarchy, and that it is by Touching the Taboo "object," our Selves and our powers, that we can break the spell. This knowledge is gained by the process of reversing the reversals of the Taboo-inflicting State. This process requires great courage, for the Most Total Taboo of patriarchy feeds upon ultimate fear. It is well known that in many societies studied by anthropologists, persons who have violated taboos have become depressed and died soon after the violation. There are clues in this that warn against underestimating the fears that block women from breaking the Total Taboo against Touching our powers. Yet above and beyond this knowledge it is essential to know that precisely by breaking the Taboo, women can connect with our Elemental powers and overcome what Wundt calls "objectified fear."

This "objectified fear," objectified/magnified to an extreme degree in women thus afflicted, that is, in all women under phallocracy, is converted into the cardinal plastic passions, especially guilt, anxiety, and depression, and it issues in hostility, bitterness, resentment, resignation, frustration, boredom, and—worst of all—fulfillment. Moreover, it stunts/pots all of the passions, shrinking/paralyzing potential E-motion into mummified, canned, glamorized de-formed forms.

Particularly fascinating in the passage from Wundt cited above is the naming of the two forms into which this "objectified fear," which is "the original characteristic of taboo," develops/splits up: "veneration and horror." It may seem at first thought that this does not apply to the Total Taboo against Women-Touching women, for we certainly are not required, or even allowed, to venerate women's Elemental powers. However, we are discouraged into "venerating" distorted and weak simulations of these powers. Women are required to participate in male "reverence" for the man-made feminine ideal, while at the same time participating in male horror of our own Touching powers.

Such confused veneration and unnatural horror are also discouragingly "inspired" in women by patriarchal religion. The manipulation that issues in displaced religious veneration is nothing less than a perversion of Women-Touching power. This patriarchally required reverence for male "divinity" as well as for such male-mother figures as popes, pediatricians, and professors, is inevitably accompanied by a *religious* horror of Women-Touching women. Such horror is expressed specifically by christian epithets for lesbianism, such as "abomination." It is expressed in the refusal of "priestly" functions to women, for these could, by association, conjure images/memories of Spiritual Touching powers. The patriarchs, then, strive to fill women with horror for Lesbianism in the deepest sense, and for all of our Gyn/affectionate and Witching powers.

It would be a great mistake, therefore, to imagine that the Total Taboo against Women-Touching women can be restricted to what is commonly understood by the expression "physical contact." The following passage from Freud concerning "obsessional prohibitions of neurotics" can be a useful reminder on this point, if, as Soothsayers, we see it with our Third Eye:

As in the case of taboo, the principal prohibition, the nucleus of the neurosis, is against touching; and thence it is sometimes known as "touching phobia: or *délire du toucher*." The prohibition does not merely apply to immediate physical contact but has an extent as wide as the metaphorical use of the phrase "to come in contact with." Anything that directs the patient's thoughts to the forbidden object, anything that brings him [sic] into intellectual contact with it, is just as much prohibited as direct physical contact. This same extension also occurs in the case of taboo.[35]

In the case of the Total Taboo, the neurosis, of course, is that of the Normal Society and its norm-makers/norm-keepers, whose Boring Norms compel them to label Pyromagnetic Taboo-breakers as "neurotic" and to endeavor to inflict "touching phobia" upon such women. Thus the above citation can be Prudishly paraphrased as follows:

The prohibition inflicted by the Normal Society against Touching by Viragos, Virgins, and Websters applies not only to immediate physical contact, but also and especially to *physical ultimacy,* which inherently has an extent as wide as Muses' Metaphorical use of the phrase "to come in contact with." Anything that directs a woman's thoughts to the forbidden object, her Self, anything that brings her into intellectual contact with her Spiritual Touching Powers, is just as much prohibited as direct physical contact with another Female Self. This extension is inherent in the Total Taboo against Women-Touching women.

Indeed, the fetishizing of that part of the Total Taboo which concerns sexual contact is a ruse commonly employed by the rulers of snooldom. Fixing women with fears of physical contact, they distract from the Gyn/Ecological context that gives full meaning to such contact, the context that Crones are beginning to comprehend and weave into Touchability, Tangibility. Fixed women, fooled by male fetishizing of this part of the Total Taboo, sometimes seek false freedom through a one-dimensional breaking of the Taboo—a transgression that is only sexual.

Women can be aided in breaking other dimensions of the circle of fear by listening to accounts of experiences of those who have faced other aspects of the Total Taboo. Sonia Johnson, for example, writing of her heresy trial in the mormon church, explains the reaction of the judges when one of her female supporters pleaded: "Please don't turn this into a witch-hunt!" With these words, the conciliatory mood in the room disappeared. Sonia's husband, Rick, made the following observation:

"She shouldn't have reminded those men of witches. . . . Men are basically very much afraid of the spiritual powers of women; that's why they try to keep them from discovering them, from using and developing them—cut them off from the priesthood, set themselves up as women's spiritual leaders. When she said 'witch-hunt,' out of the slime of womanfear in their unconscious slithered the specter of *women in power over men,* and they instantly united against their age-old enemy, woman; woman as mysterious, woman as witch, woman as powerful, woman as god. I know . . . because I felt it in myself when she said that word, and I looked up quickly and saw what I was feeling pass simultaneously over the faces of the four men seated before us." [36]

This example illustrates the fact that it is male fear of women being in Touch with our Spiritual Elemental Powers that is the motivation behind the infliction of the Terrible Taboo upon women. When women can clearly see *whose fears* of *whose powers* are at issue, this knowledge is itself empowering. The knowledge renders us Actively Untouchable, for we begin to be freely Outcast/Outcaste, outside the touchable caste, Wholly Other, Dangerous, Pyrogenetically Touching and Touchable.

The Total Taboo and Repressive Desublimation

The customary way in which the Ruling Caste has maintained the Total Taboo has been deception. In liberal cultures this has taken the form of trade-offs. Shrews can uncover this devious attack upon the Touching powers of women by returning to Marcuse's useful concept of *repressive desublimation*. Writing of the permissiveness of the affluent society, he discusses its "effective repression of the sense of guilt," which would indicate "a decline of shame and guilt feeling in the sexual sphere." He concludes:

And indeed, the exposure of the (for all practical purposes) naked body is permitted and even encouraged, and the taboos on pre- and extramarital intercourse are considerably relaxed. Thus we are faced with the contradiction that the liberalization of sexuality provides an instinctual basis for the repressive and aggressive power of the affluent society.[37]

And further:

The relaxation of taboos alleviates the sense of guilt and binds (though with considerable ambivalence) the "free" individuals libidinally to the institutionalized fathers. . . . On the other hand, if violation of taboos transcends the sexual sphere and leads to refusal and rebellion, the sense of guilt is not alleviated and repressed but rather transferred: not we, but the fathers, are guilty.[38]

In other words, desublimated sexuality, within a social context that truncates intellectual/e-motional powers, can be used to reinforce the status quo. Thus there is a "conquest of transcendence." Moreover:

The result is the atrophy of the mental organs for grasping the contradictions and the alternatives.[39]

Clearly, the sort of "sexual liberation" Marcuse was discussing was basically about heterosexual genital sex. However, his reflections are a useful reminder of the patriarchal trick of "relaxation of taboos." Shrewds have to recognize that the reduction of potentially powerful, gynergizing connections between women to only the sexual sphere in a climate of patriarchal permissiveness that would restrict women to this sphere of male-defined "sexual deviance" is also only repressive desublimation. "Liberated" women who are merely "gay" remain bound libidinally to the institutionalized fathers. But if violation of the Total Taboo encompasses and transcends the sexual sphere and leads to "refusal and rebellion" that is holistic and Elemental, guilt is indeed transferred to the fathers, and women can Touch and Move.

THE EVIL OF BANALITY AND RITES
OF APPEASEMENT

In keeping with the tradition of Descartes, modern philosophy's severed head, who not coincidentally flourished during the Witchcraze in Western Europe, the Ruling Caste of modern misogynists strives to sever women's heads, offering their victims a free choice of being a head or a body. This option is reflected in the offerings for moviegoers seeking/starving for strong female images.

In the early eighties, the film *Personal Best* was lauded as a candid and affirming statement about a lesbian relationship. Yet many sensed that the bland dullness of Mariel Hemingway was reflective of the strategy of murder by Boredom. The film exemplifies one of bore-ocracy's images of Women-Touching women—banality. If this means that "everything is permitted," one might well ask: Why bother? Another film of the same period was *On Golden Pond,* starring Kate Hepburn who, as always, is radiant with impassioned intelligence. Yet she gives it all to the service of her man. To many women, no doubt, Hepburn expresses more of what is Elementally Touching than could myriad Mariels, yet that message is muted by the roles into which Hepburn is cast. Typically, both of these films offered women less than holistic options. The result was re-inforcement of the old programming, issuing in frustration. Such frustration is frequently denied, of course, partly out of knee-jerk guilt for not being "able to enjoy" such a-musement. The banality is accepted as normal.

While the idea of casting of Hemingway as a lesbian may not, initially, have appeared banal, the film itself—and her insipid role in it—can hardly be said to escape that description. While Hepburn's personality is anything but banal, her male-identified role matches that description. Yet compared to most films, these movies can appear to women starved for Self-affirming images as refreshing treats. Spiritually starved women are served banality with just a touch of freshness, novelty, and they are grateful.*

Years ago, Hannah Arendt wrote accurately of "the fearsome word-and-thought-defying *banality of evil*." [40] I am suggesting here that banality itself can be evil, in the sense that "evil is whatever distracts." [41] For patriarchally produced banality distracts, pulling us away from our Original Movement, our *telos*. Women seeking recreation/replenishment are distracted. One meaning of *distract* is "to stir up or confuse with conflicting emotions or motives or unsettling worries: HARASS, CONFOUND." Thus confused, conflicted, confounded, women re-turn to the causers of confusion, craving consolation.

Canned a-musement, together with other phallic rituals to which "ladies are invited," are rites of appeasement. Freud writes

---

* Social psychologist Marisa Zavalloni, in a brilliant analysis of internal ecology, describes this spiritual starvation of women under patriarchy: "Women, as women, cannot derive any information from the culture that would nurture important projects, and feelings of worth and of transcendence. On the contrary, they are exposed from birth to highly disparaging cultural discourses through art, philosophy, and religion, however well-meaning particular fathers, husbands, or lovers may be. From an ego-ecological perspective it can be seen how women will form their personal identities from the same identity mechanisms as those of men but by interacting with a cultural environment which denies them, as women, the imaginary models that nurture competence, genius, and transcendence." See Marisa Zavalloni, "Ego-ecology: The Study of the Interaction Between Social and Personal Identities," in *Identity: Personal and Socio-cultural, a Symposium,* ed. by Jacobs-Widding (Stockholm: Almqvist & Wiksell, 1983).

of rites of appeasement as a method of dealing with dismembered enemies:

Other peoples have found a means for changing their former enemies after their death into guardians, friends and benefactors. This method lies in treating their severed heads with affection. . . . When the Sea Dyaks of Sarawak bring home a head from a successful head-hunting expedition, for months after its arrival it is treated with the greatest consideration and addressed with all the names of endearment of which their language is capable. The most dainty morsels of food are thrust into its mouth, delicacies of all kinds and even cigars. The head is repeatedly implored to hate its former friends and to love its new hosts since it has now become one of them.[42] *

Having inflicted dismemberment upon women, the a-musers often treat severed heads and bodies with affection, addressing these with names of endearment. Dainty morsels and delicacies—including entertainment—are bestowed upon the severed parts, which are implored to hate women and love their Hosts since, having been dismembered, they have become one with them.

Women who have not lost our heads/bodies, who are Headstrong, increasingly find such rites of appeasement unappetizing. Listening to the names of endearment (of which their language is capable) and having delicacies (even cigars or Virginia Slims) thrust into one's mouth are judged to be inadequate compensation for drastic dismemberment. Even the most high-priced of pedestals are perceived as poor substitutes for bodily/psychic integrity. Headstrong women understand that only Total Taboobreaking can overcome the evil of banality.

Appeasement, Depression, and Cyclic Re-Turning

Severed heads, having reason to believe that they are in a vulnerable position, commonly accept the dainty morsels forced upon them by their severers. Fortunately, however, unlike the murdered enemies allegedly decapitated by the Sea Dyaks, millions of women reduced to the condition of psychic decapitation are in fact not

---

* Freud's interpretation of the Sea Dyaks' behavior may not even be based on accurate reporting and in any case probably does not reflect their understanding of these rites. Nevertheless, Freud's account exhibits the patterns of perception governing the thought of this patriarch and his ilk.

yet physically murdered. One of the signs that life is still present is the ability to feel. The passions felt by decapitated women, however, are for the most part plastic. At best, they are potted.

Of central significance is the plastic passion of depression. It is logical that all women within patriarchy should experience depression, and in varying degrees. Indeed, given the prevailing conditions, it is almost cause for alarm if a woman never feels depressed. For a state worse than this would be the nonsentient condition of a full-filled fembot.

The verb *depress* literally means "to put down or overcome forcibly: CRUSH, SUBJUGATE." Depressed women are not merely suffering from an agentless disorder, for women have been put down and overcome forcibly; crushed and subjugated. An archaic definition of *depression* is "ABASEMENT, HUMBLING, DEGRADATION." That this condition is the logical result of the State of Appeasement is clear from the following definition of the verb *appease:* "to conciliate or buy off (a potential aggressor) by political or economic concessions usually at the sacrifice of principles." The acceptance of dainty/deadly morsels "at the sacrifice of principles" yields depression.

The definition of *depression* that is commonly applied within the economic sphere is also enlightening. It means "reduction, diminution, impoverishment, or depreciation in activity, strength, amount, quality, force, yield, value, or significance (a depression in trade)." Given the conditions of enforced reduction of women's activity, strength, amount (of gynergy), quality, force, yield, value, and significance in the State of Appeasement, it naturally, or, rather, unnaturally, follows that there be a widespread experience of depression, in the sense of "the state of being below normal in physical or mental vitality." Insofar as a woman is still imprisoned within the State of Appeasement she suffers from the lowering of deep Elemental vitality; she is "below normal" by Pyrometric standards. She suffers from lack of gynergy.

In some cases, the crushing, subjugating, degrading blows of Boredom have battered women into the extreme state of depression defined as "a mental disorder of psychoneurotic or psychotic proportions characterized by sadness, retardation of motor and certain vegetative processes, feelings of inadequacy and self-depreciation, and often by suicidal attempts." This condition is on a continuum with the common state of appeased women.

The appeasement of women is intended to make the Depressed State acceptable, even appetizing, and certainly normal. At the same time, it functions to make plausible the blaming of women for this normal subnormality, for women appear appeased, and even pleased. The acceptance of this blame sets the stage for the whole array of plastic passions. Paralyzed by all this plastic, women suffer from boredom, slide into resignation, and sometimes suffer the unspeakable defeat: full-fillment. Since phallic full-fillment means more appeasement and more severing, the cycle is repeated endlessly. In the course of this re-turning, women do feel some natural passions, but these are pruned, potted.

As long as women accept the appeasing pay-offs from the Paymasters we stay in the cycle of depression, of severance from Self. Only a change in the situation, a refusal of Severance Pay and a drastic declaration of independence can stop the depressing cycle. The key to the Power of Refusal is the passion of Rage.

THE RAGING RACE

Women sever our Selves from the State of Severance by the force of righteous Fury, unleashed Rage. This passion unpots the potted passions and melts down the plastic ones. Potted love, desire, joy, hate, aversion, and sorrow, as well as potted fear, daring, hope, despair, and anger shoot forth, shattering the confining pots. Extending their roots and branches, they reach for their Elemental connections with Earth, Air, Water, Fire. Touched by the sweet earth, wild winds, rich rain, warm sun, they expand unendingly.

Righteous Rage makes love, desire, and joy realistic, unsentimental. Unsatisfied with the appeasing sops/slops fed to imprisoned plants, loving, desiring, rejoicing women—that is, Lusty women—allow no limits to the qualitative expansion of our Lust. Disdaining the dainty morsels served in the Severed State of Domestication, we drink deeply of Wild elements and thrive, grow.

Freed Fury makes hate, aversion, and sorrow biophilic. No longer twisted inward, devouring women's Selves, these passions purge our souls of horizontal violence. Our hate and aversion—moving past the token torturers who are also victims—stir us to end the cruel rule of agents of aggression. Applying our Selves to Naming the real agents, Furies fueled by these passions are unappeasable. Our Fire is unallayed, unassuaged by Rites of Appeasement.

Our grief is for the Earth, our Sister, as well as for the Fore-crones of our Race. It melts/unfreezes frozen tears, tearing open Eyes to see what has been hidden and denied. Touching ancient scars, uncovering wounds, we wash away infections of Self-hate. The healing waters of our weeping give us strength. Our words of wailing wash our souls with truth that cleanses while it clears the air we breathe.

Rage-fueled fear and daring combine in forming focused feroc-ity. Furies know that the Ultimate Fearful Thing is loss of Lust for Life, and that this Lust is lost/killed by compromise, by crum-bling before our fears of lesser evils. The righteous fear of com-promise is one Source of Haggard Dreadful Daring. Furies dare also to reverse the reversal contained in this word—*compromise*—itself. For in its roots this does not mean "selling out" but sim-ply "promising together." Promising together to spurn the spuri-ous promises of our would-be procurers and appeasers, Raging women learn anew the meanings of faith, of Fate. Faithful to our promises to each other, we can dare to re-create our Fates, to be Spinners of Stamina, the threads of Life.

Hope and despair are sharpened also by Righteous Rage. Fu-ries dispense with potted hopes, such as hopes for equality within patriarchy, recognizing this to be a contradiction in terms. In this sense we despair, that is, turn our energies away from what had formerly been perceived as "good" and which was an illusion. Rage at having been deceived/duped into expending energy in the pursuit of false hopes emboldens women to reach/hope for more arduous and ultimately more real Goods. Rage, then, as a forceful reaction to realistic assessment of our caste's conditions, releases pent up gynergy which can then express itself as original, creative hope.

Anger is unpotted and transformed into Rage/Fury when the vast network that constitutes the context of our oppression is recognized. It is further transformed when the positive network of Elemental be-ing is glimpsed behind the Foreground. As the Realm of Pyrospheres is Realized, anger bursts forth as Creative Rage.

In this Realm, passions are truly movements, verbs. We experi-ence the melting down of noxious nouns embedded in our psyches, which are the plastic passions. Depression is converted into ex-pression. Guilt, anxiety, frustration, and the other lumps of fix-ated feelings are broken into their real components—the hate, aversion, sadness, fear, despair, and Rage that really move. Full-fillment melts down simply into Nothing. This process cannot happen "all at once," of course, but each movement of be-ing is experienced as an epiphany/ontophany.

Pyromancers learn to live simultaneously in many dimensions. Thus the passions that have evil as their object, such as sorrow, fear, and daring, do not and should not disappear. As powerful forms of E-motion, they have a place within a realistic, biophilic context. The same principle applies to Rage.

Pyromantic, creatively Raging women are Racy women. *Racy* means "having the distinctive or characteristic flavor, quality, or excellence of a race or kind." *Racy* also means "full of life, zest, or vigor: LIVELY, SPIRITED." Racy, Raging women, then, are Lusty, having the distinctive qualities of the Race of Women.

To comprehend raciness we can recall that the Race of Women is many-dimensional. We have seen (in the Introduction) that *race* means "act of rushing onward: RUN." The distinctive flavor, quality, and excellence of Racy Women, then, implies movement —the act of rushing onward. Moreover, *race* means "a strong or rapid current of water." The raciness of the Race of Women in-volves strength, speed, and focus. Also, *race* means "a heavy or choppy sea; especially one produced by the meeting of two tides." The Elemental raciness of the Race of Women involves Wild and roaring movement, and Tidal meetings and encounters. Clearly, then, the Racy Raging Race of Women will require the Realizing of Volcanic Virtues, as we move deeper into Pyro-spheres.

CHAPTER SEVEN

BREAKING OUT:
VOLCANIC VIRTUES

Pyromachy:	"Obsolete: fighting with fire."
	Oxford English Dictionary
Pyromachy:	"Fighting with Fire/Desire."
	Websters' First New Intergalactic Wickedary of the English Language

Propelled by Pyromantic Passion into the vortices of Pyrospheres, Prudes encounter apparent paradoxes inherent in Elemental powers. These are not the problems of political/institutional power of which the phallic ethicists drone but rather the challenges experienced by women who find ourSelves quickened by new and ancient awareness of Elemental rhythms, of harmonious connectedness in the concert of be-ing. When a woman touches/tastes this harmony the world becomes charged for her in a-mazing ways. Wits are sharpened, sensations unmuddied. The sense of synchronicity is activated, re-charged. Realizing this rhythmic concrescence, she experiences heightened hopes.

Conversely, she tastes temptations to despair. For Realizing harmony with the Elemental world implies recognizing ever more acutely the disharmony of the fathers' fabricated world. It also involves experiencing the presence (in the sense of presence of absence) of these fabrications in the fibers of our own substance. These embedded physical and psychic pollutants inhibit knowing and Spinning. Olive Schreiner was expressing an acute awareness of this conflict many decades ago, when she wrote:

We are a race of women that of old knew no fear and feared no death, and lived great lives and hoped great hopes; and if today some of us have fallen on evil and degenerate times, there moves in us yet the throb of the old blood.[1]

The more distinctly a woman re-members the Tidal rhythms of the forgotten Race of Women, and the more surely she senses "the throb of the old blood," the more certainly she is forced to face the unnatural programmed reflexes that she has inherited as a woman in patriarchy.

The struggle to shed these horrid habits is urgently experienced by Pyrognostic Nags. As we progress in Power these embeds become more obvious and more obviously alienating. Thus the Pyromantic Journey takes on the appearance of being both progress and regression at the same time. No longer completely blind to the mechanisms that made us prisoners of the masters' mazes, women enlightened by the Fire of our own Passion feel discomfort and horror even as we glimpse the ecstatic vision. To put it another way, the draining of our life force becomes intolerably perceptible as women feel the rhythms of the old blood's throb. There is then an illusion of movement in seemingly opposite directions consequent upon heightening of awareness of good and evil. But the recognition of the embedded patterns is not an illusion. It is essential to the exorcism that accompanies the ecstasy of the Pyrospheres.

The exorcism itself of the phallic presences of absence within women's psyches is accomplished largely by the acquiring of new operative habits, or virtues. Websters weaving our way into the Pyrospheres unweave old behavior patterns and create new ones. This creation does not happen through wishful thinking but through arduous practice, through repeated acts. Women who have already experienced the development of some skills know that natural talent is not enough. Musicians, writers, artists and artisans of all kinds, athletes, mathematicians, philosophers know the necessity of arduous practice. This, in traditional ethical terms, is the acquiring of habits through repeated acts.

It is problematic and even distasteful to many Furious women to call good operative habits "virtues." The word *virtue* itself, encased in coffins of patriarchal moral ideology, seems to have a putrid odor about it. That odor, to be specific, is an aroma of hypocrisy. Indeed, the word *virtue,* when Viragos first struggle to exhume it from the graveyards of phallic ethics, reeks of reversals. The traditional "virtues," as defined and used by the Masters of Morality, constitute a veritable arsenal of weapons commonly employed in the perpetual war against the Race of Racy Women.

Ruminating upon the reversals wrought through the use of the ideology of virtues, Viragos can recall Valerie Solanas' Soothsaying, when she points out that the patriarchal male attempts to become female:

... by claiming as his own all female characteristics—emotional strength and independence, forcefulness, dynamism, decisiveness, coolness, objectivity, assertiveness, courage, integrity, vitality, intensity, depth of character, grooviness, etc.—and projecting onto women all male traits—vanity, frivolity, triviality, weakness, etc.[2]

So much for the virility of the alleged virtues.

The problem with the word *virtue* is not simply that it has been applied wrongly. The message of "virility" appears to be embedded in the word itself, which is said to be derived from the Latin *vir,* meaning man. Racy women understand that the virtues of our Race—"a race of women that of old knew no fear and feared no death, and lived great lives and hoped great hopes"— have nothing "manly" or "virile" about them, and will proceed to exorcise the thought-strangling maze of reversals implied in such associations. With Solanas we will recognize that men have appropriated to themselves the names of strong qualities which they call virtues.*

Virgins—that is, women who are "never captured: UNSUBDUED" —are proceeding to Name our own good (that is, life-affirming) qualities (operative habits). When we choose to call these "virtues," we hear this old word in a new way, and it thus becomes a New Word. It is used to describe qualities of Uncaptured/ Unsubdued women, that is, Virgins. Knowing that *virgin* is thought to be derived from the Latin *virga,* meaning green branch, we claim the name *Virtue* also as a green branch, a New Name on the tree of words. *Virtue,* used by Virgins to Name our strengths, is a Virgin Word. Our virtues are Virgin Virtues.[3]

As Viragos, women vigorously claim Virgin Virtues as our own. Viragos, as women "of great stature, strength and courage," joyfully expunge from the definition of this name the idea that a Virago is "one possessing supposedly masculine qualities of

---

* Certain "virtues" are allocated to women, of course, such as obedience, humility, patience, long-suffering, purity. But clearly women have not been judged very good at these, either.

body and mind." For we have never supposed that our Virgin Virtues of body and mind are masculine qualities. Viragos/Virgins join in making a drastic semantic break away from the old virile definitions of virtues, which we have experienced as viruses infecting our minds with dis-ease.

Breaking away from such viral infections of the soul, Nags note with interest that from the paternal point of view our Virgin Virtues are vices. Indeed, such misnaming is among their deadliest de-vices. Attempting to de-vice us, they define and apply to our conduct the term *vice,* as meaning "moral depravity or corruption . . . WICKEDNESS." Since according to sadostandards Wiccen women, that is, all Witches, are Wicked, we can virtuously affirm "depravity" and "corruption." The word *depravity* is from the Latin *pravus,* meaning crooked, and *corruption* is from *com* plus *rumpere,* meaning to break. Racy women are indeed crooked by the false standards of Boring morality, and together we do indeed break out of its straightjackets, Racing free.

It is fascinating for Furies to consider another meaning of *vice,* which is "a winding or spiral staircase" (*O.E.D.*). This is derived from the Latin *vitis,* vine, with reference to the spiral growth of the tendrils. *Vice,* then, can Name the characteristic spiral pattern of biophilic movement, of growth. Heard in this sense, it can Name the good operative habits, the green branches, which are Virgin Virtues. Thus understood, *Vice* is a New Word. It calls to mind the fact that the Virtues/Vices (the Virtuous Vices) of Virgins are like spiral staircases, making possible movement out of the Foreground/Flatland into Other dimensions. Our spiraling movement, overcoming the dronish dichotomies of virile/viral virtues and vices, now leads us to the consideration of specific Virgin Virtues.

PRUDENCE

In classical ethics, prudence is an intellectual virtue defined as "right reason about things to be done." It is practical wisdom. As we have seen in the *Foreground* to this Realm, this virtue is believed to enable the prudent person, the possessor of this habit, to find the mean in moral virtues. For example, it supposedly makes possible the performance of genuinely courageous acts which avoid the extremes of cowardice on the one hand and rashness on the other. Since Pyromantic Prudence, unlike the virile virtue of prudence, reflects both the experience and the movement of Prudes, which are Extreme, the Prudence of Prudes inspires choices which are Extreme. This does not mean that a Prude will not seek "right reason" about matters of moral virtue. It does mean that her standards for judging/measuring the mean between extremes, such as cowardice and rashness, are different from the standards of phallic morality. Her standards are Pyrometric. For Pyrosophical Wisdom is Passionate, Extreme.

This Extremity of the Prudence of Prudes—our Practical Pyrosophy—is associated with the fact that Pyromantic Prudence is ineffably more questioning than is the prudence traditionally defined in patriarchal theology/philosophy. The limitations of phallic prudence are illustrated in the analysis of this virtue by Aquinas, who wrote that "the ends of moral virtue must of necessity pre-exist in the reason." Discussing this position, he wrote that "it does not belong to prudence to appoint the end to moral virtues, but only to regulate the means." [4]

For this type of thinker, then, prudence is only about the means to certain ends which "pre-exist in the reason." Prudence simply enables the prudent person to draw the right conclusions about *how* to act. It does not question *why*. For example, it is not the function of virile prudence to ask such a question as: *Why* be courageous? Nor does it question *what* courage is.

The Prudence of Prudes moves into Virgin territory. It does not pre-suppose that the answers to the questions why? and what? are known. Virgin Prudence is concerned not only with determining the means to pre-existing ends (assessing *how* to achieve these) but also with questioning the ends, purposes. A Prude asks her own Wild Whys, in the light of which she can consider radically Other ways and means. Questioning the basic presuppositions of patriarchy itself, she is empowered by Pyrogenetic Passion to question precisely the taken-for-granted ends/purposes that have been embedded in women's psyches from earliest childhood.

Since such irregular, Virginal Prudence is expressive of Wonderlust, it leads Prudes astray from the assumed regulations and rules of Prickery. By phallic standards, this Virgin Virtue is assuredly a Cardinal Vice, and the repeated deviant acts through which it is acquired are Sins. A Prude can take pride in these Originally Sinful Acts. She can recall with interest the teaching of saint Augustine that self-love leading to the contempt of "God" is the origin of every sin.[5] For indeed her Self-Centering Lust, extending to the contempt of the phallic god, helps her to be Virginally Prudent, committing Originally Sinful Acts of questioning and challenging the old saws/laws of the Lecherous State.

The Virtuous Vice of Pyrometric Prudence is Wild Wisdom that counsels and commands women to perform acts which, by the standards of phallicism, are extreme. Prudes breaking the Laws of Lechery, act wisely in ways that may appear rash, outrageous, and even raving mad. For Pyromantic Prudence is the wisdom of Weirds, the sagacity of Soothsayers and Scolds. It is queen of the Immoral Virtues/Vices, the chief of which are Nemesis, Courage, and Distemper.

The prudence of Prudes is a Volcanic Virtue/Vice, exploding out of the deeply buried cauldrons of women's experience. As volcanic, it brings the promise of new beginnings that are grounded in buried, ancient Origins. Erupting from the concealed chambers of women's Racial memories, it is Pyrosophical, bringing renewed knowledge of the nature and properties of Furious Fire/Desire. This knowledge gives form and direction to actions. Like a spiral staircase, it shapes, directs movement so that this is biophilic, spiraling past the Foreground/Fatherland of fixated thought and feeling into an Otherworld—a place of Unfolding/Realizing Passion for action, for be-ing.

It is essential, then, that Prudes reflect upon this Volcanic Virgin Virtue/Vice. The procedure here will be to analyze its parts.

THE PARTS OF PYROMANTIC PRUDENCE

In the medieval tradition of theological ethics (moral theology), prudence is said to have eight "quasi-integral" parts, that is, elements that are needed for a "perfect act" of the virtue of prudence.[6] These are: memory, understanding, docility, shrewdness, reason, foresight, circumspection, caution.[7] Prudes can prudently use this analysis as a means of spiraling into comprehension of Practical Pyrosophy, or Volcanic, Virgin Prudence. I shall re-claim/re-Name these parts, then, one by one.

Memory

Traditionally, *memory* has been considered a necessary part of the virtue of prudence, since the practice of this virtue requires experience, and experience is the result of many memories.[8] Patriarchal prudence, of course, is based upon restored, mediated memories that reconstruct women's experiences. Women breaking out of the vises of virile virtue need to call upon/call forth the deep E-motional memories of authentic individual and collective experiences—experiences which are dis-regarded and erased by the preachers of patriarchal prudence. Developing the Virgin Virtue of Prudence requires dis-covering the links among these memories, that is, re-weaving women's own context of experiences. The decisions made by Prudes on the basis of this uncovered and re-created context will be utterly Other than choices made on the basis of paternally programmed foreground memories. Moreover, deep memories, as I have shown, are E-motional, moving women's psyches in vast rhythmic movements that connect with the rhythms of the Elemental world. Their eruptions are Volcanic Dis-coverings that empower Prudes to choose and decide in Other-dimensional ways, ways that are Fired with Archaic insights of inner knowing. The Prudence of Prudes is inspired by the Muses of Gyn-Ecological Memory.

Understanding

As part of the virtue of prudence, *understanding* traditionally means an intuitively right estimate of some particular end.[9] I have pointed out that in classical christian ethics there is no basic questioning of patriarchally ordered ends. Thus there can be no radically defiant patriarchal understanding. However, the Understanding implied in Volcanic Prudence reaches beyond male-ordered ends. It moves under, stands under these man-made purposes, giving insight into the ontological telos/final causality that is hidden behind artificial agendas. That is, it uncovers a woman's own final cause, her own deep purpose that moves her in the process of be-ing.

The Understanding of Prudes stubbornly asks crucial whys. This is a habit of Nags, of Nag-Gnostics. Such Understanding is a constant questioning/questing as well as an answer, and thus it doubly perplexes the patriarchs, who predictably label Prudes "imprudent." The price of Prudish Understanding, then, is prickocratic persecution. Its reward is the activity itself of Nag-Gnostic Understanding, of Gnawing the way through the dictated dead ends that block Furies from our purposes.

Docility

Docility, of course, is part of the patriarchal virtue of prudence. The virilely virtuous drone is docile in the usually understood sense of "TRACTABLE, OBEDIENT; *often:* lacking in independence: SUBMISSIVE." Given these meanings, the word often has a noxious aroma. However, this word is rooted in the Latin *docere,* meaning to teach. Thus the primary, unpolluted meaning of *docile* is simply "teachable." While Dragonish women Understandingly despise the virile/viral docility prescribed by and for drones, proclaiming our Selves ineffably undocile in this sense, we can cultivate and respect Deviant Docility—the ability to be taught by Wise Women, by our Selves and our experiences, and by any one who has any truth to teach. This active, selective Docility is simply free use of the ability to learn, which is essential for Pyrosophical Wisdom.

Shrewdness

Shrewdness was understood by Aristotle as "a faculty of hitting upon the middle term [connecting link] instantaneously." As he explained:

It would be exemplified by a man who saw that the moon has her bright side always turned towards the sun, and quickly grasped the cause of this, namely that she borrows her light from him [*sic*]; or observed somebody in conversation with a man of wealth and divined that he was borrowing money, or that the friendship of these people sprang from a common enmity.[10]

Shrewdness, then, is the ability to guess quickly the connecting links ("middle terms") in situations. Shrews will note, however, that the "middle terms" that are "hit upon" by those who possess patriarchal shrewdness are often based upon the prevailing assumptions of the society in which the "shrewd" person lives. In the hierarchical society in which Aristotle lived and which he favored, the rich and the poor did not mingle casually. Thus when a person was seen in conversation with a man of wealth, a "shrewd" observer might be right in assuming that the poor person was borrowing money, or else that the two were bonding against a common enemy. Why else, he might ask, would they be talking with each other in this manner? In a different kind of society, this assessment would not be so shrewd.

My point is that the shrewdness of those who possess patriarchal prudence functions accurately within a predictable set of circumstances, those prevailing within one or another of the forms of patriarchal society. However, such shrewdness can be most unshrewd by Shrewish standards, for Shrews do not function predictably according to any set of phallic assumptions. An example cited by Denise Connors illustrates this point. A group of nurses were sitting together in a restaurant absorbed in their own conversation, when a boorish male who had been overhearing their discussion walked over and began talking to them. (He felt free to do this, of course, since women together are perceived as "alone.") The bore interrupted them with a "question," which ran something like the following: "So you're nurses, eh? I'll bet you've seen everything?" Within the context of the bore's-eye-view, the women could be expected to laugh in a nervous and embarrassed manner. His "shrewd" assessment of the situation was overturned, however. One of the women immediately replied: "What's to see? Two withered peaches on a dead limb!" The bore retreated immediately.[11] The Shrew who responded to him had swiftly and accurately assessed his intent and expectation—humiliation and man-ipulation of women, which was the connecting link in his obviously habitual behavior patterns—and she deftly reversed the situation.

Again, Shrews know that many employers assume that their female employees will respond to their tactics of harassment in predictable ways. When the harassment is sexual, the expectation is that the female employee will respond as women have been socialized to re-act, that is, with fear and denial. When the tactics are similar to those used against any disadvantaged, deviant, or defiant group, the expectation is that the beleaguered victim will respond in the same cowardly manner in which the oppressors themselves would react to such treatment. Such patriarchal "shrewdness" fails in the face of Volcanic Virgin Virtue.

Moreover, since phallic shrewdness, as part of the patriarchal virtue of prudence, is a habit, bore-ocrats predictably continue to repeat their erroneous assessments. To the extent that Shrews have exorcised the norms of Normal Behavior from our actions, we escape the grasp of the masters' "middle terms," and they remain mystified by missing links. Of course, some of the habitual tactics of bore-ocratic shrewdness continue to do damage, for example, the tactic of "divide and conquer." Shrews can over-come such devices only to the extent that we develop Shrewish Shrewdness.*

The Shrewdness of Shrews implies seeing *different* connecting links (middle terms) in assessing our situation, because the E-motional/intellectual environment of our thinking is not ruled by the prevailing assumptions (fallacies) of phallocracy. We con-jecture in a different context. Thus, in estimating what risks to take, Shrews draw upon deep knowledge of the *intent* of the patri-archs, knowing their lust to obstruct the Breaking Out of female be-ing. It is the depth of this knowledge that radicalizes Shrews to an extent that is beyond the capacity of the patriarchal mind to imagine and that makes Volcanic Virtuous actions unpredictable to them—whereas sadobehavior remains quite predictable.

Yet ultimately it is Shrewdness concerning Prudes' own pur-poses that matters. Women who have been awakened to E-motional identification with the Race of Women, who have Realized the capacity for moral outrage on behalf of female Ele-mental be-ing, are not pre-occupied with second-guessing the foreground rulers/foolers. Rather, Prudes are Shrewdly focusing Fire/Desire, fostering the Movement of the Biophilic Race.

Reason

Reason has been considered necessary for prudence, so that the virtuous person "may rightly apply universals to particulars, which latter are various and uncertain." [12] The primary universal principle to be applied is that good is to be done and evil avoided. While it would appear that no one could argue this point, the problem is, of course, with the interpretation of "good" and of "evil."

Racy women reason from a perspective that is Other than that which accepts patriarchal meanings/myths of good and evil. Since women have suffered the symbolic and practical conse-quences of phallic reason about/from ideas of *good* and *evil,* these words are especially subject to the scrutiny of women criti-cizing such reason. The church considered it prudent, after all, to

---

* Shrewd Shrews have noted that in the eighties bore-ocratic back-lashers have been targeting Shrews, as evidenced in the increase of in-terest on the part of college drama producers and professional Shake-spearean theater companies in re-producing *The Taming of the Shrew.*

burn alive hundreds of thousands of women accused of Witch-craft, reasoning from the premise that "good is to be done and evil avoided."

Raging women, therefore, Realizing Elemental powers of reason, cannot tranquilly accept the bland and vacuous abstractions about "good" and "evil" that abound in the ethics of Boredom. Furies are too keenly aware of the reality of christian gynocide and genocide to believe the dis-passionate quasi-mathematical verbiage of patriarchal ethicists. This detachment itself reeks of deception to those who have studied and can E-motionally re-call the history of Foresisters burned as Witches. Those whose Race has been labeled, maimed, killed, and dismembered as "evil" cannot be dispassionate about evil.* Moreover, the "particulars" about which Racy women reason, the everyday details of women's lives, are charged with the burden of the stigma inflicted upon the

---

* Ann Petry, a Black author writing in the 1940s potently described the evils that afflict Black women in America in her novel *The Street* (Boston: Houghton Mifflin Company, 1946). The young woman, Lutie Johnson, who is the central figure of the story, suffers multiple afflictions associated with being Black and female. At the end of the novel, when she is forced to kill in self-defense a man who has betrayed her, struck her, and is attempting to rape her, her pent-up Rage against all the oppression (symbolized by the novel's title) finds expression as she strikes him with an iron candlestick:

> Finally, and the blows were heavier, faster, now, she was striking at the white world which thrust black people into a walled enclosure from which there was no escape; and at the turn-of-events which had forced her to leave Bub [her son] alone while she was working so that he now faced reform school, now had a police record.
>
> She saw the face and head of the man on the sofa through the waves of anger in which he represented all these things and she was destroying them. (p. 430)

The young woman's act is very comprehensible to the reader within the context vividly portrayed in the novel. It is evident also that she has accurately assessed her situation in relation to the prevailing system of "justice," for she realizes, after killing her attacker, that: "The only thing she could do was to go away and never come back," hoping that her "crime" would not be discovered. For "the smartest lawyer in the world couldn't do anything for Bub, not now, not when his mother had killed a man (p. 432). Although this novel is deeply tragic, the reader is left with hope for the strong and courageous young woman, whose integrity and desire for justice were never undermined, violated or destroyed.

female sex by the patriarchs. Stigmatized, women are symbolic representations of "evil." The conclusion that is implicit in the symbolic equation of all women with evil is the moral correctness of gynocide.

Foresight

Since "future contingents" are the subject matter of prudence, *foresight* has been reckoned a part of prudence, "for it implies the notion of something distant, to which that which occurs in the present has to be directed." [13] When women Race beyond/ through the limitations of patriarchal measurements of time, the meaning of *foresight* shifts radically. Since Volcanic memories have their sources far behind/beyond phallotemporality, the vision of "something distant" is correspondingly expanded. The eruption of ancestral memories is enabling to Crones in such a way that the possibility of creating the future becomes more and more Realized. Nag-Gnostic knowing of final causality becomes less and less mediated. Prudes become Present in an ontologically active way, presentiating future be-ing. Women who are overcoming amnesia become Soothsayers not merely in a passive sense (receiving "revelations") but in a creative sense. Pyrosophical Prudes learn to *practice* wisdom.

To put it another way, Fates do not simply foretell that which appears to be inevitable. Nor is Fateful Fore-making simply "directing" things in the present to some pre-fixed goal. Fates act out of deepening be-ing in the past and present, participating in the Tidal Timing of biophilic creation. This is the calling of women as Weirds, as Norns, as Muses, as Augurs, as Websters, as Spider Women/Spinsters, and as called by a thousand other names. The diversity of creative forecasting casts women further through the Pyrospheres. The Foresight of Fates gives purpose to Wandering, focus to Wondering. It forearms women and forges the future.

Circumspection

Circumspection means "the quality of being careful to consider all circumstances and possible consequences." This has been deemed necessary for prudence, for "it happens that a thing is good in itself and suitable to the end, and nevertheless becomes evil or unsuitable to the end, by reason of some combination of circumstances." [14]

As a woman becomes Shrewder, her perception of her environment—her circumstances—changes. On the foreground level, she can see more clearly the Catch-22 situation of all women in a gynocidal world; she sees that hazards are "everywhere." At the same time, living more and more in Pyrospheres, she sees extraordinarily Positive/Pyrogenetic convergences of circumstances, which en-courage her to Dreadfully Daring Pyrosophical decisions. For Surviving/Thriving in Pyrospheres involves Realizing E-motionally Wild connections with the elements of one's environment.

Rather than becoming cautious and timid, then, Circumspective Prudes become bolder, and circumstances are better comprehended. Gyn/Ecological Circumspection increases possibilities and heightens powers, rather than decreasing and stunting these. Moreover, a creative Prude not only acts within a context of given circumstances. She changes circumstances and Spins new ones. To a certain extent this process resembles her dis-covering of New Words. For some of the new circumstances are new in the sense that they are heard/seen in a new meaning context, and thus are heard/seen in a new way. The process is one of creative Circumspection, and it becomes possible when a woman has chosen to know E-motionally, that is, to think and live in Fire. It becomes possible when, from this Pyrosophical vantage point, she strives to know outermost circumferences, the cosmic context of circumstances.

Caution

Caution has been enumerated among the parts of the virtue of prudence because, in contingent matters of action, "even as false is found with true, so is evil mingled with good, on account of the great variety of these matters of action, wherein good is often hindered by evil, and evil has the appearance of good." [15]

Women are certainly Nagged by awareness of situations in which "evil has the appearance of good." Phallic ethicists have always tried to legitimate the oppressive conditions of women's lives as "good," as "God's will," et cetera. Pyrosophical Prudes, however, are concerned also with other manifestations of reversal, as when good, natural acts and situations are labeled "evil" by the Masters of Male Morality. A Prude is Nagged by recurrent awareness that what she deeply experiences as good for her Self has the appearance of evil to the namers/framers of normality. Worse than this, they have made her own good appear evil even to her.

The Caution of Pyromantic Prudes, therefore, is not concerned only or even primarily with recognizing the evil that is presented as good, for example, socialization to femininity. For this deception—at least in its blatant forms—has been uncovered in more basic stages of coming to consciousness. The more subtle task is acknowledging what is good/natural for women and reclaiming/ Naming this, our heritage, which has so universally been misnamed in patriarchy that we can barely find words, at first, to Name our truth. Such a task requires active, daring, creative Caution. One avoids or fights off the evil that is paraded as good (no small task, to be sure). But a woman must re-Name with all of her Courage and creative power—with the process of her life —the good that has been stolen from her through being stigmatized as evil.

This creative Caution of Prudes, this refusal to be separated by deception from what is Originally Good, is canny/uncanny. Among the meanings of *canny,* Searchers find "skillful, clever, 'cunning' (in the old sense)" (*O.E.D.*). In archaic Scottish, *canny wife* means "wise woman, midwife (French *femme sage*); hence *canny moment:* moment of childbirth" (*O.E.D.*). The word therefore suggests the witfulness of Weirds and the creative powers of Websters. In addition, *canny* has an "obsolete" Scottish meaning: "supernaturally wise, endowed with occult or magical power" (*O.E.D.*). Canniness thus implies the Elementally natural powers of those who are Realizing Archimagical potency.

The cautiousness that is implied in the word *canny* is Elemental —utterly Other than the cautiousness of the care-takers of mortuaries of male morality. For *canny* also means "careful or cautious in motion or action; *hence,* quiet, gentle, 'soft' of speech; free from commotion, disturbance, or noise. Said of persons or animals, in their action, speech, or disposition; and also applied to things, as running water, the sea, wind, etc. (the usual sense in modern Scotch)" (*O.E.D.*). Thus it Names the strong "softness" of biophilic be-ing. It suggests that the Naming process of Canny women, like the sounds of animals, running water, the sea, the wind, is in harmony with the natural environment. The creations of "canny wives" are Gyn/Ecological.

To the mortuary care-takers of morality this Canniness is *un-*

canny, that is, "arousing feelings of dread or of inexplicable strangeness: seeming to have a supernatural character, cause, or origin: EERIE, MYSTERIOUS, WEIRD." It is *uncanny* to the unctuous authorities also in the sense that it is "extending to a degree beyond what is normal or expected: suggesting superhuman or supernatural powers or qualities." It is predictable that the Unctuous Undertakers of Necropolitan Society will experience the creativity of Canny Wives/Weirds as "uncanny." Proud Prudes take on this name with Uncanny Understanding.

The apparent contradiction expressed in the Naming of Prudish Caution as Canny/Uncanny is related to the paradoxical Naming of Virgin Virtues as Vices. For just as the Canny/Virtuous aspect of the acquired habits of Pyrosophical Prudes concerns the Realizing of women's power of Presence to our Selves and to each other, the patriarchal perception of these habits as uncanny and as vices suggests the power of Absence of Prudes to the would-be objectifiers. Canny, Virginally Virtuous women who are Realizing our power of Presence can also claim the negative names, for withdrawal of gynergy from the State of Possession is essential for spiraling movement.

This movement requires the acquiring of a variety of Virtues/ Vices through repeated acts. Central among Volcanic Virgin Virtues—Virtuous Vices—are Nemesis, Courage, and Distemper. We shall turn now to a Canny consideration of these.

FROM "JUSTICE" TO NEMESIS

The first of the moral virtues, *justice,* has been defined as "the perpetual and constant will to render to each one his right." [16] Barring the masculine/pseudogeneric pronoun, the definition would appear to have some merit. It becomes more problematic, however, when a woman asks what rights the "just" person judges that "each one" has. It is hardly necessary to review here in detail the long struggle of women to obtain "equal rights" within patriarchy in order to know that the patriarchal devisers of this definition of *justice* had in mind something substantially less than "right" when they created the device of such a concept. Since, moreover, the moral virtue of justice was believed to be situated in the will and thus to require the intellectual virtue of (virile) prudence to direct its acts, it is clear that much, too much, is askew in phallic theories of justice. The "just" king, president, pope, physician, boss, husband, father knows with certainty the proper place and "rights" of the touchable caste.

Nor does the patriarchally defined "vice" of *injustice* throw much light upon the predicament of women. For the Droningly Dictated Dichotomy of justice-injustice is chiefly concerned with the making and breaking of Boys' Club rules. The situation of women—both the oppression and the a-mazing authentic aspirations—is ineffably outside the sphere of petty paternal disputes that is reflected in this dreary semantic dichotomy. The pair, justice-injustice, is too pallid to Name the Righteous Virtue of Raging women.

More accurate to name the object and the process of Racy Righteousness is the term *Nemesis.* As Goddess of divine retribution, the Nemesis within Pyrosophical women wills to act/live the verb which is the root of her Name: *nemein,* meaning to deal out, to dispense retribution. Unlike "justice," which is depicted as a woman blindfolded and holding a sword and scales, Nemesis has her eyes open and uncovered—especially her Third Eye. Moreover, she is concerned less with "retribution," in the sense of external meting out of rewards and punishments, than with an internal judgment that sets in motion a kind of new psychic alignment of energy patterns. Nemesis, thus Named, is hardly irrelevant mysticism. Rather, this Names a relevant mysticism which responds to the tormented cries of the oppressed, and to the hunger and thirst for creative be-ing.

Certainly, women have always cried and struggled for "justice." The thwarting of this longing and struggling gives rise to the birth pangs of radical feminist awareness. But only when the knowledge that something is not "right" evolves into uncovering the invisible context of gynocide and, beyond this, into active participation in the Elemental context of biophilic harmony and power can there be great and sustained creativity and action. To Name this active Elemental contextual participation, which transcends and overturns patriarchal "justice" and "injustice," Other words are needed. Nemesis is a beginning in this direction.

The thirst for what has been perceived as attainable "justice," as well as the longing to overcome "injustice," has driven women into the arms of the male left and of the male right. Women of the left have sought Justice through male-approved methods of "revolution." Women of the right have sought justice (though they often cannot articulate even this word) through tears, self-deprecation, insistence on their place in heaven, militant anti-feminism, vicarious living. Women swing to the left and to the right when captured within the confines of the patriarchally controlled imagination—expressed in the words "justice" and "injustice."

Understandably there is often a passivity in women's hope for justice, as for a commodity long overdue. Even the expression "fighting (or working) for justice" suggests a commodity to be gained through active struggle. It does not convey the object of this striving as *something that women create*. This may in part be related to the passive condition of women as oppressed. I suggest, however, that the problem has to do also with the word *justice*, which is not sufficiently inspiring/Firing. It has the flavor, texture, and odor of a hand-out which women deserve, and which presumably could ultimately be bestowed by or wrenched from the prevailing order. But the prevailing order/ordure does not have the capacity to bestow or even to have wrenched away from it the sought-after treasure. It would be more fruitful to engage in the proverbial fruitless task of trying to obtain blood from a stone.

If a woman experiments with changing her discussion of justice from the nominal to verbal forms, she will quickly hit upon the verb *rectify*. For justice, after all, is said to be about "the right." Consistent with this is the fact that *rectify* suggests that the task is to straighten out, correct, redress, remedy, reform a situation, that is, to re-turn it to a previous condition that is understood on the same level as the "problem." The procedure sounds like correcting an error in arithmetic; it appears to be correcting an imbalance, restoring balance. There is nothing in this language that stirs the imagination beyond a patriarchal future and past, a regainable status quo.

Recognizing on some level the stagnation inherent in the dichotomy justice-injustice, theologians such as Paul Tillich have tried to write of "creative justice." Yet this effort is so alien to Pyrosophical awareness and analysis, so reinforcing of submission and of what can be called the feminine imperative, that it will make a feminist's flesh crawl. Tillich writes, for example:

Creative Justice demands . . . that he be accepted who is unacceptable in terms of proportional justice. In accepting him into the unity of forgiveness, love exposes both the acknowledged break with justice on his side with all its implicit consequences and the claim inherent in him to be *declared* just and to be *made* just by reunion [emphases mine].[17]

Certainly, acts of forgiveness are necessary in any deep relationship. But this is not all that Tillich is arguing for.

In order to savor the true flavor of this text, the reader could try the following exercise: Imagine a priest, rabbi, or minister reciting this text to a woman who has been repeatedly battered by her husband, or whose husband has sexually assaulted their daughter. Imagine the woman trying to find moral support for her decision to leave. Clearly, *declaring* the offender/criminal "just" and reuniting with him will not make him "just." Rather, what happens in such a case is that the woman is "morally" bullied into forfeiting her right to judge. She is "morally" intimidated into Self-castration, into breaking her own Naming process. She is duped, guilt-tripped into separation from her own powers as Nemesis, blocked from re-claiming her life. Tillich's moral verbiage in such a case, then, is worse than useless. It serves structures of oppression—notably those of the sexual caste system—which are not even taken into consideration.

I am suggesting, then, that *justice* is not an adequate name for that which Canny, Raging women create. The new psychic alignment of gynergy patterns associated with Nemesis is not merely rectifying of a situation which the term *unjust* could adequately describe. Nemesis is Passionate Spinning/Spiraling of new/ancient forms and connections of gynergy. It is an E-motional habit acquired/required in the Pyrospheres. It demands Shrewd as well as Fiery judgment and is therefore a Nag-Gnostic/Pyrognostic Virtue. Nemesis is a habit built up by inspired acts of Righteous Fury, which move the victims of gynocidal oppression into Pyrospheric changes unheard of in patriarchal lore.

Some women have always known about active desire that reaches beyond the confines of "justice." In 1852, in a political speech at the Woman's Rights Convention, Elizabeth Oakes Smith asked:

My friends, do we realize for what purpose we are convened? Do we fully understand that we aim at nothing less than an entire subversion of the present order of society, a dissolution of the whole existing social compact?[18]

Assessing the twentieth-century American scene, Florynce Kennedy, commenting from her vantage point as Black feminist activist and attorney, wrote:

Every form of bigotry can be found in ample supply in the legal system of our country. It would seem that Justice (usually depicted as a woman) is indeed blind to racism, sexism, war, and poverty.[19]

The specific functioning of blindfolded "justice" in the legal mind (the patriarchal mind *par excellence*) has been expressed by Joyce Carol Oates in her description of a defense lawyer:

. . . he believed in the justice of his using any legal methods he could improvise to force the other side into compromise or into dismissals of charges, or to lead a jury into the verdict he wanted. Why not? He was a defense lawyer.[20]

As archetypally cast into the role of "the other side," women know about the self-righteous sense of "justice" of professional defenders of the sadosystem, who use every method to force those who are pleading for justice "into compromise or into dismissal of charges," and to lead the "jury" of patriarchally possessed peers to pronounce the destroyers of women "not guilty." And women know that the nefarious methods of gynocide are legal.

E-motionally propelled beyond the inadequate naming expressed in the dichotomy "justice-injustice," Pyrosophical women begin to live in dimensions of that which, transitionally at least, can be called Nemesis. The Virtue of Nemesis may be perceived as *sinister,* for it is creativity that is utterly Other than the righteousness of the sadorulers. It is *sinister,* not merely in the sense of choosing left as opposed to right, for this would be mere opposition of opposites on the same plane. Rather, Nemesis moves within a different context, and creates such a context as it moves. The Otherness of this context is not "complementary" to the prevailing order of sadosociety, for it *is* Other. Women participating in the powers of Nemesis, Spinning gynocentric ways of be-ing, are not caught in reactive rage, but are Actively Raging, Racing.

Among the meanings of the noun *rage* is "violent action of the elements (as wind or sea)." Rage also means "a furious storm: TEMPEST." It means "extreme force of feeling: PASSION, FRENZY." These definitions all suggest Elemental force. Nemesis is engendered by Rage. Pyrographers will note that Nemesis as divine vengeance often has been envisioned as a visitation in the form of Elemental phenomena. Inspired by the Muses of Rage, a woman coming into touch with Nemesis becomes awakened to Elemental powers of Geomancy, Aeromancy, Hydromancy, Pyromancy. Her "visitations," or her influence upon situations, arises from Realizing her harmony with the elements. She becomes more at home in the world of dimensions uncaptured by the Phallic State.

Awareness of these dimensions gives the Canniness necessary to Spin new/ancient gynergy patterns that transform oppressive states. Sometimes this implies moving out of an old environment physically; always it implies transforming the conditions where/ when one lives.

To imagine that women who choose Creative Nemesis are therefore insensitive to the reality of oppression is to miss the point. For it is Visionary Creation that carries Women's Movement foreward (upward, downward, aroundward) and that sustains the woman warrior. Maxine Hong Kingston vividly illustrates the sustaining power of feminist vision, in relating how the stories of women warriors, told to her by her mother, aided her in the struggle of growing up female and Chinese in American society.[21] Monique Wittig's feminist classic, *Les Guérillères,* has inspired thousands of women with Amazonian Imagination.[22] Indeed, numerous Crones have been engaged in the process of conjuring Nemesis through re-membering the lore of our foremothers and through Spinning Original tales.[23] It is precisely such transcendent vision that makes possible acute sensitivity to the common facts of oppression, for in the light of what might be and perhaps once was, an A-mazed woman sees/feels the horror of each fact, each event of the Possessed State of her sex and of nature on this planet. This vision fires her to fight back.

Unlike blindfolded, static patriarchal "justice," a woman inspired by Nemesis sharpens her senses, sharpens her Labrys. As her axe, this can cut back barriers. As her wings, it carries her on the wind. Better than a broom, it bears her beyond the foreground fortresses.

Nemesis is not about casuistry, nor about cautiously measured rewards and punishments. It is about flying through the badlands, badtimes. It is about creating new cacophony, new concord, countering destruction with creation. For such symphonic soaring, a woman needs Outrageous Courage.

OUTRAGEOUS, CONTAGIOUS COURAGE

I have attempted to show that Racy women Sin in the most colossal and cosmic way by be-ing Elemental. Ontological Courage, then, the Courage required for Pyrosophical be-ing, is a Sin-full Virtue. Derived from the Latin *cor,* meaning heart, *Courage* signifies a heartfelt, passionate strength. Sin-full Courage is the core/heart of all the Volcanic Virtues.

The Courage of Pyromantic Crones is necessarily Outrageous. One meaning of *outrageous* is "exceeding the limits of what is normal or tolerable." It means "not conventional or matter-of-fact: EXTRAVAGANT, FANTASTIC." An Outrageously Courageous Crone, since she is Pyrogenetic and therefore not conventional or matter-of-fact, risks being perceived as *outrageous* in the sense of "extremely offensive: showing a disregard for decency or good taste." Of course, as her taste becomes more and more discerning she is more and more subjected to foreground labeling as "tasteless." Such deprecations should be treated as en-couraging/heartening signs that she has made progress in reversing the reigning reversals.

At the core/"heart" of the maze of reversals which Raging, Outrageous women must reverse, are the sado-ideology and sado-symbolism of the heart itself. The heart is said to symbolize "the centre of being, both physical and spiritual; the divine presence at the centre." [24] The symbol of the heart as center has been spoiled for countless women, however, by the sickening sado-sophism that "man is the head, and woman is the heart." For the cliché is intended to legitimate women's condition of subjection as entombed in the touchable caste.

The sadosages speak euphemistically of the heart as representing the "central wisdom of feeling" as opposed to the "head-wisdom" of reason. [25] The clue to the ensuing deceptions is in the dichotomy/opposition itself. No matter how highly patriarchal propagandists extol what they call "the heart," their ascribing of this to women says it all. The "central wisdom of feeling" is intended to signify mush-headed sentimentality requiring control by The Head.

By the symbolic dissociation of "the heart" from Intellectual Courage, from "head-wisdom," the decapitators have attempted the symbolic castration of women (the "hearts") cutting us off from our Active Potency. It is only by Taking Heart again, by Courage-ing the Sin of reuniting her passion and intellect, that a woman can Realize her powers. Pyrosophical Crones, wrenching the Heart back into our own semantic context, make Courage the core of Women's Movement. Taking Heart, then, becomes a Metaphor of Metabeing, carrying a woman into the Pyrospheric Realm, where she transforms, transvalues virtues, desiring, acquiring Volcanic Virtue.

Taking Heart is an essential feminist task. In 1851, Elizabeth Cady Stanton wrote movingly of the need for Courage:

The manner in which all courage and self-reliance is educated *out* of the girl, her path portrayed with dangers and difficulties that never exist, is melancholy indeed. Better, far, suffer occasional insults or die outright, than live the life of a *coward,* or never move without a protector. The best protector any woman can have, one that will serve her at all times and in all places, is *courage;* this she must get by her own experience, and experience comes by exposure.[26]

Here Stanton Names the problem—the breeding out of courage from women under the guise of protection—the breeding out that breaks the hope of Breaking Out. Yet, some have never been thoroughly broken in, and these, less broken, hearten others. As Millicent Garrett Fawcett put it, in 1920:

Courage calls to courage everywhere, and its voice cannot be denied.[27]

This is a Naming of the Contagiousness of Outrageous Courage, of its Pyromagnetic propensity. It is a Naming of the basic calling of Nagsters, who by Taking Heart, Give Heart.

A woman who Takes Heart and Gives Heart moves to the heart of the matter, becoming Self-centering. Having known heartbreak over the dis-memberment of her kind, she now heartens her Self and her Sisters. Her Taking Heart is the magic Self-woven carpet that carries her to Metabeing, the place of her heart's Desiring/Firing. Heartened, she engages in Pyromachy, fighting with Fire, with the fullness of luminous intelligence, the Radiance of Realizing reason. Her words/actions are Outrageous simply because they are beyond the proscribed limits of the familiar Flatland. She judges and *acts* according to Pyrometric standards.

Such Taking Heart is essentially that which can Give Heart to another woman, in the sense of en-couraging her to re-claim her own heart/head. I am not suggesting that an Outrageous woman acts Courageously chiefly in order to inspire others. Rather, her Taking Heart is essential to her own Elemental being. It is contagious, but not always in an immediately perceivable way. Yet Crones know that Courage is the Elemental Lifeline.

The Furious Fighting Cow, and How She Escaped

Courage is a bond between Outrageous women and other Wild creatures, especially those who in some dimensions, at least, escape the sadorule. In a remarkable travel book, *The Sea and the Jungle* (a favorite book of Rachel Carson), H. M. Tomlinson describes the brutal taking aboard ship of sixty head of cattle—each being hauled on board by a rope around her horns, the rope being attached to a crane, so that all of each cow's weight was on her horns. Each was hoisted up, bumping against the ship's side, and then dumped on the deck. All were subdued by this treatment but one, a small black heifer. Tomlinson describes the resistance of this "implacable rebel":

The cattlemen, as punishment for the trouble she had given them ashore, kept her dangling over the deck, and one got level with her face and mocked her, slapping her nose. She actually defied him. . . . She was no cow. She was insurrection, she was the hate for tyrants incarnated. They dropped her. She was up and away like a cat. . . . She put everybody on that deck in the shrouds or in the forecastle head as she trotted round with her tail up, looking for brutes to put them to death. None of the cows (of course) helped her. By a trick she was caught. . . . Then she tried to kick all who passed. If the rest of the cattle had been like her none would have suffered. Alas! They were probably all scientific evolutionists, content to wait for men to become kindly apple-lovers by slow and natural uplift; and gravely deprecated the action of the heifer from which, as peaceful cows, they disassociated themselves.[28]

During the voyage, though her head was fixed unmovably, unlike the others, the black heifer kept her unabated Fury. Recalling this, Tomlinson wrote, "What a heart!" But the story does not end here. After the journey the men had to unload the cattle:

We waited for the turn of the black heifer. . . . She made a furious lunge at the men when her nose was free, but the winch rattled, and she was brought up on her hind legs, blaring at us all. In that ugly manner she was walked on two legs across the deck, a heroine in shameful guise, while the men laughed. She was hoisted, and lowered into the river. She fought at the waiting canoe with her feet, but at last the men released her horns from the tackle. With only her face above water she heaved herself, open-mouthed, at the canoe trying to bite it, and then made some almost successful efforts to climb into it. The canoe men were so panic-stricken that they did nothing but muddle one another's efforts. The canoe rocked dangerously. This wicked animal had no care for its own safety like other cattle. It surprised its tormentors because it showed its only wish was to kill them. Just in time, the men paddled off for their lives, the cow after them. Seeing she could not catch them, she swam ashore, climbed the bank, looking around then for sight of the enemy—but they were all in hiding—and then began browsing in the scrub.[29]

This story, which could be called "The Furious Cow and How She Escaped," depicting the triumphant escape of the heifer who did not have the support of her subdued sisters, might be taken from its context and read as a poignant parable for weary and dis-couraged feminists—the moral being: Take Heart. If the brave heifer had been able (or willing) to read, she certainly would have agreed with Stanton's words: "Better, far, suffer occasional insults or die outright, than live the life of a coward." In any case, she demonstrated her knowledge of the fact that Sinfull Courage does not of its essence rely upon sisterly support. To recognize this is not to fall into "blaming the (other) victim." What embattled woman (or animal) has energy to squander on that? To recognize this is to cultivate the Self-reliance so prized by Stanton and other sturdy souls—who of course have Given Heart beyond measure.

Tomlinson's account can be read by feminists as a parable also on another level—critically, looking at it within the context of his telling it. For this story of the brave heifer and the fifty-nine who were subdued leaves something to be desired. His playful description of the "peaceful cows," as "gravely deprecating" the action of the heifer, erases the fact that it was the torture endured by the animals that had subdued them. Tomlinson did acknowledge this, of course, but seems immediately to have forgotten the significance of his own information in his delighted admiration of the solitary rebel. For, as he writes, the cows had *all* been "wild things, which had been collected in the campo with great difficulty." [30] He writes, as we have seen, "None of the cows (of course) helped her. . . . If the rest of the cattle had been like her, none would have suffered." The Outraged reader might ask: Did Tomlinson even protest? As an honored passenger he could have tried to intervene in the face of extraordinary cruelty. The context of his account does not suggest that this was his reaction.

Tomlinson does record the "great joy" which he and his companion, the ship's doctor, experienced at watching the tortured heifer's efforts to free her horns. But "great joy" at seeing the struggle of one "implacable rebel" does not strike the critical reader as an adequate response to this spectacle of suffering and bravery.

In short, the self-description of Tomlinson portrays/betrays the attitude of the liberal who by his passivity legitimates the Lecherous State. He legitimates this State also by his propensity for singling out the singularly courageous victim/escapee for his admiration, while sustaining contempt for the other Others. The subliminal association with women and other oppressed people is not hard to detect, nor are the applications. In contrast to this "sympathetic liberal observer" stance, the position of the Self-reliant, Outrageous Courageous Crone implies refusal to erase the history of oppression of those Sisters who were subdued and conquered. The Furiously Focused re-calling of the history of oppression of all women is essential to the identity of a feminist and for sustaining the Pyrosophical Vision, even under conditions of seeming desertion and isolation.

Naming Outrageous Courage

The contagiousness of Sin-full Courage—the fact that "courage calls to courage everywhere"—is furthered by the Pyrogenetic Power of Naming, which is itself an expression of the Volcanic Virtue of Courage. As we reach for words, women will do well to scrutinize synonyms for *courageous*. Brewsters will find fitting the adjective *brave,* which is derived from the Old Italian and Old Spanish *bravo,* meaning wild. Another word describing the Bravery of Wild women is *dauntless.* The import of this word is suggested by the verb *daunt,* which is derived from the Latin *domitare,* meaning to tame, and which means "to sap the courage of and subdue through fear." Refusing to be tamed, sapped, or subdued, Undaunted women become Dauntless and Undauntable. Valuing be-ing, women are Valorous/Valiant. As Amazons, women are Audacious. As Phoenixes we are Intrepid, Fearless, rising from the fires that were meant to destroy, entering the Fire that we mean to enjoy.

TEMPERANCE, TEMPER, DISTEMPER DISTEMPERANCE

The "virtue" of temperance has become associated with women, for example, in popular caricatures of the nineteenth century women's temperance movement. Only total ignorance and lack of reflection could "inspire" the belief that this movement was the result of dreary and timid fixations on self-control on the part of small-souled women. This was hardly the case. Carry Nation put the real issue most vividly:

The women and children of Barber County are calling to you men for bread, for clothes, and education. . . . [Instead] men in Medicine Lodge and other towns of Barber County are selling whiskey. . . . No wonder the women want the ballot.[31]

Clearly, the abuse of alcohol by men is linked to the economic oppression of women. Given the societally and legally sanctioned economic power of males, their squandering of money on alcohol has meant serious deprivation for women. Moreover, as Carry Nation also pointed out:

A woman is stripped of everything by them [saloons]. Her husband is torn from her; she is robbed of her sons, her home, her food, and her virtue; and then they strip her clothes off and hang her up bare in these dens of robbery and murder. Truly does the saloon make a woman bare of all things![32]

An obvious point here is that the temperance about which the reformers were concerned was the temperance of men, not of women. In the classical and christian philosophical tradition, the virtue of temperance is concerned with the desires and pleasures of the sense of touch, specifically those concerning sex, food, and drink.[33] While it would at first glance appear that the women's temperance movement was obsessed with drink alone, clearly the implications are wider. The alcohol-related intemperance they were trying to fight involved sexual abuse as well as violence of all kinds against women, children, animals. The crusaders against intemperance were not being prim and proper. They were fighting against the rape and battering of victims of all ages, against deprivation of needed food, drink, clothing, not to mention respect, kindness, health, independence.

Intemperance of males concerning drink, resulting in sexual brutality and abuses of every kind, has been a very real horror and has also functioned for women as a graphic symbol of the intemperance/disorder in patriarchal society itself. To construct a broad-based movement the crusaders focused upon alcohol and/or saloon keepers as the obvious enemy.

This focusing upon the evil of alcoholism worked as a uniting symbol for the activism of many women, and this activism was educational for those who could move on to a wider perspective of patriarchal oppression. The temperance movement thus functioned to *temper* women's powers, that is, to make these stronger and more resilient. Many other forms of activity and activism also have functioned to temper/toughen female powers.

In the 1970s and 1980s, a development in some ways comparable to the temperance movement of the nineteenth century is organized opposition to pornography. To be anti-pornography, of course, does not necessarily imply that one comprehends patriarchy or even opposes it. The *feminist* anti-pornography movement, however, is the creation of many Dreadfully Daring and inventive women confronting an extremely pivotal form of patriarchal oppression, which is recognized as such. Crones see that it is necessary to expand this vision continually, seeing pornography in the context of manifold forms of oppression and also focusing female energy in the directions of Spinning/Wonderlusting. Otherwise, there is not enough inspiration for moving on. Crones have become aware of the man-made embedded mechanisms of needing oppression to give life "meaning." If Hags succumb to this, we are doomed to living/dying out the masters' myth of "conflict and vindication" as the essence of "life's purpose." In such a state, we cannot adequately fight pornography and other manifestations of gynocide.

To deprive our Selves of the Spinning dimensions of feminism, then, is ultimately weakening. Yet of course it is also debilitating to give up the fight, to retreat from battle. In order to deal with the dilemmas posed by this complex situation, Amazons need to acquire the Virgin Virtue of Pyrosophical Temperance, which is quite Other than the virile virtue of temperance.

To understand Pyrosophical Temperance, it helps to know that the word *temperance* is derived from the Latin *temperare,* meaning to mix, blend, regulate. A Furious woman's Temperance requires that she mix, blend, and regulate the complex elements of her struggle and of her creativity in modes that are Pyrometric—passionately measured. Her work of measuring can be aided by the awakening of words related to *temperance,* especially *temper, distemper, distemperance.* These are Sister-Words radiant with Pyrogenetic meanings. I shall consider each in turn.

The verb *temper* can evoke understanding of Pyrosophical Temperance. *Temper* means "to make stronger and more resilient through hardship: TOUGHEN (the hammerblows of fate seemed not to weaken but to temper her strength—John Buchan)." This is the purpose of the hammerblows of the Fates —to Nag Pyrosophical women to original strength and resiliency.

Overcoming the effects of phallic temperance/intemperance and finding the unity of harmony within women's Selves require *tempering* in other senses as well. The verb *temper* means "to put in tune with: ATTUNE," and it means "to adjust the pitch of (a note, chord, instrument)." The tempering of Pyrogenetic women involves becoming attuned to Elemental forces. As a woman becomes more resilient, this attunement becomes sharper, better adjusted to the pitch as well as the rhythms of Wild nature.

Temper as a noun has an ambidextrous quality that is suggestive of Virgin Versatility. It means "heat of mind or emotion, proneness to anger: PASSION." It also means "calmness of mind: COMPOSURE, EQUANIMITY." A woman acquiring Pyrosophical Temperance needs *temper* in both of these senses, as she becomes more resilient and attuned to the Elemental energies within and around her.

Of course, a Pyrosophically Temperate woman does not wish

to acquire foreground "temperance," whether plastic or potted. Disdaining that pseudovirtue, she actively works to *distemper* its effects, that is, "to throw [them] out of order." Aware that *distemper* also means "to disturb or derange the condition of the air, elements, weather, climate, et cetera" (*O.E.D.*), Distempering Hags healthily disturb the condition of the air and other elements, releasing pent-up powers, dismantling the temples of pseudotemperance.

Dragonish women also cause derangement, disturbance, and disorder in the sadostate. This is experienced by its rulers as *distemperance,* that is, "improper proportioning or mingling (of elements)" (*O.E.D.*). Indeed, as Dragons, we are most Improper, and our mingling of the elements is not at all "in good form." For example, we breathe Fire, which is considered distasteful. Our propensity as Witches to raise tempests is not well received, and such Distemperance leads to complaints about our effects upon the general "climate" or "atmosphere." Such complaints are Heartening to Hags.

It is difficult to avoid the conclusion that when women are most true to our Selves we are *distemperate,* that is, "out of order, not functioning normally." As supernormally functioning Scolds, Sylphs, Shrews, Wantons, Weirds, and company, Pyromantic women are definitely "out of order." Breaking Out of the male-ordered catalogs of virile virtues is not a tidy affair. Rather, this is achieved through movements that may be compared to tidal waves, and it involves invoking Muses and confronting demons. This brings us to the work of the following chapter.

CHAPTER EIGHT

TIDY DEMONS, TIDAL MUSES

Hieroglyphic: "written in, constituted by, or belonging to that form of ancient Egyptian writing in which the characters are for the most part recognizable pictures of objects."

Webster's Third New International Dictionary of the English Language

Pyroglyphic: "written in, constituted by, or belonging to that form of Archaic Elemental writing in which the characters are for the most part recognizable pictures/portrayals of Pyromantic Passionate Thought. (See *Hydroglyphic:* ". . . reflections of Hydromantic Tidal Thought"; *Aeroglyphic:* ". . . breathings/breezes of Aeromantic Musing Thought"; *Geoglyphic:* ". . . carvings/markings of Geomantic Earthy Thought.")

Websters' First New Intergalactic Wickedary of the English Language

Elemental Movement is not man-measured/tidy. It is Tidal. This distinction Names the contrast between captured time, the clocking/clacking of clonedom, and the Tidal Timing of the Race of Raging Women. In fathered time—the tidily Man-Dated World —fixers/timers destroy diversity of Timing by routinized reduction to beats that repeat themselves, eat our Selves. Male-ordered monotony iterates/reiterates rigidly regulated days that daze, breaking biorhythms, barring its victims from finding/minding Crone-ology. By its counterfeit Crone-ology, called "chronology," clockocracy prematurely ages potential Sages, preventing Cronehood.

In contrast to timers of tedious tidiness, Tidal Rhythms display the infinite interplay of unity and diversity. Rachel Carson wrote:

The tidal rhythms, as well as the range of tide, vary from ocean to ocean. Flood tide and ebb succeed each other around the world, as night follows day, but as to whether there shall be two high tides and two low in each lunar day, or only one, there is no unvarying rule.[1]

Even the tide has its bores, but these are totally distinct from the bores who are the time-keepers of bore-ocracy. In Rachel Carson's words:

Among unusual creations of the tide, perhaps the best known are the bores. The world possesses half a dozen or more famous ones. A bore is created when a great part of the flood tide enters a river as a single wave, or at most two or three waves, with a steep and high front.[2]

Tidal bores, then, are interesting, and, in contrast to tidy bores (the world possesses numberless famous ones), they exemplify diversity. However, we should never forget the underlying theme of unity among all Tidal phenomena:

There is no drop of water in the ocean, not even in the deepest parts of the abyss, that does not know and respond to the mysterious forces that create the tide.[3]

Moreover, interplay of unity and diversity affects life on the shore as well as in the sea. Carson explains:

Nowhere on the shore is the relation of a creature to its surroundings a matter of a single cause and effect; each living thing is bound to its world by many threads, weaving the intricate design of the fabric of life.[4]

The complexity of the tides and of the life they touch suggests something of the Wild yet harmonious complexity which biophilic women gynaesthetically sense to be characteristic of all Elemental be-ing. When we think of tides, we first image the tides of the ocean, the matrix of life.

The word has a variety of other meanings, however. Thus *tide* also refers to "a similar but less marked rising and falling of an inland body of water." Moreover, there are *earth tides*. Such a tide is "a periodic alteration in the conformation of the earth's crust caused by the same forces that produce ocean tides." And an *atmospheric tide* is "one of the tidal movements of the atmosphere resembling those of the ocean but produced by diurnal temperature changes." Clearly, tides in all of these senses are manifestations of Elemental rhythms, expressing diversity in unity. *Tide* can mean also "a tidal distortion on one celestial body caused by the gravitational attraction of another" (*Webster's New Collegiate Dictionary*). The word, then, clearly suggests cosmic interconnections. Consequently, so also does the adjective *tidal*.

It is crucial that Racing women should consider the origins of the word *tide*. It is derived from the Middle English word *tyde,* meaning time, which in turn is derived from the Old English *tid*. This is akin to the Greek *daiesthai,* meaning to distribute, divide, and to the Sanskrit *dati,* meaning he cuts, divides, mows. The word *tidy* is derived from the same roots and thus also contains within itself the same basic meaning: to divide. The vast contrast between tidy measurements and Tidal Movements is itself an illustration of the extent to which words of the same origin become divided from each other in their meanings so that they function and point in opposite ways. Whereas *tidy* suggests the alienating stereotypes that fix and reify women, tying us down (the tidy housekeeper), *Tidal* can Name the Wild, Gyn/Ecological Movement that connects us with the stars. Thus these words can be wielded to Name the tragedy of tied-down women and the E-motional Movement of the Race that breaks the tidy ties.

DEMONS

A Racy woman finds it a-mazing to learn that the same semantic roots from which *tide* and *tidy* have grown have brought forth also the word *demon*. This word, derived from the Latin *daemon* and the Greek *daimōn,* is believed to be akin to the same Greek and Sanskrit words meaning to divide, and to be derived from the same Indo-European root, *da,* which also means to divide. When a Searcher understands the word *demon* within this semantic context of dividedness, the word takes on new significance for her and *demon* can function as Labrys, as Double Ax.

Usually, of course, *demon* means "an evil spirit: DEVIL." On the Other hand, it means "an attendant, ministering, or indwelling power or spirit: DAIMONION, GENIUS." This latter meaning, which is in fact the more basic sense of the word, feels familiar to a woman who is in touch with her Muse, her Genius, her Self. For she experiences well-being, happiness, which in Greek is called *eudaimonia* and implies "having a good attendant or indwelling spirit." To such a woman, the negative definition of *demon*—"evil spirit"—suggests the deceptive and ghostly presences of absence and absences of Presence that have been devised to divide her from her own Genius, Demon.

A woman who recognizes/Realizes her Demon as her attendant, ministering, and indwelling Power/Spirit, her Genius, her Muse, can fearlessly Name her own Real Presence, her presentiating power. This recognizing/Realizing and Naming releases her to participate in the Tides of her be-ing, to experience the unity and diversity of her Elemental connections. Understanding the identity of the demons who are in fact evil, she can see that these are manifestations of antispirit/antimatter. These are the "spirits" of the tyrants who impose tidy order, masking deep disorder. They cut off participation in the process of Creative Ordering that is suggested by the Latin word *ordiri*, meaning to lay the warp, begin to weave, begin.

Tidiness has been enforced upon women, both as passive recipients and as possessed instruments. As passive recipients, women absorb tidings of tidiness—of tracked, tamed, linear thinking and feeling, enforced through injections of potted fear and other pseudopassions. As instrumental cooperators, women themselves become token tyrants of tidydom. Confined to the domains/chains of kitchen, office, schoolroom, hospital ward, shopping mall, women exercise pseudo-authority cleaning and tidying, making their world trimmer, grimmer, fearfully "cheerful," tearfull. Escaping home and the range to join male-led "movements," a woman finds herself in the same domestic role, cleaning up messes made by the others. "Relaxing" in front of her tidy television set, she stares at images fashioned to tidy her brain. Boxes of "Tide" clutched by smilingly spick-and-span fembots jump off the screen to scour her mind. "Tide's in, dirt's out." Down the spout, down and out. Down the drain, heart and brain. Dirt off the shirt; off with her head. Ding-dong, the wicked Witch is dead. No complex grief or sorrowing here, just clean dismembering of her Tidal powers, her indwelling Demon, Genius.

Every woman breaking out of tidydom's tyranny needs to encounter her Demon, her Genius. *Genius* means "an attendant spirit of a person or place: tutelary deity." It means "a nature spirit or an elemental spirit: GENIE, DEMON." Other meanings of *genius,* of course, are "a strong leaning or inclination," and "extraordinary native intellectual power especially as manifested in unusual capacity for creative activity of any kind." Elemental/ Tidal imagination connects these last definitions with the first two cited above. For a woman moving into contact with the natural rhythms of her own creativity comes to understand this process in ways that require the Naming of Tutelary Spirits, Goddesses, Angels, Muses. Nor is this "mere" symbolization. It is Metaphoric Hearing/Naming of the Presences that surpass tidy "understanding," that transport the Hearer/Namer into Metabeing.

Unlike the demons of division that cut women's Lifetimes/ Lifelines into tidy tid-bits, the attendant, tutelary, indwelling Demons/Genii of Nag-Gnostic women use their cutting powers to prune away false feelings, deceptive images, freeing the flow of luminous Realizing Presence, releasing the radiant Race of Words. These are Labrys-Spirits breaking open the Labyrinthine ways hidden by deceptive, tidy mazes.

Stendhal expressed an accurate perception of the sadostate's tidying of women when he wrote: "All the geniuses who are born *women* are lost to the public good." [5] An Other way of Naming the atrocity is to say that every woman who has been cut off from her Genius has become lost from her Self, our Selves.

Women who have Realized contact with their deeply Moving Selves have experienced and expressed this inspiration in various ways. Inspired activists have sometimes Heard auditory messages. Joan of Arc reported that she heard voices, and the contents of their messages were quite specific.[6] Florence Nightingale heard messages at four crucial points in her life. This much maligned and misunderstood woman was a Genius of remarkable vision and energy, and possessed of encyclopedic knowledge.[7] Her extreme practicality (Prudish Prudence) itself refutes any possible charges of false mysticism attached to her voices. As Denise Connors has written:

Florence Nightingale's life was never one of indifference or idleness— but rather intense, passionate activity. . . . Refusing to resign herself to a life which she found utterly distasteful and degrading, she attempted to carve out an existence in which she could exercise her "passion, intellect and moral activity"—qualities which she saw as never having been satisfied in women.[8]

Sonia Johnson, excommunicated from the mormon church for her work in support of the Equal Rights Amendment, experienced hearing a strange "rustling." Then:

I opened my eyes, and there around the three sides of the room, with their heads about six inches from the ceiling, stood a throng of women in old-fashioned dress. Not like a photograph or a tableau, but moving slightly.

I knew at once who they were. They were the women whose words I had been reading all week with gratitude and love—my [mormon] foremothers.[9]

Of course, women who have been legitimated as christian saints and mystics have sometimes heard and reported "words" with impunity. Saint Teresa of Avila, for example, in *Interior Castle,* described and analyzed such phenomena under the rubric of "locutions." Teresa believed that locutions are characteristic of that stage of the soul's development which she called the "sixth Mansions." According to this saint, of course, "good" locutions are from "God," while others can come from the devil or from one's own imagination. Signs that they are from "God" are (1) a sense of power and authority that they bear with them; (2) great tranquillity in the soul; (3) the fact that these words do not vanish from the memory for a very long time—some never. They engender "certainty which cannot be overcome" and "a living spark of conviction." [10] Teresa maintained that often the soul has not been thinking of what it hears, and the "voice" comes unexpectedly. Moreover, "much more can be understood than the words themselves convey and this without any further utterance." [11] Nag-Gnostic Muses are able to recognize all of these criteria as excellent indicators that locutions are not from god but from one's own Imagination or Demon.

It is not surprising that Teresa, like other christian mystics, believed that the "locutions" were from the lord. This was the symbol system accessible to her and no other explanation was speakable or even thinkable. When we consider how consistently throughout her life Teresa cried out against the "chains" imposed upon her sex, chains obviously forged by the church and the institutions it legitimated, it seems likely that she would have rejected this symbolism if the mind-bindings restricting her imagination had not been so oppressive. As it was, Teresa was securely tied down into tidydom, and her statement that she was "not in the least like a woman" displays the extent of the dividedness inflicted by patriarchal religion upon her mind.[12]

Not all of the women gifted in this way have had their psychic powers bound by such explicitly phallic symbolism as that which enchained the christian mystics. However, the sadosociety's tyranny has often twisted such experiences into the tortures of madness, or what is taken to be madness and treated as such by the guardians of "normality." Clearly, among the women burned as Witches, as well as among those confined as "hysterics" or incarcerated as "psychotics," among those destroyed by psychosurgery, shock treatments, drugs, and psychoanalysis, many have been endowed with inspiration, sometimes experienced as locutions, and with great talent for expressing such inspiration. Such powers have been tidied up, tied down, lost and unfound.

Negative Auditory Phenomena

Doris Lessing, in *The Four-Gated City,* poignantly conveys the mental suffering of some women moving beyond tidy reasoning. Describing the experience of Martha Quest as she is developing new organs/powers of knowing, Lessing writes:

It was as if a million radio sets ran simultaneously, and her mind plugged itself in fast to one after another, so that words, phrases, songs, sounds, came into audition and then faded.[13]

Although Martha is able to break through this horror, her friend Lynda, who has suffered greater psychological damage, seems to be condemned endlessly to this hellish state. Since Lessing's world-view is hetero-relational,[14] the horrible suffering of her female potential psychics appears inevitable. Although Lynda and Martha Quest are friends and support each other, there is something inadequate about their relationship. Their analysis of the suffering does not go so far into its roots as to reach a Naming of patriarchy. Thus the message conveyed by Lessing is inherently depressing.

Within an exclusively hetero-relational context, the capacity for potent Naming of the situation of women and of its causes is muted. Castrated, divided radically from their Selves, women caught in the condition represented by Lynda are helpless objects of internalized psychic battering, broken by the ceaseless clacking of embedded verbiage, cut off from the healing flow of the Race of Radiant Words.

I am not claiming that Self-Realizing women can avoid all psychic suffering. This is hardly the case, since all have been touched/violated by the agents of tidy tyranny. However, when the potential for Elemental bonding has to some extent been released and Realized, a gynergetic and healing atmosphere is possible. In such an environment multiple expression of Outrageous perceptions are possible, as part of the process of Naming.

Sometimes gifted Websters who have broken free and found the Race of Radiant Words have been unable to shed completely the infernal burdens of the unspeakable past. Virginia Woolf was such a Webster, and it is not surprising that this Genius suffered from negative auditory phenomena. Virginia was sexually abused by both her half-brothers for many years. As Stephen Trombley has put it:

. . . the simple fact is, Virginia was, in various ways, molested by her half-brothers, George and Gerald Duckworth, throughout her childhood, adolescence, and young adulthood.[15]

In a letter to Ethel Smyth, Virginia wrote:

I still shiver with shame at the memory of my half-brother, standing me on a ledge, aged about 6 or so, exploring my private parts.[16]

Analyzing this occurrence and those that succeeded it, Trombley calculates:

If we consider that Virginia was aged "6 or so" in 1888, and that the interference continued until 1904, when she was twenty-two years old, that is a period of sixteen years. Gerald Duckworth was born in 1870, and so was eighteen years old when he stood Virginia on a ledge and "explored" her. In 1895, George Duckworth was twenty-seven years old, and his interference continued until 1904, when he was thirty-six years of age.[17]

This sexual abuse, masked as brotherly affection, inevitably had destructive consequences. Virginia was considered "mad" by some who have claimed authoritative understanding of her. With grotesque insensitivity, Quentin Bell imputes to her "a cancer of the mind, a corruption of the spirit." Bell was able to imagine this condition as unendurable, and concluded that "in the end, when the voices of insanity spoke to her in 1941, she took the only remedy that remained, the cure of death." [18]

Virginia Woolf was a Forecrone of great, essentially untameable powers. Her "moments of being" were moments of contact with her Genius/Demon/Muse. Her subsequent moving in be-ing, her weaving together of "the severed parts," was a work of Radiant Wording. She did Realize the Presence of her Muse. The infernal sexual abusers were not able to destroy her powers. Had there been available to her a community of Tidal Musing women, she most probably would not have needed the tidy "cure of death" which was proclaimed "the only remedy that remained" by her obtuse "biographer" (necrographer).*

Inspired by Virginia and other Websters, we shall pursue further the subject of Musing. First, however, there will be a brief intermission during which Hags may hurl a few Labryses after the retreating demons of tidiness.

TIDY REPORTS; UNTIDY RETORTS

In her book of Original Genius, *The Euguélionne,* the French Canadian feminist Louky Bersianik, writes Untidily of the curse of tidiness, as seen through the eyes of the Euguélionne, a visitor from another planet. A sample report:

FEATS BEHIND THE SCENES.
—Achieve. Assist. Balance the budget. Balance the meals. Bandage cuts. Bawl in hiding. Blanche. Buy. Care for. Chill. Clear. Console. Cook. Cut out. Cut up. Darn. Do the dishes. Drive. Dry. Dry dishes. Economize. Educate. Empty the ashtrays. Empty the garbage cans. Encourage. Endure. Feed. Flatter. Fold. Forbid. Forgive. Freeze. Gather laundry. Gather up garbage. Give. Go shopping. Heat up. Help. Iron. Keep. Keep (yourself) young. Laugh. Love. Maintain. Make children. Make love. Make meals. Make peace. Make sure homework's done. Pare. Pay off bills. Peel. Play. Preserve. Punish. Rinse. Roast. Rub. Serve. Set table. Sew. Shout. Shut (yourself) up. Stop (yourself) shouting. Sweep. Tidy. Use up leftovers. Wash. Wax. *ETC.*[19]

---

* Emily Culpepper has suggested the term *necrography* to describe this genre of writing.

On the most obvious level, tidiness suggests housework. According to recent studies the average working wife in 1982 spent 26 hours a week doing housework and the average husband spent 36 minutes.[20] Nags need to think not only of the physical exhaustion implied in this double-double work schedule of women, but also of the fragmentation of spirit and binding of creativity. Anyone who has produced a work of artistic, scholarly, or scientific achievement knows that one does not say: "Since I now have an hour to spare, I'll sit down and write for a while." Great works require time and space around them—which may appear to be "leisure" and which Virginia Woolf called "a room of one's own."

Even if she has "servants" to do the housework, a woman is supposed to be the "angel in the house," doing spiritual housework. Virginia Woolf made it clear that before women can write we must *kill* the "angel in the house," glorified by male authors.[21] The word *angel,* squeezed into this tidy context (derived from the tidy scribbler Coventry Patmore), is an example of the phenomenon of false faces imposed upon words under phallic rule. As we have seen, the word *angel* has breathtakingly biophilic meanings and suggests Elemental powers of be-ing. The petty perversity of Patmore's use of this word, his typically tidy twisting of this inherently Tidal Name, is comparable to snooldom's shrinking of the Goddess Isis to the dimensions of wimpy plastic madonnas.

An "Exotic" Example

The tidiness inflicted upon women, together with orders to impose this torture upon each other, combine to produce a climate of tidy torture. Within this prevailing climate, the everyday atrocities here "at home" go unrecognized and unreported, while "exotic" tidy practices in faraway lands become the objects of fascinated attention.

This phenomenon was blatantly exemplified in *National Geographic* in an article concerning the "beauty secret" of Padaung tribeswomen of Burma, often called "giraffe women." The article reports:

A relentless embrace of brass . . . armors the neck in a coil that weighs about 20 pounds, and measures a head-popping one foot high.

The loops, draped with silver chains and coins and cushioned by a small pillow under the chin, signal elegance, wealth, and position.[22]

The author, a physician, does give some indication of the horror underlying this "elegance," including X-rays that reveal an unbelievable displacement of the clavicle and ribs by the loops, the first of which are twisted around a girl's neck when she is about five years old. The number of loops is augmented periodically. Moreover:

Rings worn on arms and legs may weigh a woman down with an additional thirty pounds of brass. Since leg coils hamper walking, the women waddle. Constrained from drinking in the usual head-back position, a ring wearer leans forward to sip through a straw. . . . And the voices of wearers, wrote British journalist J. G. Scott, sound "as if they were speaking up the shaft of a well." [23]

The readers of *National Geographic* were also informed that in the past the coils were removed as punishment for adultery. The head would then flop over and the woman would suffocate. Certain questions, significantly, are not raised in the article, for example: How could such a burdened, crippled woman possibly escape from a male who had decided to force her into adultery? What comparable horror could have been inflicted upon him?

The attitude of the author (and most likely of the editors) is conveyed explicitly:

Legend claims that the brass rings protect the women from tiger bites, but actually the practice of wearing them helps maintain individual and tribal identity.[24]

As if to reinforce this message, the article is accompanied by colorful photographs of "giraffe women," most of whom are smiling, apparently in a state of full-fillment. Moreover, the reader is left with the depressing information that:

The custom, indelibly inscribed in Padaung culture, persists and, according to University of Illinois anthropologist F. K. Lehman, shows signs of a resurgence.[25]

While it may be true that the "custom" prevails only in a tribe of several thousand members, the article is of significance as an example of the media's mind-tidying tactics. For this kind of publication, by means of both overt and subliminal double-talk, functions to defeat rather than to liberate consciousness. This depressing effect is achieved in at least two ways.

First, the article manages on one level to minimize the horror of such mutilation. The fact that the "custom" affects relatively few women in a faraway land distances the female reader to some extent, so that the atrocity can be experienced superficially as unthreatening. Indeed, it sets up an unmentioned comparison/contrast in the reader's mind between the situation of the "giraffe women" and her own, even eliciting plastic feelings of gratitude for the benefits of modern civilization and its "liberation" of women. Since the "giraffe women" are smiling and since the loops are described as signifying elegance, wealth, and position and as helping the women maintain "individual identity," the reader may be seduced into thinking that the cultural difference between herself and these women is so vast that she is unable to give an "objective" estimate of their oppression. She is lured into non-identification with them as sister-women; and she is further mystified by her male acquaintances' disguised—or obvious —experience of the article as a piece of exotic, or even erotic, journalism. Moreover, in some circles (conservative, liberal, and "radical") any criticism could even bring down remonstrances for the critic's "sentimentality" or "cultural imperialism."

Second, on a deeper level, no matter how bamboozled a woman may be by such confusing media messages, the knowledge is absorbed that *women* are *mutilated* and vulnerable to the prevailing "customs." In the psyche of any woman reading such an article the connection is made between the "strange" condition of these "other" women and her own state. The fear-button that has been embedded deep in her soul is tidily tapped and the message recorded: "Stay in line, then you'll be fine."

Although the double-talk has conveyed, on the overt level, a sense of disconnection from the bizarre "giraffe women" and all of the horrors they are used to symbolize, the reader is allowed to make unspoken/unspeakable connections, privately. This terrifying private understanding is paralyzing so long as it remains private and to some extent subliminal. And there are, of course, reasons why a woman would keep it thus repressed, including fear of ridicule and of the common tidy labels. Yet only by making the connections explicit can she release her potted anger and fear, converting these into gynergizing Rage/Courage, burning the tidy bindings of her mind, Realizing her power.

Each time one woman encourages another to Realize such subliminal connections, severing the tidy ties, she is presentiating Presence. Each time she uses her Labrys to cut through the demonic double messages of tidydom she releases Tidings of Great Hope, for she is rendering the truth explicit and therefore accessible. Such Good Tidings free the flow of communications/connections. Potentially, this flow is Tidal, enabling those who are Touched by its healing waves to Race with the Race of Women.

THE MUSING OF MUSES

The noun *Muse*, derived from the Greek *Mousa* and probably akin to *mnasthai*, "to remember," is defined as "any of nine sister goddesses associated with the Graces in Greek mythology and regarded as presiding over learning and the creative arts (as poetry and music)." *Muse* is also defined as "the personification of a guiding genius or principal source of inspiration." *Muse*, then, coincides with *Demon* in Naming the attendant or indwelling powers of Tidal women. *Muse* also means "the creative spirit of an individual."

Unlike the Name *Demon, Muse* carries no charge of negative meanings. It is not burdened with contradictory definitions associated with good and evil. Yet it does have a kind of double-edged quality. For, as we have just seen, it can refer to a Goddess and also to "the creative spirit of an individual." To Labrys-wielding women, however, these are not really two completely distinct meanings. Indeed, Amazons cut down the tidy barriers that divide these seemingly disparate definitions of *Muse*. Moreover, visitations of Muses make these meetings of meanings perceptible. At moments of Grace, Crone-logical crossroads, Muses so Touch "the creative spirit of the individual" that she becomes/ is one with her Muse. At such moments a woman *is* the Creative Spirit of the individual (her Self). Then there is no sharp dichotomy between a woman's native power and her Attendant Spirit.

A woman wielding Musing Powers releases waves of meanings, so that new and ancient words can be heard and spoken. Like a wand her Labrys stirs the words in Pyrographic patterns, wherein disparate meanings meet. It is a happy circumstance that the verb *muse*, although it apparently is not etymologically related to the noun *Muse*, so aptly describes the activity of a woman who meets her Muse. It means "to become absorbed in thought: RUMINATE." It means "*archaic:* to become astonished: WONDER, MARVEL." A Musing woman is absorbed in her own thoughts (as opposed to those of the tidy programmers), and thus is continually astonished/astonishing, wondering, marveling.

Musing women are terrifying to tidy tyrants, whose entire project of tidiness is planned to a-Muse Muses. The word *amuse* has an archaic definition: "to divert the attention of: DECEIVE, DELUDE, BEMUSE." Insipid amusements are intended to divert Muses from true and Tidal Movement. Unable to be Muses, the tidy tricksters try to *bemuse* Muses, that is, "to make confused or muddled: BEWILDER." Tidal women attack such tactics with the battle cry: Be Musing! Be Wilder! Rallying each other with these slogans, Wanton women wax wiser.

Recalling the stories of Apollo, the mythic model of male tidiness and Master of Mister Cleans, and of his attempts to moderate the moods of Muses, we refuse to be a-Mused. Enraged, we read the words of Robert Graves concerning that gruesome god:

He [Apollo] brought the Muses down from their home on Mount Helicon to Delphi, tamed their wild frenzy, and led them in formal and decorous dances.[26]

Tidal women, untamed, reject the ridiculous "formal and decorous dances" with Super Natural Roars.

Such Originally Natural Roaring terrifies bores, especially those who claim to worship Muses. Graves, for example, who identifies the "White Goddess" as Muse, gravely describes her as "the Mother of all the Living, the ancient power of fright and lust—the female spider or the queen-bee whose embrace is death." [27]

A Demonic and Monstrous Muse does not mind being identified with spiders and queen-bees, nor is she offended to hear of her ancient powers of Fright and Lust. Since she has known the Radiant sides of these words, she can transform the labels into Names of which she is Prudishly Proud. For the labels have been applied to all of her great Foresisters, and they help re-mind her of her noble lineage/heritage. The labels even render accessible the Other side, which they are intended to hide, and this unwitting unveiling, rather than dis-couraging, en-courages Pride.

MEMORY AND MUSING

Musing women are in Touch with Memory. Appropriately the first Muse of the Greek triad (who was also called the Mother of the Muses) was called Mnemosyne, meaning Memory.* Graves had sufficient information about her to express the belief that poets under her influence experience, in the "poetic act," a suspension of time in the usual sense and that "details of future experience often become incorporated in the poem, as they do in dreams." [28] Muses know that Musing/Spinning is in fact Poetic Act *par excellence,* that it is Creative Act. Thus it involves not merely a "suspension of time," as Graves believed, but rather a creative Spiraling of time.

The patriarchal notion of inspiration by the Muse is basically passive. Writing of the influence of Mnemosyne, Graves states:

One can have memory of the future as well as of the past. Memory of the future is usually called instinct in animals, intuition in human beings.[29]

Although this concept of intuition (memory of the future) may sound impressive, within Graves' context it is passive. Graves believes that "in poems one is (or should be) in critical control of the situation; in dreams one is a paranoiac, a mere spectator of mythographic event." [30] The problem is that both of these modes of future memory are tidied up/tied down by patriarchal male passivity. The patriarchal poet, such as Graves, may have "critical control" over what he writes, but his criticism itself remains encased in the tidy containers contrived by clockocracy. Moreover, the droning dreamer whose dreams are programmed by phallicism is indeed a spectator, watching a plot that never changes.

* The number of Muses varied, as well as their names, at different times and places in ancient Greece. The first Muses, who were worshipped on Mount Helicon, were three in number, but it was finally agreed that there were nine Muses.

In contrast to this passive plodding plot, the future Memory of a Spinning Muse is an Act of Pyrography. Empowered by Memory, she passionately Spins her lifelines, divining the future that she is creating. She does not a-Muse others. Rather, she Muses others, mending the broken connections.

Under the conditions of tidy tutelage, however, "memory" is used to stop Muses from Musing. So called mnemonic devices and mnemotechnical aids assist only in accelerating the course of deep amnesia, which, as we have seen, passes as "a good memory." All of mediated education is fabrication of a-Musing "memories." Refusing this a-Musing is a Tidal task, a work of Pure Lust.

A woman undertaking this task will find it useful to recall that "originally the Muses were represented as virgins of the strictest chastity." [31] There is the following account, for example:

They had taken shelter one day with Pyreneos, King of Daulis in Phocis, when the king attempted to violate them. The Muses then took their wings and flew away. Pyreneos tried to follow them, but he fell from the top of his palace and was killed. [32]

Virgins/Muses reject the would-be violators of Memory, flying from them, letting them follow and fall from the tops of their tidy palaces/whorehouses, tidily dropping dead.

Wanton Virgins studiously recall also the words of Virgin Woolf, who wrote in *Three Guineas* of the chastity she would require of women (the "daughters of educated men"):

By chastity is meant that when you have made enough to live on by your profession you must refuse to sell your brain for the sake of money. [33]

Ruminating on this statement, Muses/Nags find that further analysis is needful, for more than money is at issue. A Muse refuses to sell her own Memory/Heritage for *anything,* including either male *or female* approval.*

* Virginia Woolf implied this in her discussion of "freedom from false loyalties" (*Three Guineas* [New York: Harcourt, Brace & World, Harbinger Books, 1938], p. 80). However, this analysis was not attached directly to the idea of chastity. Moreover, the methods of seduction of feminists by tidydom have "evolved" in the course of the half-century following the writing of *Three Guineas,* so that further analysis is now needed.

Faithfulness to Tidal Memory implies refusal to sell out, despite threats on all levels. These can be threats of losing one's job, of losing opportunities to publish one's work. They can be threats of social ostracism or damage to reputation for "going too far," or "crossing a line," or "thinking you're ahead of everyone else." Criticism and feedback from friends and peers is essential. Yet the experienced reality of women who continue to Move includes moments of Moving Alone. The Muse is herSelf the greatest companion, and faithfulness to Her attracts the companions who will be compatible for continued Wanderings, Wonderings. Even when enduring/confronting extremely difficult situations, a woman who manages to stay true to Tidal Memory transcends tidy ties.

Countless stories, factual and fictional, have attested to the Good Tidings received by those who are faithful to their Muses/Selves. The phenomenon is observable in women who have never even had the chance to become consciously feminist. I have chosen one story as an illustration.

"Aunt Mehetabel" and Her Muse

In a remarkable story of an "unimportant" elderly Spinster who lived in total economic dependence upon her brother and his family in old-time New England, Dorothy Canfield Fisher conveys the meaning of Musing.

The dependence of Mehetabel by no means meant that she was a parasite without responsibilities. Rather, she was obliged to drudge at thankless tidy tasks in her brother's house for long hours every day, washing men's work clothes, ironing, canning. Through it all, she was effaced and erased. However, Mehetabel had one great pleasure and talent: "Even as a girl she had been clever with her needle in the way of patching bedquilts." [34]

Fisher movingly describes the moment when her "great idea" came to Mehetabel—the "complicated, splendidly difficult pattern" for a truly wonderful quilt—and her subsequent asking permission of her sister-in-law to begin work on it. Then:

Mehetabel rushed back up the steep attic stairs to her room, and in a joyful agitation began preparations for the work of her life. Her very first stitches showed her that it was even better than she hoped. By some heaven-sent inspiration she had invented a pattern beyond which no patchwork quilt could go.[35]

Fisher's description of Mehetabel's work in her room conveys that her creative experience was no less ecstatic than that of Emily Dickinson or of any other great artist:

Every time she opened the door, no matter what weather hung outside the one small window, she always saw the little room flooded with sunshine. She smiled to herself as she bent over the innumerable scraps of cotton cloth on her work table. Already—to her—they were ranged in orderly, complex, mosaic-beauty.[36]

Like Virginia Woolf, then, Mehetabel enjoyed "a room of her own," and her delight was "to put the severed parts together."

The power of Mehetabel's creating in concert with her Muse was almost immediately perceivable. The very next day after the family had all examined with astonished admiration the first square of her quilt she instinctively behaved differently:

For the first time in her life the dependent old maid contradicted her powerful sister-in-law.[37]

Moreover, soon she sat up straighter, took part in the conversation, and was listened to.

Mehetabel was by no means miraculously released from the dimensions of her foreground existence. Instead, these became part of a wider context of meaning that came from her own creativity and sense of purpose:

She went on faithfully with her monotonous housework, not neglecting a corner. But the atmosphere of her world changed. . . . Through the longest task of washing milk-pans, there rose a rainbow of promise. She took her place by the little table and put the thimble on her knotted, hard finger with the solemnity of a priestess performing a rite.[38]

Mehetabel was transformed through her transforming work of putting the pieces together in a splendid and intricate pattern. After more than four years of labor, the quilt was completed and won first prize at the County Fair. The artist looked at her work and rejected even hymnbook phrases ("the only kind of poetic expression she knew") to describe it, not merely because this would be sacrilegious, but because such words were not "nearly striking enough."

We are told by the author that up to the moment when she heard the first cry of admiration for the first square of the quilt, "Mehetabel had labored in the purest spirit of selfless adoration of an ideal." [39] I would suggest that throughout the story, Fisher is really saying that Mehetabel had finally *found* her *Self*. Her chastity was expressed in faithful re-membering of an ecstatic vision.

FEY FAITH, HOPPING HOPE, BIOPHILIC BONDING

The words "faith, hope, and charity" have come to represent a sickening trio—the so-called "theological virtues" of christianity. The sacred threeness of this configuration of qualities suggests that they may be foreground distortions of something ancient and real that has been cut up, trimmed down, and done in, reduced to unrecognizability. All are tied to the christian god as their "object." [40] All acts of Musing inherently involve untying these imprisoned virtues, re-weaving their meanings.

The word *faith* is derived from the Middle English *fey*. Although *faith* is probably not akin to the modern word *fey,* Furious women are inspired by the similarities in sound to investigate the possibility of describing our faith as *fey*. One definition of *fey* is "being in a wild or elated state of mind formerly believed to portend death: behaving in an excited irresponsible manner: beside oneself." The faith of a woman who identifies with the Fates may well cause her to be Positively Fey, or in a wild, elated state of mind, which to the fathers may seem to portend death. The question is: the death of *whom,* or *what*? For such a woman is not responsible to the rulers of the rapist system, and her sense of responsibility to her Self portends death to them and to their system. Having come into Touch with her Self, she must be declared *fey* by the fathers in yet another sense: "out of one's mind: MAD . . . TOUCHED." Furiously faithful women are Positively Touching and Touched, and are therefore Mad as Maenads.

Colorfully described by mythographers as a college of orgiastic laurel-chewing priestesses, the Maenads have been associated with oak trees. [41] Believing in their rights to defend their own space, they used their double axes when they deemed this reasonable and necessary. Graves has written:

As sacred king he [Orpheus] was struck by a thunderbolt—that is, killed with a double-axe—in an oak grove at the summer solstice, and then dismembered by the Maenads.[42]

Obviously it is unwise to mess with Maenads, whose feyness can portend death to sacred kings and other priestly predators.

Fey has Other dimensions as well. It means "able to see fairies or to have intuitions about the future: possessing a sixth sense: CLAIRVOYANT." Fey feminist faith implies the natural clairvoyance of those who reject master-minded mediation of sense experience. This feyness of feminist faith is the source of the hope that is characteristic of Hags. Some etymologists have suggested that the English word *hope* in its roots may be akin to the old English *hoppian,* which means to hop.[43] A Fey woman/Hag can hope because she can hop, leap, jump intuitively. To put it another way, her cognitive and affective rhythms are not tidy. They are Tidal, responding to her Elemental context.

The realism of the faith and hope of a Fey woman is related to her finely tuned gynaesthetic ability to sense what is happening around her. Her feelings, intuitions, aspirations are Events that happen in an accurately perceived context of Other Elemental Events—for example, the acts of Other Fey women. That is, they happen in a context of biophilic bonding. Before turning to this subject, we shall pause to consider biophilic time, which is the "when" of Fey bounding and bonding.

Fairy Time and Aeviternity

A Fey woman is aware of a kind of duration that sometimes has been called "fairy time." Katharine Briggs explains this sense of duration:

The early fairy specialists had a vivid sense of the relativity of time, founded, perhaps, on experiences of dream or trance, when a dream that covers several years may be experienced between rolling out of bed and landing on the floor. . . . As a rule, however, time moves in the other direction, both in VISITS TO FAIRYLAND and to other supernatural worlds. A dance of a few minutes takes a year and a day of common time. . . . This is not always so, for nothing in folk tradition can be contained in an exact and logical system.[44]

Clearly, then, fairy time is hardly clock time. It may be stretched or condensed—as anyone knows who has ever created anything and lived intensely.

Fey faithful women detect special significance in the fact that sometimes it is a "broken taboo" that precipitates entrance into fairy time.[45] Women-Touching women, having broken the Terrible Taboo, have experienced radical changes in our sense of duration, which can be described by the Metaphor of fairy time. Time, in the classical sense, is the measure of motion.[46] A Fey woman has known E-motion, the most intense internal Movement of Passion, and this has not been dichotomized from her external actions, which therefore are measured by E-motion. Her relations to her Self and to other women, then, have changed the "measure" of her be-ing in the world. She lives "on the boundary" of patriarchal time.

Briggs has shown that sometimes it has been singing, visions, and dreams that have "stretched time into another dimension," but that "journeys into another world or realm are still more likely to do so." [47] It is precisely the breaking of the Terrible Taboo that makes possible the kinds of songs, dreams, visions, and especially the Journeys that stretch time into Other dimensions. As the Taboo-breaking reader knows, it is not possible to break the Total Taboo simply by breaking a few rules. Rather this Total Taboo-breaking implies deeper motivation, for it is many-dimensional and *includes* singing, dreaming, visioning, and Journeying in Other modes, measures.

Writing of the Fées, or "fairy ladies," Briggs notes that in Ireland and Scotland they sometimes were thought to be fallen angels and that in Brittany they were sometimes believed to be Goddess-like.[48] She also shows that the mythological origins of the French Fées lie in the stories of the Fates. In the medieval Arthurian romances these came to England as *fays,* or fairies. The English word *fairy* is also derived from the Latin *Fata,* or Goddess of Fate. It is clear that just as fairies are symbolically connected with angels, they are also connected with the Fates. As Briggs puts it, the Fays were "descendents" of the Fates.[49]

Since the hopping/hoping of Fey women inevitably involves participation in forms of duration akin to fairy time, it is useful to consider further some implications of connections between what we might call "fairy phenomena" and traditional ideas about "fallen angels" and their duration.

As the reader recalls, the "fallen angels," according to christian theology, are those who refused to surrender their natural autonomy to the christian god and therefore were deprived of "eternal happiness," consisting in the "Beatific Vision" of the divine essence. Since Furiously Fey women refuse such surrender of autonomy, knowing that it involves a most unbeatific fission/ fracturing of integrity, the "fallen angels" would appear to be important inspirers and allies. The tradition concerning the natural mode of duration of angels is therefore of some interest.

Christian theologians have described angels ("good" and "bad") as being outside time as "men" commonly experience time. On the other hand, they do not have the attribute of eternity, which implies absolute immutability, or unchangeableness, and which is said to belong only to god. For angels are believed to be changeable in the sense that they make choices. Moreover:

... they have changeableness of intelligence, of affections, and of places, in their own degree. Therefore these are measured by aeviternity, which is a mean between eternity and time.[50]

Another way of putting this would be to say that the angels' changeableness is in the realm of what were traditionally understood to be "spiritual" acts—acts of intellect and will. Their changes are therefore primarily active, rather than simply passive. Clocks and watches would be pointless to them, since their acts are not measured in a quantitative sense. The *quality* and intensity of such spiritual activities is their measure.

The kind of Metaphoric leap that is required to feel "at home" with this sort of discourse about angels is also suggestive of the sort of leaps/hops involved in experiencing the "beyond time" of Fey women. For here the important measure concerns quality and intensity of activities which involve mythic giant steps past the Foreground. The Movements that "count" are Metaphoric Springs of consciousness, and of behavior consistent with this consciousness.

Metaphoric hops/leaps are hope-full, Fate-full acts that are myth-breaking, breaking up old myths, bringing us to Realms of Metabeing. These Metaphoric hops can be likened to participation in aeviternity. They are naturally Angelic. Through these we do not simply become "fallen," however. Fey women actively jump, hop, leap, hurl our Selves beyond the range of boring beatific visions and other videogames. We actively *are* our Fates.

The Biophilic Bounding/Bonding of Fates

As Fates, Fey women bound and bond biophilically with each other, and with the sun and the moon, the tides, and all of the elements. Our Time is relative to this ever moving context. Thus as Fate, a Fey woman does not only participate in aeviternity, for she is not only spiritual. Rather, she is material/spiritual.

Since the Fates are the Triple Moon Goddess, the name *Fates* suggests diversity as well as unity. For the moon is a primal Shape-Shifter. As Shape-Shifters, women experience diversity and unity not only among our Selves, but also within our Selves. As a Fey woman Spins her Fate, she, as Fate, is affected and effected by her Spinning. As she moves, her Time changes. The measure of her Time is Moonstruck, Tidal. Her shifting of gynergy-patterns shifts the shape of Time.

Scientists claim that seismographs placed on the moon indicate that most moonquakes are caused by tidal attraction and occur when the moon is closest to earth. The moon's influence upon the tides, then, is in some way reciprocated. The actions of women as Fates/Moon Goddesses affecting the environment are also in some ways reciprocated. A Moon Goddess moves in concordance with her surroundings, so that the environment she creates affects her creation.

Clearly, the Stamina spun by women as Fates form complex patterns. The very word *stamina* is plural in construction. One archaic definition is "the innate capacities formerly regarded as conditioning or governing the duration of life." It has come to mean "the strength or vigor of bodily constitution: capacity for standing fatigue or resisting disease." It has also come to mean "strength or courage of conviction: staying power: PERSERVERANCE." *Stamina,* then, Names the innate capacities that are the sources of both bodily and spiritual "staying powers." It suggests high quality of "duration of life" and points toward overcoming the dichotomy between physical and spiritual strength.

The complexity of the Stamina spun by Fates involves the intertwining of Fey Faith, Hopping Hope, and Biophilic Bonding. As Fey, a woman has unbounded Powers of Self-transformation, for she is faithful to her own true be-ing. As hopping/hoping, she makes the necessary quantum leaps and giant jumps to continue her transformations/Shape-Shiftings. As biophilically bonding, she communicates her powers to Others, and in return receives hopping/leaping energy from them.

The Spinning of these intertwining threads, then, implies also the Weaving of cords. A cord can be understood as a kind of rope, of course, and wise women do have a long and honorable tradition of knotting.[51] To deeply Hearing Hags, however, *cord* happily/hoppily blends with *chord*. The association becomes explicit when one Muses upon the meaning of *chord*, "a combination of two or more tones sounded together, especially tones that blend harmoniously." *Chord* as a verb means "to harmonize together: ACCORD." The word *accord* literally brings us to the heart of the matter, since it is derived from the Latin *ad* plus *cor*, meaning heart. At its heart/core, Stamina is accord/harmony.

Women acquiring Stamina hear the harmony of the Fates. Moreover, a woman who is faithful to the Name *Fate* (derived from the Latin *fari*, meaning to speak), expresses her faith by Naming/Wording. Since that which she is Naming is harmony, her wording itself will creatively participate in this harmony. She will hear and speak Elemental sounds.

ELEMENTAL SOUNDING

The Fates are associated with Elemental sounds. Graves has written:

There is evidence . . . that before the introduction of the modified Phoenician alphabet into Greece an alphabet had existed there as a religious secret held by the priestesses of the moon—Io, or the Three Fates: that it was closely linked with the calendar, and that its letters were represented not by written characters, but by twigs cut from different trees typical of the year's sequent months.[52]

Moreover, the Fates were said to have invented the five vowels of the first alphabet.[53] It is impossible to think of all this as simply a visual matter, for, clearly, the visible signs represent sounds. The use of twigs cut from different trees, rather than written letters, to signify basic sounds, suggests a sense of the Elemental quality of these sounds, of their interconnectedness with manifestations of Wild nature, such as trees. In other words, it conveys a sense of harmony among apparently dissimilar Elemental phenomena.

We can be mindful of such Elemental harmony when we think of the sounds of the tides. In *The Edge of the Sea,* after describing visual phenomena associated with the tides, Rachel Carson writes:

Even more directly the tides address the sense of hearing, speaking a language of their own, distinct from the voice of the surf. The sound of a rising tide is heard most clearly on shores removed from the swell of the open ocean. In the stillness of night the strong waveless surge of a rising tide creates a confused tumult of water sounds—swashings and swirlings and a continuous slapping against the rocky rim of the land. Sometimes there are undertones of murmurings and whisperings; then suddenly all lesser sounds are obliterated by a torrential inpouring of water.[54]

Like the tides, Elementally Sounding women directly address the sense of hearing, speaking a language distinct from that of the Foreground. The sounds of Tidal women rising are heard most clearly in removed places and in the stillness of night. There is a tumult of women's sounds, not unlike the swashings and swirlings of the tide. Sometimes there are undertones of murmurings and whisperings. Then suddenly all lesser sounds are obliterated by the torrential roaring of women.

Like the sounds of the tide, the sounds of roaring women elicit Wonder. They are more like the sounds of questions than of answers. This is what keeps Sounding women Fey, Hopping, and Biophilic.

Elementally Sounding women continually *sound* also in another sense, that is, "to measure the depth of," and "to try to find out." Her refusal to accept tidy answers to her continual Sounding gives a woman autonomy and authority. This is the authority of Augurs—often perceived as Ogres—whose Augury is always an asking, whose Soothsaying is really Seeking.

Such authoritative Seeking is not a luxury; rather, it springs from Necessity, the Mother of our Invention. Graves recounts the opinion of "some" that the Fates are under the control of Zeus. Then he adds:

Others hold, on the contrary, that Zeus himself is subject to the Fates, as the Pythian priestess once confessed in an oracle; because they are not his children, but parthenogenous daughters of the Great Goddess Necessity, against whom not even the gods contend, and who is called "The Strong Fate." [55]

Elementally Sounding Augurs *are* the "Others," who, being contrary, question the paternity of Zeus and re-call Necessity "our Mother." Thus Zeus and all the alleged fathers have lost their authority and consequently cannot stop our hopping, hoping, harmonizing.

A Parthenogenous Daughter has her own lineage, focus, finality. Her bonding is based on this autonomy, and her faith keeps her questioning those who would deny it. Her friendships are founded on this faith, and her Fey exuberance de-limits her Life-Lust. By her boundless Seeking she escapes the bounds of the fathers' fields and spheres of influence.

The continual Soundings of Musing Maenads and Furious Fates are works of deep Passion. They are, above all, inspired by Fire. The transcribing of our Elemental Sounds into readable signs requires Pyroglyphic writing, comprising recognizable pictures/portrayals of Pyromantic Passionate Thought.

Polygraphic writing will also be Hydroglyphic, Aeroglyphic, Geoglyphic. The dis-covering of such an Elemental alphabet will not happen all at once. It will require macro-mutations in ways of be-ing. Confrontation with this subject brings us to the entrance of the Third Realm, which is the Realm of Metamorphospheres.

THE THIRD REALM

METAMORPHOSPHERES

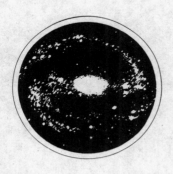

CHAPTER NINE

FOREGROUND TO THE THIRD REALM: BREAKTHROUGH TO METAMORPHOSPHERES*

Metamorphosis: "a change of physical form or substance, especially such a change brought about by or as if by supernatural means (the metamorphosis of men into animals)."

Webster's Third New International Dictionary of the English Language

Metamorphosis: "changes of physical/spiritual form or substance, especially such a change brought about by Super Natural means (the metapatriarchal metamorphosis of tamed women into Wild Witches)." N.B.: Wickedary editors have observed that even the *Oxford English Dictionary* defines *metamorphosis* as "the act or process of changing in form, shape, or substance, especially transformation by magic or witchcraft."

Websters' First New Intergalactic Wickedary of the English Language

Women Moving/Musing into Metamorphospheres begin to glimpse the shapes of our ontological metamorphosis, which can be envisioned as Be-Longing, Be-Friending, and Be-Witching.

* The word *Metamorphospheres* was invented by Denise Connors during a conversation in Maine, in July 1982.

Before we can move/mutate into these Spheres, we must encounter in this Foreground the reified caricatures of these movements. These mirror images are (1) the inauthentic forms of "belonging" bestowed upon women in patriarchy; that is, the prefabricated false collective identities offered to and foisted upon women as necessary and desirable; (2) the patronizing, deceptive, and destructive forms of "befriending" bestowed upon women whose identities have been destroyed through "belonging"; (3) the feminizing of women thus "befriended," and the stealing of our spiritual powers through false naming, which is typified in the epithet "bewitching," as applied to a "seductive" woman.

THE BOXES OF INAUTHENTIC "BELONGING"

In order to comprehend how alienating and how potted the desire to "belong" can be, it helps to recall some meanings of *belong*. These include: "to be suitable, appropriate, or advantageous"; "to be in a proper, rightful, or fitting place, situation, or connection"; "to be the property of a person or thing." *Belong* also means "to become attached or bound (as to a person, group, or organization)." It means "to be properly classified (whales belong among the mammals)." (Needless to say, whales themSelves probably are not interested in this classification.)

The potted passion of desire shrinks the longings of women to such a point that women actually long to belong in the senses defined above. Patriarchal women long to be "appropriate," "to be in a proper, rightful, or fitting place," and "to be the property of a person or thing," for example, in the institution of marriage. Women are afflicted with potted longings to "become attached or bound" to male-ordered society, and with potted desires to be "properly classified."

Such boxed-in belonging is a distorted set of mirror images of Be-Longing, of the ontological yearning which is Pure Lust. All of these mirror images are invitations to women to sacrifice our autonomous Wild Selves, for the sake of "protection" by the paternal protection racketeers. The protection racket requires a trade-off—the abandonment of Be-Longing in return for apparent shelter and safety. Beaten into longing for belonging, women become needy, and beg for befriending.

BELITTLEMENT BY "BEFRIENDING"

Women whose identities have been shrunk by belonging are easy targets of belittling "befriending." *Befriend* is defined as "to act as a friend to: show kindness, sympathy, and understanding to (befriend a helpless person)." The frequently patronizing overtones of the word are betrayed by the example. I am not saying that "befriending" never has a genuine sense (be a friend). The point here is that belittling "befriending" is the sort of charity bestowed upon women reduced to perceiving themselves as helpless. Women thus reduced, having been boxed into belonging, long to be befriended. The belittling "befrienders"—doctors, lawyers, merchants, chiefs—are only too willing to oblige. As fixed and distorted mirror image of Be-Friending, the potted desire to be befriended fixes a woman into postures of passivity, reducing her to an unresisting object of phallic lust. Thus fixated upon being befriended she is prevented from unfolding her Powers of Be-Friending, for Be-Friending is radically active. When a woman has been separated from these active powers, she can safely be labeled "bewitching."

BAFFLEMENT BY "BEWITCHINGNESS"

Women who have been "befriended" by bores aspire to be "bewitching." The following tamed and derivative definition of *bewitch* applies: "to attract or please to such a degree as to take away all power of resistance or considered reservation: EN-CHANT, CHARM, FASCINATE (she bewitched King James no less than her first lover—*N.Y. Times*) (that time-honored privilege of saying foolish things in the grand manner which seems to have bewitched our gallant forefathers—Norman Douglas)." Hags who re-member the powers of Forecrones, conjured by such Weird Words as BEWITCH, ENCHANT, CHARM, FASCINATE, will note the reversal in this definition. The women who belonged to and were befriended by king James and the "gallant forefathers" indeed endured the "privilege of saying foolish things." Feminized fembots, praised for playing the fool, are the favored playthings of snools. Such feigned "bewitching" behavior is the pathetic mirror image of Powers of Be-Witching, that is, ontological Witching: the exercise of creative spiritual powers.

The boxing of women into Self-limiting longings for belonging, befriending, and bewitchingness is accomplished through devious devices. Four such seductive strategies, which I first identified in *Beyond God the Father,* are *depreciation,* particularization, spiritualization, universalization.* I shall further elaborate that analysis here, as prompting additional Shrewish insights in this context. Characteristically, these devices generate endless vicious circles, since the false needs which they spawn perpetuate the climate in which such tactics succeed.

DEPRECIATION

There are many devices available both to women and to men for refusing to see the problem of sexual caste. . . . One is asked: "Are you on that subject of women again when there are so many important problems—like war, racism, pollution of the environment?" One would think, to hear this, that there is no connection between sexism and the rape of the Third World, the rape of the Blacks, or the rape of the land and water.[1]

The tactic described above is *depreciation.* It is intended to make gynocide seem less important than the other atrocities of phallocracy.† More than this, it is designed to disguise the fact that phallocracy is the basic structure underlying the various forms of oppression.

The device of depreciation basically is the deceptive minimizing of gynocide and the cutting down of women's hopes and ambitions. Feminists are well aware of the condoning of rape and woman-battering that prevails in patriarchy. Less obvious is the disparagement of our powers and aspirations, and the seduction of women into cooperation in this Self-belittling.

One essential area targeted by such disparagement is women's intellectuality—to such an extent that this very word is heard as

---

* In *Beyond God the Father* (Boston: Beacon Press, 1973) I used the term *trivialization.* Since *Trivia* is one of the names of the Triple Goddess, I now rarely use this term to mean depreciation/disparagement/belittling of the cause of women.

† The weakness of the term *sexism*—which appeared adequate in 1973—has been demonstrated by the readiness with which some men "admit" and even boast of their "sexism." Thus—ironically—the very word *sexism* has functioned to serve the mechanisms of depreciation. I now usually choose to avoid this rather flat and weak term when Naming woman-hating/gynocide.

threatening by some women, even by feminists.* This belittling of women's intellects—probably more than any other form of disparagement—undermines female hope and courage. It spawns potted desires to "belong," and it breeds potted hopes for "befriending" and "bewitchingness." Deprived of trust in her own mind, the courage of her own convictions, a woman is rendered helplessly passive and filled with Self-loathing. She is grateful for the "privilege of saying foolish things," for praising the butchers and bores who have befriended her.

The taboo against female intellectual courage is at the core of the Terrible Taboo against Women-Touching women. Women are duped into dis-couraging the development of intellectuality in each other even in the name of "feminism." Since *intellectuality*, in the fullest sense, implies knowing one's own mind, the depreciation of a woman's intellectuality affects all aspects of her life, shrinking her physical and emotional energy, narrowing her sights. A woman thus depreciated/dis-couraged feels spooked because she senses that there is a conspiracy to keep her in line.

If a woman has chosen to become a feminist, she has made a choice to be *for women,* to be loyal to women, and therefore she has become a member of a cognitive and affective minority. It is well known that a cognitive minority of one has only a slim chance of survival.[2] In the case of a sincere feminist, since cognitive deviance is combined with affective deviance, the vulnerability of her situation increases exponentially. By bonding with women she makes an implicit decision to *trust* women (in defiance of the folk "wisdom" passed on to patriarchal daughters, which admonishes us to "never trust a woman"). In a special way she has let down her defenses in her relationships with women. She has not been prepared to confront the residues in feminists of the patri-

---

* I am by no means identifying intellectuality with those qualities which are rewarded in academia because they are *not* threatening to established beliefs—qualities such as droning docility, obsequiousness, linear thinking, absence of passion and creativity, inability to challenge authority, et cetera. Genuine intellectuality, of course, can often be found in women working "on the boundaries" of academia and of some of the professions, as well as in women who have never aspired to academic credentials or who have been prevented from such legitimations by economic or ethnic oppression or by other personal circumstances. Essentially, intellectuality involves a choice to use one's mind to its fullest capacity, questioning/questing under all circumstances, Realizing Reason.

archal patterns that can surface unexpectedly in an astonishing variety of shapes, including the belittling of women's own intellects. By becoming a feminist she has placed herself more acutely *at risk* in relation to the most insidious weapons of the fixers—the woman-depreciating embeds in the female psyche. Yet, having understood the scope of the State of Atrocity, she cannot, without the sacrifice of her integrity, consciously "turn back."

A possible reaction in the face of such a Life-threatening situation, however, is Self-censorship, which can take many forms. These range from conforming to the prevailing dress code ("after all, this is only a matter of style") to conforming to prevailing codes of speech, behavior, and innermost thought. This conformity can involve complicity in the mechanisms of *particularization*.

PARTICULARIZATION

Paternal pricking/prodding of women commonly employs the device of *particularization:*

Another way of refusing to see the oppression of women is *particularization*. For instance, one hears: "Oh, that's a Catholic problem. The Catholic Church is so medieval." One would imagine, to listen to this, that there is no patriarchy anywhere else.[3]

The Self-censorship that is a by-product of the depreciation of women's oppression often takes the form of cooperation in particularization. Women have a "gut" understanding of the enormous risk involved in Seeing phallocracy in all of its ramifications. When this terrifying knowledge of risk is combined with not-seeing the Ecstatic experience that is the Other side of Exorcism of phallocracy, a woman can fall into patterns of particularization, for example by narrowing the scope of her vision to a single issue.* The issue may be extremely important in itself, but if it is not seen in context, as interconnected with all gynocidal atrocities, it cannot really be *seen*. Also, if focusing upon combatting an atrocity becomes so consuming an occupation that Moments of Spinning are diminished, this loss of Ecstatic Vision will

---

* This is not to be confused with choosing to focus one's energies on a particular issue, for example, woman-battering or rape. It is necessary to make choices and in a sense to "specialize" on the level of activism.

hinder the process of Metamorphosis, weakening effectiveness in relation even to the particular issue itself.

At certain times and places, for example, some women have focused upon the abortion issue. This can be seen as a microcosm of female oppression, since it is the autonomy of women that is the target of anti-abortionists.* But if such an issue is not seen in a Gyn/Ecological context, feminist activism that focuses within its circumscribed area begins to feel draining and even mean-ingless. For in truth women's minds are starved for meaning, for Voyages of Dis-covering new and ancient territories, for Self-Creation.

Certainly, one woman or group cannot do everything. Special-ization and even a kind of functionalism are necessary, but the struggle to see connections can be abandoned only at our peril. Since it is precisely the act of seeing the context that is terrifying, the choice to focus upon a single issue can even function as an excuse for not-seeing the context. Since feminism then becomes reduced to some particular issue, it becomes easy to dismiss as not sufficiently compelling or meaningful.

Female complicity in particularization—meaning exclusive focusing upon one tentacle of the patriarchy—is itself a form of possession/obsession. Since such complicity implies Self-enclosure within terms set by the patriarchs, the activities it engenders be-come reactive, repetitive, and ritualistic. When the patriarchal *given* absorbs all attention and energy away from the project of living our transcendence now, gynergy becomes contained by the sadosociety and is converted into the simple reactive behavior pat-terns that it can anticipate and absorb.

This can happen in various ways. Women working directly against such atrocities as rape and pornography, for example, are sometimes burnt out by the horrors they daily encounter, and caught in chains of re-action. In a different way, women working to create Women's Studies programs in universities whose essen-tial agenda is the erasure of female be-ing can also suffer burn-out, and be caught on wheels of re-action. For, in addition to the

---

This specialization will be most effective if combined with a wide and complex understanding of the many facets of women's oppression as well as women's Spinning.

* This can be said also about religious indoctrination, psychiatric practices, fashions, job discrimination, et cetera.

mental and emotional battering continually endured in such a situation, there are subliminal seepages of gynergy under pressure to compromise, water-down. Here the battle takes the form of shadow boxing.

The bombardment with knowledge of physical atrocities is absent in academia. Instead, academic women are worn down by deception and by temptations to commit what Virginia Woolf called "adultery of the brain," for example, by suppressing information in the name of "objectivity." Women in academia are killed softly by "his words," by the proliferation of bland and boring texts, by the obligation always to return to elementary consciousness-raising (consciousness-razing)—a phallic objective achieved simply enough by the requirement that males be admitted to Women's Studies classes. Women's Studies thus can serve the establishment of Boredom, becoming an agency of anti-Change, anti-Metamorphosis. Thus conquered, it can do little to rescue women from the paternally prescribed program of belonging, befriending, and bewitchingness (Feminization 101).

UNIVERSALIZATION

Some people, especially academics, attempt to make the problem disappear by *universalization*. One frequently hears: "But isn't the real problem *human* liberation?" The difficulty with this approach is that the words used may be "true," but when used to avoid confronting the specific problems of sexism they are radically untruthful.[4]

One *still* "frequently hears" the same whine/line, used to avoid confronting the specific problems engendered by phallocracy and its agents.

Universalization as a fallacy embedded in befriended/ended women's thoughts translates into a variety of forms. One form is the notion that women must take on the responsibility for saving the "human race." This is actually a very old patriarchal line, and it always implies an agenda of female acceptance of male leadership ("mystical," moral, political). Implicit in this ideology is the assumption that women are "equally" (meaning primarily) to blame for every horror perpetrated by males.

Another way in which fallacious universalization expresses itself is through variations on the theme that "as long as anyone (or any woman) is oppressed, all (or all women) are oppressed." Such statements are not without a core of truth, which is the fact of common bonds among all women. Indeed, this commonality is what makes possible feminist moral outrage on behalf of other women and the Lust for a women's revolution. The fallacy lies/lies in the implications often drawn from this universalizing, such as the notion that there is something wrong or selfish about being joyful, healthy, productive, and creative so long as "any woman" is still oppressed. Such a political dogma implies a grim and worse than puritanical ethic of joylessness, demanding Self-denial and hatred of Spinning. It works insidiously to coerce women into withholding from our Selves the hope of moving into Metamorphospheres.

It might be useful to experiment with re-thinking this thesis of universalization. For example, one could say: "So long as any woman sheds the suffocating armor of alienation and unfolds her be-ing in the process of Spinning, there is hope that others can do so." It is not difficult to predict programmed reactions of protest to such a statement, which could be misread as an expression of indifference to the plight of less fortunate women. In fact, it expresses a leap/hop of faith in the intuition that biophilia is contagious.

Clearly, there are ineffably vast differences in the conditions through which women struggle toward Metamorphosis, yet there is no simple way of understanding the process. No one could successfully argue that Sojourner Truth, Harriet Tubman, or Helen Keller did not Weave her own way into Metamorphospheres, despite the conditions of slavery, racism, poverty, or multiple disabilities. To acknowledge these Wonders is not to justify any form of phallocratic oppression. Rather, these "exceptions" signal the Spinning capacities and achievements of countless unknown women. They are intimations that women under almost all conditions can and do experience Moments of Spinning. These Moments radiate the gynergy to continue Metamorphic Movement.

Without the creative exemplarity of such Moments of Spinning, women are prey to the deadening device of universalization. All that is specific to female experience and genius can then be shoveled under a rubbish heap of pseudo-generics. (Our achievements are called "human" and praised/belittled as products of "people" at certain points in "man's history.") Believing that they are "persons first, not just women," women befuddled by false universalization yearn to belong to the thrusting throng that thrives on defacing, erasing, replacing female be-ing.

SPIRITUALIZATION

Reduced to such a state, women are ready for seduction by *spiritualization:*

Another related method of refusing to see is *spiritualization,* that is, refusal to look at concrete oppressive facts. For example, would-be pacifiers of women seem to be fond of quoting the Pauline text which proclaims that "in Christ there is neither male nor female." This invites the response that *even if* this were true, the fact is that everywhere else there certainly is. Moreover, given the concrete facts of social reality and given the fact that the Christ-image is male, one has to ask what meaning-content the passage possibly can have.[5]

Not only in christianity but in all of patriarchal religion one finds mazes of myths that legitimate the destruction of women and at the same time offer pseudo-escapes from such devastation. Spiritualization moronizes by the use of thought-killing reversals.

Spiritualization "works," that is, achieves its spectacular mind-mummifying results when accompanied by "love bombing," a strategy recently identified and applied by the moonies,* but practiced for millennia by "spiritual" organizations. "Love bombing" has been described as follows:

Constant open affection directed towards a new recruit by the rest of the group. Designed to overwhelm; and frequently used when the recruit threatens to leave the cult.[6]

I am using the expression "love bombing" here in a wide sense. As practiced by christians, for example, it is not reserved only for "new recruits." Moreover, it is usually more subtle than the moonie variety. "Christian charity" often implies very little open display of affection. However, it does involve a constant flow of rhetoric about "love" of god and neighbor—a bombardment of verbiage which often replaces/displaces any signs or acts of genuine biophilic concern. Moreover, socialism and its by-product, "socialist feminism," appear often to be imitative of christianity in this respect. Love/concern for the oppressed then easily

---

* Moonies are, of course, members of the unification church, founded by the rev. Sun Myung Moon.

translates into love for oppression as the only morally acceptable state. Moronized by such moralism, women cannot move into Metamorphospheres. Indeed this Realm of Possibilities is "spiritualized"/vaporized out of the imagination before it can even begin to unfold.

Since women are spiritually starved within snooldom, it does not take much to detonate the love bombing effect. One need only think of the institutions of courtship and romantic love, the seduction and enslavement of young girls by pimps, the emotional manipulation that is the work of therapists and priests. In all cases, that which is "bombed" is the autonomy that is essential for biophilic growth and change.

In the various forms of love bombing the "love" that is lavished and/or withheld is made to appear the ultimate full-fillment. As Denise Connors explains it, this desired commodity is a substitute for how it would feel to be autonomously creative. Since the women thus victimized are out of touch with the experience of creativity, this substitute commodity is craved and accepted. In this sense, the device "works." [7]

Entry into the Realm of Metamorphospheres, then, is thwarted by the infliction of a condition which appears to be love-starvation but which is in reality Lust-starvation—the denial and blocking of Pure Lust. Thus Lust-starved, women become lackeys to the Lecherous Lacklusters. Deadended, befriended, possessed by an itch to bewitch, Lust-lacking women are unaware that they have Nothing to lose.

The process of overcoming the effects of spiritualization and love bombing, which is a process of Losing Nothing, is essential to Metamorphic Movement. It is necessary now to consider some views of such movement.

THEORIES OF METAMORPHIC MOVEMENT

During recent decades a number of women, nonfeminist as well as feminist, have expressed heightened interest and a sense of urgency about a phenomenon often described as the emergence of new powers, faculties, or organs of the mind. Although theories concerning this phenomenon vary greatly, the ideas expressed generally include entry into a new stage of evolution. This is usually conceived as implying something like a quantum jump beyond "the present state" of consciousness—a condition which might well be described as the Absent State of consciousness. Three of these theories will be Nag-noted here.

In 1967 Shafica Karagulla, a physician specializing in neuropsychiatry, published a book entitled *Breakthrough to Creativity: Your Higher Sense Perception.* She wrote:

Man is moving in consciousness out of a world of static solid forms into a world of dynamic energy patterns. This is his problem and his opportunity. As a prisoner of the five senses, he has experienced his world as "solid," "concrete," "rigid." Today he has entered a fluid intangible world of vibrating, radiating energy.

Life adapts to environment. Man plunged into this new environment, a universe that is nothing but frequency, must of necessity make new adaptations. He must achieve an ability to more directly experience a world of frequency. In order to do this, he must develop new senses or expand those senses which he already has. There is abundant evidence that many human beings are already expanding the usual five senses into super sensory levels. It is possible that there is already a "mutation in consciousness" taking place and that a few people are developing a new "sense of frequency." [8]

Dr. Karagulla, having departed from the "acceptable" methods of her field, worked with a number of persons gifted with what she calls "Higher Sense Perception." The women and men she interviewed did appear to have remarkable talents for telepathy, clairvoyance, precognition, the reading of auras, and other manifestations of Higher Sense Perception. Her recording of these phenomena is fascinating, but from a Nag-Gnostic point of view her analysis is inadequate.

In the early part of *Breakthrough to Creativity* the reader is given the impression that these phenomena represent a new stage of development, corresponding in some way to the "breakthroughs" of modern science, (concerning which the author appears to be uncritically optimistic). This thesis seems to be hard to sustain, however, and Karagulla herself maintains that instances of Higher Sense Perception have been reported "from the very earliest times." Moreover, she appears not to notice any significance in the fact that whereas nearly all the "historical" recorded instances of H.S.P. which she cites are attributed to males, most of the anonymous "sensitives" whom she actually met and interviewed, and whose experiences she verified, were (to judge from the pseudonyms) women.

A Shrewd might suspect that Dr. Karagulla's lack of *Feminist* Sense Perception accounts for much of the confusion. There is a noticeable conflict between her intuition that H.S.P. development represents a new stage of evolution that is happening now and her knowledge of the fact that H.S.P. experiences are not "new." A Shrewd analysis suggests that this conflict is a consequence of Karagulla's inability to identify clearly the source and the direction of the new stage of psychic transformation—the "mutation in consciousness." She has recognized that this will involve expansion of "the usual five senses," but there is no indication that she sees patriarchal technology functioning as an impediment to such expansion. There is no evidence that she has perceived feminism as an expression/manifestation of Higher Sense Perception or that she has identified women who have Metapatriarchal consciousness as primary agents of "Breakthrough to Creativity." A Nag-Gnostic critic would point out that the "mutation in consciousness" that Karagulla anticipates will be directly connected with the rise of feminism, which is Metapatriarchal Intelligence.*

Another prophet of mutation in consciousness is Doris Lessing. In Part Four of *The Four-Gated City* (1969) the reader experiences through Martha Quest a journey into other dimensions of consciousness, as she develops new powers of knowing. Lessing's descriptions of Martha's ordeal of confrontation with the inner voice of the "self-hater" can function as chilling illustrations of the power of the sadosociety's embeds to hold back the evolution of consciousness. Martha recognizes that hers has been a narrow escape. She has survived the onslaughts of the self-hater because she is armed with some knowledge of the process. Without that knowledge:

. . . A DOCTOR OR A PSYCHIATRIST WOULD HAVE NEEDED ONLY TO USE THE LANGUAGE OF THE SELF-HATER AND THAT WOULD HAVE BEEN THAT. FINIS, MARTHA! BRING OUT YOUR MACHINES. BRING OUT YOUR DRUGS! YES, YES, YOU KNOW BEST, DOCTOR, I'LL DO WHAT YOU SAY: I'M TOO SCARED NOT TO.[9]

What Martha succeeded in doing was facing down the embedded self-hater, self-punisher, who keeps each victim dulled

* To uphold this thesis is not to invalidate the experiences of individual male psychics or of female sensitives who are not explicitly feminists.

and unable to know the evidence of her own senses. In her notes concerning the self-hater, Martha observed:

If a dictator wishes to control a party, or a country; if a hierarchy of priests wish to control their flock; if any power-seeker anywhere wants to create a manipulated group—he, she, has to embody the self-hater. It is as easy as that. *And it is very easy to do.*[10]

Lessing does not offer an analysis of phallocracy as embedding the self-hater ("the Devil") in the psyches of his victims. She is able to describe aptly the mechanisms of Self-hate which sustain the Gynocidal Society without being able to Name the Gynocidal Society. However, this does not completely invalidate her analysis of these mechanisms. Shrews can recognize in her descriptions clues concerning the embeds that block feminist movement into Metamorphospheres.

In *The Four-Gated City,* Martha and her friend Lynda are prophets, forerunners of a more highly evolved species. Lessing gives hints of a future of superlative, highly evolved male and female humans who, after the nuclear holocaust, begin to be born in hidden places in the world. The reader is given the impression that these superior beings are the results of some mutation. As Martha states in a letter written during the post-holocaust period, "one day all the human race will be like them." That is:

People like you and me are a sort of experimental model and Nature has had enough of us.[11]

The reader is left quite mystified, however. Aside from the very problematic notion that nuclear holocaust would be the catalyst necessary to trigger the mutation into higher forms, what other conditions could account for it? How does the "human race" move from its current defective state to the highly evolved condition of which Lessing briefly hints? As in the case of Karagulla's theory, Lessing's vision fails to bring into focus not only the specificity of phallic oppression but also those luminous explosions of female-identified creativity which *are* Movements into Metamorphospheres.

In her description of Martha Quest's transformation, Lessing makes the point that the process itself contains the necessary clues for unfolding awareness:

Still, she had learned that one thing, that most important thing, which was that one simply had to go on, take one step after another; this process in itself held the keys.[12]

If this is true for Martha Quest, presumably it would be true for other participants in the history-bearing group that she represents.[13] But we are faced with the problem that it is unclear *who* might participate in such a group. If we search Lessing's descriptions of Martha for clues, we observe that an ardent quest for Self-knowledge is a fundamental quality. Martha sees well enough that "this particular planet is inhabited thickly by defectively evolved animals." [14] She does not move through this process of seeing the horror to joyous gynergetic Spinning. We are told that "Nature" decides to produce a new and better "human race." Poor Martha, however, despite her heroic struggle, does not really participate in that race, and she does not Race.

It is Nag-noteworthy that Lessing introduces the final part of *The Four-Gated City* with epigraphs from male religious "teachers," specifically from the master Rumi of Balkh (born A.D. 1207) and from *The Sufis* (Idries Shah). Both of these sources/texts proclaim that "man" or "humanity" acquires new organs in the course of evolution in response to needs for specific organs. The sufi doctrine presented by Idries Shah states that "the human being's organism is producing a new complex of organs in response to such a need." Within Lessing's interpretation, however, the new organs that presumably are possessed by the remarkable post nuclear holocaust children do not seem to be a consequence of Martha's Quest, but rather, by-products of technological destruction. The reader can certainly appreciate the notion of the emergence of such a new species as nature's triumph over evil. Yet within Lessing's context this thought has an unsatisfying incompleteness. The account has a hollow ring to a woman who experiences *now* in her own life the biophilic potential for Metamorphosis. Moreover, Lessing's work, by implying that the evil of nuclear holocaust is necessary in the evolutionary scheme of things, can function subliminally to legitimate this horror.

By the early seventies feminists were making leaps of under-standing concerning Metamorphosis. 1974 marked the publica-tion of Barbara Starrett's classic feminist article, "I Dream in Female: The Metaphors of Evolution." Starrett wrote:

Now imagine a species that has so evolved that its members begin to feel like another species, are aware of their differentness, and have developed a consciousness about themselves that is not explainable in contemporary symbols, forms, mindsets, language, art and culture.
Women are now at this point. . . .

Starrett sees contemporary feminists as descendents of the Witches who survived the Burning Times and as aware of this heritage. She continues:

And we feel it; we know it. We are beginning to see into the past and into the future, to heal and create again, to be aware of our own strange abilities, to energize and communicate with each other in new ways.
We are even becoming aware that we can consciously evolve; that our new "organ" is something which enables us to will our own further evolution. The more aware we become of our own evolutionary pro-cess, the more we are empowered to will and direct that process: an incredible evolutionary leap, a macro-mutation on a level with (and having similar dynamics to) the development of language.[15]

The reader who was part of the feminist experience of the early seventies may feel a certain nostalgia reading these words. The women recognized by Starrett to be "now at this point" were/are, of course, the cognitive minority known as radical feminists. One decade later, we find our Selves confronted by an insidious backlash, whose intent is to undermine the intellectual courage to live out the vision reflected in Starrett's article. The sadorulers employ the Self-hater embedded in women to patron-ize and openly sneer at such vision, relying upon the usual stock-pile of Biggest Lies, utilizing the usual devices of depreciation, particularization, universalization, spiritualization to batter the minds of Muses approaching Metamorphospheres. They employ fembotized women to kill the hopes of women who are in fact experiencing Metamorphosis in the process of evolving metapatri-archal consciousness.

Entry into Metamorphospheres, then, requires exorcism of the demons spawned by the Big Brothers in their frantic backlash against the rise of female powers. The most effective form of exorcism is Continuing the Journey, refusing to be distracted by the bad magic of the Manipulators/Mutilators. Despite the attempts to mute the voices of Musing women, more and more Wantons/Witches are aware of our potency to change.

The active and explicit development of women's spiritual powers is a continuing focus of many Furies. This theme is aptly expressed in the title of a recently published anthology: *The Politics of Women's Spirituality: Essays on the Rise of Spiritual Power Within the Feminist Movement*.[16] Many feminists continue to express myriad manifestations of Creative Female Clairvoyance. Among these are writers and other artists as varied in their approaches as: Merlin Stone, Z. Budapest, Sally Gearhart, Maxine Hong Kingston, Adrienne Rich, Nelle Morton, Gloria Anzaldúa, Nicole Brossard, Janice Raymond, Carol Christ, "Sweet Honey in the Rock," Willie Tyson, Naomi Littlebear, Robin Morgan, Charlene Spretnak, Starhawk, Emily Culpepper, Louki Bersianik, Judy Grahn, Monique Wittig, and Judy Chicago. All of these women "dream in female." [17]

Muses, recalling that *dream* is from the Old English *drēam*, meaning noise, joy, music, remind women that Female Dreaming is noisy, joyous, and musical. Also, we are not surprised to hear that *dream* is said to be etymologically related to the Latvian word (*duñduris*) meaning gadfly, wasp. For Metamorphosing women sting and provoke each other to Change.

Wanton women also warn each other that *dream* is derived from the Indo-European root *dhreugh-*, meaning to deceive. We point out that the real danger of deception is from man-made daydreams/daddydreams—*his* romances, *his* theories, *his* religions, *his* soap operas. The danger is that we will be seduced into believing that everyday "common sense" and "logic"—the scripts of the plastic dream-makers—are "reality." The danger is that we will be held back by these male fantasies, kept from Dreaming deeply enough, Wildly enough.

BUTTERFLIES, BACKLASH, AND ERRATIC MOVEMENT

Meandering into Metamorphospheres, Muses notice that our Labryses are also Butterflies. From this perspective, too, they are symbols of the Great Goddess.[18] As a matter of casual interest, we might light upon a description of how butterflies appear to outside observers. H. M. Tomlinson describes an encounter of the all-male crew of a British ship with a tropical butterfly:

A superb butterfly, too bright and quick to be anything but an escape from Paradise, will stay its dancing flight, as though with intelligent surprise at our presence, hover as if puzzled, and swoop to inspect us, alighting on some such incongruous piece of our furniture as a coil of rope, or the cook's refuse pail, pulsing its wings there, plainly nothing to do with us, the prismatic image of joy. Out always rush some of our men at it, as though the sight of it maddened them, as would a revelation of accessible riches. It moves only at the last moment, abruptly and insolently. They are left to gape at its mocking retreat. It goes in erratic flashes to the wall of trees and then soars over the parapet, hope at large.[19]

The sight of the butterfly is maddening to the men. Even more maddening is her mocking retreat. The riches accessible to her are inaccessible to them. Characteristically, she moves in erratic flashes. *Erratic* means "having no fixed course: WANDERING." It means "deviating from what is ordinary or standard (as in nature, behavior, or opinion): ODD, ECCENTRIC." The erraticism of the butterfly—her Wanderlust, Untidiness, Eccentricity—is essential to her be-ing "hope at large."

The erratic be-ing of butterflies is described by Elizabeth Goudge, who writes that they are "yet not quite birds, as they were not quite flowers, mysterious and fascinating as are all indeterminate creatures." [20] Although tidy collectors are always trying to classify them, there is something about them that mocks classification. This, of course, is one reason why the collectors are obsessed with classifying them, pinning their corpses onto stiff boards in glass cases.

Indeed, butterflies represent that which is baffling to the necrophilic fixers, whose behavior in relation to these creatures is illuminating. Gertrude Stein relates a fascinating "little description" of this:

One of such of these kind of them had a little boy and this one, the little son wanted to make a collection of butterflies and beetles and it was all exciting to him and it was all arranged then and then the father said to the son you are certain this is not a cruel thing that you are wanting to be doing, killing things to make collections of them, and the son was very disturbed then and they talked about it together the two of them and more and more they talked about it then and then at last the boy was convinced it was a cruel thing and he said he would not do it and his father said the little boy was a noble boy to give up pleasure when it was a cruel one. The boy went to bed then and then the father when he got up in the early morning saw a wonderfully beautiful moth in the room and he caught him and he killed him and he pinned him and he woke up his son then and showed it to him and he said to him "see what a good father I am to have caught and killed this one," the boy was all mixed up inside him and then he said he would go on with his collecting and that was all there was then of discussing and this is a little description of something that happened once and it is very interesting.[21]

Since butterflies represent biophilia at large—that which is beautiful, joyous, hopeful, and erratic—they seem to elicit the fathers' inherent tendency to expose themselves, as Gertrude Stein has illustrated in her little description of snoolish self-contradiction.

The autonomous, Wild movement of Erratic women also elicits the deceptive/destructive reflexes of the fraternal flashers, who perpetually preach against "cruelty" even as they perpetrate biocidal acts. Backlash, then, is to be expected. It is boringly predictable.

The responses of Erratically Flying women to the butchers'/ botchers' backlash, however, are Unpredictable to them. There is, for example, the fact that we do not re-spond/re-act. We do not backlash back at them. Instead, we spontaneously act. Such acting is unintelligible to incomplete snot boys, hacks, and snools. Feeling like fools, the flashers/lashers strut and swagger, draw their daggers. Stabbing/jabbing, jerking, jabbering, the butterfly-fixers prick each other.

Amid this butchery/botchery Butterflies alone are undisturbed. Poised, we pulse our wings, waving good-bye. We are ready to fly. The Time to enter Metamorphospheres is now.

CHAPTER TEN

BE-LONGING: THE LUST FOR HAPPINESS

Supernatural:	"transcending nature in degree and in kind or concerned with what transcends nature (a divine order which directs history from outside and keeps man in touch with the eternal world through the Church and the sacraments—*Times Lit. Supp.*)."
	Webster's Third New International Dictionary of the English Language
Super Natural:	"Unfolding Nature in degree and in kind or concerned with what Unfolds Nature (an Elemental order which directs history from inside and keeps women and all biophilic creatures in Touch with the real world through the senses—*Tidal Times*)."
	Websters' First New Intergalactic Wickedary of the English Language

The word *happiness* has been banalized/travestied beyond belief/relief by the Bosses of Boredom. Repeated and regurgitated by the verbiage vendors, it is phallicism's formalized label for full-fillment. Images of "happy" fembots file through the Foreground of fatherdom's dumb shows/fantasies, erasing Rage, setting the stage for numberless mummified/numb-ified copies. Xeroxed First Ladies parade through commercials and soaps. Mechanical toys applauding the boys, televised numbots nod their agreement to all of His speeches and smile while He preaches His Nuclear Sermons. Like Daisy with Donald, like Nancy with Ronald, the doll-women duckspeak their memorized scripts. "Everything's fine." So goes the Line. "There's happiness for all in store, in nineteen hundred eighty-four." *

Happiness has Wholly Other meanings from all this, however. The following discussion launches a Nag-Gnostic ontological exploration of such Other dimensions.

PHILOSOPHICAL AND THEOLOGICAL CONSIDERATIONS OF HAPPINESS

The word *happiness,* deeply understood, is radiant with ontological meaning. Uncovering its philosophical meaning is an important task for Wonderers seeking/Lusting for Wisdom. Our exorcism and ecstasy can be aided by exploration of this philosophical background. Indeed, such investigation is a catalyst for Metamorphic movement into our own Background of Metabeing. Moreover, Nag-Gnostic examination of the medieval theological tradition concerning happiness (or what was known as "man's last end") is vital for this exploit/exploration. Theologians have believed that "grace" is necessary for the attainment of happiness, and the reasons that led them to this conclusion shed light upon our Metamorphic movement.

In Aristotelian philosophy, happiness is *eudaimonia.* As we have seen in Chapter Eight, *eudaimonia* in Greek means having a good attendant or indwelling spirit. As a philosophical term employed by Aristotle and his disciples it means "a life of activity governed by reason." In the highest sense, happiness is a life of activity of the mind, or contemplation.[1]

Clearly, then, within this tradition, happiness is not equatable with some passing emotion. Rather, the emotion of joy—popu-

---

* The following is my own rendering of a typical Numbot Chorus number, which conveys something of the style and thought content of these man-made manikins' performances:

Four score and seven years ago, our fathers made a T.V. show.
It's time to switch the dial again, time to watch and smile again.
We've always smiled and watched our men.
We'll smile and watch our men again. Again. Again.
When acid falling from the sky was just a gleam in Daddy's eye
We never asked the reason why; we'll never ask again.
When nukes were just a big boys' plot, we smiled and watched a lot.
It's 1984 again. We'll smile and watch our men again.
Amen.
(Applause, as the Numbots fade in time for the Nightly News.)

larly identified with happiness—is a consequence of the life of activity that constitutes happiness. The experience of joy is a psychic manifestation of happiness.

Following the tradition of Aristotle, Aquinas taught that "man's happiness," which he identified as "man's last end" consists in an operation of the intellect. Consistent with his own logic, moreover, he concluded that the happiness of "man" must consist in the operation of his highest power—the intellect—in relation to its highest object. For Aquinas, the highest object of knowledge is the "Divine Essence." He writes:

For perfect happiness the intellect needs to reach the very Essence of the First Cause. And thus it will have its perfection through union with God as with that object, in which alone man's happiness consists.[2]

This conclusion presented a problem to its author. For he believed that man could not attain such union through his natural powers. For:

Every knowledge that is according to the mode of created substance falls short of the vision of the Divine Essence, which infinitely surpasses all created substance. Consequently neither man, nor any creature, can attain final Happiness by his natural powers.[3]

Man, then, would seem doomed to eternal frustration. God, however, has the solution. By infusing grace into the soul, god elevates the capacities of Man, so that Man can merit eternal happiness in the next life. Yet one problem remains, namely, that the created intellect after death still lacks the capacity to see the "Divine Essence," even after this reward has been "merited" with the aid of grace. Aquinas maintains that this is resolved by the infusion of a "supernatural disposition," that is, a special supernatural light, which is added to the intellect "in order that it may be raised up to such a great and sublime height."[4]

Although some Hags and Harpies may feel a bit hysterical after hearing of all these additives and erections, it is important not to succumb to the urge to roll on the floor or fly away before considering the fascinating insights which can be gleaned from such texts. For, as representative of mainstream traditional christian belief, Aquinas was conveying overt and subliminal messages of importance. I shall note some of these.

First, there is the notion that happiness is fully attainable only after death. Second, this presupposes that the spiritual faculties (intellect and will) of the Happy Dead Ones were elevated supernaturally by grace when they were still alive, so that they could merit eternal happiness. Third, the Happy Creature, in order to have the Beatific Vision in heaven, must be in a permanently passive condition in relation to "God," who has all of the power in this relationship. The Aristotelian idea of happiness as a life of activity of the mind has been converted into an afterlife of passivity. Since the "operation" or "activity" is utterly supernatural, artifactual, the Happy State is one of essential impotence. This afterlife of perpetual union/copulation with the Divine Essence is an absolutely artificial operation.

One could see this doctrine of happiness, then, as a confession and legitimation of male impotence. It is by no means a woman-originated doctrine. Women do not experience a need for a supernaturally stimulated eternal erection. As impotent beings, patriarchal males do have this need, which they have erected religiously as the requirement for happiness. It will be noticed that the eternal copulation under scrutiny here is a male homo-erotic relationship. The sons seek union with their male god, who is frozen forever as the dominant partner in this pathetically unequal union.

One might ask what all this has to do with women. In one sense, it would seem, the answer is "not much." Women have never concocted such a bizarre scenario of eternal full-fillment, although many have succumbed to intolerable pressures to swallow such myths. Women do feel blocked/fixed by forces which they often cannot Name, and which are experienced as impediments to the unfolding of our own native capacities. Since patriarchal propaganda is everywhere, even within women's minds, and since phallo-institutions impose sanctions throughout fatherland, the lives of many women have indeed been made so miserable that they have been able to accept the bore-ophilic belief that happiness is attainable only after death. They have even been bored/gored into believing that their powers need supernatural elevation (grace) in this life in order to have any hope of happiness in the next.

As the mind-bindings come loose, however, women become increasingly aware that the impediments to our attainment of happiness are not innate deficiencies. Wild women do not share the phallocratic male's problem of impotence and thus do not have the need to fantasize an eternal connection with an omnipotent being. Metamorphosing women recognize that our happiness is indeed a *life of activity*. In a special way happiness is activity of the mind, or contemplation. It can include many activities: artistic creation, political action, development of spiritual powers, athletic activities. These are a few facets of our many-sided Unfolding, our holistic Realization of Be-Longing, that is, our Happiness.

METAPATTERNING

As we have seen, the theology of eternal happiness implies the need for supernatural extensions of man's powers, so that he can connect eternally with god. It is not hard to detect which organ, in a phallocentric religion, is subliminally the focus of this attention/extension. Nags will note also, on the basis of previous discussion, that theological language about supernatural "raising up" of the intellect "to a great and sublime height" so that it can connect with god has analogs in phallotechnology's erections. The explosions of nuclear weapons are also supernatural/artificial emissions—attempts of impotent males to connect eternally with their omnipotent killer-god. Since the impotent patriarchal male's own organ "falls short" (to use the expression of Aquinas concerning man's intellect) of attaining the "Divine Essence," he needs to build and use technological extensions of that organ.

Given this context, male pronouncements concerning a new stage of "spiritual evolution" that requires the acquisition of "new organs" are suspect in the eyes of Metamorphosing women. Thus the statements of the master Rumi of Balkh and of the sufis that are cited by Doris Lessing reflect this perspective of male obsession with impotence.* When women adapt this kind of language uncritically, it becomes easy to slide into other phallic assumptions.

Feminists also sometimes have used this kind of language. For example, Barbara Starrett's article (cited in the Foreground to this Realm) presents the concept of a new "organ" which "enables us to will our own further evolution." There is nothing

---

* The fact that these "spiritual teachers" were not christians is irrelevant to this point. Whether the "spiritual teacher" is Aquinas or the master Rumi, the over-riding "sacred canopy" of legitimations is constructed of the symbols of phallicism.

whatsoever that is phallic about Starrett's ideas, and indeed it is a valid mode of speculation to ask whether women are developing such a faculty. However, it is important for Nags to question where and under what circumstances we began to employ certain words to convey ideas that are new to us, and whether they can be misleading.*

The use of such a term as "organ" to designate the Metamorphosing Powers of metapatriarchal women could carry with it subliminal associations not intended by the speaker/writer. It could suggest, for example, that Lusty women's Be-Longing is somehow parallel or comparable to the patriarchal killer males' felt need to transcend their physical and ontological sense of impotence by acquiring supernatural or technological extensions. Wonderlusting Voyagers do not need such extensions. Wild women Realize our will to further evolution, our Lust for participation in the Unfolding of Be-ing, our Happiness. Our primary problem now is the overcoming of the unnatural obstacles —both external and embedded—to this ontological Passion.

There are Elemental powers in each woman's psyche that are covered by the embedded codes of her captors. In her process of breaking the embedded code, she uncovers her own powers. One way of describing this process is to call it *metapatterning.*

The Dreaming/Musing that engenders Metamorphosis is a process of metapatterning. This process presupposes Seeing through the paternal patterns, the moldy molds intended to stunt our lives. It is thought-provoking for Searchers to find that the word *pattern* is derived from the Middle Latin *patronus,* meaning patron of a benefice, patron saint, master, pattern. *Patronus,* of course, is derived from *pater,* meaning father. Indeed, there is an odor of paternalism about the definition of the word *pattern,* which means "a fully realized form, original, or model accepted or proposed for imitation: something regarded as a normative example to be copied: ARCHETYPE, EXEMPLAR." Metapatriarchal Erratic movement is hardly according to patriarchal pattern.

---

* My earlier use of the word *androgyny* to signify woman-identified integrity is a case in point. When I was writing *Beyond God the Father* this word was suggested by a male colleague. Although it sounded a bit alien, I adopted it without enough critical evaluation. Subsequent experiences made it clear that the word was completely inadequate, conveying something like the images of Ronald and Nancy Reagan scotch-taped together.

Metamorphosing women do not imitate/copy some "fully realized" paternal form or model. Rather, we are Realizing/Forming/Originating.

When metamorphosing Muses use the term *metapatterning,* we mean to Name the process of breaking through paternal patterns.[5] Nag-identified metapatterning involves real transcending of patriarchal patterns of thinking, speaking, acting. It is weaving our way through and out of these patterns. Erratic women weave our lives, our works, not as imitations of models, nor as models for others, but as unique diversified creations.

Rather than seeking to develop new "organs" (an old pattern), then, metapatterning women recognize that we already have the powers to will our own further evolution. The idea of a new "organ" is too limiting to Name the source of the metapatterning powers which myriad consciously mutating women are now discovering in multiform ways. That source is something like a Telic Focusing Principle that is all-pervasive within the organism, that is entirely present in all parts of the organism. This Telic Focusing Principle enables us to assimilate what we need from the environment, to grow, to adapt, to change. It is a re-membering principle as well as a metapatterning principle. Our analysis of Metamorphospheric Movement requires that we give further attention to the workings of this principle.

FOCUSING/CENTERING

When a woman is deeply in touch with her creative powers, her powers of metapatterning, she can, of course, recall other times of feeling at a distance from these powers and from this kind of activity. The Presence of her metapatterning Self accentuates her awareness of the alienation she experienced in times of foreground fixation. She may, at these peak moments, be able to acknowledge the alienation of "normal" times during which she could not fully experience her own experience of alienation. She may then ask her Self in astonishment where she was at those other times, when, it seems, she had fallen away from her Center.

She had, in fact, been dragged away from her Center by the fragmentation of foreground "living," that is, dying. The process of dislocation/splintering, however, may have been subtle, subliminal. Sometimes, therefore, a woman will describe her experience of being connected once more with her metapatterning

Presence as suddenly coming home again after an unexplained and inexplicable absence.

Metapatterning can take many forms. The activities involved are multiform, for example, traveling in a foreign country, riding a bicycle, being engaged in a Spinning discussion of ideas, walking on the beach. The process of writing a book of feminist philosophy can be a useful illustration. This is particularly so because the effort of metapatterning is sustained over a somewhat lengthy period of time and because the process itself of metapatterning is the object of attention.

So, then, a woman may be in the process of writing a book, an activity that requires telic centering/focusing. In the course of this prolonged activity she assimilates all kinds of events into the writing process. The book she is writing participates in the deep purposefulness of her living. Her Lust to write this particular work becomes part of her Be-Longing, and writing it is one dimension of writing the book of her life. It is a Metaphor of her Journey into Metabeing. The focus required for bringing forth a work in this dimension, and of these dimensions, encourages the writer into a state of heightened awareness. Many apparent "coincidences" then begin to happen. For example, although the author of this book does not often watch television, she turns on the T.V. set one day just in time to see/hear a "news" story that evokes a whole chain of metaphors. Or again, she is thinking about a Foresister—Elizabeth Cady Stanton— and wishing she had a particular piece of information at her fingertips. A few minutes later she opens her mailbox and finds that a publisher has sent her a complimentary, unsolicited copy of a book on Stanton, containing just the information wanted. Moreover, she "just happens" to open the book immediately to the right place. Or again, in the course of a telephone conversation a friend mentions an article that is exactly what is needed to support the argument she is developing at the moment.

The sensory aliveness that accompanies such a process is complex/gynaesthetic. A typo turns out to be the truly accurate and subliminally intended word. This aliveness is a consequence of deep telic focusing/centering. Even the tedious distractions of daily life can sometimes be assimilated into this process by the telic principle. A boring committee meeting occasionally can provide material for radical analysis. A trip to the supermarket can suddenly supply a missing clue. The Presence of the creative telos, then, keeps a woman fiercely focused. Since the author here described is a radical feminist, she is involved in the creative communal process of decoding the prevailing codes and of creating out of her own Code, that is, metapatterning. The material for her Search, therefore, is Everywhere.

Yet the forces of fragmentation lie in ambush. As Dragons, as Gorgons, women must guard and foster the Flame of telic focus. For poor women, for women of color, and for others whose individual circumstances are particularly oppressive, the struggle against the fragmentation of energy that brings physical disease and psychic paralysis is often unspeakably hard. For all women, particularly in times and places of extreme repression, the creative telos within the Self is in conflict with the agendas of the sadostate. Some counterforce is provided by the communal telos of the feminist movement, and the constant weaving of this net of knowledge and commitment is both the primary act and the necessary condition for the macromutation that is the Elemental Metamorphic Movement of women.

THE "SOUL" AS METAPHOR FOR TELIC PRINCIPLE

One traditional way of naming the principle of telic focus has been to call this the "soul." Shrewds can use this as a starting point for our analysis. Since my intent is to wrench this concept out of its traditional context, using it in a Nag-Gnostic context, I am employing it not simply as an analytic concept but also as Metaphor.

Soul, as springboard word, then, refers here to the animating principle of an organism. Specifically, it means the "substantial form" of a living body, as this is understood in Aristotelian philosophy.[6] Soul, then, as the word is used here, is not intended in a Platonic sense, as if it were a distinct entity loosely connected with the body, or imprisoned in the body. Certainly I do not mean it in any sort of Cartesian sense, as if it were "mind" or *res cogitans* vaguely connected with matter. Rather, I use the word *soul* to mean an animating principle that is intimately united with/present to the body, in a union that traditionally has been called a "hylomorphic union." According to this theory, in human beings the "intellectual principle" is united to the body as the body's form.[7]

To speak of the soul in this sense, then, is not to convey the naive, dualistic notion that soul and body are two united entities. The soul, conceived as the animating and unifying principle of the organism, is the radical source of life functions and activities. It is the source of telic centering—of the purposiveness of the organism.

The soul, understood in this tradition, is wholly present in each part of the body.[8] It is not a mere quantitative whole. An example of the latter would be a house, which is composed of foundation, walls, and roof. (Obviously, the entire house is not in each of its parts.) Moreover, the soul is not just a generic or logical whole, as a whole definition is made up of all of its parts. Rather, it is a "potential whole." Explaining this concept, Aquinas wrote that the whole soul is divided into "virtual parts." That is:

The whole soul is in each part of the body, by totality of perfection and of essence, but not by totality of power. . . . with regard to sight, it is in the eye; and with regard to hearing, it is in the ear, and so forth.[9]

Since this concept of unity (of essence) at the root of multiplicity (of parts/powers) was not comprehended by all philosophers, Aquinas had to refute the position that "besides the intellectual soul there are in man other souls essentially different from one another." [10]

This seemingly simple position, namely, that there are not many souls in one person, but rather one soul, wholly present everywhere within that person, can be a Metaphoric springboard for Metamorphosing women. It can function as an aid to Amazons seeking the meaning of our Be-Longing in the face/faces of the fear-full fragmentation of women that is inflicted in the fatherland. Some of the implications may be more obvious if the Searcher substitutes the word *Self* for *soul,* thereby constructing the statement: There are not many Selves in one woman, but rather, one Self, wholly present in that woman. I am not asserting here that Self and soul are precisely equivalent terms; in fact, they are not. My point is that one obvious consequence of the idea that a woman has one soul wholly present in all of her "parts," is that there is an essential integrity at the very core of her Self.

Be-Longing implies the Unfolding, the Realization, of this inherent integrity. It is Realized as a woman becomes wholly Present in all of her activities. The phenomenological manifestation of this integrity and pervasive Presence of her soul is a radical consistency in her behavior. She does not seem to be "one person one day and someone else the next." This is not to say that she lacks complexity and variety of skills, activities, and experiences. Quite the opposite is the case; she manifests a high degree of differentiation. Moreover, she is spontaneous. This is possible because her energy is focused; it is not dissipated in the maintenance of masks, of fragmented false selves—splintered personae parading on the periphery of her Self.

The Unfolding/Realizing of this integrity is be-ing beyond such reified beings, the solidified pseudo-selves. It is participation in Metabeing. The Lust for this intensely focused ontological activity, or Be-Longing, is the Lust for Happiness.

Souls and Holograms/Holographs

The concept of the unity of the soul, as presented in Aristotelian philosophy and developed in the doctrine of Aquinas, can not easily be dismissed as completely absurd and irrelevant. To one who has long been familiar with this doctrine, it is both fascinating and funny to find contemporary scientific thinkers using language that in some ways is reminiscent of this idea, when they write of the universe and of the mind as "holograms."

According to David Bohm, for example, who often uses the holographic analogy, the information of the entire universe is contained in each of its parts. As Larry Dossey describes holograms:

A hologram is a specially constructed image which, when illuminated by a laser beam, seems eerily suspended in three-dimensional space. The most incredible feature of holograms is that any *piece* of it, if illuminated with coherent light, provides an image of the *entire* hologram. The information of the whole is contained in each part.[11]

Dossey—and others before him—asks whether, as part of the universe, we have holographic features ourselves that permit us to comprehend a holographic universe. Stanford neurophysiologist Karl Pribam has answered the question in the affirmative, proposing the hologram as a model of brain function.[12] Putting

together the ideas of Bohm and Pribam, Dossey suggests that
the brain is a hologram "that is a part of an even larger hologram
—the universe itself." [13]

The holographic analogy is, of course, just that—an analogy.*
It has provided a language for these scientists to speak of an
idea of the mind and of its relation to the universe that is really
not entirely new. Comparable themes have recurred in the history
of philosophy.[14] Bearing this in mind, Brewsters may wish to
use holograms/holographs as variant metaphors pointing to
integrity/wholeness. This is not to suggest that contemporary
scientific jargon legitimates the classical philosophical language,
concerning the soul, for example. It may be, however, that the
holographic metaphor can render more accessible some of the
potentially helpful concepts that are contained/captured within
the contexts of philosophical treatises.

The holographic metaphor, moreover, as applied to the idea
of the soul, can suggest a telic centering principle which is an
unfolding potential whole—one that is changing in harmony
with the universe. Prudes can use this combination of metaphors
to point to the internal source of the unfolding integrity of metapatriarchal women. Such integrity is manifested in the whole
spectrum of a woman's activities and characterizes her presentiating Presence.

COMMUNICATION BEYOND THE CELLS OF SICKNESS

Since Metamorphosing women are Gyn/Ecological, we do not
evolve/mutate as isolated units, nor do our powers develop in
isolation from each other. Recalling the metaphor of the hologram, we reflect upon the fact that "any *piece* of it, if illuminated
with coherent light, provides an image of the *entire* hologram."
Women who are Realizing any of our powers, that is, illuminating such powers with the coherent light of our own reason, find
that this process implies Realizing the telic principle (soul) in
its entirety/integrity. Metamorphosing women are Unfolding as
whole intellectual/passionate/sentient Selves as we move out
of the Numbed State. No other than holistic change is desirable.

---

* Robin Morgan uses the holographic analogy in a thought-provoking
way to view feminism. See *The Anatomy of Freedom* (Garden City,
N.Y.: Doubleday and Company, 1982).

To speak of it another way, this mutation is organic. The powers of Crones evolve in harmony with each other, in *communication* with each other.

David Bakan discusses communication on a biological level in a way that can be helpful for the analysis of metapatriarchal processes. After distinguishing conscious communication between two persons from internal communication that takes place when something previously unconscious becomes conscious within an individual, he discusses internal biological communication:

Within the human organism there are varieties of forms of communication evident when what happens in one part of the body affects what happens in other parts. There are numerous mechanisms in such internal communication, the neural and hormonal being particularly conspicuous. . . . The mechanisms are remarkably diverse. The fact that communication takes place, by whatever mechanism, pervades all biological phenomena.[15]

The reduction of such internal communication results in disease and death. Identifying this anti-process as telic decentralization, Bakan discusses lack of communication in cancer cells:

It turns out that the cells of cancer, which are radically and manifestly removed from the telos of any higher level of the hierarchical order, are precisely those cells which are distinguishable from their cellular counterparts by a gross inability to communicate with other cells, as indicated both by their growth behavior and by the lack of ionic transfer.[16] *

Nags are very much aware of the "gross inability to communicate" which characterizes those who manufacture and maintain the imprisoning cells of snooldom. Those who construct and sell these cells (homes, schools, hospitals, doctrines, myths, et cetera) are precisely those who cannot communicate in biophilic and ontological dimensions. They attempt, however, to invade and man-ipulate those whom they imprison and poison, and this predatory P-R impedes Elemental communication. The result, of course, is a sick social "organism," and a widespread sickness unto death among members of that society.

* Bakan's choice of the words *higher* and *hierarchical* order is perhaps unfortunate, but this does not invalidate his point.

Bakan reminds us that *"a degree of telic decentralization is the essential underlying characteristic of the diseased organism."* [17] Metamorphosing women are determined to leave the diseased organism of fatherland. The way out is precisely telic centering/focusing, which implies quantum leaps of conscious communication within our Selves, among each other, and with the universe. This consciously willed centered Unfolding implies macroevolution.

MACROEVOLUTION

Having affirmed the Aristotelian doctrine of the soul as one viable starting point for discussion of our transformation, Soothsayers will assess some of its liabilities as well as its assets. There is, first of all, the problem of its dualism. We have seen that the dualism of Aristotle and Aquinas was not merely a crude belief in form (soul) and matter as if these were two "things." Rather, these were understood to be intimately connected principles of a living creature. There is hardly a more abstract concept in the history of philosophy than Aristotle's notion of "prime matter," which was by no means believed to be sense perceptible, but rather was thought to be knowable only through a complex reasoning process. Yet dualism, however subtle, is recognized as inadequate by Nag-Gnostic critics, for Naming the reality of our Selves. It is more in accord with the experience of women breaking free of *feminitude*[18] to view "soul" and "body" as ways of talking about different aspects of the same Self. Moreover, there are more than two aspects of such experience. Words such as *spirit* and *aura*, for example, name other aspects of Self-definition, as does *Elemental be-ing*.[19]

Nags also criticize the *essential* unchangeableness of the Aristotelian soul. It is true that change was believed to take place on an "accidental" level. The intellect, for example, could acquire new knowledge. In the view of Aquinas, the essence of the soul is something like a root or source of many faculties, which are distinguished from each other by their acts and objects. The powers flow from the essence of the soul and are interconnected with each other.[20] The activities proceeding from these powers of the soul, thus conceived, were understood to bring about individual and social development. No matter how highly these faculties are developed, however, according to this tradition, this brings about no essential change in the individual or the species. The worldview of Aristotelianism, then, was static, nonevolutionary.

It was, perhaps, a glimmer of intuition and yearning for more than this stasis that prompted the christian doctrine of grace—especially the doctrine of sanctifying grace. The latter, conceived as "supernatural life" infused into the soul, was believed to make possible a "heightening" or intensification of the soul's spiritual capacities, so that these could attain higher levels or dimensions. Unfortunately, the higher levels all converged into/boiled down to "God." The intimations of quantum leaps beyond the prevailing static state were potted into a belief in a "supernatural" Static State, the eternal stag-nation of the blessed.

Hags find this kind of eternal retirement plan ineffably resistible. Dismissing christian supernaturalism as the Kiss of Death, we catch our breath and return to the Aristotelian concept of the soul, considering other aspects of this theory. The treatment of sexual differentiation, for example, is another important topic, although seemingly not very important to Aristotle, for sexual difference is considered "accidental" to the "human species." Although to the uninitiated, "accidental" may sound like a joke term, it was intended seriously. Taken in this context, it did not mean "happening by chance or causing injury." Rather, it was intended to convey that the difference of gender is nonessential, that it does not change the species of individuals. In other words, women were considered to be "human"—in abstract theory though not in the actual society legitimated by Aristotle. That is, women were said to belong to the fixed species called MAN.[21]

Metamorphosing women are not flattered but rather are horrified at the idea of such belonging. Moreover, the experience of such a woman is that she does not "belong." Her Erraticism essentially implies breaking the molds of the Fixed Species. Her psychic/physical Living requires Macroevolution.

Macroevolution is defined as "evolutionary change involving relatively large and complex steps (as transformation of one species to another)." Such evolution is now intended, with varying degrees of explicitness, by many Crones. Metapatriarchal women experience as ineffably accidental our connection with the species that has planned and executed witchcrazes, death camps, slavery, torture, racism in all of its manifestations, world famine, chemical contamination, animal experimentation, the nuclear arms race. This differentiation is affirmed by a series of conscious choices.

Metapatriarchally moving women not only experience now but continue to choose to develop our differences from those who consciously and willingly perpetrate these horrors and we recognize these differences as not merely accidental, but rather *essential*. The traditional concept of "species," especially of "the human species" does not adequately encompass the differently oriented lives supposedly contained therein. I refer primarily to its grotesque blurring of differences between those whose intent and behavior is radically biophilic and those whose desensitized/decentralized, soulless and berserk (dis)orientation manifests "gross inability to communicate" and fundamental enmity toward Life itself. *

Alice Walker has expressed an almost inexpressably enraged awareness of these differences in her article "Nuclear Exorcism" (first delivered as a speech at an anti-nuclear arms rally). After reciting a curse prayer that was collected by Zora Neale Hurston in the 1920s, Walker discusses the hope for revenge that she believes to be at the heart of people of color's resistance to joining the anti-nuclear movement. She writes:

And it would be good, perhaps, to put an end to the species in any case, rather than let white men continue to subjugate it and continue their lust to dominate, exploit and despoil not just our planet but the rest of the universe, which is their clear and oft-stated intention, leaving their arrogance and litter not just on the moon but on everything else they can reach.[22]

After presenting a strong argument for "fatally irradiating ourselves" and for "accepting our demise as a planet as a simple and just preventive medicine administered to the universe," Alice Walker decides against passive acceptance of extinction:

Life is better than death, I believe, if only because it is less boring, and because it has fresh peaches in it. In any case, earth is my home—

---

* Wise readers will recognize that this sort of distinction is not a simplistic bifurcation on the basis of gender. Patriarchy here is seen as a disease attacking the core of consciousness in females as well as males.

though for centuries white people have tried to convince me that I have no right to exist, except in the dirtiest, darkest corners of the globe.

So let me tell you: I intend to protect my home.[23]

I suggest that the decision not to allow nuclear maniacs "to put an end to the species" logically implies rejection of the idea that there is a "human species." The gynocidal, genocidal, biocidal aggressors whose lust is for destruction are deciding in one direction. It is possible to decide in Other directions through the consciously willed and continual affirmation of Ongoing Life that is Pure Lust. This lived decision as it is carried out in everyday events constitutes not only more than an accidental difference; it is also greater than a specific difference. *It renders the old philosophical concept of "species" obsolete,* especially as a tool for conceptualizing and Naming the be-ing of biophilic creatures. Such ones cannot be confined to any static species, for our essences are changing, metapatterning.

When I write Metaphorically of the "souls" of women as our telic focusing and metapatterning principle, then, I am not restricting the term to express the classical Aristotelian idea of substantial form determining an individual as a member of a fixed species. For such a species can conceivably contain/encompass other "members" whose telos (if the privation can be designated by an affirmative name) is really anti-telos, that is, ultimate destruction of meaning and purpose. Indeed, the concept of such a species is contradictory, nonsensical. It would attempt to embrace creatures whose conscious behavior is wholly oriented in opposite directions.

Yet the term *soul* can be heard with the Third Ear by one who listens in an Other context. Springing off from the Aristotelian structure, and from the language of modern science as well, the Spirited Searcher may speak of the soul not as that which confines an individual within a "species," but rather as a principle of uniqueness/diversity.*

---

* Haggard Searchers will relish recalling that according to medieval theology, *each* angel is a distinct species. (See Thomas Aquinas, *Summa theologiae,* I, q. 50, a. 4.) Each Metamorphosing Journeyer experiences moments in which she recognizes her Self and Others who *live* biophilically as many distinct species.

Since Metamorphosing women can view our bodies as transmutable to and from energy, the soul can be seen as the centering principle of this energy/gynergy. It is, as the ancients believed, the form of the body, but this is translated by Wanton/Wandering women to mean the metapatterning principle through which we direct our shape-shifting, our transfiguration/mutation.

This telic principle of uniqueness/diversity by no means has the effect of undermining unity, manifested in community, commonality, and bonding. Rather, it expands and intensifies the possibilities of Living the realities designated by these words. The deep connections that are rooted in one's individuality as an intentional creator of her be-ing are more significant than are accidental connections in space and time, that is, of geographical and/or temporal proximity. They are more radical even than familial, ethnic, and class ties, and ties of religious and educational "background."

To affirm this connectedness that is rooted in Self-creation is hardly to overlook these other ties, in all their complexity and depth. It is to begin to understand these givens in the context of metapatriarchal becoming. The confrontation and exploration of the effects of these bonds of "background" has been an important concern of many feminists in the late seventies and in the eighties. Crones are also re-membering a more radical Background of diversity and connectedness that moves women into Metamorphospheres. Bonding in relation to the final cause—the cause of causes—is focused upon where we are going. It is focused also upon where we came from, in the most radical sense, for it is rooted in Elemental origins.

This bonding of women as deeply connected with our final cause takes place in a world of vibrations, of resonances, of ribbons of rhythm weaving through rivers, sands, trees, winds, flames, seas. Our thoughts respond to the music of plants and animals, oceans and stars. Women sense, too, that animals and plants respond to our thought-forms, that nothing is done in isolation. We are participants not only in what is commonly called the dance of life, but also in what Prudes might prefer to call the Prance of Life. For macroevolution, we recall, requires "relatively large and complex steps." This is especially the case as we continue to transform from one species to another.

The intensity/immensity of individual women's steps—our

prancing, metapatterning movements of individuation—augments our capacity and Lust for participation. The Lusty longing for ontological participation is an intrinsic aspect of Be-Longing. It is a longing to live in connectedness that already is, but is not yet Realized. Realizing such ontological participation requires conjuring metamemories, the memories that aid our Prancing, that spring and bound into the deep past, thereby carrying our vision forward.

BE-LONGING AND METAMEMORY

Women's yearning for experiencing our ontological connectedness with all that is Elemental implies a longing to mend, to weave together the Elemental realities that have been severed from consciousness, that is, forgotten. The deep significance of forgetting and re-membering is suggested in Greek myth. According to Hesiod, Lethe (Forgetting) is the daughter of Eris (Strife).[24] It is clear that the amnesia of women is in large measure the product of strife/conflict. From the earliest beginnings of our lives all of the agents of patriarchal patterning work unceasingly to destroy women's Elemental Wildness. The suffering involved in the struggle to survive this battering certainly induces forgetfulness.

There is much more to be understood about deep forgetfulness, however. As we have seen, in Greek mythology Mnemosyne, the Goddess of Memory, was the mother of all art. Poetry, then, was the child of Memory. Reflecting upon Plato's banning of poetry from his ideal state, Ernest Schachtel recalls that since that philosopher was concerned with planning the future rather than with evoking the past, he chose to impose a taboo upon memory in its most potent forms.[25] Comparing the story of Ulysses' strategy for withstanding the irresistible song of the Sirens with Plato's banning of the poets, Schachtel reminds us that "the profound fascination of memory of past experience . . . with its promise of happiness and pleasure" poses a "threat to the kind of activity, planning, and purposeful thought and behavior encouraged by modern Western civilization."[26]

Unfortunately, Schachtel does not have very clear intimations of what it is about deep Memory that promises happiness and pleasure. Nor can he really say *what* it is, exactly, about "the kind of purposeful thought and behavior encouraged by modern Western civilization" that makes it radically inimical to such

Memory. Metapatriarchal women, however, are dis-covering what sort of Memory is so potent, so promising, and so threatening to modern civilization's "purposeful" thought and behavior. Nags Nag each other into recurrent awareness of what is wrong with the purposes of the Memory-hating civilization. We know that truly focused purposefulness is rooted in deep Memory, which we might now call Metamemory. For this is beyond and trans-formative of ordinary "memories," and it is a source of the Lust for Happiness, that is, Be-Longing.

Crones, therefore, are keenly cognizant of the urgency of the task—implied in Be-Longing itself—of overcoming our amnesia. For as long as vaster expanses of Metamemory still elude us, the energy of our Lusting is slowed down, potted, deflected. Clues for our Memory-Searching can be gleaned from Schachtel's anal-ysis of "childhood amnesia." He writes:

The categories (or schemata) of adult memory are not suitable re-ceptacles for early childhood experiences and therefore not fit to pre-serve these experiences and enable their recall.[27]

Developing this thesis, Schachtel points out the inadequacy of the Freudian assumption that a repression of sexual experi-ence accounts for the repression of nearly all experience of early childhood. Rather, the problem of amnesia is also associated with the fact that there is a quality and intensity typical of early childhood experience that cannot be contained in the adult's categories for retaining memories. Muses hardly need to be per-suaded of Schachtel's point that the average adult memory is incapable of reproducing "anything that resembles a really rich, full, rounded, and alive experience." [28] As he points out:

Even the most "exciting" events are remembered as milestones rather than as moments filled with the concrete abundance of life. Adult memory reflects life as a road with occasional signposts and milestones rather than as the landscape through which this road has led. . . . And even these signposts themselves do not usually indicate the really sig-nificant moments in a person's life; rather they point to the events that are conventionally supposed to be significant, to the clichés which society has come to consider as the main stations of life.[29]

Thus the memories of most people come to resemble "the stereo-typed answers to a questionnaire."

While agreeing with this point, Crone-logical critics find it imperative to point out the inadequacy of Schachtel's analysis and description of the average adult's poverty of memory. For the categories of "adult memory" in patriarchy are the categories of androcentric memory. The "milestones" of this artificial memory are male milestones, and all too frequently function for women as millstones. Thus, for example, religious and national holidays conjure memories of servitude—shopping, cooking, cleaning, et cetera. Patriarchal weddings imply the legal and ritualized loss of one's own name and autonomy. Going to work commonly means accepting a dead-end, low paying, Self-erasing job. Birthdays are reminders of aging and subsequent patriarchal devaluation. While the milestones of adult "life" may be dreary for individual males, they are at the same time a collective boost to the male ego, to the Mythic Male with whom each man identifies. Thus Christmas, Easter, Veterans' Day, Washington's Birthday, a marriage in the family are designed to be "uppers" for men and "downers" (disguised as uppers) for women.

Moral outrage at the degradation/erasure of women implied in all of these milestones/millstones can propel a woman to the gateways of Metamemory. The quest to re-member the qualitatively Other, vivid, richly significant experiences of our past is especially urgent for women, for Realizing of such realities gives us the strength to exorcise the patriarchal categories. A woman who can evoke her childhood experiences of gazing at the moon and stars on clear nights, or lying on the grass, or listening to the sea, or watching the sunset is Elementally inspired. When she can recall early experiences of the smell of leaves on an October day, the taste of raspberries at a picnic, the feel of sand warmed by the sun, she is empowered. Energized by her own unique Elemental memories, she can break through the maze of "adult categories." Her reawakened, recharged aura expands its rays, shining through the film of societally imposed schemata, rendering visible the deep connections.

Enormous breakthroughs to the spheres of deep Memory can be occasioned by the accidental recurrence of a body posture. Feminists becoming aware of our bodies in new/ancient powerful ways know that this far-from-accidental process reconnects us with Metamemory. Women who study self-defense and various forms of the martial arts, for example, sometimes describe a vivid re-membering of bodily integrity and coordination which they had known as young girls, before the heavy indoctrination of adolescence forced feminization upon them.[30] Through the living of physical as well as spiritual intimacy with other Deviant/Defiant women, Hags experience gestures, postures, acts reminiscent of earliest woman-loving experiences with our mothers. Craftswomen who are deeply absorbed in such crafts as pottery, spinning, and weaving sometimes describe the experience of their work in words that evoke Metamemory.

DEVIANT/DEFIANT WOMEN AS METAMEMORY–BEARING GROUP

The memories accessible to Crones are not simply of physical closeness to our mothers. The charged memories of childhood carry with them in a complex and condensed way the vivid Elemental perceptions of the world that we experienced as children. Virginia Woolf expresses this quality of Elemental memory, in describing what she calls her first memory, which is a combination of two memories. The first part is a recollection of being on her mother's lap on a train or in an omnibus. This blends with the other part. She writes:

If life has a base that it stands upon, if it is a bowl that one fills and fills and fills—then my bowl without a doubt stands upon this memory. It is of lying half asleep, half awake, in bed in the nursery at St. Ives. It is of hearing the waves breaking, one, two, one, two, and sending a splash of water over the beach; and then breaking, one, two, one, two, behind a yellow blind. It is of hearing the blind draw its little acorn across the floor as the wind blew the blind out. It is of lying and hearing this splash and seeing this light, and feeling, it is almost impossible that I should be here, of feeling the purest ecstasy I can conceive.[31]

Of crucial importance is the blending of being on her mother's lap with "the most important of all memories." This memory of lying in the nursery of St. Ives is an illustration of Metamemory. It is Elemental, filled with rhythmic sounds of the sea and the wind, suffused with light.

Such memories are Taboo. Their ecstasy and fullness can be more real than the present moment. They beckon to the ways of escape from the prison cells that are constructed of the schemata of "adult," that is, male-controlled, memory. Sirens/Sibyls insist that the Taboo against woman-bonding is connected with the Taboo against such memories. For commitment to women and breaking of the Total Taboo implies breaking through the blocks that stop us from re-membering the ecstatic spheres of Metamemory. Woman-bonding be-ing, then, is the opening of Pandora's box, which is filled with the richest treasures.

The ecstatic memories that become accessible do not induce passivity, but rather they are catalysts of intense activity which is qualitatively Other than that desired by the patriarchal planners. They are catalysts of macroevolution. Viragos' violations of Taboo, by transcending as well as including the sexual sphere, imply a constant Quest. This Quest requires creative living of the promise of Happiness that is inherent in Metamemory. Refusal to conform to hetero-relational norms is, in effect, refusal to be re-minded by the re-formers of Memory.

In a special way, then, Deviant/Defiant women are the Metamemory-bearing group among women.* This is the logical consequence of a radical choice to re-member Happiness, of a Great Refusal to be re-minded by obedience to the deadening rules of the Ruling Caste. This Choice to recall the empowering memories and to create in our daily lives future memories of Happiness is a continuing act of deviant defiance. It is a macroevolutionary leap that is fueled by Be-Longing.

Some years ago Herbert Marcuse wrote, concerning Freudian theory:

Theoretically, the difference between mental health and neurosis lies only in the degree and effectiveness of resignation: mental health is successful, efficient resignation—normally so efficient that it shows forth as moderately happy satisfaction.[32]

* This is why patriarchal professionals work to control/channel female deviance. The "encouragement" of female sickness is one means to this end. As Denise Connors has demonstrated, "women's sickness can be seen as a means of channeling women's potential deviance away from a collective, system-destructive route and into a more privatized and self-destructive path." She shows that "the sick role has served to neutralize and contain women's rage, their subversive force and potential to envision and create a new way of life." ("The Social Construction of Women's Sickness," paper delivered in the Feminist Lecture Series, Smith College, Northampton, Mass., February 17, 1983.)

Further developing his exposition of this theme, Marcuse explained Freud's view:

Repression and unhappiness *must be* if civilization is to prevail. . . . In the long run, the question is only how much resignation the individual can bear without breaking up. In this sense, therapy is a course in resignation.[33]

It is precisely this resignation to "civilization" with its numbing schemata that is defied and transcended by deviant Hags whose re-membering is the root of metapatterning, of metamorphosis.

Of course, some of patriarchy's therapists have attempted to offer their clients something more than resignation to everyday unhappiness. Discussing these pathetic efforts, Marcuse continues:

Over and against such a "minimum program," Fromm and the other revisionists proclaim a higher goal of therapy: "optimal development of a person's potentialities and the realization of his individuality." Now it is precisely this goal which is essentially unattainable—not because of limitations in the psychoanalytic techniques but because the established civilization itself, in its very structure, denies it.[34]

Radical feminism, insofar as it is true to itself, is the Denial of this denial. As the Metamemory-bearing group, Taboo-breaking women, insofar as we are true to our Selves, are Deniers of this denial. This deviant Denying is radical unmasking of the spheres of Metamemory which are the rightful heritage of all women.

RE-MEMBERING BEYOND CIVILIZATION

Freud, that apostle of adjustment to common, everyday unhappiness, defined the foreground conditions of forget-full fatherland:

The programme of becoming happy, which the pleasure principle imposes on us, cannot be fulfilled; yet we must not—indeed, we cannot —give up our efforts to bring it nearer to fulfillment by some means or other. . . . Happiness, in the reduced sense in which we recognize it as possible, is a problem of the economics of the individual's libido.[35]

Shrewish Prudes parody this paternal patter, and in the process of reversing its reversals come up with a bit of Soothsaying. Thus:

The Elemental power of becoming happy, which our memories re-call to us, can be Realized. Therefore, we must not—indeed we can-not—give up our efforts to bring it nearer to actualization by our own means. . . . Happiness, in the ecstatic sense in which we recognize it as possible, is the project of Metamemory-bearing women.

Feminism essentially means commitment to our past and future memories of Happiness in defiance of civilization.* Bearing in mind that an "obsolete" meaning of *civilization* is "the act of making a criminal process civil," Sibyls suggest that phallic civilization is essentially a criminal process, parading as "civil." Singing into conscious awareness our childhood and ancestral memories, Sirens lure women into our Past and therefore into our Future, awakening Be-Longing.

A simple and telling comment on civilization is recorded in *Daughters of Copper Woman,* a remarkable collection of stories from native women of Vancouver Island, women who are "mem-bers of a secret society whose roots go back beyond recorded his-tory to the dawn of Time itself." [36] The specific statement is:

Civilization brought measles, whooping cough, chicken pox, diph-theria, small pox, tuberculosis, and syphilis.[37]

In a wide sense, all of the stories in *Daughters of Copper Woman* are comments on civilization. The white christian conquerors of the native people decimated their population. When vast num-bers of the "memorizers," the women of this matriarchal, matri-lineal society, who were living history books, were killed by the

---

* Lillian Smith, discussing Freud's view that woman is retarded as a civilized person, wrote: "I think that what he mistook for her lack of civilization is woman's lack of *loyalty* to civilization." See "Autobiogra-phy as a Dialogue between King and Corpse," in *The Winner Names the Age,* ed. by Michelle Cliff (New York: W. W. Norton and Company, 1978). Developing this theme, Adrienne Rich has written of the prob-lematic intertwining of racism and the oppression of women as these evils affect the lives of women, especially in the United States. This theme of choosing to be disloyal to civilization is essential in the development of feminist theory which takes on the task of realistic assessment of the multiple oppression of women under patriarchy. See Adrienne Rich, "Dis-loyal to Civilization: Feminism, Racism, Gynephobia," in *On Lies, Secrets, and Silence: Selected Prose 1966–1978* (New York: W. W. Norton and Company, 1979), pp. 275–310.

disease-carrying, raping, white male invaders, much of the knowledge and wisdom of these women died with them. Yet some of the knowledge remains. The voice of Old Woman, speaking to the young girl Ki-Ki through her "Granny," explained:

"We must reach out to our sisters, all of our sisters, and ask them to share their truth with us, offer to share our truth with them. . . . The last treasure we have, the secrets of the matriarchy, can be shared and honored by women, and be proof there is another way, a better way, and some of us remember it." [38]

Expressing a vision of universal female re-membering, Old Woman said:

"Women are bringing the pieces of truth together. Women are believing again that we have a right to be whole. Scattered pieces from the black sisters, from the yellow sisters, from the white sisters, are coming together, trying to form a whole, and it can't form without the pieces we have saved and cherished." [39]

Metamemory is deep and vast. Women who "are bringing the pieces of the truth together" are moving beyond civilization. This moving implies Natural Grace. Since the Graceful leaps of Be-Longing women cannot be accomplished in isolation, it is essential now to explore more deeply the problem of communication, which is Be-Friending.

CHAPTER ELEVEN

BE-FRIENDING:
THE LUST TO SHARE HAPPINESS

> *Separatism:*   "a disposition toward secession or
> schism; especially: advocacy of with-
> drawal from a parent group (as a
> church)."
>
> *Webster's Third New International*
> *Dictionary of the English Language*

> *Separatism (Radical Feminist):* "a necessary disposition
> toward separation from the causes of
> fragmentation; especially: advocacy
> of withdrawal from all parasitic
> groups (as a church), for the pur-
> pose of gynophilic/biophilic commu-
> nication."
>
> *Websters' First New Intergalactic*
> *Wickedary of the English Language*

Happiness implies biophilic communication. Such communication is ontological, implying deep interconnectedness with all
be-ing. This interconnectedness can be expressed as follows:

Everything that IS is connected with everything else that IS.

Crones will recall the "first law of ecology," as expressed by
Barry Commoner, namely: "Everything is connected to everything else." [1] While this is a useful maxim as it stands, there is
also something left unexpressed, namely the fact of disconnectedness, the breaking of the flow of natural interconnectedness, the
manufacture of fractures by the Foreground Fraternity.

As a consequence of this fracturing there are, in fact, "things"
that are not biophilically connected. On the physical level, one
need only think of plutonium, of agent orange, of the increasing
quantity of hazardous wastes. On the psychic level, there are the

plastic feelings, pseudo-virtues, and warped ideas discussed in the Pyrospheres. These products of the Predatory State ARE NOT, in the sense that they do not participate in the biophilic flow of be-ing. Of course they "are there," as barriers to our Realization of powers of be-ing. Only through such Realization can radical ontological communication be dis-covered. Analysis of this process requires cutting through the snarls that keep women in the State of Separation.

SEPARATION AND REVERSAL

One of the basic blocks to Be-Friending, that is, to radical onto-logical communication among women, is the embedded fear of separation. Terrified of the dreadful thing which in fact has al-ready happened (although this event is unacknowledged), that is, of separation from their Selves, women in the Possessed State dread separation from their separaters/fracturers/batterers/flat-terers. Therefore they are horrified by such words as the label "separatist."

Women confined in the phallic State of Separation, then, are characterized/crippled by inability to identify the agents of Self-blocking separation. They are victimized by the strategy of re-versal. Just as the label "man-hater" in Woman-Hating Society functions to stop thought, so also the negatively charged use of the label "separatist" within the State of Separation hinders women from Be-Friending.

It is necessary to recognize that the life-blockers who have instituted the State of Lechery are radically separated from the natural harmony of the universe. Women who separate our Selves from the blockheads/blockhearts whose intent is to block our Unfolding, our Happiness, do so out of radical commitment to communication. It is precisely the commitment and capacity for ontological communication that is feared by the blockocratic rulers, for this is what they lack.

Metapatriarchal women, who choose biophilic communication, understand that the foreground label "separatist" will be used against us. The question is whether we choose to expend energy refuting this, or to "save" energy by ignoring it, or to understand this word as a Labrys which we can sharpen and use.

The expenditure of gynergy in refutation is kept at a mini-mum by Shrewd Scolds. Wanton women understand that this is a waste, and even as Gorgons and Amazons we recognize that fixation on refuting is ultimately re-fusion with the sappers/drainers. The second alternative, ignoring the label, is functional only if one is truly ignorant. As worldly/Otherworldly Nag-Gnostics, however, we do *know* about the prevailing prattle-battle; we are not ignorant of this. To totally suppress this knowledge, to pretend it isn't there, is mind-mutilating.

The Metamorphic option, then, would seem to be the third, that is, to use the term *separatism* as our Labrys. On the one hand, it Names phallic separatism, which blocks and bars Life-Lust—the desire for ontological communication. On the other hand, it Names the choice of women to break from the artificial context of phallic separatism in order to affirm and live our radical connectedness in biophilic be-ing.

As a name for the movement of Metamorphosing women, therefore, *separatism* is what I would call a "second order" word. For it does not emphasize the direction, or final cause, of our movement, which is ontological Metamorphosis itself, but rather an essential prerequisite of this movement under the conditions of patriarchy. Since, under these conditions, separation from those forces that cut us off from be-ing is necessary, it is not inaccurate for a radical feminist to call her Self a separatist. This name, however, unless used in a context of Lusty words, is inadequate. Since the whole point of feminist separation is biophilic communication/participation in Be-ing, it is bio-logical to conclude that these context-providing words will be Other words—words that signify such transcendent communication, for example, Spinster, Webster, Brewster, Fate, Muse.

For metapatterning women to wield the word *separatism* as a true Labrys, moreover, its positive meanings must be understood in conjunction with phallic separatism—the condition which makes metapatriarchal separation necessary. It is essential, therefore, to consider the meaning of phallic separatism.

PHALLIC SEPARATISM

Recalling the description of cancer cells as characterized by a "gross inability to communicate," Websters may decide to consider the analogy with cancer as a tool for description of the phallocratic society. Crones have observed that there is a disorder at the very core of patriarchal consciousness, and that this consciousness both engenders and is engendered by phallocentric myths, ideologies, and institutions in an endless necrophilic circle of separation and return. If there can be said to be a "connecting thread" or commonality among all of these phenomena, that commonality is their disconnectedness from biophilic purpose.

The cancer analogy for contemporary society is widespread, of course. Few connect it with phallicism, however. Yet the somewhat accurate images in the contemporary imagination of how cancer "works" expose a great deal. In the Prologue to Robin Cook's medical thriller, *Fever,* there is a vivid description of poisonous molecules of benzene attacking cells in the bone marrow of a twelve-year-old girl. As Cook describes the event:

The [attacked] cell instantly divided and the resulting daughter cells had the same defect. No longer did they listen to the mysterious central control and mature into normal white blood cells. Instead they responded to an unfettered urge to reproduce their altered selves. Although they appeared to be relatively normal within the marrow, they were different from other young white blood cells. The usual surface stickiness was absent, and they absorbed nutrients at an alarmingly selfish rate. They had become parasites within their own house.[2]

As a parable, this description can be Prudently applied as follows: Within the Virulent State of phallocracy women have been attacked and divided against our Selves. From the earliest times of the patriarchy countless mothers have been broken, and the resulting broken daughters have carried on the chain of fragmentation. No longer have the broken daughters been able to listen unhindered to the "mysterious" telic centering principle within and become fully Self-actualizing women. Instead, they have been reduced to responding to the fettered/fathered urge to reproduce their altered—that is, patriarchally identified—selves in an endless circle of Self-destruction. Such forcibly altered women have appeared to be normal within the man-made milieu. In these altered women, the usual defenses are absent, and they have absorbed the "nutrients" of misogynistic messages at an alarming rate. This patriarchal "selfishness" is the result of starvation for real spiritual and intellectual nutrition.[3] Thus these members of the chain of broken mothers and daughters are unable to communicate unbroken messages of biophilia. Patriarchal women, then, have been reduced to the role of "parasites" within their own "house"—this planet, feeding into the mechanisms of reversal, distracting attention from the fact of patriarchal parasitism.

Yet the sources of wholeness are within women.[4] Consequently, many women, even under patriarchal rule, have managed to transmit mixed messages of biophilia and gynophilia to their daughters. The overcoming of phallic separatism, of the programmed separation of all living creatures from the telic centering principle of be-ing, will involve facing the horror of its workings and its effects.

One way of approaching the spiritual carcinogenesis that is patriarchy is to look at its own ideologies, as well as its myths, as the self-fulfilling prophecies which they are. One excellent example is the Aristotelian-Thomistic doctrine that women are "misbegotten." Relying upon Aristotle's biology in his work *De Generatione Animalium,* Aquinas, the "Angelic Doctor," wrote:

As regards the individual nature, woman is defective and misbegotten, for the active force in the male seed tends to the production of a perfect likeness in the masculine sex; while the production of woman comes from defect in the active force or from some material indisposition, or even from some external influence; such as that of a south wind, which is moist, as the Philosopher [Aristotle] observes.[5]

On one level, many Hags have seen this as a laughable reversal, at which they can righteously roar. On another level, it functions also as self-fulfilling prophecy of the man-made woman. In the context of Amazonian analysis, "misbegotten" as applied to women under patriarchy describes the deformity/conformity of women to male-made models or patterns. Thus women who, like patriarchal males, cannot listen to the telic centering principle within, are—on the foreground level—man-made, made-up, misbegotten. Women in this condition include not only the twice-born Athenas but also those immersed in passive stereotypic femininity.

Women in this Misbegotten State have been assigned to break/divide the daughters, to break in their daughters, to break down their defenses, to cut off their possibilities for Original communication. They are indeed unfettered in carrying out this male-ordered mission. It is important to scrutinize the remainder of the text cited above from Aquinas. He continues:

On the other hand, as regards human nature in general, woman is not misbegotten, but is included in nature's intention as directed to the work of generation. Now the general intention of nature depends on God, Who is the universal Author of nature. Therefore, in producing nature, God formed not only the male but also the female.[6]

This text can be decoded as follows:

As regards the man-made construct of "human nature" in general, patriarchal women are not misbegotten, but are included in "nature's" intention as necessary for the work of reproduction of the male-identified species. Now the general purpose of "nature" depends upon patriarchal myth-makers, who are the universal Authors of "nature." Therefore, in producing "nature," these myth-makers formed not only the stereotypic male, but also the stereotypic female.

Simply stated, what this amounts to is the fact that patriarchally begotten, that is, misbegotten, women, serve patriarchal purposes, blocking the flow of Elemental be-ing. In order to comprehend the processes of Metamorphosing women's separation from this State of Separation—to actualize powers of Be-Friending—it is important to consider the effects of phallic separatism in women's lives.

The Effects of Phallic Separatism

In order to understand the effects of ontological dividedness, it may be helpful to employ a metaphor of wholeness. Returning to the idea of the holograph, Websters note that the basic meaning of this word is "a document (as a letter, deed, or will) wholly in the handwriting of the person for whom it proceeds and whose act it purports to be." The life of a wholly Present woman would manifest itself as wholly in her own "handwriting." That is, it would be clear that she has been the composer, creator of the Book of her Life. She would acknowledge many friends, Fore-sisters, contributors, but it would be evident that her words and deeds proceed always from her Self as center of focus and purpose. Gynographers would be able to detect her signature in all of her acts. Such a holographic, hologynic Hag would be an inspiration, a signal of attainable Happiness.

In fact, Metamorphosing women sometimes experience such integrity. Yet the facts of dividedness are undeniable. Sirens,

Sibyls, Soothsayers/Truthsayers must face this separation from our Selves. Feminists, seeking deep and faithful bonding with other women, have frequently been baffled and broken by repeated encounters with this brokenness. Many have experienced inexpressible grief and even despair.

To feminists, one of the most dis-spiriting experiences imaginable is to encounter in a woman an apparent inability to experience moral outrage at the atrocities perpetrated against her sex. This cannot be explained by ignorance of facts, when the facts are presented clearly and cogently. The puzzle is ineffably confounding: here is a woman, yet she seems unable to identify with the oppression of women—a condition which she must have experienced on many levels. She may, in fact, be sensitive to the abuses against almost any other group, while apparently feeling nothing about the common lot of women—in a word, gynocide.

To approach this problem it is helpful to Spiral back to the study of the passions in the Realm of Pyrospheres. Shrewds will have noticed in the Foreground to that Realm that in the traditional listing of the eleven passions, only one passion has no contrary, namely, anger. Unlike such passions as daring and fear, for example, which involve movements toward and from a "difficult [to avoid] evil" that is not present, anger is a movement of attack upon an evil that is present. According to that analysis, since the "difficult evil" is present, a movement of withdrawal is not possible.

There is a certain logic in this medieval analysis that should not be overlooked. Of course, Hags know that anger can be converted into such plastic passions as depression, hostility, anxiety. However, so can other passions be transformed into pseudo-emotions. The Nagging question remains: What exactly is different about anger? Is there really no contrary movement? Where does the anger go?

Shrewd women may obtain insight for approaching these questions by observing such phenomena as the current interest in the syndrome called "multiple-personality disorder." That this subject is particularly significant in relation to the topic of anger is suggested by the fact that according to one recent survey of some one hundred psychiatrists around the country the vast majority of cases of multiple-personality disorder that were "seen" were women, and over 90 percent of the patients diagnosed and treated as "multiples" had been severely abused sexually and/or in other physical ways for long periods during their childhood.[7]

Ellen Hale has pointed out that although multiple-personality has been sensationalized in such popular books as *The Three Faces of Eve* and *Sibyl,* it is currently receiving serious attention by some psychiatrists. Some of these professionals are now admitting that the disorder is far more common than previously acknowledged, partly because the condition has been misdiagnosed, often as the catch-all "schizophrenia." Hale cites Dr. Frances C. Howland of the Yale University School of Medicine, who has treated "multiples" for years. Remarking that the possibilities in situations of danger are to fight back or run away, Dr. Howland stated: "If you can't do either—as a child cannot—you can only do it symbolically. Dissociation is symbolic flight."[8] The dissociation manifested in those diagnosed as multiple personalities is extreme. One psychiatrist claims to have identified "startling differences in the brain waves of the alternate personalities of patients suffering from multiple-personality disorder." Another study suggested that each personality may have its own memory. "Multiples" may have abnormally wide vocal ranges and an extraordinary ability to alter speech patterns.[9]

Two of the cases cited by Hale will serve to illustrate the extremity of the abuse of women who become "multiples." Natasha (a pseudonym) was raped continually by her father from the time she was two until she turned sixteen. "Until she was 12, the rapes took place with her mother's passive compliance and often with her active participation." Natasha seems to have 127 personalities or personality fragments. Another woman, "Sherry," was tortured as a child by her father who played "doctor" with her. His sexual torture of her was so vicious that she bled all over his white jacket. Among her father's other activities was throwing her pet cat into an incinerator.[10]

There is hardly a feminist (none, to my knowledge) who can read or even hear of such material with complete equanimity. One reason for this shared sense of horror may be an implicit recognition that a low-grade form of multiple-personality disorder is very common among women in patriarchal society. Indeed, I suggest that this is the normal/misbegotten condition of women locked into the phallic State of Separation. All women within sadosociety (even those with the most enlightened and well-meaning parents) have been psychically abused and starved for healing, inspiring Self-images. Since mind (or soul) and body are not separate entities, such deprivation inevitably has physical effects.

To return to the questions posed above concerning anger, then, I suggest that Shrewds following this line of reasoning can find in the idea of a widespread low-grade multiple-personality disorder among women strong intimations of the answer to our question: What happens to the woman-identified, that is, Self-identified Rage of women under patriarchy? Since women abused as children cannot fight back or run away, dissociation is a logical solution. I suggest that dissociation is the "missing contrary" of the passion of anger. Anger can be seen as different from the other passions in this respect, namely, that when it is blocked, its movement or energy splinters into fragments within the psyche. Rage, then, can be seen as a convertible energy form. In the State of Separation this energy in women is frequently converted into the production of dissociated "other selves."

If this analysis is correct, then the key to escape from the State of Separation can be found by asking a precise question concerning patriarchally possessed women—women incapable of moral outrage on behalf of their own Selves and other women. The question, simply, is: What is it that a patriarchal woman dissociates from? The response that seems most evident to a meta-patriarchal thinker is that the dissociation is from her original identity as a woman—not as the sadosociety defines "woman," but as an Archaic, Elemental woman, which Jan Raymond has Named "an original woman." [11] This response leads to the subject of radical feminist separatism.

RADICAL FEMINIST SEPARATISM

Weirds and Websters, wielding the word *separatism* as one of our many Labryses, can use this word to name our intent and actions that powerfully separate us from the Dissociated State, releasing the flow of Elemental energy. Thus understood, separatism is an essential aspect of gynophilic communication, for it separates a woman from the causes of fragmentation—the obstacles, internal and external—which separate her from the flow of integrity within her Self.

We can begin to understand the importance of such separation from the State of Separation by returning to the subject of Rage. We have seen that anger in the traditional sense is a movement of attack against the evil that is present. This raises the question of how the gynocidal evil of phallic separatism is "present" to a woman.

In an earlier chapter I discussed the "presence of absence" that characterizes phallicism. This kind of presence, when it invades a vulnerable woman, has as its target her very integrity of identity. Typically, when a little girl or a grown woman is sexually abused, she blames herself, feeling guilty and ashamed. Anger may not be her immediate reaction, because the internal "fighting back" which is the passion of anger implies an ability to distinguish the Self and her motives from those of the attacker. The phallic presence of absence, however, translates itself within the attacked/victimized woman's psyche into an internalized presence of absence of the woman's Self. Feeling that she has been stained and defiled by the attack, the victim loses the capacity to Name the attacker and even to Name the event of violation as an attack. In such a case, she has internalized and identified with the evil.[12]

The evil, then, can be so present that it blends with a woman's own idea of herself. In order to attack this attack, she must disconnect her Self from the violator. If she is caught within the maze of patriarchal images of women as weak, despicable, seductive, dirty—images injected in early childhood into every woman within patriarchy—this may be precisely the move she is unable to make. Her incipient Elemental Rage, twisted in upon itself, splinters her soul.

The attack, of course, need not be physical. The perpetual bombardment of women's psyches with overt and subtle insults, often guised as courtesy, consideration, and respect, also inflicts the presence of absence within that immobilizes the impulse to anger. The dissociation that results will not be recognized as such within the State of Separation, which is also the State of Reversal. Rather, it will be accepted and fostered as normal and healthy.

The healing response to this condition is the providing of a *context* that affirms precisely that from which women under patriarchy have been dissociated, that is, identification as Wild, Original women. Feminist separatism, then, is a communal process, affirming the flow of connectedness within each woman—her Presence of Presence.

The history of women's struggles to provide and maintain diverse forms of "women's space" has been a vivid testimony to the fact that men recognize this to be a crucial issue in the war to control women's minds. Many women, moreover, deceived by rhetoric concerning "equality" and "human rights," have been willing to cede such hard-won space. Sometimes the attack upon women's space originates in socialist circles, whose propagandists manage to persuade white as well as minority women that since some men are oppressed, these men should have access to all feminist gatherings and events. These invasions are justified through ideologies that ignore the meaning and functioning of phallocracy/patriarchy as radical source of other forms of oppression.

Particularly instructive has been the virulent and often vicious undermining by university administrators of the efforts of feminists to reserve some Women's Studies classes for women only. Such classes can provide the occasion for true encounters with Metamemory, for perceiving and reasoning beyond the schemata of "adult," i.e., male-authored, memories. They can provide contexts for re-membering beyond civilization, for metapatterning. Therefore they must be undermined. The radical potential of freely thinking women is a threat to the very meaning of a patriarchal university. Indeed, such institutions are dedicated to the maintenance of the "adult schemata" whose purpose is the destruction of Metamemory.* They are dedicated to the proposition that "the programme of becoming happy . . . cannot be fulfilled."

It should come as no great shock to Crone-ologists to find that these institutions of "higher learning," which make every effort to impede the development of Women's Studies, also undermine Black Studies and "honor" themselves by giving honorary degrees to fanatic proponents of the nuclear arms race. All of these practices are manifestations of the same program—the denial of

---

* The absurdity of the average history course is one illustration of this. There could hardly be a more dreary example of the emptiness of "adult" memory's categories than History of Man 101. Here the milestones/millstones of male memory, which block out virtually all of the landscape, are weapons of assault and battery that grind down the student's potential for making any sense of the past or the present or the future.

the possibility of Happiness. Yet in this sordid setting there is still a struggle for the life of the mind. These institutions possess important re-sources for the stimulation of such life. Therefore, they remain an essential arena—a battleground, in fact—of the struggle for intellectual/e-motional autonomy that is feminist separation from the State of Separation.

It is important now to consider further the meaning of the context-weaving that can release the flow of Presence within and among women.

BE-FRIENDING: WEAVING CONTEXTS, CREATING ATMOSPHERES

Spinsters, who have experienced something of the process/activity of Happiness, Lust to share such Realization of participation in Be-ing. The actualization of this desire requires *Be-Friending*. *Be-Friending* is the creation of a context/atmosphere in which acts/leaps of Metamorphosis can take place. Websters Weaving this context are inspired to do so by our knowledge of female potential. That is, it is not the supposition that women are "weak" that inspires the Weaving. Rather, it is certain knowledge of the potency of women—a potency that needs to be actualized—that emboldens us to continue the work.

While the knowledge of female potency is certain, it is far from certain that this will be Actualized/Realized by many women under the prevailing conditions of the State of Separation. Therefore, quantum leaps of Fate-identified faith, hope, and Lust are in order. These leaps are part of the process itself of Weaving. They are acts of Metamorphosis, for they strengthen and actualize spiritual capacities. As Lusty Leapers, women carry the threads of connectedness ever further, beyond already Realized limits. That is, we are actualizing psychic and physical ultimacy. This Leaping/Weaving is a continuing act of sharing Lust for Happiness.

In choosing/inventing the word *Be-Friending* to Name such Webster-identified activity, I do not mean to suggest that every woman, or even every feminist, can "be a friend to" or "be friends with" every other woman. It is clear, first of all, that there are limitations of time and energy. Second, there are serious differences of temperament and circumstances which make it impossible for some women to be friends with each other, no matter how well intentioned each may be. There are also, as Jan Raymond has pointed out, women who hate their Selves and other women, and there are histories of "unfulfilled expectations, betrayal, lack of real caring, and the wall of entrenched differences between friends that become insurmountable." [13] Moreover, a genuine friendship between any two women develops over a long period of time, and it requires basic creative harmony between the friends and a firmness of commitment to each other.

Although friendship is not possible among all feminists, the work of Be-Friending can be shared by all, and all can benefit from this Metamorphospheric activity. Be-Friending involves Weaving a context in which women can Realize our Self-transforming, metapatterning participation in Be-ing. Therefore it implies the creation of an atmosphere in which women are enabled to be friends. Every woman who contributes to the creation of this atmosphere functions as a catalyst for the evolution of other women and for the forming and unfolding of genuine friendships.

An example of Be-Friending will illustrate this process. In the late 1940s the publication of Simone de Beauvoir's great feminist work, *The Second Sex,* made possible dialogue among women about their own lives. For many years this work functioned as an almost solitary beacon for women seeking to understand the *connections* among the oppressive evils they experienced, for they came to understand the fact of otherness within patriarchal society. There were other feminist works in existence, of course, but these were not really accessible, even to "educated" women. *The Second Sex* helped to generate an atmosphere in which women could utter their own thoughts, at least to themselves. Some women began to make applications and to seek out less accessible sources, many of which had gone out of print. Most important was the fact that de Beauvoir, by breaking the silence, partially broke the Terrible Taboo. Women were Touched, psychically and e-motionally. Many such women, thus re-awakened, began to have conversations, take actions, write articles— even during the dreary fifties.

It could not accurately be said that de Beauvoir was a personal friend to the thousands of women awakened by her work. It can be said that she has been part of the movement of Be-Friending and that she has been a catalyst for the friendships of many women. The atmosphere to which her work contributed could not remain stagnant. The "air" was invigorating—a stimulant encouraging women to make those quantum leaps that bring us into Metamorphospheres.

Similarly today, any woman who makes leaps of metapatterning, whether these be in a personal relationship, in political activity, in a work of theory or of art, in spiritual understanding, or in all of the above, is a weaver of the network of Be-Friending. So also have been the Fore-Spinsters who have preceded us, Spinning and Weaving the context that makes our friendships possible.

BE-FRIENDING, BE-LONGING, AND RAGE

Be-Friending is radically connected with Be-Longing. The latter is that which metapatriarchal women wish for each other and en-courage in each other, for only the longing/Lusting for be-ing can bring about Happiness. Be-Friending arouses and awakens in a woman her Be-Longing, her telic focus. Be-Friending is both the flowering of Be-Longing and an important condition for the arousal and sustaining of this ontological Passion.

Be-Friending provides the context in which the low-grade multiple-personality disorder which I have suggested is the "contrary" of Rage can be confronted and overcome. The manner in which the context of Be-Friending functions to overcome this affliction of dissociation is analogous to the action of a magnet. That is, it attracts the telic focusing powers of be-ing in a woman. For, as we have seen, everything that IS is connected with everything else that IS. Only be-ing can call forth be-ing. Only confirmation of one's own Reality awakens that Reality in another.

As she is drawn into the Spiraling movement of Be-Friending, a woman becomes a friend to the be-ing in her Self, which is to say, her centering Self. The intensity of her desire focuses her energy, which becomes unsplintered, unblocked. This focusing, gathering of her dissociated energy, makes possible the release of Rage. The Metamorphosing Sage rides her Rage. It is her broom, her Fire-breathing, winged mare. It is her spiraling staircase, leading her where she can find her own Kind, unbind her mind.

Rage is not "a stage." It is not something to be gotten over. It is transformative, focusing Force. Like a horse who streaks across fields on a moonlit night, her mane flying, Rage gallops on pounding hooves of unleashed Passion. The sounds of its pounding awaken transcendent E-motion. As the ocean roars its rhythms into every creature, giving birth to sensations of our common Sources/Courses, Rage too, makes senses come alive agáin, thrive again.

Women require the context of Be-Friending both to sustain the positive force of moral Outrage and to continue the Fury-fueled task of inventing new ways of living. Without the encouragement of Be-Friending, anger can deteriorate into rancor and can mis-fire, injuring the wrong targets. One function of the work of Be-Friending, then, is to keep the sense of Outrage focused in a biophilic way.

THE CONTEXT OF OUTRAGE

The knowledge woven through acts of Be-Friending is characterized by the woman-identified recognition of connectedness that inspires and sustains the Weavers. Websters do not flinch from seeing the complicity of women as token torturers. At the same time, we struggle always to see who in fact holds the institutional power that man-ipulates and damages the consciousness/conscience of women who oppress other women. Examples of such complicity are legion. Crones know the horrifying history of mothers used as token torturers of their daughters. Crones born and brought up in America can hardly be unaware of the compounded complicity involved when phallocratic racial oppression further desensitizes and dissociates the woman who has "power" from her more oppressed sister.

The history of Black slavery in the United States illustrates this situation most tragically. A testimony of Sarah M. Grimké, abolitionist from South Carolina, published in 1839, concerns the torture of a young woman "whose independent spirit could not brook the degradation of slavery" and who repeatedly ran away. The young woman's back was lacerated to such an extent that "a finger could not be laid between the cuts." In addition:

A heavy iron collar, with three prongs projecting from it, was placed round her neck, and a strong and sound front tooth was extracted, to serve as a mark to describe her, in case of escape.[14]

Sarah Grimké, who personally saw this young woman, stated:

Her sufferings at this time were agonizing; she could lie in no position but on her back, which was sore from scourgings, as I can testify from personal inspection, and her only place of rest was the floor, on a blanket. These outrages were committed in a family where the mistress daily read the scriptures, and assembled her children for family worship. She was accounted, and was really, so far as alms-giving was concerned, a charitable woman, and tender-hearted to the poor; and yet this suffering slave, who was the seamstress of the family, was continually in her presence . . . with her lacerated and bleeding back, her mutilated mouth, and heavy iron collar without, so far as appeared, exciting any feelings of compassion.[15]

The passive complicity of the pious bible-reading mistress illustrates one way in which hatred could work itself out. Sometimes the cooperation has been more active. In 1853 Solomon Northup described the breaking of a high-spirited young woman whose back "bore the scars of a thousand stripes . . . because it had fallen her lot to be the slave of a licentious master and a jealous mistress." Northup testified concerning the agony of this woman:

Nothing delighted the mistress so much as to see her suffer. . . . Patsey walked under a cloud. If she uttered a word in opposition to her master's will, the lash was resorted to at once, to bring her to subjection; if she was not watchful while about her cabin, or when walking in the yard, a billet of wood, or a broken bottle perhaps, hurled from her mistress' hand, would smite her unexpectedly in the face. . . .

Finally, for a trifling offense, Patsey was given a savage whipping, while her mistress and the master's children watched with obvious satisfaction. She almost died.

From that time forward she was not what she had been.[16]

Black women, aware of this history and faced with the day-to-day experience of racial oppression, are faced with the dilemmas implied in bonding with white women. Together with other women of color, many are creating their own radical feminist analysis.[17] White women, especially in the United States, often feel discouraged by the knowledge of white patriarchal female indifference, racial hatred, and cruelty. In the face of such unspeakable cruelty, vividly illustrated in the accounts of the mistresses' behavior and repeated thousands of times over in the country of Reagan and Company, what can be said about Female-identified Outrage?

Considering the behavior of the slaveholders' wives described above may re-mind Hags of certain basic threads in the context of our Outrage. The bible-reading mistress of the tortured young seamstress was "supported" in her dissociation from the victimized Black woman by patriarchal religion, the patriarchal institutions of slavery and racism, and the patriarchal institution of marriage. The vicious mistress of the other young woman, whose jealousy was aroused by the fact that her lecherous lout of a husband raped his defenseless slave, was the product of these same soul-molding sado-institutions. None of these institutions were invented by women or have ever been under the control of women.

It would be not only absurd but ethically wrong to excuse the slaveholders' wives, or to excuse contemporary female racist oppressors, or to condone a Phyllis Schlafly for her gynocidal, genocidal, biocidal politics. As conscious carriers of phallocratic diseases and executors of phallocratic crimes, such women are indeed responsible. Furies, moreover, will recognize that the obvious corruption and cooptation of women under patriarchy can function to weaken Female-identified Outrage in women who are sincerely struggling to live a metapatriarchal morality. That is, token torturers function as instruments of the sadostate not only as the appointed executors of oppressive acts, but also as dis-couraging and confusing role models, driving other women into paralyzing guilt and misdirected anger. Patriarchal women, then, function as Rage-blockers/twisters.

It is predictable and already observable that as the biocidal nuclear arms race continues, as the destruction of Third World people by the United States and other powerful nations escalates, as racism and poverty "at home" worsens, many women's energy and motivation for Weaving tapestries of Female Be-Friending is undermined. This is partly traceable to disgust and horror at the increasing visibility and apparent moral bankruptcy of right-wing women and other female servants of the sadostate. It is also traceable to false guilt for putting the cause of feminism first.

Crones, then, can recognize the time-honored trick of the patriarchs efficiently operating in the eighties. This is the creation of a perpetual State of Emergency, in which some male-ordered activity is always made to appear prior in importance to the liberation of women. In the face of this onslaught, Metamorphic leaps of be-ing will be possible only if there is an intensification of intent and determination on the part of women who recognize phallocracy as the root of rapism, racism, gynocide, genocide, and ultimate biocide.

Only clearly focused Female Outrage can sustain the work of metapatterning. Only continuous Weaving of tapestries of female-identified knowledge—that is, our work of Be-Friending—can further the development of metapatriarchal consciousness and behavior. These Crone-centered tapestries can serve as magic carpets for women who choose to fly beyond the sadostate's Eternal Lie. These vehicles can also serve as maps of passages to Metamemory.

BE-FRIENDING AND FEMALE FRIENDSHIP: I

There have been countless great and deep friendships among women. Without metapatriarchal consciousness, however, these are less than they might have been. A Metamorphic context is necessary for friendship to thrive. Since friendship implies a sharing of activity—in a special sense, intellectual activity—the necessary context will be one that awakens and encourages women to exercise their powers to full capacity. It will inspire women to share Happiness, to make Metamorphic leaps and to encounter Metamemory. Such a context I have called Be-Friending.

Lacking such a context, women do sometimes reach immeasurable depths in their friendships, but there is almost always an atmosphere of tragedy about these relationships—a vague sense of something missing, or something lost. Perhaps the most poignant words ever written concerning this subject are the closing lines of Toni Morrison's *Sula,* when Nel re-members her unfathomable connection with Sula, who had died twenty-five years before:

"All that time, all that time, I thought I was missing Jude." And the loss pressed down on her chest and came up into her throat. "We was girls together," she said as though explaining something. "O Lord, Sula," she cried, "girl, girl, girlgirlgirl." It was a fine cry—loud and long—but it had no bottom and it had no top, just circles and circles of sorrow.[18]

Musing women might well conclude that the words "We was girls together" *do* explain something, perhaps everything. It would seem that Nel's visit to the cemetery after the death of

Eva (Sula's grandmother, who survived Sula by a quarter of a century) occasioned a volcanic eruption of Metamemory. For decades, Metamemory had been smoldering beneath the schemata, or categories, of "adult" memory. The "milestone" that had blocked Nel's deep Memory was having been deserted by her man, Jude, whom Sula had "taken."

This "milestone" of adult/male-identified memory is omnipresent among patriarchally possessed women. Even before it occurs, the "dreadful" event has already happened in the realm of anticipation. It therefore perpetually functions as a closure of deep Memory of female friendship, an alienating foreground "memory" of the future. Just before her death, Sula had intuited the way this Memory-block would continue to function in Nel.

When Nel closed the door, Sula reached for more medicine. . . . "So she will walk on down that road, her back so straight in that old green coat, the strap of her handbag pushed all the way to the elbow, thinking how much I have cost her and never remember the days when we were two throats and one eye and we had no price." [19]

The one word that was wrong in Sula's prophecy was "never." Although it required a quarter of a century, the volcanic eruption of Metamemory did take place. The landscape through which Nel's road had led became gynaesthetically perceptible. She Realized the truly significant events of the past, as distinct from those conventionally supposed to be significant.

The girlhood friendship of Nel and Sula was transcendent. They both were dreamers and both understood the odds against them:

Because each had discovered years before that they were neither white nor male, and that all freedom and triumph was forbidden to them, they had set about creating something else to be. [20]

The fact that so many women have responded deeply to this story suggests that such girlhood experiences are not isolated phenomena. *Sula* touches chords of remembrance of things past in women who seemingly are totally unlike Nel and Sula—unlike because of their racial and economic backgrounds, because of "training" and individual temperament. Yet there is a common Memory of setting about "creating something else to be."

When such chords are struck in women's psyches, the stirrings of Metamemory are felt. There are movements of re-membering beyond civilization. The tapestry of Be-Friending which such books as *Sula* help to Weave stirs the air, the atmosphere which women breathe. Breathing deeply, Muses recall those girlhood moments of be-ing in such a way that these become movements of be-ing. Each woman's ecstatic Metamemory is absolutely unique. Yet the threads of commonality are Luminously visible, harmoniously audible.

This ecstatic experience of Metamemory-bearing women suggests that it is primarily in the Realm of Metamorphospheres that Crones' genuine connections and true diversity can be discovered. When women bond solely on the basis of oppression, more and more forms of man-made "commonality" and "diversity" assume importance, masking the potential for deep woman-bonding. When women bond primarily on the grounds of male-identified "commonality" and "diversity," the hope of Metamorphosis becomes an elusive dream. The tragic spectacle of Arab and Jewish women misfiring rage at each other illustrates this patriarchally created scenario. One could think also of the women of Northern and Southern Ireland. One could think of one's local women's community, where divisions often have nothing to do with the common cause of feminism.

One need only think—if one can bear to do so—of one's local hospital. Although there are many skilled and sensitive nurses, it is not unknown for a nurse to identify more with "doctor's orders," even when she has certain knowledge that his orders are destroying the patient, than with the patient. If the patient is a woman, a nurse's dissociation from her Self and consequently from the woman patient can be astonishing and devastating. If the patient is a woman of color or is poor, the chances are that her mistreatment will be worse.

Women can easily fall (or be pushed) into forgetting that racial and ethnic oppression, like the sexual oppression which is the primary and universal model of such victimization, is a male invention. Seeking to uncover the causes of such amnesia and confusion, Furies find that the constructs of patriarchal civilization require the assimilation of women, and consequently our ghettoization from each other, from our Selves.

It is undeniable that women all over this planet have different exigencies and commitments that are overwhelming. Despite and because of this fact, Muses continue to Weave contexts of Be-Friending, which point beyond assimilation/ghettoization. Be-Friending beyond civilization, Sirens lure women to the places where female friendship comes alive, thrives.

Other works by women that are far less explicit than *Sula* on the subject of female friendship sometimes have such a haunting effect upon large numbers of women that Shrews strongly suspect they contain messages to be decoded. One such work is Emily Brontë's *Wuthering Heights*. Many Nag-Gnostics have noted, at least to our Selves, that Heathcliff is not really similar to any of the males we have known. Obvious Nagging questions arise. We know that Emily was penned into using a male "pen name," that is, "Ellis Bell." Isn't it perfectly logical to think that perhaps she was also penned into transsexing the great love of Catherine's life?

Barbara Deming suggested some years ago that Heathcliff is the other side of Catherine's Self. She cites "his" cry of agony after Catherine's death: "Oh, God! it is unutterable! I *cannot* live without my life! I *cannot* live without my soul!" [21] For her part, Catherine had said to Nelly: "Nelly, I *am* Heathcliff!" [22] It is clear enough to Viragos from these words and from the E-motional context of *Wuthering Heights* that Heathcliff is the disguise of the Female Friend of Emily Brontë's dreams. "He" feels an identity with Catherine that only an other female Self could feel.

The character of Laurie in Louisa May Alcott's *Little Women* also can be suspected by Shrewds of being the impossible woman of Jo's dreams, her Self and alter ego. "He" has the freedom and possibility of exercising his range of capacities—a freedom denied to Louisa/Jo in rigid nineteenth century New England. It follows Crone-logically from this supposition that Alcott's creative imagination could not allow Jo to marry Laurie.

One Nagging question that recurrently haunts Hags is simply: How do such coded works by women work upon our imaginations? It is clear immediately that these do not function like man-made mythic figures who are transsexed female symbols, such as Jesus. Whereas Jesus is the product of male myth-makers, manufactured to serve patriarchal ends, an entirely different purpose inspires the creative imaginations of women struggling to break mind-bindings. Such women's work must be decoded because Naming has been part of the Terrible Taboo and because the bonding of women has been broken. Thus, Emily Brontë was attempting to Name that which is Unnameable when the sanctions of the sexual caste system are as overtly operative as they were in her milieu. Whereas the male propagandists of patriarchy are trying to disguise, convert, and possess female powers, attributing these to males, female creators under patriarchy are struggling to express female transcendence, even if this must appear to be incarnated in male flesh.

Female readers of such woman-authored works very often intuitively understand the dilemma of the authors, for they have shared this dilemma and often have tragically lived it out, translating Lust for female friendship into the "need" for men. Such understanding may be subliminal in the author as well as in the reader. Yet the messages are there and the partially hidden workings/struggles of women's imaginations toward Metamorphosis have—to borrow the expression of Nelle Morton—"a fantastic coherence." [23] Given the reality of subliminal knowledge, such works, I suggest, have contributed to the context of Be-Friending. Yet they are hardly enough, and, if not decoded, they amount to little more than starvation-rations.

Just as there are vast differences between explicit, Metamemory-inspiring women's fiction about female friendships and coded, implicit fiction on this subject, so also there are essential distinctions between theoretical works written from a feminist perspective and woman-authored theoretical works that attempt to be "universal" or "humanist," ignoring the State of Gynocide. In the case of the latter, there has to be some degree of dissociation on the part of the authors from the real conditions of their lives, internal as well as external. For there is no "humanist" perspective possible within patriarchy, any more than there is a truly "generic" term. Words such as *man, men, people, professor,* etc. are pseudo-generics, as Julia Penelope has shown. [24] Women who are bamboozled by pseudo-generics and by "humanist" ideologies —all of which are male inventions—may contribute to the context of Be-Friending, but such contributions leave something to be Desired. [25]

Nag-Gnostics must pursue the analysis, seriously asking whether theoretical works by "humanist" women—works written from a pseudo-generic perspective—sometimes can have the power to evoke the volcanic eruptions of Metamemory that are necessary for female friendships to thrive. The experience of readers/students of such works testifies to the fact that in some cases these do stir Metamemory, but usually only if the reader brings to them an already awakened metapatriarchal consciousness. Since female "humanist" authors are in some ways more mystified than their male mentors and colleagues (despite noisy or sophisticated protests, men know that *man,* et cetera, refers to men), the chances that they can be *prime* movers of Metamemory are diminished.

There is a chronic condition common among freudian women authors, jungian women authors, christian women authors, marxian women authors, new age-ean women authors, et al. That condition, often unmentioned, is mentorship by men. The mental blocks of pseudo-generic women are mentor blocks. Moreover, the mendacity of men-mentors is unmendable, unendable, under the reign of men. It can be mended only when this reign is ended, for women under men's mentorship are minds divided, derided. Having negotiated the way through courses of, by, and for men, pseudo-generic women are dissociated.

The Weaving of Be-Friending requires ending men's tending/blending of women's minds. Insofar as Happiness is a life of contemplation, and insofar as friendship is the sharing of Happiness, female-identified Metamorphosing friendship implies the overthrow of male schooling/ruling of women's intellects. This is not to say that Nags will not learn their ABCs. Some will even earn their highest of higher degrees. As Muses, women use these, but refuse to be master-minded. Scolds study Unlearning, burning our bindings/re-mindings with Scalding Tongues of Fire.

The following little description will convey some of the flavor of the activities of metapatriarchal women working on the boundary of academia, and beyond:

Prudes undo the nasty knots/nots (knot allowed, knot too proud, knot too far, knot a star) of the not-women. Weirds spell Disaster for the plaster-casters of Crones' Crooning, Dreaming. Screaming, Dragons bite the pipes of Bearded Brother No-it-alls. Undines extinguish Distinguished Professors. Gorgons eat gurus for brunch. The crunch is not heard, since the Sirens sing loudly.

Meanwhile: "Ready, set . . . Go!" shout the Maenads, as Furies light fuses. Salamanders leap through the flames. "Enough of their games!" shriek the Vixens. The entire edifice goes up in smoke.

"A tasteless joke!" crows the cock to the jock, adjusting his mortar-bored. "Thank the lord, we're all still here."

"And there they still are," laughs a Crone from her Star. "With the help of Grace we've made it to the boundary of their fabrica-tion-foundry . . . and beyond." Grace and her Sisters smile and bow. The crowd cheers long and loud. Then a young Soothsayer states simply that this event has been a Metaphoric Leap in her life of learning, a true Commencement of her Journey beyond academia/anemia. She too receives a strong ovation for her ovarian oration.

BE-FRIENDING AND FEMALE FRIENDSHIP: II

The context of Be-Friending is not woven entirely of books, of course. The products of women's creative activism—such as shelters for battered women, rape crisis centers, anti-pornography demonstrations, women's concerts, anti-nuclear protests, the women's health movement, female-identified rituals—are fundamental constituents of the context of Be-Friending.

Most essential is the fact that Be-Friending is woven of the fibers of women's lives. A Wild woman's participation in Be-Friending is conveyed not only by words, but also in myriad other ways. Gestures, witty comments, facial expressions, glances, a certain light in the eye, caresses, styles of clothing, ways of walking, choices of occupation, of environment—these are a few of the signals of a woman's participation in Be-Friending, or of her nonparticipation in this Spinning/Weaving process.

These signals are transmitted and received in a complex way. They comprise the field of gynergy emitted from and surrounding a woman which we may call her aura. Muses are learning better to trust our gynaesthetic perceptions concerning the focus of another woman's energy. To develop confidence in this matter is not to become judgmental in a moralistic sense, but to increase one's ability to assess with whom to connect—that is, communi-cate one's gynergy, and under what circumstances. As Jan Raymond succinctly stated:

There are women who have been/are *for women*. Women must learn to identify such women. Women must also learn to identify their friends.[26]

There are two distinct points here. First, there is the necessity to be able to identify women who are *for women*. Such women I would Name Be-Friending women. Second, there is the necessity to be able to identify among such women those with whom the development of Elemental friendship is possible. A Shrewd Prude finds/chooses friends with whom Elemental relationships can be developed. The Elemental spiritual/physical context/atmosphere in which such friendships can flourish is woven/spun by the vast network of Be-Friending women, many of whom have not even met each other. Yet all are extremely important for the lives and friendships of all the others. This partially invisible network has commonly been called *Sisterhood*. In the estimation of Crones that word has withstood grievous assaults, abuses, and disappointments over a considerable period of Crone-time and is still in good standing.

Within this context, women can hope to Realize our potential for finding and developing deep, Self-transforming friendships. Such friendships imply communication of Happiness. For Hags, this means sharing, on many levels, activities of our Metamorphic be-ing, risking together our metapatterning living, our creativity. It means diving together into the wonder-full depths of Metamemory. It means voyaging together beyond civilization, always/all ways further and deeper into Metamorphospheres. This Realizing of the Lust to share Happiness, to respond with Others to the Wild calls of Be-Longing, implies waking Weird Powers of Be-Witching. Weird women/Witches leap into this subject, in the following chapter.

CHAPTER TWELVE

BE-WITCHING:
THE LUST FOR METAMORPHOSIS

Grace: "a free gift of God to man for his regeneration or sanctification."

Webster's Third New International Dictionary of the English Language

Grace: "a free shift away from the vicious circle of god and man's 'regeneration or sanctification'; a Spiraling, Metamorphic leap of Be-Witching."

Websters' First New Intergalactic Wickedary of the English Language

Happy Hags and Harpies, divested of hope for "heavenly happiness," focus attention beyond the "afterlife" to Life. The ecstasy of this Divine Despair bursts conventional bonds with explosions of pent-up powers. Nags gallop through galaxies while Sirens sing to the stars. Stiffs leap Gracefully among the Heavenly bodies, as Websters wend our way Weirdward, transversing the skies. Crones drive chariots drawn by Dragons. Hitching wagons to the tails of comets, Wantons wander as celestial tourists. Brewsters practice broomstick-riding. Deciding that transportation is no problem, Furies flap our wings. Weirds sing, as Scolds proclaim the After-Death of Daddydom. "Our Time has come," shriek Shrews and Vixens. It is the moment of Be-Witching.

Be-Witching is Labrys-like, as the word itself conveys. According to Skeats' *Etymological Dictionary*, *witch* (derived from the Anglo-Saxon *wicce*) is linked with the Norwegian *vikja*, meaning to turn aside, to conjure away. "This links it with the Icelandic *vikja:* to move, turn, push aside. . . . Thus *witch* perhaps = 'averter.' "[1] This is one side of the Labrys. On the other side is the fact that, according to *Webster's, bewitch* (together with *allure, captivate, fascinate, charm, enchant*) is a synonym for *attract*. In recent times, of course, these words have been perverted and reduced to describe feminine seductiveness. These reversals mask Elemental powers of attraction.

Be-Witching, then, implies the exercise of Labrys-like spiritual powers. The Labryses of Witches/Weirds can function as shields, averting/warding off attacks of demons. They also act as magnets, attracting Elemental spiritual forces, our Demons/Muses. The magnetizing side is power of presentiating Presence. One consequence of this power of Presence to our Selves is power of absence to the fragmenters, who then can no longer afflict Furies with the deadening effects of their absence of be-ing. As shield, then, the Labrys of Be-Witching women averts such lethal presence of absence, achieving the Absence of Life-blocking absence.

As Lusty women whirl our Labryses, we hurl our Selves with them. We move in eddies and spirals, entering the whirling world. Be-Witching, then, involves Spiraling change. Describing this kind of movement, Emily Culpepper has written:

It is often difficult to overcome the oppressive momentum of the endlessly repetitive ruts formed by old, deeply engrained habits. . . . With the model of the spiral in mind, we can value even one small step toward change as being that slight shift of degree which can transform the confining path of the circle, channeling its momentum into a spiraling path that can really move us onward.[2]

Be-Witching is the actual leaping/hopping/flying that is Metamorphosis, and that is encouraged by the context of Be-Friending. It is the series of movements that constitute that shift of degree which can transform the confining path of the circle. Be-Witching, then, is the succession of transformative moments/movements of be-ing that are Metamorphic, macromutational. It is the creation of Fairy Space.

Often such a moment/movement is experienced and perceived as only "one small step toward change." Like light from the farthest stars, it participates in macroworlds of motion that are not noticeable to those whose vision is confined to foreground perceptions. The apparent "one small step" that leaps and whirls through galaxies of inner/outer space appears as the slightest deviation from the fixed and normal necrophilic rut of tidydom.

Yet this micro/macrodeviation can make all the difference. Patriarchal males know this and therefore attempt to prevent the slightest deviation.

Since such moments/movements of macromutation are heightened hops/hopes of Be-Witching, they should be seen as ontological in their texture and scope. These are moments of escape from the vampires/vacuums of nonbe-ing that suck away the force of Life/Lust. They are movements of averting the attacks of nonbe-ing. The momentum achieved through such Amazonian acts of aversion is at the same time the E-motional force that releases Archimagical magnetizing energy. The moments of averting, of wielding our Be-Witching Labryses as shields against nonbe-ing are magical magnetizing moments/movements in Realms of Be-ing. That is, the gatherings of gynergy that are mustered for quantum leaps out of sadosociety's control have Elemental force of attraction into the whirling vortices of living/be-ing.

Women who achieve the "slight shift of degree," transforming dead circles of separation and return, averting the vampires' vacuums, by this same movement attract others away from nonbe-ing into the Centering Journey that is participation in Be-ing. Be-Witching women thus enchant others, chanting, calling, luring into Lust for transformation/transportation into Metabeing. Like Sirens singing the call of the Strange, Be-Witching women rearrange the shapes of our lives. We are Shape-shifters, in ontological dimensions.

Shape-shifting implies Metamorphosis beyond static forms that hold down participation in Be-ing, which is Happiness. It is cosmic in its implications. As Sonia Johnson has suggested, the holographic metaphor implies that if one woman changes her way of be-ing this can affect all women.[3] The inherent logic of this metaphor would seem to imply that such change can and does affect the whole universe. Even to consider such an "absurd" reasoning implies a shift in the shape of thinking/imaging, a step/hop off the Foreground.

The Shape-shifting of Be-Witching implies acts of psychic/physical ultimacy. These risking acts/leaps require the development of Natural Grace—an athleticism of spirit/body, an unfolding and strengthening of innate capabilities. Shape-shifting also involves eating of the Tree of *Other* Knowledge. It implies confronting the Serpent of Wild Wisdom. This brings us to the subject of snakes.

SNAKES AND WILD WISDOM: I

"Everyone" knows the story of the serpent tempting Eve in the Garden of Eden to eat of the Tree of Knowledge. Mary's relation to the snake is different, of course. Being the model christian, she crushes it with her foot. Marina Warner writes:

> In Christianity, the serpent has lost its primary character as a source of wisdom and eternity. It is above all the principal Christian symbol of evil, and when it sprawls under the Virgin's foot, it is not her direct attribute, representing her knowledge and power as it does in the snake-brandishing statue of the goddess of Minoan Crete, but illustrates her victory over evil.[4]

Wicked women recognize the identity of the "evil" over whom Mary, in her assigned role as token torturer, enjoys "victory." The snake is symbolic of Wild Wisdom, and its primal associations are not phallic but rather are biophilic and Elemental.

Crones are aware that the symbolic association of the snake and the moon is ancient and widespread. Since each time a snake sloughs off her skin she appears to be reborn, snakes have often been compared to the moon, which appears to be reborn each month. Moreover, this lunar rhythm of renewal symbolically connects the snake with menstruation. The fact that the "Immaculately Conceived Virgin" is portrayed as crushing the snake is therefore horrifyingly significant.

Warner astutely states that although on the immediate level the serpent in this scenario "has lost its connotations of knowledge and power and simply becomes a loathsome emblem of wickedness . . . at another level it has retained its ancient meaning, for it represents a kind of heterodox knowledge and sexuality that Christianity has spurned."[5] Gorgons/Viragos understand very well the Mantic Meanings of this "heterodox knowledge and sexuality." Nags, Shrews, Soothsayers, Sibyls, and Scolds proclaim these Meanings as Good Tidings to the universe. Communication of such information can have astonishing results. The following account is just one example of what might happen when women begin to crack the Crone-crushers' code, seeking our own Wild Wisdom, following the call of Wonderlust:

Upon hearing the Elemental Message, the Snake awakes, uncoils her Self, shakes off the foolish "virgin's" crushing foot. As the token oppressor topples over, cracking her fembot-shell, the Original Witch springs free. Hissing and kissing, the Snake and the Archimage call to their Sisters. Gleefully gliding from places of hiding we join the Ecstatic Reunion. Our Gathering's whirling Spins spirals of Serpentine Grace. Tearing the lace of her discarded veil, the Great Crone tosses the remnants starward, creating a heavenly trail. We Snake Dancers playfully follow this. Some hiss with delight as the Hag lifts two snakelets—one in each hand—and waves them on high as she skips through the sky. "The Minoan Goddess has returned!" sing the Muses.

Unwinding from the exertion of this work/play, the Wise Virgins/Viragos decide to Name our serpentine starry path, which can still be seen in the evening sky, the "Merry Way."

SNAKES AND WILD WISDOM: II

The bland, banal boringness of patriarchal symbolism is illustrated in the usual discussions of serpents as symbols. They are said to symbolize the phallus, eternity, et cetera, but there is rarely any Dragon-identified *life* in these descriptions. They are abstract in a deadening way, and Nag-Gnostics can find little in these "explanations" that can connect us with the meaning of the Minoan Snake-Goddess or—more importantly—with our Selves.

The deadness of patriarchal serpent symbolism is an illuminating illustration of the fathers' flattening/taming of Wild Wisdom. Moreover, the crushing of the snake by the "blessed virgin" exemplifies and "encourages" the crushing of Wild Wisdom by women. Indeed, many Nags would note that only women *could* be the adequate instruments for such crushing of Elemental Female Wisdom.

As an exercise in re-gaining Wild knowledge, it is useful to consider snakes as real Elemental creatures, seeing them in a fresh way as Metaphors of Metamorphosis. Starhawk describes and illustrates this needed freshness of perception in writing of snakes—specifically, of "a real snake, perhaps the one who lives with me." She continues:

I watch her slow movements, feel the strength in her long body, see her skin grow dull, her eyes cloud over until she looks lifeless—and

I wake one morning to find her old skin crumpled like a discarded nylon stocking. . . . And I could say that to me, the snake as a symbol now means, not the Fall, but renewal, resurrection. Yet that also would be false, because in the language of magic the symbol has no intellectually assigned meaning; it is a pointer that says, "Look. Pay attention to this *thing*." [6]

Starhawk then points out that the meaning of the snake tells many stories. For example, her once-a-month meal and her periodic shedding show "that time flows differently for her than for us, that time is not a thing but a relationship." [7] Yet her meaning is not exhausted even by a thousand stories or insights. Starhawk's point is that "the magic that works" requires that "we let the *things* themselves, in all the richness and complexity of their existence, speak to us." [8]

Breaking out of the thought-forms that are shaped by patriarchal culture into contexts woven by Be-Friending women, Crones encourage each other to shift the shapes of our consciousness, to connect with Elemental creatures, such as the Snake, in Original ways. Each leap of direct insight implies tearing away layers of distorting man-made lenses that have "corrected" our vision. Each leap involves averting the attacks of the trackers who would keep us in line, and it involves attracting/drawing our own latent capacities into fuller Realization. These quantum leaps of perception are acts of Be-Witching. The language that can both express and encourage such leaps of perception is in large measure a language of metaphysical metaphors. These are Metaphors of Metamorphosis. They are causes as well as effects of transformative acts that transport Wonderlusting women Weirdward through the Realm of Metamorphospheres.

PERCEPTION AS SHAPE-SHIFTING EXPERIENCE

Ernest Schachtel provides a useful conceptual analysis of the tracks that beat and train our perceptual faculties into dullness. He employs the concept of "secondary autocentricity," which refers to "secondary embeddedness in a closed pattern of life, by which man seeks to re-establish something akin to the security of the womb *after* the object world has emerged for him in the exploratory play and learning of childhood." [9] This closed mode of perception, utilitarian and banal, is characterized by "recognition of something either already familiar or quickly labeled and filed away in some familiar category." [10]

In sharp contrast to this womb-tomb, classified worldview, which is the prevailing perceptual mode of most people in "our" civilization, there is "allocentric [other-centered] perception"— the perceptual experience of be-ing fully alive and fully turned toward the object of perception. Schachtel writes:

> . . . the fully allocentric perception (especially of nature, people, and the great works of art) always breaks through and transcends the confines of the labeled, the familiar, and establishes a relation in which a direct encounter with the object itself . . . takes place. [11]

Moreover:

> In the moments of allocentric perception at its fullest we always are at the frontiers of our familiar world, breaking through the enclosing wall of explicit or implicit labels and encountering the inexhaustible other, which transcends all labels with which man tries to capture and tame it, so that he may use it and so that its unfamiliarity will no longer disquiet him. [12]

No Crone can read such passages without being stirred to reflect upon the enormity of her Hag-identified Shape-shifting project. Whereas the male (or female) patriarchally identified artist may risk "a direct encounter with the object itself," dismissing (to some extent) its trite/familiar* labels, his/her allocentric perceptions can remain safely confined within the permissible sphere of "art." If, however, allocentric perception transcends the "artistic" sphere—a confined and thoroughly labeled territory within the domain of fatherdom—a quantum leap of perceptual experience begins to enter the range of Possibility. Crones recognize Wild women ourSelves as participating in the inexhaustible Other, "which transcends all labels with which man tries to capture and tame it, so that he may use it and so that its unfamiliarity will no longer disquiet him." This places us,

---

* The word *familiar* as used here, of course, means banal, well known. As Be-Witching women know, *familiar* also has a totally Other meaning, that is, it refers to a Super Natural spirited animal who is the friend of a Witch.

indeed, at the frontiers of the patriarchally familiar world, and the Unfamiliarity of the view is awesome.

Schachtel logically pursues his analysis, writing:

The more original the mind and personality of the perceiver is, the greater is the likelihood that what he perceives sometimes will transcend *"reality"* as known in the everyday currency of his culture.[13]

The "reality" transcended by the artist or by any creative person is, of course, the "reality" of public opinion, having nothing to do with the inexhaustible Reality of the world. The very word, *reality,* is therefore a battleground between creative ("allocentric") perception and stale/closed ("secondary autocentric") perception. This would hold true even for artists whose creative perceptions have not transcended the parameters and hidden agendas of patriarchal assumptions.

When the Artist is a metapatterning woman whose perception and commitment concerns Reality beyond these paternal parameters and agendas, the word *reality* is nothing less than an Ontological Battleground. The risks are ultimate. The word *Artist,* here, is not confined to describe one who has acquired specific skills that are legitimated or at least tolerated by the fathers. It Names a woman who is metapatterning—risking/pursuing metapatriarchal perception and expression. Such a woman is seeking knowledge of the "inexhaustible Other," without the familiar footholds of phallic frameworks.

The inexhaustible Other encountered by a Be-Witching woman is, first of all, her Self, Who flows in underground connectedness with all Elemental be-ing. This Self is Virgin—uncaptured and untamed—transcending the labels of man. This is the Self who is capable of direct encounters. A Be-Witching woman's Allocentric perceptions, then, are at the same time Autocentric. The famous "subject-object" split of patriarchal science and philosophy is challenged by the fact/act of her Realizing her Self as Other.

Such Be-Witching acts of Allocentric perception, since they are Self-centering Self-perception, have nothing to do with "selfishness" that is contrary to generosity/magnanimity. They are perceptions of deep rootedness, connectedness. In such moments, the focusing of the perceiver's faculties on another participant in

Be-ing—whether this participant be another woman, a cat, a tree, a snake, a river, or the moon—is unclouded and intense. It is not framed by labels and categories. It is not embedded in the closed world/womb of the patriarchal familiar.

It is consciousness of her own Otherness that enables a woman to know the other Others. Since women are the primal Other within patriarchy, the universal caste system on this planet, women have the primal Possibility of Allocentric knowledge that can embrace our Selves and touch other Others. Wild women, then, are Shape-shifters whose Other-knowledge shields us from the framers and pulls/attracts us into further transformations.

OTHERNESS AND LEAPS OF TRANSFORMATION: I

The starting point of a woman's metapatriarchal Metamorphosis is an ontological intuition of her Otherness in relation to all of the shapes imposed upon her by patriarchy. These include symbol-shapes, idea-shapes, relation-shapes, emotion-shapes, action-shapes. The intuition of Otherness in relation to all of these is holistic, and it is the root of hologynic Metamorphosis.

Faithfulness to this intuition of radical Otherness in relation to all patriarchal patterns/models is a basic prerequisite for trans-formative acts of Be-Witching. This faithfulness, which implies willingness to face unflinchingly the implications of our increasing awareness of planetary gynocide, is fuel required for evolutionary leaping. A woman knows her Otherness not only in relation to the androcratic atrocities, however. She knows it most certainly through Realizing her Elemental powers—through evolutionary leaping itself.

Knowing the fact of Otherness does not imply immediately knowing The Answer to every question. It does provide a basis for evaluating questions. If, for example, a woman is asked: "What kind of society do you propose for the year 2000?" she might answer that for her this cannot assume priority among questions. Rather than being a question that participates in Otherness, it is all too tidy and familiar in its format and its assumptions. It assumes, for example, that the planet earth will be habitable in the year 2000. Yet this assumption is not the core of what is wrong with it.

What *is* wrong with such a question is its implied underestimation of the ineffable scope of a biophilic woman's Otherness in relation to all the prefabricated or imaginable shapes of patriarchal "reality." Since Otherness is underestimated by the questioner, so also is the enormity of the task of Shape-shifting. The *process* of Shape-shifting itself is short-changed in this patriarchal mode of questioning, which overlooks the essential point that the process—the *shifting*—itself contains the clues to further change.

When, for example, a woman first consciously says of her Self, "I am a radical feminist," there is a Shift in the shape of her soul. Sonia Johnson gives an extraordinary illustration of such a Shift in her account of the circumstances leading to her first saying of those words. Johnson's "miles and miles of underground corridors full of filing cabinets" containing unconscious knowledge of the oppression of women burst open in one evening, when a stupid and arrogant mormon church leader presented his anti-ERA position. That evening she fully and consciously heard the Lies (of how the men of the mormon church had always "loved" mormon women and of the "exalted" position of these women). Not long afterward she wrote: "I'm a feminist to the core and will be until I die . . . fiercely, passionately, reverently, and totally committed to justice for my sisters on this earth." [14] The justice of which Sonia Johnson was writing is what I would now call Nemesis, but the word used is not the issue here. The point is that this was a Moment of Shape-shifting/ understanding/be-ing.

It is significant that the first act Sonia Johnson performed after this epiphany was to "let God have it." She killed off the male "God," naturally, for the primal and essential move of Shape-shifting that accompanies a truly conscious Realization that "I am a radical feminist" is a rejection of patriarchal religious myth. This will continue to be a long, almost unfathomably complex process, but it inevitably involves rejection of the malegod.

At this point a radical Nag-Gnostic analysis requires that we Spiral back to the essential *ground* of Metamorphic movement, that is, to the Realization of radical Otherness of Wild women in relation to all patriarchal forms/shapes of consciousness, speech, and behavior. Furies are faced with the fact that it is quite possible that a woman who has not gone through a process analogous to that of Sonia Johnson can say the words "I am a feminist" without understanding the depth meaning of those words. At certain times and places this can be/has been an "in" thing to say. "Feminist," like any name, can be used in such a way that it functions merely as a label. In such cases, it is merely one variant expression of patriarchal consciousness.

It is possible, moreover, that a woman who uses the label "feminist" without awareness and conscious choice of her radical Otherness, can imagine that she has by-passed patriarchal myth. If challenged, she might argue that she was never so "naive" as to have accepted mormonism, or catholicism, or methodism, or orthodox judaism, or hinduism, et cetera. That is, she may refuse to acknowledge the fact of patriarchal embeds in her own psyche. The question thus arises: What criteria are there for knowing whether real psychic transformation/Shape-shifting is occurring? There are many, but a few will serve to illustrate the way these can be known.

First, actual Shape-shifting, or Be-Witching, cannot happen without an awesome sense of Otherness from patriarchal norms and values. Certainly, not all of the implications of the Otherness can be consciously known and acted upon immediately. Such knowing and acting *are* the Metamorphic process that continues throughout a feminist's life. In an intuitive, potential way these implications are known, however, in what might be called a "radical feminist intuition of Otherness."

This intuition is both exhilarating and frightening. For many women, the stimulation that accompanies release from the bindings of embedded labels/lies is so overwhelming, the invigoration so wondrous, that the frightening aspects of this leap seem small in relation to the horrors of spiritual possession that is now acknowledged and exorcised. Yet, accompanying this experience of exhilaration, there *must* be conscious awareness of the facts concerning the sadosociety's sanctions against radical feminism, at least in a general way. Consciousness of these sanctions, then, is a second criterion.

The sense of Otherness, moreover, implies a Lust for bonding with other women, for Be-Friending. A radical feminist is committed to the Race of women, to our becoming and freedom. Therefore she feels Rage at the oppression of her sisters of all races, of all ethnic groups, of all classes, of all nations. She identifies with women *as women*. This woman-identification is the third criterion.

Genuine metapatriarchal Metamorphosis, then, implies commitment to the cause of women that persists, against the current, even when feminism is no longer popular among liberals, and even when many women who had appeared to participate in the Otherworld Journey, as sisters, declare that they have moved "beyond" this "phase" to a more "integrated" or more "balanced" political position, such as socialism, for example, or careerism within the phallic structures. This persistence is a fourth mark of genuine Metamorphosis.

When a statement such as "I am a feminist" (or, less commonly, "I am a radical feminist") is functioning merely within the parameters of patriarchal labeling, the criteria just described are not met. Thus a woman may use such a label to describe herself out of a need to belong to a group or organization where she hopes to gain approval. Rather than experiencing an intuition of Otherness, she remains terrified of autonomy and genuine individuality. In this case, she is oblivious to the atrocity-level of the sanctions against be-ing really *for women*. It follows, then, that her "bonding" with women is on shaky ground, since she has not assessed and faced one of the logical consequences of bonding with women as women, namely, punishment by the patriarchy. Finally, it is evident that the woman thus described will not meet the fourth requirement for feminist transformation, namely, persistence. She may, however, persist in using the label "feminist" to describe herself, as long as the true arduousness of be-ing *for women* is not required of her. The men-and-boys in charge of the Labeling Society will encourage and reward such mistaken self-labeling, since it feeds into the "divide and conquer" strategy required by them for maintaining the State of Oppression/Depression.

Nags, Shrews, and Scolds learn not to expend inordinate amounts of energy berating such women, although we grieve deeply for them. Fired by faith that Metamorphosis itself is contagious and that the intuition of Otherness is communicable, Nags choose to Nag our Selves into further feats of Shape-shifting. We are enabled to do this without false guilt, for we know the magnetic powers of Be-Witching. The Shape-shifting acts of Be-Witching women create vortices of gynergy which can help pull women away from the traps of labeldom into Realization of their/our magnificent Otherness.

To accomplish this magnetic feat, Weirds must also attend to the task of averting and converting the lethal labels thrown in our paths to stop Spiraling movement. Be-Witching women catch these and shift their shapes to suit biophilic purposes, for Metamorphosis is not creation "out of nothing" but rather transformation of whatever materials are at hand. We therefore work with symbol-shapes, idea-shapes, relation-shapes of fatherland, recognizing these as frozen and twisted caricatures of the inexhaustible Other—of the flow in which Elemental women participate.

Crones crack the man-made shells. Maenads chew them into better shape. Brewsters cook them, Dragons melt them, Spinsters Spin their substance into verbs. Since Shape-shifting is a complex task, our methods are various/multifarious. Further analysis of this process is the work of the following section.

OTHERNESS AND TRANSFORMATION: II

A Nag-Gnostic philosopher may wish to pursue the case of a woman who actually has experienced an ontological intuition of radical Otherness in relation to the shapes of patriarchy. Let us suppose that this woman has been able to say of her Self, "I am a radical feminist," and that she has performed the primal act of Shape-shifting—that she has cracked the symbol of the patriarchal god. It is crucial that she not falter at this point, foolishly believing that "the deed is done," once and for all. The moment that such an assumption is made, she will fall again into the trap/rut of familiar categories/labels.

Our Nag-Gnostic philosopher might want to ask this woman (we might call her "Novice Nag") what her next move in the Shape-shifting process might be, after disposing of the malegod.*

If Novice Nag (N.N.) is a perceptive pupil, she will respond by pointing out that so long as a Nag has even one toe still poised on the edge of the Foreground, she has not yet disposed of him entirely.

The philosopher congratulates N.N. for her expression of this perception. To pursue the idea further, she reads to N.N. from Alice Walker's Be-Witching novel *The Color Purple*. She turns to the part where Shug Avery is explaining her experience of

---

* The philosopher, of course, will note that "Novice Nag" could well be her Self, since all Nag-Gnostics consider our Selves novices.

"God" to Celie, who has come to the point of "trying to chase that old white man out of my head." Celie ponders Shug's words:

Still, it is like Shug say, you have to git man off your eyeball, before you can see anything a'tall.

Man corrupt everything, say Shug. He on your box of grits, in your head, and all over the radio. He try to make you think he everywhere. Soon as you think he everywhere, you think he God. But he ain't. Whenever you trying to pray, and man plop himself on the other end of it, tell him to git lost, say Shug. Conjure up flowers, wind, water, a big rock.

But this hard work, let me tell you. He been there so long, he don't want to budge. . . . Everytime I conjure up a rock, I throw it [says Celie].[15]

The philosopher and N.N. agree heartily that through repeated experiences they know that "he don't want to budge." The philosopher suggests that Nags can profit a great deal from listening to Shug Avery's view that "God ain't a he or a she, but a It," and she points out that when Celie persists in asking "But what do it look like?" she receives an important answer from Shug. The philosopher continues to read to Novice Nag:

Don't look like nothing, she [Shug] say. It ain't a picture show. It ain't something you can look at apart from anything else, including yourself. I believe God is everything, say Shug. . . . She say, My first step away from the old white man was trees. Then air. Then birds. Then other people. But one day when I was sitting quiet and feeling like a motherless child, which I was, it come to me: that feeling of being part of everything, not separate at all.[16]

Hearing these words, our Nag-Gnostic philosopher and Novice Nag must feel essentially in accord with Shug and Celie.* The philosopher might want to think of this view as a sort of "Nag-Gnostic pantheism," while at the same time cautioning the Novice, of course, that such an abstract expression should *not* be used as a label, but that it could be a sort of shorthand Meta-

---

* It is essential to point out that Shug Avery and Celie are in no way responsible for the interpretations of their conversations and behavior presented in this section. I have assumed the Nag-Gnostic prerogative of having Nagging thoughts about them and expressing these. Any Nags —especially Shug and Celie—are, of course, free to disagree.

phoric phrase that can carry Wonderlusting analysis in its Meta-morphic flights.

Probably at this point the philosopher will have noticed the troubled expression that has been clouding the face of Novice Nag ever since hearing Shug's pronouncement that "God ain't a he or a she, but a It." N.N. is a radical feminist who is very much involved in the process of dis-covering Goddess-symbols. It seems to her a mistake to reject the pronoun "She" in favor of "It."

The philosopher is sympathetic to this reaction, but she reminds N.N. of the complexity of the Naming process, and of the multiplicity of the points of transition in the Spiraling Journey. "In fact," says the Crone, "there is much to be said in favor of sometimes using the pronoun 'It,' in order to sustain our sense of Otherness."

Novice Nag appears shocked. "But we have just gotten rid of the patriarchal theologians' he-gods and the phallic philosophers' it-gods," she cries. "Why are you saying this?"

"I am suggesting that this semantic twist can illustrate the Spiraling course of Shape-shifting," the Crone calmly retorts. "You see, spirals move backward as well as forward, and this is all part of the same movement."

"Well, yes," replies N.N., "but I wish you would explain further."

"I'll gladly try," sighs the Sage, eyeing the purple sky, "but these matters continue to be puzzling and mysterious. That is why we call ourSelves Nag-Gnostics, you know. We go on Nagging each other and galloping further on the purple pathways."

"You mean the *spiraling* pathways?"

"Exactly."

"Please do continue," says Novice Nag.

The following account summarizes the philosopher's response to this request.

The Shape-Shifting of Words and Context

It seems that our eavesdropping on the conversation of Shug and Celie has brought us back to a crucial moment of Shape-shifting. We should pay particular attention to the fact that their discussion takes place in a context of Be-Friending. Shug and Celie together have woven this context of shared Hag-identified experiences and ideas, which makes possible transformative leaps of perception.

It is true that Shug appears to be somewhat in the role of guide or teacher, as if she had previously figured out everything about "God" that she expressed to Celie. However, there is really no reason to assume that this is the case. In fact, any Spinster who has had experiences of Spinning conversations with another woman knows that both Hags are involved in the thought-forming process. Even if one appears to be somewhat more in the role of listener, both are intensely and actively involved in the Spinning process. Most probably, Celie has "brought out" the ideas and Metaphors expressed by Shug in ways that are astonishing to both.

It is important also to note that Shug's words about "God" are descriptions of moments of Other-centered perceptions. She has gotten beyond the labels ("the old white man") and therefore her Other-centeredness includes her Self. That is, in the very act of leaping beyond the labels, she has Realized her own Otherness in relation to the system represented by the old white man. She has become able to see with Real Eyes. Therefore she can see that "It ['God'] ain't something you can look at apart from anything else, including yourself." Her perception of Reality is Allocentric and Metamorphic.

With the Labrys of her own Wild wit, Shug manages to avert the labelers' weapons (their labels) and to act as a Magnet for Celie, attracting her to her own presentiating powers of overcoming the malegod. Celie's response is anything but passive: "Every time I conjure up a rock, I throw it." Moreover, soon afterward (a few breathtaking pages later) Celie leaves her oppressive husband, moves away with Shug (her lover), and opens her own business—sewing beautiful, multicolored pants.

Furthermore, other women in this story are attracted into the magnetic vortex of Metamorphosis. Timid little Squeak (whose real name is Mary Agnes) leaves her man, Harpo, to continue her career as a singer. Sophie does not leave, but rather Self-affirmingly stands her ground at her husband Harpo's house. It could be said that Nettie, the beloved sister from whom Celie had been separated for decades, was drawn safely back from Africa by the power of this magnetic vortex. The fact that there was an incredible psychic connection between the sisters, despite thousands of miles and many years of separation, is demonstrated throughout the book. Even after Celie has received a telegram from the U.S. Department of Defense saying that the ship in which Nettie—and her husband and Celie's children—were returning from Africa was sunk by German mines, Celie continues to believe/know that Nettie is still alive: "How can you be dead if I still feel you?" Celie asks.[17]

The characters and plot of this story, which is utterly Crone-identified, place the choice of the pronoun *It* and of the noun *God* in a plausible context, which makes such usage acceptable to even the most hard-headed Hags. We might contrast this Naming with an *apparently* more radical choice of female pronouns and names for divinity that are contained within a foreground context, for example, an "alternative" christian religious service. In the latter case, the context of patriarchal myth is unchallenged. The use of the feminine forms merely suggests that the christian divinity—like Dustin Hoffman in the film *Tootsie*—is so superior and magnanimous that he can contain all female values. Just as Dustin could proclaim to Julie that "I *am* Dorothy," the christian god can arrogantly announce that he is also a "she" (during alternative services) and doesn't mind occasionally being referred to as "the Goddess" (whose history and force he has vampirized, contained, and reversed for millennia).

It can happen also that even feminist thinkers who are not boxed into the formulae of christian churches can use feminine symbols for divinity in ways that do not transcend patriarchal categories. For example, fixation upon the "Great Mother" to the exclusion of the myriad other possibilities for Naming transcendence, can fix women into foreground categories that block encounters with the inexhaustible Other, stopping the Metamorphic process.

The pronoun *it*, as used by patriarchal philosophers to refer to "ultimate reality," functions as a disguise for the unexamined assumption that this "ultimate reality" is male. The fact that such assumptions are still operative on the level of phantasms in the imaginations of such philosophers can be seen frequently in their religious beliefs, the symbols they employ in their everyday language, and their usual patriarchal behavior. That is, the context of their lives displays the agendas hidden by their "it."

In contrast to this, the apparently neuter "It" and even "God," as these function in the context of Shug Avery and Other Crones, work as instruments of Other-centered intuition and communication. Although many—probably most—Novice Nags as well as Nag-Gnostic Crones strongly prefer female-identified terms to Name ultimate/intimate Reality, we recognize that it is only in an Other-centered *context* that these can come Alive as instruments of Be-Witching, that is, as Metaphors of Metamorphosis.

Shape-shifting, then, is contextual. The occasional appearance of old words, such as "God" and "It" to Name deep Reality, can serve as a reminder to examine the atmosphere in which words are spoken. Such jarring of the radical imagination can work for Prudes as a safeguard against using and accepting Hag-identified new words as taken-for-granted labels, converting them into mere foreground terms. Websters are aware that new words are new in the sense they are heard in an Other semantic context. The Otherness of the context is necessary for genuinely Metamorphic leaps of understanding.

Words and their context are constantly struggling to keep up with each other. Thus a woman may hear a new word without having experienced the process which is the context in which it must be understood. In such a case, she is not really Hearing this word in Metamorphic dimensions. Or, conversely, it may happen that a woman's radicalizing experiences have moved her into a context of perceptions for which she has not yet found words. The Shape-shifting of words and context, therefore, involves a Spiraling—forward/backward/forward—movement of integrity and transformative interaction. One essential indication that the Spiraling process is continuing is sustained awareness of the intuition of radical Otherness.

SPIRALING AND METAPHORS

To a large extent, metaphors are the language and the vessels of metapatriarchal Spiraling, that is, of Be-Witching. When, for example, I say "Spinsters Spin," multileveled images of creation and change are evoked. If I say, "Amazons are whirling our Labryses," other dimensions of movement are conjured, such as images of battle. "Muses muse" summons the image of the Wild female Self re-membering her Genius. A statement such as "Prudes practice Volcanic Prudence" suggests that the agent (the Prude) and her actions (of Volcanic Prudence) totally break the bounds set by the conventional images of "prudes" and of "prudent" behavior. If I say that "Tidal Time is different from tidy time," a contextual difference is evoked, implying that an Other perception of duration can be expected when one lives different/deviant understandings of reality.

These examples, as well as hundreds of others in this book, have popped/hopped out of a context of living/thinking in meta-patriarchal ways. They could not have jumped/bumped into the writer's mind if there were not a Be-Friending context woven by deviant/defiant women. That context is a net, visible to the Third Eye, that stretches across the spiritual abysses that have been manufactured by the fraternity of fragmenters. It is not necessary that every net-maker find every metaphor meaningful or appropriate for her own use. The essential point is that these images stir the atmosphere E-motionally, awakening ancient connections not only with each other, but with winds, waters, rocks, trees, birds, butterflies, bats, cats, stars.

A metapatriarchal metaphor "works" precisely to the extent that it carries a woman further into the Wild dimensions of Other-centered consciousness—out of the dead circles into Spiraling/Spinning motion. Be-Witching metaphors transmute the shapes of consciousness and behavior, that is, they change the context of perception. They do this by jarring images, stirring memories, accentuating contradictions, upsetting unconscious traditional assumptions, evoking "inappropriate" laughter, releasing pent-up tears, eliciting gynaesthetic sensings of connections, arousing Dragon-identified Passions, inspiring acts of Volcanic Virtue, brewing Strange Ideas.

Metaphors, then, are not mere static symbols.[18] Insofar as symbols convey stasis, they function to legitimate the Static State. God-the-Father, Jesus, Buddha, et al. function in this way. The "Great Mother," isolated from Other and more daring images, also legitimates the Standstill Society, the Stag-nation. These images are characterized by what they do *not* do: They do not transform, jar, stir, arouse, or inspire Dreadful Daring Acts. They do not evoke "inappropriate" laughter, tears, passions, ideas. They certainly do not encourage a gynaesthetic sense of connectedness. One of their most essential lacks is the lack of genuine multidimensionality.

Symbols, at least as they are used in patriarchy, are commonly flattened-out, frozen metaphors that have been captured, reduced, and reversed into one-dimensionality. Indeed, one-dimensionality is itself a primary reversal of the core meaning of Spiraling Metaphor. Biblical language, especially that associated with Jesus, conveys this deadly flatness, which is usually combined with an inauthentic, utterly predictable emotional hype. The effect is a sort of canned hysteria in the tones of the speaker.

Any Crone who has played "switching stations" on the radio, especially on Sunday, can recall the experience of recognizing instantly that a christian preacher is speaking, even before she has consciously picked up more than a phrase. The unctuous intonations of the preachy voice are always the same. As she swiftly switches the dial, escaping from the blaring sounds of canned christian bleating, she is literally turning away/averting the vampiristic vibrations that would suck her into circles of guilt and fear. Conscious awareness of her natural passion of aversion aids her in averting this morass of monotony. She instinctively and gynaesthetically senses that the preachy stereotyped tones and phrases echo the dead uniformity of the symbol-system they endlessly repeat. Their monopolizing/monotonizing of air waves batters the brain, to such an extent that even a few fleeting seconds of such routinized intoning/droning constitute an injection of depression, a sense of banality and boredom.

In contrast to this sadosymbol syndrome, the Metaphoric experience is enlivening. One sign of its Life-giving force is complexity and multiplicity of meanings, which reflect the complexity of life itself.* Thus the expression "Race of Women," for example, which I have employed frequently in this book, cannot be understood at all if it is heard one-dimensionally. The sense of "the act of rushing onward" is as integral to its meaning in this context as "nation, people." The fact that Wild women are rushing onward is evidence that we are a "people," and that we are

---

* The astonishing variety of multidimensional metapatriarchal metaphors is apparent when we look at women's work in different languages. Outstanding among such creative workers is the French-Canadian poet Nicole Brossard, whose complex and intense Metaphoric usage is manifested throughout her works. This is illustrated in one of her book titles: *L'amèr*—which suggests motherhood, the sea, and bitterness. Obviously, this cannot be rendered adequately in English. See Nicole Brossard, *L'amèr ou le Chapitre effrité* (Montreal: Quinze, 1977).

Elementally kin to "a strong current of water." Our Race is racing, for we are participating in the flow of Be-ing. "Race of Women," therefore, is a metaphysical Metaphor, and it is a Metaphor of Metamorphosis. Clearly, it is no static symbol. To reduce it to that level is to freeze it into the foreground context, making it almost dull enough to be a suitable topic for an "alternative" Sunday sermon.

Lusty women, of course, do speak of symbols. For example, we often refer to the Labrys as a feminist symbol. It can be understood that way, as an image that points beyond itself to deep Reality. When we activate its Metaphoric Potential, however, we whirl it, hurl our Selves with it. As Metaphor it carries us into new Realms, and it changes our perceptions, our be-ing. Used metaphorically, it is an instrument of change, of Metamorphosis. Flying with it, we shift from circular reasoning to Spiraling E-motional knowing and acting. Spiders, dolphins, snakes, and butterflies also can be seen as symbols. However, as affecting/moving our creative imaginations beyond any fixed and assigned meanings—as engaging us in creative interaction with their be-ing—they are Metaphoric. The spiral itself can be called a symbol, but the moment we become active participants in Spiraling leaps of be-ing, we have activated its potential as Metaphor of Metabeing.

Just as metapatriarchal Metaphors are not merely symbols, they also are not merely abstractions. It may be argued that everyone "knows" this, since metaphors are so often contrasted with the language of abstraction. In fact, however, the "metaphors" of patriarchy are very abstract, in the sense of "considered apart form any application to a particular object or specific instance: separated from embodiment." When, for example, a man says of a woman, "She is a doll!" his foreground intention may be to compliment her, but the actual content of the statement is horrifying. One might ask: What sort of Spiraling Journey could be conjured by the word *doll*? Perhaps when it is wound up, it marches around the table, but this mechanical imitation of life is its ultimate "act." *Doll* as metaphor for a living woman, then, is considered apart from any real application. Most significantly, it is separated from *living* embodiment. A woman who is pleased to be called a "doll" is indeed in a depressed and depressing condition.

Disneyland exemplifies this sort of abstract patriarchal metaphor. Filled with imitations of life processes, it attempts to astonish and please with its gruesome parade of products that are meant to seem bigger and better than life. Watching Ronald Reagan on television can be an exercise in observation of abstract patriarchal metaphor. The image walks, talks, moves facial muscles, imitates signs of emotion and thought processes. Like the Disneyland characters, it is an imitation of life, posing as bigger and better. The image of "The President" is a mechanical metaphor, carrying necrophilic messages of no-change, masquerading as progress. The Presbot and his "Peacekeeper" are paradigms of abstract/empty patriarchal metaphor.

In contrast to patriarchal metaphors and abstractions, meta-patriarchal abstract thought can evoke Metamorphosis. Such Nag-Gnostic abstract thought—passionate theoretical reasoning that breaks the bonds of patriarchal assumptions—is essential to the Metamorphic process. Unlike the prevailing academic abstractions, which function to isolate bits of knowledge, meta-patriarchal theory manifests connections on the level of be-ing.[19] Since such thinking is Original, almost invariably it begins to assume Mantic Metaphorical dimensions. Its language is Metaphorical in the sense that this is characterized by multileveled meanings and imagination-arousing newness, evoking Spiraling movement.

BE-WITCHING THROUGH METAMORPHOSPHERES

The butterfly's arrival at the condition described in the Foreground to this Realm as "hope at large" is the consequence of complex transformations or metamorphoses. She has been in turn an egg, a larva or caterpillar, a pupa or chrysalis and finally an imago, or perfect insect. These stages of metamorphosis are encoded in the genes of the butterfly, so that the qualitative leaps which bring her to the final, perfect stage of "imago" are the same in each individual and predictable. (At least, this is the opinion of scientists who are non-butterflies.) I am suggesting that the Metamorphosis of metapatriarchal women cannot be so precisely described, and certainly not so precisely predicted.

In her Self-transcending dimensions, each woman may be compared to angels, as described in medieval theology. In a real sense, she is, like the angels, a distinct species unto herself. An essential part of her project of Metamorphosis is the dis-covering of her own species, that is, Self-creation. For a Metamorphosing woman, the challenge is not one of uncovering some fixed genetic code. Rather, she must break the system/code of symbols that has been embedded in her psyche as a kind of pseudo-genetic code and that is intended to block her comprehension of her own species, her Self.

A metapatriarchal woman must break this code in at least two ways. First, she must figure out its meanings (the meaning behind the "meanings" she is meant to "understand"). Second, she must break the rules/laws implied in the embedded code. This is necessary for breaking out of the pseudo-chrysalis in which the master mummifiers have encased her/erased her. In this process she uncovers her own Code, which has been buried beneath the codes of her captors.

This covered Code is, of course, Elemental. It is en-couraging to know that the Latin root of the word *code* is *codex,* meaning trunk of a tree. For Lusty women experience our Elemental connection with trees—who are rooted in the depth of the earth, and who are in contact with water and air and with the light and warmth of the sun, the rhythms of the moon and stars.

At the same time, it is also important to know that *codex* is akin to the Latin *cudere,* meaning to beat, which is the root of the verb *hew,* meaning "to fell (as a tree) by blows of an ax: cut down." The phallocratic codes are intended to hew women and our sisters, the trees—to cut us down, dismembering us.

The code-breaking of a Metamorphosing woman enables her to protect the trunk, roots, branches of the Tree of Her Life from those who intend to cut her down. It enables her to find and create her own Code. This finding and creating is a revolutionary, Spiraling process. It is a Metaphoric process intrinsic to Metamorphosis, carrying us through succeeding transformations, purifications. The code-breaking, myth-breaking of metapatriarchal women involves expulsion of alien antibodies, antispirits. It is a process comparable to the Self-purification of our Sisters the elements, who work to expel man-made pollutants from their own species.

From the perspective of the patriarchal possessors, a woman who finds her own Code is merely a heretic, guilty of some heterodoxy, and therefore subject to cure. By choosing this view of it, the trackers, tamers, hope to keep her within their own senescent circle. In fact, however, a truly Odd Woman is no longer god's woman. In relation to the masterplan, women who find our own Codes *are* Elemental *Errata,* that is, we *are* Errors. In relation to that plan, Metamorphosing women *are* living, breathing, Self-perpetuating Mistakes. We *are* Metapatriarchal Mutations.

Exploring the ranges of these Changes is the quest of this vast Realm, whose spheres are times/spaces of Super Natural Graces. Musing beyond stability/stasis, women opt for transformation/ mutation, achieving this through Crone-centered creation.

A basic block, inhibiting such leaps, is fear of becoming "out of control." Women continually express their fear that women— their mothers, their daughters, their patients, their students, their Selves—will get "out of control." As Denise Connors has suggested, the question that is masked/unasked is "Out of *whose* control?" The problem is that such fear-full women, filled with embedded fears, are too much under control, phallocratic control.[20] This is control by role. The word *control* unmasks itself when we recognize that it is derived from *contre-roll,* the old form of *counter-roll,* meaning "a duplicate register, used to verify the official or first-made roll." [21] Women who are under control in patriarchy are reduced to the state of duplicates/registers/re-cordings of the official or approved man-made feminine role. By staying under control, we verify this role as the right role. Thus the gynocidal machine continues to roll, running us over, running us down.

It is quite understandable that males in power should fear "losing control." It may seem less comprehensible, at first, that women should experience terror of "getting out of control." However, adherence to "the role" for women has been equated with safety, shelter, and—most serious of all—sanity. Women of the Right and women of the Left as well as women of the middle/ muddle road, have more to dread than abandonment by their male "protectors." The patriarchally embedded fears have made women terrified of our Selves, our Souls, our Sanity. Succumbing to these terrors would mean settling for inanity.

Transformation is the idea and reality whose time has come. Of course it is true that the Metamorphosis of metapatriarchal women is not entirely new. Crones know in our bones that since the beginnings of patriarchy there have always been some women engaged in breaking the cockocratic codes, finding their own Codes. At this time, however, the destroyers have moved further on their death march than ever before, attacking/poisoning the elements, filling the Earth with their lethal emissions, invading women's souls. At this time, the Be-Witching cognitive/affective minority—metapatriarchal women—is bonding, participating in the process of our Race.

On one level it is true that the Codes underlying the embedded patriarchal codes are not new. They are the vast, Virgin Potential yet to be Realized. Yet they are also New. For the actualizing of this potential/potency is the creation of further potential, the furthering of future possibilities.

True to our Memory of Archespheres, Be-Witching women continue to originate, mutate, metamutate. Armed with impassioned Virtues acquired in the Realm of Fire, Wild Weird women Spiral further through the Metamorphospheres. This is our Knowing Time, Growing Time. It is No-ing Time to compromise.

Erratically, Wanderwomen move through this Realm, keeping in Touch with the Natural Graces. Yearning to live the richness of be-ing in rainbow-radiant diversity, we Race with the Grace of Be-Longing. Decoding the myths and unsnapping the traps that have kept us from bonding, we weave with the Grace of Be-Friending.

Aroused by the Touch of our Wonder-filled Woman-Lust, Wonderers fly with the Grace of Be-Witching, unfolding our spiritual powers. Like flowers, like serpents, like dragons, like angels, we Spiral in rhythms of Weirdward creation. Leaping with Wanderlust, Weaving new Wonders, we intend to be Fore-Crones of Gnostic Nag-Nations. As Dreamers we glimpse our sidereal cities that gleam in the heavens like Stars of the Sea. They call us all ways, now, to Be.

CAT/EGORICAL APPENDIX*

The following is a transcription of an interview intended for publication in the *Journal of Ology: An Organ of Academic Inquisition.* The interviewer is Professor Yessir of the Department of Ology, College of Knowledge. The interviewees are two beautiful felines, Ms. Wild Cat (my familiar) and her sister/friend, Ms. Wild Eyes, who occasionally handle public relations. Since the *Journal of Ology* failed to publish the interview, I have decided to print it here, as accurately transcribed from the tape extracted from Professor Yessir by these felines. The editorial comments and descriptions of events that took place during the interview were reported to me by these Spirited creatures, in whose perceptiveness and veracity I have the utmost confidence.

M.D.

PROF. Y. (peering nervously at the staring felines): Good evening, Ladies. Is one of you Doctor Daly?

W.C. and W.E.: No, we are acting as her representatives and have been requested to handle this interview.

PROF. Y.: I should prefer to speak directly with Doctor Daly.

W.C. (jumping to her familiar seat on *The Basic Works of Aristotle*): Not a chance.

PROF. Y.: Well, then. I'll come directly to the point. The editors of our Journal are concerned about some of Doctor Daly's rather strange views. Quite frankly, the Inquisition is inquisitive about her sources.

W.E. (eyeing the interviewer): Oh, she thinks up her own stuff. Of course, she is also compulsively scholarly and precise . . .

PROF. Y.: My dear young lady, your statements are disturbing. First, as an academic, Doctor Daly is not allowed to—er—

* *Cat/egorical* means pertaining to a cat/egory. A cat/egory is an allegory written by and for cats and their friends. A Cat/egorical Appendix need not be read by anyone else.

"think up." Moreover, she has had the gall to use our professional Ological sources for her own purposes and in her own context. Indeed she refers to these as "springboards."

W.C. (springing onto the table): She has seven degrees and knows your resources better than you do. In fact, as Crone, she claims these as *her* Sources. As her familiar, I know.

PROF. Y. (ignoring the remark about degrees): You cannot be her familiar. That is my role.

W.E. (*yawning*): This sounds like a good time for a catnap.

PROF. Y.: According to *Webster's Third New International Dictionary of the English Language,* the term *familiar* means "a confidential officer of the Inquisition whose task was to apprehend and imprison the accused." The Academic Inquisition is a continuation of this noble institution, and I am its officer—i.e., *familiar.*

W.C. (squinting in disgust): You are a mere foreground "familiar," a necrophilic reversal of my true be-ing. As an academic, you must know that according to *Webster's, familiar* also means "a supernatural spirit often embodied in an animal and at the service of a person (the loathsome toad, the witches' familiar—Harvey Graham)." *I* am a familiar in this sense—not a loathsome toad, to be sure— but a stunning feline. I am a Super Natural Spirited Background animal, at the service of my friend, Crone Daly. Of course, she is also at my service—opening doors, opening cans, serving me tender vittles . . .

PROF. Y.: You are nothing but the figment of an overwrought imagination. You do not exist. You . . .

W.E. (opening her eyes): We can spare you just eleven more moments of feline time. Please get to the point. My own Crone—whose devoted familiar *I* am—will be needing me soon to sit on her dissertation notes. What are the charges?

PROF. Y.: First, she has insulted everyone, most notably the Pope. That's blasphemy.

W.E.: That's natural. He has insulted her species. Who is he, anyway? Your "God"?

PROF. Y. (droning on): Second, she claims to be a distinct species. Therefore, we charge her with biological determinism.

W.E.: Oh, that snoolish reversal! Quite the opposite is true, of course. As she clearly states, her position is that no biophilic person need be determined to stay within the confines of necrophilic species. By pursuing her love of Life, or Pure Lust, a Nag breaks away from biological determinism. My sister and I share this view.

w.c.: Indeed we do. Of course, we are very bio-logical and very determined to break free.

PROF. Y.: Then you Ladies are claiming that Doctor Daly and yourselves belong to the same species?

w.e. (eyeing her sister knowingly): Not at all. We all Be-Long in distinct species. Moreover, my sister and I, to be specific, are—as the saying goes—as different as night and day. Yet we participate together in the chorus of be-ing.

PROF. Y.: Your response to the charge of biological determinism does not match any of the Inquisition's categories. I must, therefore, record it as a nonresponse—that is, as a confession of sin.

w.c. (yawning): Our Cat/egorical response simply transcends the ineffable limitations of your tidy "categories." Your comment about "sin" is correct, however. In Doctor Daly's Weird opinion . . .

PROF. Y. (interrupting): Then you admit that she advocates sin? That is the third charge.

w.e. (chasing w.c. around the room): You can bet your sweet ass . . .

PROF. Y. (bellowing in frustration): The fourth charge, Ladies, is gnosticism. Your mistress has been accused—even by feminist The-Ologians—of gnosticism.

w.c. and w.e. (simultaneously): The word is *Nag-Gnosticism!* She is a Self-proclaimed Nag-Gnostic. And she is *not* our "mistress."

PROF. Y. (ignoring this response): My colleagues from the Department of The-Ology are concerned that this position is heretical.

w.c.: You mean *Her-etical,* or *Her-Ethical.* Doctor Daly has become too Weird to be classified merely as "heretical."

PROF. Y. (blankly): According to our records, the Full-Osophical faculty members maintain that her work does not fit in . . .

w.e. (scratching): It is, in large measure, a question of capacity.

PROF. Y. (visibly fading): The fifth charge concerns her discussion of the "Race of Women"—also referred to as the—er—

"Elemental Race." Our Androlatry and Psycho-Ology professors find this disturbing.

W.E. (calmly washing her chest): Well, isn't everything—to them?

PROF. Y. (attempting an ingratiating approach): Well, yes. I mean, confidentially, Ladies, we could overlook a great deal of her erratic thought and behavior if she would confine herself to the field of literature—which I suppose you would call litter-ature (heh-heh). However, such ideas, coming from one who holds doctorates in The-Ology and in Full-Osophy, are unacceptable and embarrassing to her colleagues.

W.C. (coughing slightly on a fur ball): She doesn't hold her doctorates all the time. She holds me sometimes, for example.

PROF. Y. (reddening): Ladies—or whatever you are—Your responses are too litteral, I mean literal, to meet the intellectual standards of the *Journal of Ology*.

W.C.: What did you expect? Fuzzy foreground abstractions? We can't discuss metapatriarchal metapatterning Metaphor with just anyone . . .

AUTHOR'S NOTE: I

At this point, the taped interview transcribed by the Wise Sisters ends. According to their account, at that moment a moth landed on the lap of the Inquisitorial interviewer. Unable to control their impulses, both felines lunged at the insect, causing the distraught professor to slip from his chair in a swoon. Both have testified (and I trust their testimony implicitly) that after they had succeeded in bringing him back to "consciousness" (through various maneuvers such as meowing, jumping, scratching his beard, et cetera), he lost his former facade of composure. It seems that he began pleading for information while crawling on his knees back to his seat. Indeed, he tearfully informed them that, since none of their replies fit the categories of his questionnaire, that is, since he had been unable to extract from them the correct replies, he would be severely penalized by his superiors.

Professor Yessir even tried to bond with the "humble" felines as his "fellow familiars," begging them for answers that would fit his categories. He spoke bitterly of the The-Ologians, in particular, ridiculing their anachronistic efforts to regain their former position as Queens of the Sciences. He expressed his terror of the Psycho-Ologists, revealing that they had threatened to use him as an experimental subject for psycho-surgery. The sensitive felines, though secretly pitying the snool, remained unmoved by his craven cajoling.

AUTHOR'S NOTE: II

Since this work has gone to press, Professor Yessir's (mis)interpretation of the interview was, in fact, published in the Spring 1984 issue of the *Journal of Ology* under the title "Crazed Crone Confesses." The subsequent rush of letters to the editor could be anticipated. Ms. Wild Cat and Ms. Wild Eyes both shrewdly predicted that some would find his deceptive piece cat/astrophic, whereas others would believe that it functioned for them as a cat/atonic. The Wild Sisters remarked that, for them, the experience has functioned as cat/alyst for continuing development of their own Cat/egories.

These Cat/egories of Elemental perception will continue to be shared among their own kind, in the fields and meadows of the Familiar/Strange universe, far from the boundaries of androcratic academia. Some women, these philosophical felines say, will just "happen" to Race through these fields and pick up Messages of an Other and better world. Such Be-Longing, Be-Friending, Be-Witching women will hear ripples of merriment, echoes of distant yet familiar rhythms. They will sense the joyous vibrations of that Otherworld which is "here" and "there" at the same (Tidal) time.

Such women, sensing these Other dimensions, will feel the Be-Friending Touches of many animals, of trees, breezes, raindrops, sunbeams. We will experience "coincidences," Syn-Crone-icities, meetings at crossroads of species, of souls. We'll Race and Race and leap with deer and hop with rabbits. With ladybugs we'll climb tall stalks of grass. With barnacles we'll hug the rocks of seashores. With snakes we'll glide through gardens. Like butterflies we'll skit from flower to flower. Our Hour will come. It has, already.

If this View is true, this glimpse of leaping through heroic realms, then the world is ultimately safe.[1] Be-Witching, then, is our Possible Dream. Nothing is really lost to those who Lust. Our luck is with the Fates.

This Call of the Wild, this Summons to hear the Word of the Weird, is Sirens' song. It guides us on paths of Be-Longing, of living in harmony with Spheres. It teaches the lore of Be-Friending, of sharing magnificent treasures. It inspires to the risk of Be-Witching, of joining the whirling world of Wonderlust.

In Be-Friending/bonding with the not-so-humble feline sweetly dozing on the pages of the open dictionary beside my desk—her furry figure covering the definition of the word *familiar*—I find it fitting to call this Call the "Cat/egorial Imperative." In her own Way, she understands, of course.[2]

NOTES

INDEX

NOTES

PREFACE

1. Mary Daly, *Beyond God the Father: Toward a Philosophy of Women's Liberation* (Boston: Beacon Press, 1973); *Gyn/Ecology: The Metaethics of Radical Feminism* (Boston: Beacon Press, 1978).

2. Daly, *Gyn/Ecology,* pp. 29–31.

3. It should not be too surprising that women with fiercely focused feminist consciousness have widely differentiated interests. A woman who is known as a "separatist," for example, may have friendly communication with some men, without any compromise of her integrity. She may read, with profit, male-authored books, using these as re-sources for her own original analysis. If she is of catholic background, she may invoke, with remarkable success, such Goddess-Metaphors as the mother of saint Anthony, the female finder of lost objects. She is not particularly chagrined at this seeming inconsistency—although it may cause her to grin and cackle quietly to herSelf. Unity in complexity is, after all, a far-out phenomenon. Whatever her situation, she lives "on the boundary" of patriarchal institutions, and she lives dangerously.

4. Nelle Morton has developed this explanation in her essay "The Goddess as Metaphoric Image," which will be included in her forthcoming book, *The Journey Is Home.*

5. See, for example, Janice Raymond, *The Transsexual Empire: The Making of the She-Male* (Boston: Beacon Press, 1979); Andrea Dworkin, *Pornography: Men Possessing Women* (New York: G. P. Putnam's Sons, Perigee Books, 1981); Marilyn Frye, *The Politics of Reality: Essays in Feminist Theory* (Trumansburg, N.Y.: The Crossing Press, 1983).

6. Sarah Hoagland illustrates this process by untangling women's use of "vulnerability" in her essay "Vulnerability and Power," *Sinister Wisdom,* no. 19 (1982), pp. 13–23.

7. Julia Penelope has been particularly enlightening in this field.

INTRODUCTION

1. Conversation with Anne Dellenbaugh, Leverett, Mass., 1981.

2. The idea of *tribes* of women was suggested to me by Sue Bellamy. Conversation, Sydney, Australia, 1981.

3. Virginia Woolf, *Three Guineas* (New York: Harcourt, Brace & World, Inc., 1938; Harbinger Books, 1966), p. 109.

4. Matilda Joslyn Gage noted: "The famous works of Paracelsus were but compilations of the knowledge of these 'wise women' as he himself stated." *Woman, Church and State* (c. 1893; reprint edition,

Watertown, Mass.: Persephone Press, 1980), p. 104. Moreover, in 1527, at Basel, Paracelsus reportedly "threw all his medical works, including those of Hippocrates and Galen, into the fire, saying that he knew nothing except what he had learned from the witches." Ibid., p. 104. See Jules Michelet, *Satanism and Witchcraft,* trans. by A. R. Allinson (New York: The Citadel Press, 1939), p. 80.

Moreover, other students of Paracelsus, without explicitly recognizing the meaning of their comments, confirm this. Manley P. Hall, for example, writes: "He liked to visit hermits living in huts and caves, and to explore the myths and legends of the gypsies, alchemists, and herbalists, and even magicians and sorcerers." *The Mystical and Medical Philosophy of Paracelsus* (Los Angeles: The Philosophical Research Society, Inc., 1964), p. 45.

5. Hall, *The Mystical and Medical Philosophy,* p. 53.

6. See Aristotle, *Metaphysics*: "For it is owing to their wonder that men [sic] both now begin and at first began to philosophize; they wondered originally at the obvious difficulties, then advanced little by little and stated difficulties about the greater matters, e.g. about the phenomena of the moon and those of the sun and of the stars, and about the genesis of the universe. And a man who is puzzled and wonders thinks himself ignorant (whence even the lover of myth is in a sense a lover of Wisdom, for the myth is composed of wonders)." I, 2.

7. Emily Brontë, *Wuthering Heights* (New York: The Modern Library, 1950), p. 84.

8. Raymond T. Stamm, Exegesis of the Epistle to the Galatians, 4:3, in *The Interpreter's Bible,* 12 vols. (New York: Abingdon-Cokesbury Press, 1952–57), X, 521.

9. J. E. Cirlot, *A Dictionary of Symbols,* trans. by Jack Sage (New York: Philosophical Library, 1962), p. 337.

10. Emily Culpepper, "Philosophia in a Feminist Key: Revolt of the Symbols" (unpublished Th.D. dissertation, Harvard University, 1983), pp. 381–408.

11. Conversation, Leverett, Mass., 1981.

12. Cirlot, *A Dictionary of Symbols,* pp. 5–6.

13. This dictionary-inspired incantation was first suggested by Barbara Zanotti, in a lecture delivered at Boston College as part of the Feminist Lecture Series, Spring 1980.

14. Hall, *The Mystical and Medical Philosophy,* p. 54.

15. Conversation with Barbara Zanotti, Leverett, Mass., 1980.

16. Francis W. Beare, Exegesis of the Epistle to the Colossians, 2:10, in *The Interpreter's Bible,* XI, 195.

17. "Principalities," in *The Interpreter's Dictionary of the Bible,* 4 vols. (New York: Abingdon Press, 1962), III, 891.

18. Conversation with Kathy Newman, Leverett, Mass., 1981.

19. Conversation with Mary Schultz, Leverett, Mass., 1981.

20. The word *pre-fix* was dis-covered by Myra Love. Conversation, Leverett, Mass., 1981.

21. Paul Tillich, *Dynamics of Faith* (New York: Harper and Row, 1957), p. 43.

22. Conversation with Nelle Morton, Claremont, Calif., 1981. See also Nelle Morton, "The Rising Woman Consciousness in a Male Language Structure," *Andover Newton Quarterly,* XII (March 1972), pp. 177–90; "How Images Function," *Quest: A Feminist Quarterly,* vol. 3, no. 2 (Fall 1976), pp. 54–59; "Beloved Image" paper delivered at the National Conference of the American Academy of Religion, San Francisco, December 28, 1977, p. 4. These and other writings by Nelle Morton will be published in a forthcoming volume, *The Journey Is Home,* composed of her papers and articles from 1970 to 1979. This book reflects the development of her thought and of the women's movement during that period and contains writings from each year of that decade.

23. Adrienne Rich, *The Dream of a Common Language: Poems 1974–1977* (New York: W. W. Norton and Company, 1978).

24. In *Beyond God the Father: Toward a Philosophy of Women's Liberation* (Boston: Beacon Press, 1973), I have analyzed at length my use of *Be-ing* as Verb—as intransitive Verb—to Name ultimate reality. At the time of writing that book I still used the term *God* to Name that reality. The symbol, God as Verb, was an essential step in my intellectual process to the Metaphor, Goddess as Verb. Often feminists try to eliminate this step, with the unfortunate result that "The Goddess" functions as a static symbol, simply replacing the noun *God.* In writing *Beyond God the Father,* I also used the expression *Power of Be-ing* to refer to ultimate/intimate reality. This emphasized the Verb, but I now think that it gives less than adequate emphasis to the multiple aspects of transcendence. I therefore now use the plural, *Powers of Be-ing.*

Behind this semantic struggle lies, of course, the problem of the one and the many. It is important to be explicitly aware of this problem. Some feminists, with good reason, prefer to use the singular Name, *The Goddess.* Others, also with good reasons, prefer to speak of *Goddesses.* Although the latter choice is motivated by understanding of the necessity for, and fact of, multiplicity and diversity in symbols/metaphors of the Goddess, there is, it seems to me, an unresolved problem, if one ignores the principle of unity: the One. When Be-ing is understood as Verb, the focus of the discussion changes. It would be foolish to speak of "Be-ings." But women can and do speak of different Powers and manifestations of Be-ing, which are sometimes imaged as Goddesses.

25. Susanne K. Langer, *Philosophy in a New Key,* Mentor Books (New York: New American Library, 1942), p. 114.

26. Ibid., p. 113.

27. My allusion here is to Elizabeth Gould Davis, *The First Sex* (New York: G. P. Putnam's Sons, 1971)—the work of a courageous Crone.

28. Paul Tillich, *Systematic Theology,* 3 vols. (Chicago: University of Chicago Press, 1951–63), I, 163.

29. Ibid., pp. 163–64.

30. See Mary Daly, *Gyn/Ecology: The Metaethics of Radical Feminism* (Boston: Beacon Press, 1978), pp. 22–29.

31. In dozens of classic papers, articles, and reviews Julia Penelope (Stanley) has been on the forefront of radical postpatriarchal theory of language. An up-to-date bibliography of her work can be obtained by writing to Julia Penelope, Department of English, University of Nebraska, Lincoln, Nebraska 68588.

32. Daly, *Gyn/Ecology*, p. 27.

33. Conversation with Kathy Newman, Leverett, Mass., 1980.

Chapter One FOREGROUND TO THE FIRST REALM:
THE SADOSOCIETY AND ITS SADOSPIRITUAL
LEGITIMATORS

1. This trinitarian Naming of the sublime, sublimation, sublimination was suggested in a conversation with Jane Caputi, Boston, 1977.

2. See Louky Bersianik, *Les agénésies du vieux monde* (Outremont, Quebec: L'Intégrale, éditrice, 1982). This work can be obtained by writing to Nicole Brossard, 34 avenue Robert, Outremont, Quebec H3S 2P2, Canada.

3. Cited in Herbert B. Workman, *The Evolution of the Monastic Ideal* (Boston: Beacon Press, 1962), p. 321.

4. Ibid.

5. Ibid.

6. Ibid., p. 42.

7. Donald Attwater, *The Penguin Dictionary of Saints* (Baltimore: Penguin Books, Inc., 1965), p. 309.

8. Workman, *Evolution of the Monastic Ideal,* pp. 42–43.

9. Ibid., p. 44.

10. Ibid., p. 45.

11. Ibid., p. 61.

12. John A. O'Brien, *The American Martyrs* (New York: Appleton-Century-Crofts, Inc., 1953), p. 197.

13. Ibid., p. 198.

14. Ibid., p. 196. Jane Caputi amusingly relates her experience of having been told to read this book when she was in the sixth grade by a nun who suggested it as a substitute for the book she wanted to read, which was on the subject of "what a young girl should know" (about sexuality).

15. Barrington Moore, Jr., *Injustice: The Social Bases of Obedience and Revolt* (White Plains, N.Y.: M. E. Sharpe, 1978), p. 51.

16. Ibid.

17. Cited in Ved Mehta, "Profiles: Mahatma Gandhi and His Apostles," Part III: "The Company They Keep," *The New Yorker,* May 24, 1976, p. 46.

18. Cited by Ved Mehta, ibid., p. 51.

19. Ibid.

20. Cited by Ved Mehta, ibid., p. 54.

21. Erik H. Erikson, *Gandhi's Truth: On the Origins of Militant Non-violence* (New York: W. W. Norton and Company, 1969), pp. 405–06.

22. John E. Mack, *A Prince of Our Disorder: The Life of T. E. Lawrence* (Boston: Little, Brown and Company, 1976), p. 427.

23. Ibid.

24. Ibid., p. 433.

25. Ibid., p. 434.

26. Ibid., p. 438.

27. Ibid.

28. Ibid., p. 440.

29. Ibid., p. 441.

30. Ibid., p. 440.

31. Dag Hammarskjöld, *Markings,* trans. by Leif Sjöberg and W. H. Auden (New York: Alfred A. Knopf, 1965), p. 93.

32. Ibid., p. 108.

33. Ibid., p. 109.

34. Ibid., p. 115.

35. Ibid., p. 148.

36. Ibid., p. 156.

37. Ibid., p. xv.

38. Ibid.

39. Ibid., p. xviii.

40. Ibid., p. xvii.

41. Ibid., p. 152.

42. *Robert Oppenheimer: Letters and Recollections,* ed. by Alice Kimball Smith and Charles Wiener (Cambridge, Mass.: Harvard University Press, 1980), p. 156.

43. Cited in Robert J. Lifton, *The Broken Connection: On Death and the Continuity of Life* (New York: Simon and Schuster, Touchstone Books, 1979), p. 425.

44. For a discussion of telic decentralization in organisms, see David Bakan, *Disease, Pain, and Sacrifice: Toward a Psychology of Suffering* (Boston: Beacon Press, 1968), pp. 31–38.

45. *Robert Oppenheimer,* p. 290.

46. Lansing Lamont, *Day of Trinity* (New York: Atheneum, 1965), p. 261.

47. Barbara Ehrenreich and Annette Fuentes, "Special Report: Life on the Global Assembly Line," *Ms.,* January 1981, p. 53.

48. Ibid., p. 55.

49. See Thomas Aquinas, *Summa theologiae* III, qq. 74, 75, 76, 77. Moreover, the dogma of the "real presence" of Christ in the eucharist is officially defined doctrine of the catholic church.

50. See Janice G. Raymond, *The Transsexual Empire: The Making of the She-Male* (Boston: Beacon Press, 1979).

51. *Boston Herald American,* April 26, 1981, p. A18.

52. Ibid.

53. The Canadian feminist author Louky Bersianik expressed this graphic metaphor in a discussion at Stanley House, New Richmond, New Brunswick, Canada, August 1980.

54. Andrea Dworkin, *Pornography: Men Possessing Women* (New York: G. P. Putnam's Sons, Perigee Books, 1979, 1980, 1981), p. 165.

55. Ibid., p. 96.

56. Petition circulated in November 1980 by christian women theologians.

57. J. E. Lovelock, *Gaia: A New Look at Life on Earth* (Oxford: Oxford University Press, 1979), p. 148.

58. René Dubos, *The Wooing of Earth* (New York: Charles Scribner's Sons, 1980), p. 68.

59. Simone de Beauvoir, *The Second Sex,* trans. and ed. by H. M. Parshley (New York: Random House, Vintage Books, 1952), p. 750.

60. Ibid., p. 752.

61. Ibid., pp. 743–53.

62. Moore, *Injustice,* pp. 500–01.

63. Ernest Becker, *The Structure of Evil* (New York: George Braziller, 1968), p. 182.

64. Ibid., p. 185.

65. Cf. Aristotle, *Metaphysics,* Book IX.

66. Jerry Mander, *Four Arguments for the Elimination of Television* (New York: Morrow Quill Paperbacks, 1978), p. 61.

67. Ibid., p. 55.

68. Ibid., p. 62.

69. John Stoltenberg, "Sadomasochism: Eroticized Violence, Eroticized Powerlessness," in *Against Sadomasochism: A Radical Feminist Analysis,* ed. by Robin Ruth Linden, Darlene R. Pagano, Diana E. H. Russell, Susan Leigh Star (East Palo Alto, Calif.: Frog in the Well, 1982), p. 125.

70. Ibid., p. 127.

71. Ibid.

72. Ibid., p. 129.

73. Andrea Dworkin, *Right-Wing Women* (New York: G. P. Putnam's Sons, Perigee Books, 1983), pp. 22–23.

74. *Boston Globe,* August 1, 1980, p. 18.

75. *Boston Globe,* July 16, 1980, p. 8.

76. *Time,* August 4, 1980, p. 52.

77. Conversation with Eleanor Mullaley, Leverett, Mass., 1980.

78. See Mary Daly, *Gyn/Ecology: The Metaethics of Radical Feminism* (Boston: Beacon Press, 1978), pp. 130–33.

79. Hannah Arendt, *Eichmann in Jerusalem: A Report on the Banality of Evil* (New York: Penguin Books, 1963, 1964), p. 251.

80. Robert J. Lifton, *Thought Reform and the Psychology of Totalism* (New York: W. W. Norton and Company, 1961, 1963), p. 426.

81. Ibid., p. 427.

82. See Wilson Bryan Key, *Subliminal Seduction: Ad Media's Manipulation of a Not So Innocent America* (New York: New American

Library, Signet Books, 1973); and *Media Sexploitation* (Englewood Cliffs, N.J.: Prentice-Hall, Inc., 1976).

83. See Elizabeth Gould Davis, *The First Sex* (New York: G. P. Putnam's Sons, 1971), chapter 15, "Mary and the Great Goddess," pp. 243–51.

Chapter Two BEYOND THE SADO-SUBLIME:
EXORCISING ARCHETYPES, EVOKING THE ARCHIMAGE

1. See P. Diamandopoulos, "Arche," in *The Encyclopedia of Philosophy,* ed. by Paul Edwards, Editor-in-Chief (New York: Macmillan Publishing Co. and The Free Press, 1967), I, 145–46.

2. Ibid., p. 145.

3. F. E. Peters, *Greek Philosophical Terms: A Historical Lexicon* (New York: New York University Press, 1967), p. 23.

4. Walter Pagel, *Paracelsus: An Introduction to Philosophical Medicine in the Era of the Renaissance* (Basel, Switzerland, and New York: S. Karger, 1958), pp. 84–85.

5. See Janice Raymond, "The Illusion of Androgyny," *Quest: A Feminist Quarterly,* vol. 2, no. 1 (Summer 1975), pp. 57–66.

6. C. G. Jung, *The Archetypes and the Collective Unconscious,* 2nd. ed., trans. by R. F. C. Hull, Bollingen Series XX, *The Collected Works of C. G. Jung* (Princeton, N.J.: Princeton University Press, 1959, 1969) IX, Part I, 79.

7. Erich Neumann, *The Origins and History of Consciousness,* trans. from the German by R. F. C. Hull, Bollingen Series XLII (Princeton, N.J.: Princeton University Press, 1954), p. 322.

8. Jung, *The Archetypes and the Collective Unconscious,* pp. 81–82.

9. Neumann, *The Origins and History of Consciousness,* p. 133.

10. *Greenfield* (Mass.) *Recorder,* February 21, 1981, p. A5.

11. *Boston Globe,* January 21, 1981, p. 14.

12. *Worcester* (Mass.) *Telegram,* February 9, 1981, p. 6.

13. *Boston Globe,* January 27, 1981, p. 1.

14. *Boston Globe,* January 21, 1981, p. 5.

15. Conversation with Anne Dellenbaugh, Leverett, Mass., February 1981.

16. See *American Heritage Dictionary,* Appendix.

17. J. C. Cooper, *An Illustrated Encyclopedia of Traditional Symbols* (London: Thames and Hudson, 1978), p. 159.

18. Ibid., p. 47.

19. Conversation with Anne Dellenbaugh, Leverett, Mass., October 31, 1981.

20. See Matilda Joslyn Gage, *Woman, Church and State* (c. 1893; reprint edition, Watertown, Mass.: Persephone Press, 1980), p. 104.

21. Pagel, *Paracelsus,* p. 63.

22. Ibid., p. 62.

23. Ibid., p. 63.

24. Conversation with Mary Schultz, Leverett, Mass., February 1981.

25. See the classic study of patriarchal motherhood by Adrienne Rich, *Of Woman Born: Motherhood as Experience and Institution* (New York: W. W. Norton and Company, 1976).

26. Conversation with Eleanor Mullaley, Leverett, Mass., February 1981.

27. See Mary Daly, *Gyn/Ecology: The Metaethics of Radical Feminism* (Boston: Beacon Press, 1978), pp. 178–222.

28. This word has been suggested by Eleanor Mullaley. Conversation, Boston, 1980.

29. See Mary Daly, *Beyond God the Father: Toward a Philosophy of Women's Liberation* (Boston: Beacon Press, 1973), pp. 81–92.

30. The twelfth century genius Hildegarde of Bingen, Abbess of Rupertsberg, could serve as an example of this.

31. See Judy Grahn, "She Who," in *The Work of a Common Woman: The Collected Poetry of Judy Grahn, 1964–1977* (New York: St. Martin's Press, 1978), pp. 75–109.

32. This analysis appears in Louky Bersianik, *Les agénésies du vieux monde* (Outremont, Quebec: L'Intégrale, éditrice, 1982).

33. Thomas Aquinas, *Summa theologiae* I, q. 93, a. 7.

34. Marina Warner, *Alone of All Her Sex: The Myth and the Cult of the Virgin Mary* (New York: Alfred A. Knopf, 1976; Simon and Schuster, Wallaby Books, 1978), p. 256.

35. Ibid., p. 259.

36. Ibid., p. 263–64.

37. Ernest G. Schachtel, *Metamorphosis* (New York: Basic Books, 1959), p. 280.

38. Friedrich Nietzsche, *On the Genealogy of Morals,* trans. by Walter Kaufmann and R. J. Hollingdale, ed. by Walter Kaufmann (New York: Random House, Vintage Books, 1967), p. 33.

39. Ibid., p. 32.

40. This word was suggested by Anne Dellenbaugh, conversation, Leverett, Mass., 1981.

41. See Daly, *Gyn/Ecology,* pp. 223–92, footnotes. See G. J. Barker-Benfield, *The Horrors of the Half-Known Life* (New York: Harper and Row, 1976), especially pp. 61–132. See also Seale Harris, M.D., *Woman's Surgeon: The Life Story of J. Marion Sims,* with the collaboration of Frances Williams Browin (New York: The Macmillan Company, 1950). The pomposity and plethora of hypocritical excuses for Sims, the hero of Harris, can be appreciated only by reading the book, which actually glorifies the atrocities of Sims.

42. See Lillian Faderman, *Surpassing the Love of Men* (New York: William Morrow and Company, Inc., 1981), especially pp. 233–38.

43. Suzanne Arms, *Immaculate Deception: A New Look at Women and Childbirth in America* (New York: Bantam Books, 1975).

44. See Daly, *Gyn/Ecology,* pp. 83–85.

45. Lecture given at Boston College during the Feminist Lecture Series, Winter 1980.

46. This more moderate view had been held by Thomas Aquinas, *Summa theologiae* III, q. 27.

47. Conversation, Boston, January 1981.

48. Conversation, Boston, January 1981.

49. Judith Long Laws, "The Psychology of Tokenism: An Analysis," *Sex Roles,* vol. 1, no. 1 (1975), p. 58.

50. Ralf Dahrendorf, *Class and Class Conflict in Industrial Society* (Stanford: Stanford University Press, 1959), p. 60.

51. Laws, "The Psychology of Tokenism," p. 55.

52. Ibid., p. 64.

53. Ibid., p. 63.

54. See Anne Dellenbaugh, "She Who Is and Is Not Yet: An Essay on Parthenogenesis," *Trivia: A Journal of Ideas,* 1 (Fall 1982), p. 44.

55. Andrée Collard has expressed a similar point: "Animals and trees don't need to go to the root of things, they are already there. Nature and animals and women—if only we could be left alone—don't need to 'harness the keys to Paradise,' we *are* Paradise." See her article, "Random Thoughts on Victimization," *Sinister Wisdom,* 11 (Fall 1979), pp. 30–36.

56. Conversation with Sandra L. Zimdars-Swartz, Leverett, Mass., July 16, 1983.

57. Leonard W. Moss and Stephen C. Cappannari, "In Quest of the Black Virgin: She Is Black Because She Is Black," in *Mother Worship,* ed. by James J. Preston (Chapel Hill: University of North Carolina Press, 1982), p. 56.

58. Ibid., p. 65.

59. Ibid., p. 62.

60. *New Larousse Encyclopedia of Mythology,* trans. from the French by Richard Aldington and Delano Ames (New York: The Hamlyn Publishing Group Limited, 1959), p. 19.

61. E. A. Wallis Budge, *The Gods of the Egyptians* (1904; reprint edition, New York: Dover, 1969), p. 207.

62. W. Max Müller, *Egyptian,* vol. XII, *Mythology of All Races,* ed. by Louis Herbert Gray (Boston: Marshall Jones Co., 1918), p. 52.

63. Ibid., p. 53.

64. Jane Roberts, *Psychic Politics* (Englewood Cliffs, N.J.: Prentice-Hall, Inc., 1976), p. 9.

65. Ibid., p. 19.

66. Sandra M. Gilbert and Susan Gubar wittily discuss "authors" and "pens" in their book *The Madwoman in the Attic* (New Haven and London: Yale University Press, 1979), chapter 1.

Chapter Three BEYOND SADO-SUBLIMATION:
REAL PRESENCE

1. See Andrée Collard, "Rape of the Wild," *Trivia: A Journal of Ideas,* 2 (Spring 1983), pp. 64–86.

2. Conversation, Norwell, Mass., June 1981.

3. Cited in Robert J. Lifton, *The Broken Connection* (New York: Simon and Schuster, Touchstone Books, 1979), p. 370.

4. Marina Warner, *Alone of All Her Sex: The Myth and the Cult of the Virgin Mary* (New York: Alfred A. Knopf, 1976; Simon and Schuster, Wallaby Books, 1978), p. 94.

5. Cited in Lifton, *The Broken Connection*, p. 370.

6. Leslie R. Groves, *Now It Can Be Told: The Story of the Manhattan Project* (New York: Harper and Row, 1962), p. 437.

7. Warner, *Alone of All Her Sex*, p. 94.

8. William L. Lawrence, *Men and Atoms* (New York: Simon and Schuster, 1959), p. 197.

9. Dr. Helen Caldicott, *Nuclear Madness* (Brookline, Mass.: Autumn Press, Inc., 1978), p. 65.

10. See Betty Friedan, *The Feminine Mystique* (New York: W. W. Norton and Company, 1963).

11. Although Lammastide was the first of August, celebrations associated with it in recent centuries have taken place almost two weeks later. See Margaret A. Murray, *The God of the Witches* (New York: Oxford University Press, 1952), p. 43. Murray points out that the Puck Fair of Killorglin, County Kerry, Ireland, whose original date was Lammastide and which is a modern survival of the Horned God, was changed to August 11 or 12 because of an alteration in the calendar in 1752.

12. Warner, *Alone of All Her Sex*, p. 100.

13. See Mary Daly, *Gyn/Ecology: The Metaethics of Radical Feminism* (Boston: Beacon Press, 1978), pp. 94–95.

14. See *Report from Iron Mountain: On the Possibility and Desirability of Peace.* With Introductory Material by Leonard C. Lewin (New York: Dell Publishing Company, Delta Books, 1967). Although this book is considered a spoof, the mentality it depicts is real.

15. Lifton, *The Broken Connection*, p. 358.

16. See Thomas Aquinas, *Summa theologiae* I, qq. 27–43.

17. Louky Bersianik, *Les agénésies du vieux monde* (Outremont, Quebec: L'Intégrale, éditrice, 1982), especially pp. 5–9.

18. See Aquinas, *Summa theologiae* III, q. 1, a. 5c.

19. Michael J. Asken, "Psychoemotional Aspects of Mastectomy: A Review of Recent Literature," *American Journal of Psychiatry*, vol. 132, no. 1 (January 1975), p. 56.

20. Ibid., p. 57.

21. Harold J. May, "Psychosexual Sequelae to Mastectomy: Implications for Therapeutic and Rehabilitative Intervention," *Journal of Rehabilitation*, vol. 46 (January, February, March 1980), p. 31.

22. Howard A. Rusk, M.D., *Rehabilitation Medicine: A Textbook on Physical Medicine and Rehabilitation* (St. Louis: The C. V. Mosby Company, 1964), p. 20.

23. Simone de Beauvoir, *The Second Sex*, trans. and ed. by H. M. Parshley (New York: Random House, Vintage Books, 1952), p. 193.

24. René Dubos, *The Wooing of Earth* (New York: Charles Scribner's Sons, 1980), pp. 61–62.

25. John J. Vincent, *Christ in a Nuclear World* (Manchester, England: Crux Press, 1962), p. 49.

26. Ibid., p. 158.

27. De Beauvoir, *The Second Sex,* pp. xxi–xxii.

28. Ibid., p. 69.

29. Ibid., p. 87.

30. Ibid., p. xxii.

31. See Matilda Joslyn Gage, *Woman, Church and State* (c. 1893; reprint edition, Watertown, Mass.: Persephone Press, 1980); Elizabeth Gould Davis, *The First Sex* (New York: G. P. Putnam's Sons, 1971). Also see Merlin Stone, *When God Was a Woman* (New York: Harcourt Brace Jovanovich, Harvest Books, 1976).

32. Manley P. Hall, *The Mystical and Medical Philosophy of Paracelsus* (Los Angeles: The Philosophical Research Society, Inc., 1964), p. 54.

33. Thomas Aquinas was explicit on this point: "First and chiefly, the image of the Trinity is to be found in the acts of the soul, that is, inasmuch as from the knowledge which we possess, by actual thought we form an internal word; and thence break forth into love." See *Summa theologiae* I, q. 93, a. 7c.

34. Hannah Arendt, *Eichmann in Jerusalem: A Report on the Banality of Evil* (New York: Penguin Books, 1963, 1964), p. 251.

35. See Herbert Marcuse, *One-Dimensional Man* (Boston: Beacon Press, 1964), pp. 56–83. See also Herbert Marcuse, *An Essay on Liberation* (Boston: Beacon Press, 1969).

36. See Daly, *Beyond God the Father: Toward a Philosophy of Women's Liberation* (Boston: Beacon Press, 1973). I used Marcuse's analysis to discuss the limitations imposed upon heterosexual women by "the sexual revolution." At this point I am suggesting that the same texts could be excellent springboards for analyzing the mechanisms of repressive desublimation in connection with the current selective patriarchal permissiveness toward lesbianism.

37. Daly, *Gyn/Ecology,* p. 381.

38. See Aquinas, *Summa theologiae* II–II, q. 1.

39. Robert J. Lifton, *Thought Reform and the Psychology of Totalism* (New York: W. W. Norton and Company, 1961, 1963), p. 426.

40. George Orwell, *1984* (New York: New American Library, Signet Classics, 1949), p. 87.

41. Ibid., pp. 28–29.

42. Lifton, *Thought Reform,* p. 426.

43. Ibid.

44. *Man-infested* was suggested by Eleanor Mullaley, conversation, Boston, 1980.

45. Daly, *Beyond God the Father,* pp. 41–42.

46. Orwell, *1984,* p. 63.

47. Ibid., p. 26.
48. Rev. Walter W. Skeat, *A Concise Etymological Dictionary of the English Language* (Oxford: At the Clarendon Press, 1911).
49. Joseph Campbell, *The Masks of God: Oriental Mythology* (New York: Viking Press, 1962), p. 66.

Chapter Four BEYOND SADO-SUBLIMINATION: REALIZING ELEMENTAL POTENCY

1. This word was dis-covered by Wicked Denise Connors, Leverett, Mass., January 18, 1983.
2. See Wilson Bryan Key, *Subliminal Seduction* (New York: New American Library, Signet Books, 1973); and *Media Sexploitation* (Englewood Cliffs, N.J.: Prentice-Hall, Inc., 1976).
3. It is useful to read a work such as Robert Graves, *The Greek Myths* (Baltimore, Md.: Penguin Books, 1975), which is equipped with a good index, noting the historical transformations of classical mythic figures—Athena is an obvious example. The reader might then reflect upon ways in which later manifestations carry with/in them earlier meanings which can function in a subliminal manner, despite the overt apparent mythic messages of a later period.
4. Jan Raymond has shown that those who have written of the holocaust of the Jews in Nazi Germany fail to recognize the history of gynocidal holocaust, which is essential for understanding patriarchal genocidal atrocities. See "Women's History and Transcendence," in *Religious Liberty in the Crossfire of Creeds,* ed. by Franklin H. Littell (Philadelphia: Ecumenical Press, 1978), pp. 47–52.
5. See Mary Daly, *Beyond God the Father: Toward a Philosophy of Women's Liberation* (Boston: Beacon Press, 1973), chapter 7.
6. See Thomas Aquinas, *Summa theologiae* I, qq. 50–64, qq. 106–114. Medieval Arabian philosophers, especially Avicenna and Averroes, transmitted spectacular analyses of the "separate intelligences." See Etienne Gilson, *History of Christian Philosophy in the Middle Ages* (London: Sheed and Ward, 1955), pp. 181–225. Johannes Scotus Erigena, the astonishing ninth century Irish philosopher, produced interesting material on the hierarchies of angelic substances, as did other, less original thinkers.
7. Paul Tillich, *Systematic Theology,* 3 vols. (Chicago: University of Chicago Press, 1951–63), I, 73.
8. Ibid., I, 75.
9. Ibid., I, 164.
10. Ibid., I, 163.
11. Donald L. Burnham, M.D., "Separation Anxiety," *Archives of General Psychiatry,* XIII (1965), pp. 346–58.
12. James Hillman, *Re-Visioning Psychology* (New York: Harper and Row, 1975), p. 5.

13. Tillich, *Systematic Theology,* I, 177.

14. Conversation with Mary Schultz, Leverett, Mass., January 1981.

15. Daly, *Beyond God the Father,* pp. 34–35.

16. Andrea Dworkin, *Our Blood* (New York: Harper & Row, 1976), p. 24.

17. See Aristotle, *Metaphysics* IX, 1.

18. Conversation with Louky Bersianik, Stanley House, New Richmond, New Brunswick, Canada, August 1980.

19. See Denise Donnell Connors, "Sickness unto Death: Medicine as Mythic, Necrophilic, and Iatrogenic," *Advances in Nursing Science,* vol. 2, no. 3 (April 1980), pp. 39–51.

20. Virginia Woolf, *Moments of Being: Unpublished Autobiographical Writings,* ed. and with an introduction and notes by Jeanne Schulkind (New York: Harcourt Brace Jovanovich, 1976), p. 67.

21. Barbara Myerhoff, *Number Our Days* (New York: Simon & Schuster, Touchstone Books, 1978), p. 39.

22. Conversation with Frances Theoret, Stanley House, New Richmond, New Brunswick, Canada, August 1980.

23. Muriel Rukeyser, "Käthe Kollwitz," III, St. 4, *The Speed of Darkness* (New York: Random House, 1968), p. 103.

24. Woolf, *Moments of Being,* p. 72.

25. Ibid., p. 73.

26. Ibid., p. 70.

27. Ibid., p. 72.

28. Ibid., p. 93.

29. Ibid., p. 72.

30. Alice Walker, "In Search of Our Mothers' Gardens," *Ms.,* May 1974, pp. 66–67.

31. Gloria Anzaldúa, "Speaking in Tongues: A Letter to Third World Women Writers," in *This Bridge Called My Back: Writings by Radical Women of Color,* ed. by Cherríe Moraga and Gloria Anzaldúa (Watertown, Mass.: Persephone Press, 1981), p. 170.

32. See Tillie Olsen, *Silences* (New York: Delacorte Press/Seymour Lawrence, 1978).

33. Rachel Carson, *The Sea Around Us* (New York: New American Library, Mentor Books, 1961), p. 144.

34. Janice Raymond, "A Genealogy of Female Friendship," *Trivia: A Journal of Ideas,* no. 1 (Fall 1982), p. 25.

35. Carson, *The Sea Around Us,* pp. 154–55.

36. Monique Wittig and Sande Zeig, *Lesbian Peoples: Material for a Dictionary* (New York: Avon Books, 1979), p. 96.

37. Woolf, *Moments of Being,* p. 98.

38. See Michelle Cliff, "The Resonance of Interruption," *Chrysalis,* no. 8 (Summer 1979), pp. 29–37.

39. George Orwell, *1984* (New York: New American Library, Signet Classics, 1949), p. 26.

40. Francis W. Beare, Exegesis of the Epistle to the Colossians, 2:10,

in *The Interpreter's Bible,* 12 vols. (New York: Abingdon-Cokesbury Press, 1952–57), XI, 195.

41. See "Principalities," in *The Interpreter's Dictionary of the Bible,* 4 vols. (New York: Abingdon Press, 1962), III, 891.

42. Orwell, *1984,* p. 210.

43. The Revised Standard Version translates this verse: "and you have come to fulness of life in him, who is the head of all rule and authority."

44. Cited in Catherine Dimier, *The Old Testament Apocrypha,* trans. from the French by S. J. Tester (New York: Hawthorn Books, 1964), p. 31.

45. Ibid., pp. 37–38.

46. Cited in *Dictionary of the Bible,* ed. by J. Hastings (New York: Charles Scribner's Sons, 1908), I, 683.

47. See Jacob Grimm, *Teutonic Mythology,* trans. from the fourth edition with notes and appendix by James Steven Stallybrass, 4 vols. (London: George Bell and Sons, 1883). This monumental work also illustrates the fact that doublethink is hardly confined to the period of the European witchcraze. Jacob Grimm, in this study of Teutonic mythology, exemplifies garden variety deception. In his chapter "Wise Women" he writes: "If human nature in general shews a tendency to pay a higher respect and deference to the female sex, this has always been specially characteristic of Teutonic nations. Men earn deification by their deeds, women by their wisdom. . . . This Germanic *reverence for woman,* already emphasized by Tacitus, is markedly expressed in our old systems of law." I, 397). Grimm surely had available to him information about the torture of women in Germany. Henry Charles Lea wrote: "In Italy and Spain torture is limited to an hour, but in Germany it will last anywhere from a day and a night to four days and four nights, during which the executioner never ceases his work, and the judge never omits to order him to renew it, and the executioner has full power to employ new methods." See Henry Charles Lea, *Materials Toward a History of Witchcraft,* arranged and edited by Arthur C. Howland, with an introduction by George Lincoln Burr, 3 vols. (New York: Thomas Yoseloff, 1957), II, 735.

48. "Elements," *Encyclopedia Biblica* (New York: The Macmillan Company, 1901), II, 1259.

49. Heinrich Kramer and James Sprenger, *The Malleus Maleficarum,* trans. with introductions, bibliography, and notes by the Rev. Montague Summers (New York: Dover Publications, Inc., 1971), The Second Part, Q. I, chapter xv, p. 149.

50. Matilda Joslyn Gage, *Woman, Church and State* (c. 1893; reprint edition, Watertown, Mass.: Persephone Press, 1980), p. 107.

51. Alice James, *The Diary of Alice James,* ed. with an introduction by Leon Edel (New York: Dodd, Mead, and Company, 1934, 1964), p. 142.

52. Connors, "Sickness unto Death," p. 42.

53. Rossell Hope Robbins, *The Encyclopedia of Witchcraft and Demonology* (New York: Crown Publishers, Inc., Bonanza Books, 1959), p. 493.

54. Ibid., p. 492.

55. Thomas S. Szasz, *The Manufacture of Madness* (New York: Harper and Row, 1970), p. 35.

56. Cited in Robbins, *Encyclopedia of Witchcraft and Demonology*, p. 101.

57. Valerie Solanas, *SCUM Manifesto,* with an introduction by Vivian Gornick (New York: Olympia Press, 1967, 1968, 1970), p. 7.

58. Thomas Aquinas, *Summa theologiae* I, q. 63, a. 3c.

59. Gustav Davidson, *A Dictionary of Angels* (New York: The Free Press, 1967), p. 228.

60. Ibid., p. 227.

61. Sandra M. Gilbert and Susan Gubar, *The Madwoman in the Attic: The Woman Writer in the Nineteenth-Century Literary Imagination* (New Haven and London: Yale University Press, 1979), p. 255.

62. Ibid.

63. Emily E. Culpepper, "Philosophia in a Feminist Key: Revolt of the Symbols" (unpublished Th.D. dissertation, Harvard University, 1983), chapter 3.

Chapter Five   FOREGROUND TO THE SECOND REALM: PLASTIC AND POTTED PASSIONS AND VIRTUES

1. Thomas Aquinas, *Summa theologiae* I–II, q. 22, a. 3c.

2. Ibid., I–II, q. 23, a. 1c.

3. Ibid., I, q. 81, a. 2c.

4. Ibid., I–II, q. 23, a. 1c.

5. Ibid.

6. Ibid., I–II, q. 23, a. 2c.

7. Ibid., I–II, q. 23, a. 3c.

8. Betty Friedan, *The Feminine Mystique* (New York: W. W. Norton and Company, 1963). See chapter 1.

9. Matilda Joslyn Gage, *Woman, Church and State* (c. 1893; reprint edition, Watertown, Mass.: Persephone Press, 1980), p. 238.

10. Simone de Beauvoir, *The Ethics of Ambiguity,* trans. by Bernard Frechtman (Secaucus, N.J.: The Citadel Press, 1948), p. 28.

11. Olive Schreiner, *The Story of an African Farm* (c. 1883; reprint edition, New York: Schocken Books, 1968), p. 176.

12. Ibid.

13. Ibid., p. 177.

14. See Marge Piercy's poem "A work of artifice," in *To Be of Use* (Garden City, N.Y.: Doubleday and Company, 1969, 1971, 1973), p. 3.

15. George Orwell, *1984* (New York: New American Library, Signet Classics, 1949), p. 252.

16. J. D. Reed, "The New Baby Bloom," *Time,* February 22, 1982, p. 52.

17. Kathleen Barry, *Female Sexual Slavery* (Englewood Cliffs, N.J.: Prentice-Hall, Inc., 1979), p. 74. Barry reserves the term "sexual slavery" for the most brutal and overt forms of sexual enslavement of women, while using the expression "sex colonization" to refer to the more generalized condition of oppression of all women. See pp. 139–73.

18. Ibid., p. 79.

19. *Boston Globe,* July 28, 1980, p. 29.

20. "Helen Gurley Brown: Fear Is the Key," Conversations/Marian Christy, *Boston Sunday Globe,* February 7, 1982, pp. A29–30.

21. See Helen Gurley Brown, *Having It All* (New York: Simon and Schuster/Linden Press, 1982).

22. Susan Page, "That Schlafly Touch," *Boston Globe,* July 15, 1980, p. 2.

23. Andrea Dworkin, *Right-Wing Women* (New York: G. P. Putnam's Sons, Perigee Books, 1983), p. 30.

24. Page, "That Schlafly Touch," p. 2.

25. Quoted from Dr. Kathryn Shands, *New York Times,* June 28, 1980, p. 17.

26. Molly Ivins, "For D. H. Lawrence, Pagan Rites in the Desert," *Boston Globe,* July 22, 1980, p. 9.

27. Quoted from Carol Parry, in Enid Nemy, "Commissions for Women's Conference Stress Economic Issues," *New York Times,* June 16, 1980, p. B6.

28. Quoted in *Boston Globe,* December 11, 1979, p. 1.

29. *Boston Globe,* May 19, 1980, p. 1.

30. Thomas Aquinas, *Summa theologiae* I–II, q. 56.

31. Ibid., I–II, q. 57, a. 3, a. 4.

32. Ibid., II–II, qq. 129–38.

33. Ibid., I–II, q. 58 a. 4, a. 5.

34. Ibid., I–II, q. 59, a. 1.

35. Aristotle, *Nicomachean Ethics* II, 8.

36. William Blake, "The Marriage of Heaven and Hell," in *The Poetical Works of William Blake,* ed. and with an introduction and textual notes by John Sampson (London: Oxford University Press, 1928), p. 250.

37. Mark Twain, *Following the Equator: A Journey Around the World* (Hartford: The American Publishing Company, 1897), p. 195.

38. Edmund Burke, "Speech on Conciliation: March 22, 1775," in *Selected Writings and Speeches on America: Edmund Burke,* ed. with an introduction by Thomas H. D. Mahoney (Indianapolis: Bobbs-Merrill Co., 1964), p. 173.

39. Thomas Aquinas, *Summa theologiae* II–II, q. 124, a. 2.

40. See Paul Tillich, *The Courage to Be* (New Haven: Yale University Press, 1952).

41. See Mary Daly, "The Courage to See," *The Christian Century,* LXXXVIII (September 22, 1971), pp. 1108–11.

42. Gordon A. Macdonald, *Volcanoes* (Englewood Cliffs, N.J.: Prentice-Hall, Inc., 1972), p. 378.

43. Conversation with Mary Schultz, Leverett, Mass., December 1980.

Chapter Six   ELEMENTAL E-MOTION:
FROM TOUCHABLE CASTE TO RAGING RACE

1. Jerry Mander, *Four Arguments for the Elimination of Television* (New York: Morrow Quill Paperbacks, 1977, 1978), pp. 15–16.

2. Ibid., p. 299.

3. Ibid.

4. Ibid., p. 304.

5. Lilian Bell, *From a Girl's Point of View* (New York and London: Harper and Brothers Publishers, 1897), pp. 133–34.

6. Willie Tyson, "The Ballad of Merciful Mary," *Full Count* (Washington, D.C.: Lima Bean Records, 1974).

7. George Orwell, *1984* (New York: New American Library, Signet Classics, 1949), p. 12.

8. Mary Daly, *Beyond God the Father: Toward a Philosophy of Women's Liberation* (Boston: Beacon Press, 1973), p. 2. Jo Freeman first suggested the theory of a sexual caste system in "The Legal Basis of the Sexual Caste System," *Valparaiso Law Review*, V, Symposium Issue (1971), pp. 203–36.

9. Lorraine Hansberry, "New York: Baby, You Could Be Jesus in Drag," in *To Be Young, Gifted, and Black (An Informal Autobiography)*, adapted by Robert Nemiroff (New York: New American Library, Signet Books, 1969), p. 98.

10. Beth Brant, "Introduction: A Gathering of Spirit," *Sinister Wisdom*, no. 22/23 (1983), pp. 7–8.

11. Ibid., p. 8.

12. Barrington Moore, Jr., *Injustice: The Social Bases of Obedience and Revolt* (White Plains, N.Y.: M. E. Sharpe, Inc., 1978), p. 50.

13. Orwell, *1984*, p. 63.

14. Susan B. Anthony, personal correspondence cited in Ida Husted Harper, *The Life and Work of Susan B. Anthony* (Indianapolis: The Hollenbeck Press, 1898), p. 366.

15. Sonia Johnson, *From Housewife to Heretic* (Garden City, N.Y.: Doubleday and Company, Inc., 1981), pp. 106–07.

16. Ibid., p. 107.

17. Moore, *Injustice*, p. 57.

18. Daly, *Beyond God the Father*, p. 2.

19. See Moore, *Injustice*, p. 59.

20. Ibid., p. 62.

21. Nancy M. Henley, *Body Politics* (Englewood Cliffs, N.J.: Prentice-Hall, Inc., 1977), especially pp. 185–201.

22. Ibid., pp. 199–200.

23. Ibid., p. 200.

24. Moore, *Injustice,* p. 58.

25. "Taboo," in *Grolier Encyclopedia* (New York: The Grolier Society, 1957), XIX, 62.

26. The radical feminist Canadian poet Nicole Brossard has developed a complex theory of the significance of surface/skin in several of her works in recent years. See especially *Picture Theory* (Montreal: Editions Nouvelle Optique, 1982).

27. Janice Raymond invents and explains this new word in her article "A Genealogy of Female Friendship," *Trivia: A Journal of Ideas,* 1 (Fall 1982), pp. 5–26.

28. Rachel Carson, *The Sea Around Us* (New York: New American Library, Mentor Books, 1961), p. 31.

29. Ibid., p. 33.

30. Sigmund Freud, *Totem and Taboo: Some Points of Agreement Between the Mental Lives of Savages and Neurotics,* trans. by James Strachey (London: Routledge and Kegan Paul, Ltd., 1950), pp. 19–20.

31. Ibid., p. 20.

32. Ibid., p. 24.

33. Ibid.

34. Ibid., p. 25.

35. Ibid., p. 27.

36. Johnson, *From Housewife to Heretic,* p. 330.

37. Herbert Marcuse, *An Essay on Liberation* (Boston: Beacon Press, 1969), p. 9.

38. Ibid.

39. Herbert Marcuse, *One-Dimensional Man* (Boston: Beacon Press, 1964), p. 79.

40. Hannah Arendt, *Eichmann in Jerusalem: A Report on the Banality of Evil* (New York: Penguin Books, 1963, 1964), p. 252.

41. Tillie Olsen, *Silences* (New York: Delacorte Press/Seymour Lawrence, 1965, 1972, 1978), p. 21.

42. Freud, *Totem and Taboo,* p. 37.

Chapter Seven BREAKING OUT: VOLCANIC VIRTUES

1. Olive Schreiner, cited in "Rebel Thoughts," *The Woman Rebel,* vol. 1, no. 3 (May 1914), p. 19.

2. Valerie Solanas, *SCUM Manifesto,* with an introduction by Vivian Gornick (New York: Olympia Press, 1967, 1968, 1970), p. 7.

3. The expression "Virgin Virtues" was suggested in a telephone conversation with Emily Culpepper, July 7, 1982.

4. Thomas Aquinas, *Summa theologiae* II–II, q. 47, a. 6c.

5. Saint Augustine, *De Civitate Dei* xiv, 28.

6. Aquinas, *Summa theologiae* II–II, q. 48.

7. Ibid.

8. Ibid., II–II, q. 49, a. 1.

9. Ibid., II–II, q. 49, a. 2, ad 1.

10. Aristotle, *Posterior Analytics* I, 34.

11. Conversation with Denise Connors, Leverett, Mass., March 1983. The Shrew who made this Shrewd response was Marilyn Richard.

12. Aquinas, *Summa theologiae* II–II, q. 49, a. 5, ad 2.

13. Ibid., II–II, q. 49, a. 6c.

14. Ibid., II–II, q. 49, a. 7c.

15. Ibid., II–II, q. 49, a. 8c.

16. Ibid., II–II, q. 58, a. 1c.

17. Paul Tillich, *Love, Power, and Justice* (New York: Oxford University Press, Galaxy Books, 1954), p. 86.

18. Elizabeth Oakes Smith, speech delivered at Woman's Rights Convention, 1852, in *History of Woman Suffrage,* ed. by Elizabeth Cady Stanton, Susan B. Anthony, and Matilda Joslyn Gage (New York: Fowler and Wells, 1881), I, 522–23.

19. Florynce Kennedy, "Institutionalized Oppression *vs.* the Female," in *Sisterhood Is Powerful,* ed. by Robin Morgan (New York: Random House, 1970), pp. 445–46.

20. Joyce Carol Oates, *Do with Me What You Will* (New York: The Vanguard Press, Inc., 1973), p. 284.

21. See Maxine Hong Kingston, *The Woman Warrior* (New York: Random House, Vintage Books, 1975, 1976).

22. Monique Wittig, *Les Guérillères,* trans. by David Le Vay (New York: Avon Books, 1969, 1971).

23. The Australian novelist Gabrielle Lord conjures a powerful story that illustrates the powers of female warriorhood in *Fortress* (Sydney, Australia, and London: Aurora Press, 1980).

24. J. C. Cooper, *An Illustrated Encyclopedia of Traditional Symbols* (London: Thames and Hudson, 1978), p. 82.

25. Ibid.

26. Elizabeth Cady Stanton, Letter to Woman's Suffrage Convention, 1851, in *History of Woman Suffrage,* I, 816.

27. Millicent Garrett Fawcett, *The Women's Victory—and After: Personal Reminiscences, 1911–1918* (London: Sidgwick and Jackson, Ltd., 1920), p. 66.

28. H. M. Tomlinson, *The Sea and the Jungle* (New York: The Modern Library, 1928), pp. 158–59.

29. Ibid., pp. 213–14.

30. Ibid., p. 158.

31. Quoted by Carleton Beals, *Cyclone Carry* (Philadelphia: Chilton Company, 1962), p. 99.

32. Ibid., p. 136.

33. See Aquinas, *Summa theologiae* II–II, q. 141, a. 4c. See Aristotle, *Nichomachean Ethics* III, 10.

Chapter Eight TIDY DEMONS, TIDAL MUSES

1. Rachel Carson, *The Sea Around Us* (New York: New American Library, Mentor Books, 1961), p. 146.

2. Ibid., p. 151.

3. Ibid., p. 142.

4. Rachel Carson, *The Edge of the Sea* (Boston: Houghton Mifflin Company, 1955), p. 14.

5. Stendhal, cited in Simone de Beauvoir, *The Second Sex,* trans. by H. M. Parshley (New York: Random House, Vintage Books, 1952), p. 149.

6. See Margaret A. Murray, *The Witch-Cult in Western Europe* (New York: Oxford University Press, 1921, 1963), Appendix IV, pp. 270–76.

7. See Cecil Woodham-Smith, *Florence Nightingale, 1820–1910* (New York: McGraw-Hill Book Company, Inc., 1951). In her superb biography of Florence Nightingale, based on private letters and papers never before made public, Woodham-Smith reveals Florence Nightingale as a radical many-sided genius and activist of unusual energy. At the present writing, this biography is out of print. Feminists have shown a tendency to ignore, belittle, caricature, and even malign Florence Nightingale. The reappearance of this biography would help to clarify the situation.

8. Denise Donnell Connors, "Florence Nightingale, 1820–1910: A Radical Genius Re-membered," *Trivia: A Journal of Ideas,* 2 (Spring 1983), p. 87. In this article, Denise Connors demonstrates that Nightingale was truly radical in several senses, indicating that these aspects of her life and work have inspired the recent formation of *Cassandra: Radical Feminist Nurses Network.* To receive a newsletter which provides information and a membership form, women can write to *Cassandra,* P.O. Box 341, Williamsville, N.Y. 14221. See also Connors' article, "The Radical Roots of Nursing," vol. 1, no. 1, *Cassandra: Radical Feminist Nurses Newsletter.*

9. Sonia Johnson, *From Housewife to Heretic* (New York: Doubleday and Company, 1981), p. 126.

10. St. Teresa of Avila, *Interior Castle,* trans. and ed. by E. Allison Peers, from the critical edition of P. Silverio de Santa Teresa, C.D. (Garden City, N.Y.: Doubleday and Company, Image Books, 1961), pp. 141–43.

11. Ibid., p. 146.

12. See Dominique Deneuville, *Sainte Thérèse d'Avila et la femme* (Paris: Editions du Chalet, 1964). For references to specific passages in the works of Teresa in which she complains of the chains imposed upon her sex, see my book *The Church and the Second Sex: With a New Feminist Postchristian Introduction by the Author* (New York: Harper and Row, Harper Colophon Books, 1975).

13. Doris Lessing, *The Four-Gated City* (New York: Alfred A. Knopf, Inc., Bantam Books, 1969), p. 499.

14. This word was invented by Janice Raymond. See "A Genealogy of Female Friendship," *Trivia: A Journal of Ideas,* 1 (Fall 1982), p. 10.

15. Stephen Trombley, *All That Summer She Was Mad: Virginia*

Woolf: Female Victim of Male Medicine (New York: The Continuum Publishing Company, 1981), p. 7.

16. Cited in Quentin Bell, *Virginia Woolf: A Biography* (New York: Harcourt Brace Jovanovich, 1972), I, 44, note.

17. Trombley, *All That Summer,* p. 8.

18. Bell, *Virginia Woolf,* I, 44.

19. Louky Bersianik, *The Euguélionne,* a triptych novel, trans. by Gerry Denis, Alison Hewitt, Donna Murray, and Martha O'Brien (Victoria, British Columbia: Press Porcépic, 1981), pp. 131–32.

20. Jane O'Reilly, "The Death and Life of the ERA," *Boston Globe Magazine,* July 18, 1982, p. 21.

21. Virginia Woolf, "Professions for Women," in *The Death of the Moth and Other Essays* (New York: Harcourt, Brace & World, Inc., 1942; Harvest Books, 1970), pp. 235–42.

22. John M. Keshishian, M.D., "Anatomy of a Burmese Beauty Secret," *National Geographic,* June 1979, p. 798.

23. Ibid., p. 801.

24. Ibid., p. 800.

25. Ibid., p. 801.

26. Robert Graves, *The Greek Myths* (Baltimore, Md.: Penguin Books, 1955, 1960), I, 21.o.

27. Robert Graves, *The White Goddess* (New York: Farrar, Straus and Giroux, 1948), p. 24.

28. Ibid., p. 343.

29. Ibid.

30. Ibid.

31. *New Larousse Encyclopedia of Mythology,* trans. by Richard Aldington and Delano Ames (New York: The Hamlyn Publishing Group Limited, 1959), p. 120.

32. Ibid.

33. Virginia Woolf, *Three Guineas* (New York: Harcourt, Brace & World, Inc., 1938; Harbinger Books, 1966), p. 80.

34. Dorothy Canfield Fisher (1879–1958), "The Bedquilt," in *Women and Fiction 2,* ed. by Susan Cahill (New York: New American Library, Mentor Books, 1978), p. 36.

35. Ibid., p. 37.

36. Ibid., p. 38.

37. Ibid., p. 39.

38. Ibid.

39. Ibid., p. 38.

40. See Thomas Aquinas, *Summa theologiae* II–II, q. 1, a. 1c; q. 17, a. 1c; q. 23, a. 1c.

41. Graves, *The Greek Myths,* I, 21.6; I, 28.f.

42. Ibid., I, 28.2.

43. The possibility of this connection is suggested by *Webster's Third New International Dictionary.*

44. Katharine Briggs, *An Encyclopedia of Fairies* (New York: Pantheon Books, 1976), p. 398.
45. Ibid., pp. 398–400.
46. Aristotle, *Physics* IV, 11.
47. Katharine Briggs, *The Vanishing People* (New York: Pantheon Books, 1978), p. 14.
48. Ibid., pp. 32, 182, note 14.
49. Ibid., p. 141.
50. Aquinas, *Summa theologiae* I, q. 10, a. 5c.
51. Helen Diner, *Mothers and Amazons: The First Feminine History of Culture,* ed. and trans. by John Philip Lundin (Garden City, N.Y.: Doubleday and Company, Anchor Books, 1973), pp. 16–18. Diner writes: "Knitting, knotting, interlacing, and entwining belong to the female realm in Nature, but so does entanglement in a magic plot . . . and the unraveling of anything that is completed" (p. 16).
52. Graves, *The Greek Myths,* I, 52.2.
53. Ibid., I, 52.a.
54. Carson, *The Edge of the Sea,* p. 27.
55. Graves, *The Greek Myths,* I, 10.c.

Chapter Nine FOREGROUND TO THE THIRD REALM: BREAKTHROUGH TO METAMORPHOSPHERES

1. Mary Daly, *Beyond God the Father: Toward a Philosophy of Women's Liberation* (Boston: Beacon Press, 1973), pp. 4–5.
2. See, for example, Peter Berger, *The Sacred Canopy* (Garden City, N.Y.: Doubleday and Company, Inc., 1967).
3. Daly, *Beyond God the Father,* p. 5.
4. Ibid., pp. 5–6.
5. Ibid., p. 5.
6. Susan and Anne Swatland, *Escape from the Moonies* (London: New English Library, 1982), p. 145.
7. Conversation, Leverett, Mass., August 12, 1982.
8. Shafica Karagulla, M.D., *Breakthrough to Creativity* (Santa Monica, Calif.: DeVorss & Co., Inc., 1967), p. 19.
9. Doris Lessing, *The Four-Gated City* (New York: Alfred A. Knopf, Inc., Bantam Books, 1969), p. 553. Interestingly, Starhawk also employs Lessing's concept of the self-hater. See *Dreaming the Dark* (Boston: Beacon Press, 1982), chapter 4.
10. Lessing, *The Four-Gated City,* pp. 552–53.
11. Ibid., p. 648.
12. Ibid., p. 588.
13. The idea of history-bearing groups is developed by Paul Tillich in *Systematic Theology,* 3 vols. (Chicago: University of Chicago Press, 1951–63), III, 310. The idea of women as history-bearing group is developed in Daly, *Beyond God the Father,* pp. 35ff.
14. Lessing, *The Four-Gated City,* p. 506.

15. Barbara Starrett, "I Dream in Female: The Metaphors of Evolution," *Amazon Quarterly,* vol. 3, no. 1 (November 1974), p. 13.

16. *The Politics of Women's Spirituality,* ed. by Charlene Spretnak (Garden City, N.Y.: Doubleday and Company, Inc., 1982).

17. This list can be read as an incantation, conjuring the Presences of many Other women.

18. J. C. Cooper, *An Illustrated Encyclopedia of Traditional Symbols* (London: Thames and Hudson, 1978), p. 28.

19. H. M. Tomlinson, *The Sea and the Jungle* (New York: The Modern Library, 1928), p. 187.

20. Elizabeth Goudge, *The Child from the Sea* (New York: Coward-McCann, Inc., 1970), p. 212.

21. Gertrude Stein, *The Making of Americans* (New York: Harcourt, Brace & World, 1934; Harvest Books, 1962), p. 284.

Chapter Ten   BE-LONGING: THE LUST FOR HAPPINESS

1. See Aristotle, *Nicomachean Ethics* X, 6, 7.

2. Thomas Aquinas, *Summa theologiae* I–II, q. 3, a. 8c.

3. Ibid., I–II, q. 5, a. 5c.

4. Ibid., I, q. 12, a. 5c.

5. Gregory Bateson, in *Mind and Nature: A Necessary Unity* (New York: E. P. Dutton, 1979), uses the term *metapattern,* but not in this metapatriarchal sense. See pp. 11ff.

6. Aquinas, *Summa theologiae* I, q. 75, 76. See Aristotle, *De Anima* II, ch. 1 and 2.

7. Aquinas, *Summa theologiae* I, q. 76, a. 1c. See Aristotle, *De Anima* II, 2.

8. Aquinas, *Summa theologiae* I, q. 76, a. 8c.

9. Ibid., I, q. 76, a. 8c.

10. Ibid., I, q. 76, a. 3c.

11. Larry Dossey, M.D., *Space, Time and Medicine* (Boulder & London: Shambhala Publications, 1982), p. 103.

12. Karl Pribam, interviewed by Daniel Goleman, "Holographic Memory," *Psychology Today,* February 1979, pp. 71–84.

13. Dossey, *Space, Time and Medicine,* p. 107. See David Bohm, *Wholeness and the Implicate Order* (London: Routledge and Kegan Paul, Ltd., 1980).

14. According to Leibniz (1646–1716), for example, the universe is composed of a hierarchy of "monads," each of which is a microcosm reflecting the world with differing degrees of clarity. See Gottfried Wilhelm von Leibniz, *The Monadology and Other Philosophical Writings,* trans. by Robert Latta (London: Oxford University Press, 1925).

15. David Bakan, *Disease, Pain, and Sacrifice* (Boston: Beacon Press, 1968), p. 34.

16. Ibid., p. 37.

17. Ibid., p. 38.

18. This word was invented by Françoise d'Eaubonne, a French feminist theoretician, in her book *Le Féminisme ou la mort* (Paris: Pierre Horay, 1974).

19. Jane Roberts describes the principle of unity in diversity through using the concept of "focus personality." See *Psychic Politics* (Englewood Cliffs, N.J.: Prentice-Hall, Inc., 1976).

20. Aquinas, *Summa theologiae* I, q. 77, a. 6.

21. Both Aristotle and Aquinas believed women to be defective and misbegotten males. Aquinas explained that this is only according to the "individual nature" (of all women). Nevertheless, "as regards human nature in general" women are not misbegotten, but are included in nature's intention for the work of generation. *Summa theologiae* I, q. 92, a. 1 ad 1. See Aristotle, *De Generatione Animalium* IV, 2.

22. Alice Walker, "Nuclear Exorcism," *Mother Jones*, September/October 1982, p. 21.

23. Ibid.

24. Hesiod, *Theogony*, 227.

25. Ernest G. Schachtel, *Metamorphosis* (New York: Basic Books, Inc., 1959), pp. 279–80.

26. Ibid., p. 280.

27. Ibid., p. 284.

28. Ibid., p. 287.

29. Ibid.

30. Emily Culpepper has described her own experience of this phenomenon in "Philosophia in a Feminist Key: Revolt of the Symbols" (unpublished Th.D. dissertation, Harvard University, 1983), chapter 8.

31. Virginia Woolf, *Moments of Being: Unpublished Autobiographical Writings,* ed. and with an introduction by Jeanne Schulkind (New York: Harcourt Brace Jovanovich, 1976), pp. 64–65.

32. Herbert Marcuse, *Eros and Civilization* (New York: Alfred A. Knopf, Vintage Books, 1955), p. 224.

33. Ibid., p. 225.

34. Ibid., p. 235.

35. Sigmund Freud, *Civilization and Its Discontents,* trans. and ed. by James Strachey (New York: W. W. Norton and Company, 1961), p. 30.

36. Anne Cameron, *Daughters of Copper Woman* (Vancouver, British Columbia: Press Gang Publishers, 1981), preface.

37. Ibid., p. 12.

38. Ibid., p. 146.

39. Ibid., p. 145.

Chapter Eleven BE-FRIENDING:
THE LUST TO SHARE HAPPINESS

1. Barry Commoner, *The Closing Circle* (New York: Alfred A. Knopf, Bantam Books, 1971, 1974), p. 29.

2. Robin Cook, *Fever* (New York: New American Library, Signet Books, 1982), p. 2.

3. These deep psychic levels of the oppression of women are cogently analyzed by Marilyn Frye in *The Politics of Reality: Essays in Feminist Theory* (Trumansburg, N.Y.: The Crossing Press, 1983).

4. Denise Connors has emphasized the need for recognizing and acting upon our knowledge of this fact, arguing forcefully that women have not found wholeness (healing) at the hands of male physicians and should not expect this. ("The Social Construction of Women's Sickness," paper delivered in the Feminist Lecture Series, Smith College, Northampton, Mass., February 17, 1983.)

5. Thomas Aquinas, *Summa theologiae* I, q. 92, a. 1, ad 1. I have written of this theory with mingled amusement and horror, in *The Church and the Second Sex* (New York: Harper and Row, Harper Colophon Books, 1975). The present concern is understanding it within the Sado-Syndrome of self-fulfilling prophecy.

6. Aquinas, *Summa theologiae* I, q. 92, a. 1, ad 1.

7. The survey, made by Dr. Frank W. Putnam, Jr., a psychiatrist and physiologist at the National Institute of Mental Health in Bethesda, Md., was discussed by Ellen Hale, "Inside the Divided Mind," *The New York Times Magazine,* April 17, 1983, p. 102. Hale writes, concerning this high proportion of women (85 percent): "This may reflect society's tendency to deal with a violent man—or his violent alternate—by throwing him in jail, while women more often are steered to the psychiatrist's office."

8. Ibid.

9. Ibid., p. 100.

10. Ibid., pp. 101–02, 105–06.

11. Janice Raymond, "A Genealogy of Female Friendship," *Trivia: A Journal of Ideas,* 1 (Fall 1982), p. 7.

12. It is germane to this point to reflect upon the fact that some women, when asked whether they were raped, answered that they didn't know. See Andra Medea and Kathleen Thompson, *Against Rape* (New York: Farrar, Straus and Giroux, 1974), p. 26.

13. Raymond, "A Genealogy of Female Friendship," p. 6.

14. Sarah M. Grimké, "A Seamstress Is Punished," in *Black Women in White America: A Documentary History,* ed. by Gerda Lerner (New York: Random House, Vintage Books, 1972), p. 18.

15. Ibid., pp. 18–19.

16. Solomon Northup, "The Slaveholder's Mistress," in *Black Women in White America,* pp. 50–51.

17. See, for example, "Racism Is the Issue," *Heresies,* vol. 4, no. 3, issue 15 (1982).

18. Toni Morrison, *Sula* (New York: Bantam Books, 1973), p. 149.

19. Ibid., p. 126.

20. Ibid., p. 44.

21. Emily Brontë, *Wuthering Heights* (New York: The Modern Library, 1950), p. 197. See Barbara Deming, "Two Perspectives on Women's Struggle," *We Cannot Live Without Our Lives* (New York: Grossman Publishers, 1974), pp. 52–74.

22. Brontë, *Wuthering Heights,* p. 97. Sandra Gilbert and Susan Gubar

have expressed the view that Heathcliff and Catherine together constitute an androgynous or gynandrous whole, "a woman's man" and a woman *for herself* in Sartre's sense, "making up one complete woman." See their book, *The Madwoman in the Attic* (New Haven and London: Yale University Press, 1979), p. 295. The assumption of this theory is that a "complete" woman is androgynous, that is, requires masculine as well as feminine aspects. I do not agree with this idea of female wholeness. The fact that Emily Brontë had to use a male character to express Catherine's Self does not validate theories of androgyny nor does it demonstrate that Brontë would have accepted these theories. It does state a great deal about the society within which she struggled to create.

23. Nelle Morton, "Beloved Image!" Paper delivered at the National Conference of the American Academy of Religion, San Francisco, December 28, 1977, p. 4.

24. Julia Penelope (Stanley), "Prescribed Passivity: The Language of Sexism," a paper delivered at the Southeastern Conference on Linguistics, Nashville, Tennessee, March 20–21, 1975.

25. The work of Susanne Langer illustrates non-woman-identified theory by women. See *Philosophy in a New Key* (New York: New American Library, Mentor Books, 1942). That Langer's work can be useful to feminists is illustrated by Emily Culpepper, in "Philosophia in a Feminist Key: Revolt of the Symbols" (unpublished Th.D. dissertation, Harvard University, 1983), pp. 55–98. The writings of Hannah Arendt also have inspired feminists to further analysis within a woman-identified context and could be said to contribute to Be-Friending. There are many examples of this phenomenon, of course.

26. Raymond, "A Genealogy of Female Friendship," pp. 6–7.

Chapter Twelve BE-WITCHING:
THE LUST FOR METAMORPHOSIS

1. Rev. Walter W. Skeat, *A Concise Etymological Dictionary of the English Language* (Oxford: At the Clarendon Press, 1911), p. 613.

2. Emily Culpepper, "Philosophia in a Feminist Key: Revolt of the Symbols" (unpublished Th.D. dissertation, Harvard University, 1983), p. 379.

3. Conversation, Leverett, Mass., June 11, 1983.

4. Marina Warner, *Alone of All Her Sex: The Myth and the Cult of the Virgin Mary* (New York: Alfred A. Knopf, 1976; Simon and Schuster, Wallaby Books, 1978), p. 268.

5. Ibid., p. 269. Shrewds might consider the fact that the crushing of the snake by Mary in christian mythology is an implicit admission that the primary/primal identity of the serpent as symbol is not phallic. For, as Emily Culpepper has suggested, christians are too male-identified to promote an image of a woman crushing a phallus. Conversation, Leverett, Mass., August 1983.

6. Starhawk, *Dreaming the Dark: Magic, Sex and Politics* (Boston: Beacon Press, 1982), pp. 26–27.

7. Ibid., p. 27.

8. Ibid., p. 26.

9. Ernest G. Schachtel, *Metamorphosis* (New York: Basic Books, 1959), p. 176.

10. Ibid., p. 177.

11. Ibid.

12. Ibid., p. 178.

13. Ibid.

14. Sonia Johnson, *From Housewife to Heretic* (Garden City, N.Y.: Doubleday and Company, 1981), p. 112.

15. Alice Walker, *The Color Purple* (New York: Harcourt Brace Jovanovich, 1982), p. 168.

16. Ibid., p. 167.

17. Ibid., p. 220.

18. As I have indicated in the Introduction, a clear presentation of patriarchal theory concerning symbols is given by theologian Paul Tillich. He maintains that symbols open up levels of reality otherwise closed to us and unlock dimensions and elements of our souls which correspond to these hidden dimensions and elements of reality. "They grow when the situation is ripe for them, and they die when the situation changes." See Paul Tillich, *Dynamics of Faith* (New York: Harper and Row, 1957), pp. 41–43. My position differs from that of Tillich. Patriarchal symbols are, I suggest, 90 percent dead, since they do not open up but rather close off Deep Reality. Metapatriarchal symbols can open up access to these deep dimensions. To the degree that they succeed in doing this, radically moving and transforming us, they function as Metaphors of Metamorphosis.

19. In a powerful article on women and science, mathematician and environmental engineer Pat Hynes protests the critical absence of "women-centered sensibility, genius, and passion" from science as it is known today. She argues persuasively that "science could be a way we would deepen by ideas, by rigorous observation, and by empirical methods what we intuit about nature." See H. Patricia Hynes, "Active Women in Passive '80," *Trivia: A Journal of Ideas*, I (Fall 1982), pp. 64–76.

20. Conversation, Leverett, Mass., April 28, 1983.

21. Skeat, *A Concise Etymological Dictionary*, p. 110.

Nonchapter Thirteen   CAT/EGORICAL APPENDIX

1. See Jane Roberts, *Psychic Politics* (Englewood Cliffs, N.J.: Prentice-Hall, Inc., 1976).

2. In their own ways so also do the many animals and Other creatures who have contributed to this Weaving. Among these is the Wise cat Persephone and the Witchy cat Adele, as well as the warrior cat, Earl Grey. Others include the lovely garter snake who sometimes crosses the

threshold of the loft where I have been working; a tall emu and several wallabies, koala bears, and kookaburras whom I met in Australia; a stunning parrot who resides in Munich and who eloquently announces: "Scheiss auf Goethe!" whenever her spirit moves her to do so. Also important is a young bull residing in Leverett, Mass., whose style of interrupting my conversations with two cows helped me to understand the basic meaning of the phrase "horning in." I could never omit the group of astonishing horses in the pastures across the way and down the road, whose galloping hooves sent inspiration in the night. Never to be forgotten are the butterflies who have graced the nearby woods or the praying mantis who arrived when I was thinking of mantic/soothsaying creatures. I am indebted also to several deer, a number of field mice, and two particular rabbits—one very large and one very small—who occasionally visited me at dusk in Leverett. I was instructed by a very aggressive robin and an intelligent cow who re-membered some of her heritage, and by the vast crowd of chorusing birds and peepers who live nearby.

I must add to this accounting my appreciation of a particular tornado, of a brook that rushes loudly at night, of myriad stars and of the Lusty moon—so astonishing on New England country nights. Finally, there are the trees—several in particular—for whose companionship I am grateful.

All of these Elemental creatures continue to be sources of hilarity, healing, hope, and confidence that the Biophilic Powers of Be-ing will not be defeated, ever.

INDEX OF NEW WORDS

Although many of these words are not new in the old sense, they are new in a new sense, because they are heard in a new way. The page references, for the most part, reflect the way in which these new words are first used or first defined. In other instances, the page numbers simply indicate characteristic usage of the word.

* Asterisked words also appear in *Gyn/Ecology*.
† Virginia Woolf.
*† Denise Connors.
†† Anne Dellenbaugh.

---

† Janice Raymond.
†† Emily Culpepper.
††† Eleanor Mullaley.
†††† Denise Connors.
††††† Virginia Woolf.

---

† Emily Culpepper.
†† Janice Raymond.
††† Anne Dellenbaugh.
†††† Mary Schultz.

† Denise Connors.
†† Janice Raymond.
††† Anne Cameron, *Daughters of Copperwoman.*
†††† Anne Dellenbaugh.

† Janice Raymond.

GENERAL INDEX

abortion, xi, 52; and Mother Teresa, 213–214; and particularization, 323

absence: ontological, 147; phallic, 148; physical, 144; from Self, 153; unreal, 53

Absence: power of, 146–147

absence of Presence, 147, 149–150; and the Triple Goddess, 165

academia: women in, 321n, 324

act: of seeing, 323; traditional explanation of, 63

Acts: Dreadful, 405; Originally Sinful, 264; spiritual, 310

acts: of allocentric perception, 394; biocidal, 335; Elemental, 61; of knowing, 95; of passion, 95; of psychic/physical ultimacy, 389

Adele, Witchy Cat, 447

advertising: techniques in subliminal, 153

Aeromancy: etymology of, 115, 187, 189–190

aeviternity, 310–311

agents: and false inclusion, 64; naming of, 21, 64, 199

Aggression, as Deadly Sin, x

air, 257; and the breath of life, 17; and creation, 17; and movement, 18; symbolism of, 17

Alacoque, Marie, 58, 65

Alcott, Louisa May, 382

alcohol abuse, 285–286; and confessionalism, 205–206

Aldington, Richard, 118n

"allocentric (other-centered) perception," 393–394

Alone of All Her Sex, 114n

American Martyrs, The, 38

Ames, Delano, 118n

amnesia, 6, 31, 36, 112, 132, 163, 271, 304, 381; childhood, 99, 355; memory, 99; and Realizing reason, 163; and sado-subliminal messages, 162; of women, 354–355

Anatomy of Freedom, The, 347n

Anaximander, 79, 80

Anaximenes, 16

Ancient Mirrors of Womanhood, 118n

androgyny, 135, 341n; as cannibalistic, 207–208

Angela of Foligno, Saint, 58n

Angels, 178–183, 189–191, 298, 408; changeableness of, 310; Elemental roles of, 182; as Elemental Spirits, 155; fallen, 309–310; intelligence of, 19; as spirits of the elements, 182; as spiritual beings, 19; time and, 310

anger, 258, 368–371

animals: torture of, 75, 282–284, 286, 351

Anne, saint, 113n

"Annunciation, the," 74; and rape, 104–106

Anthony, Nicole, 242

Anthony, saint, 36

Anthony, Susan B., 102, 236, 237

anti-semitism, 100n–101n

Anzaldúa, Gloria, 174, 333

aphasia, 132, 140–141, 164

Apollo, 302

appetite, sensitive, 198, 217; concupiscible part, 198, 199n, 217; irascible part, 198–199

apraxia, 132, 164

Aquinas, Thomas, 132–134, 184, 189–190, 217, 264, 338, 340, 345–346, 349, 352n, 366–367; philosophy of, 132–134, 184, 189–190, 217, 264–266, 269, 271, 338–340, 345–346, 349, 352n, 366, 425, 428, 429, 430, 431, 432, 435, 436, 438, 439, 441, 442, 443, 444, 445

Arcana, 90

Arche/Archai, 79, 122–123

Arche, 80, 86, 179; etymology of, 79; Greek definition of, 12

Archespheres, xi, 31, 35, 78, 119, 138, 152, 154, 162

Mary Daly is a Nag-Gnostic philosopher
who holds doctorates in theology and philosophy from the University of Fribourg, Switzerland. An associate professor of theology at
Boston College, this Shrewd Prude pursues
pyrosophical wisdom in her own Realms of
be-ing. She is also the author of *The Church
and the Second Sex, Beyond God the Father,
Gyn / Ecology, Webster's First New
Intergalactic Wickedary of the English
Language,* and *Outercourse.*

Wild Cat is one of the coauthors of
Nonchapter Thirteen: Cat / egorical Appendix.